Metaphysics

Metaphysics: An Introduction combines comprehensive coverage of the core elements of metaphysics with contemporary and lively debates within the subject. It provides a rigorous and yet accessible overview of a rich array of topics, connecting the abstract nature of metaphysics with the real world. Topics covered include:

- Basic logic for metaphysics
- An introduction to ontology
- Abstract objects
- Material objects
- Critiques of metaphysics
- Free will
- Time
- Modality
- Persistence
- Causation
- Social ontology: the metaphysics of race.

This outstanding book not only equips the reader with a thorough knowledge of the fundamentals of metaphysics but provides a valuable guide to contemporary metaphysics and metaphysicians.

Additional features such as exercises, annotated further reading, a glossary, and a companion website at www.routledge.com/cw/ney will help students find their way around this subject and assist teachers in the classroom.

Alyssa Ney is Associate Professor of Philosophy at the University of Rochester, USA. She is editor (with David Albert) of *The Wave Function: Essays in the Metaphysics of Quantum Mechanics* (2013).

Metaphysics

An Introduction

ALYSSA NEY

Routledge
Taylor & Francis Group

LONDON AND NEW YORK

First published 2014
by Routledge
2 Park Square, Milton Park, Abingdon, Oxon OX14 4RN

and by Routledge
711 Third Avenue, New York, NY 10017

Routledge is an imprint of the Taylor & Francis Group, an informa business

British Library Cataloguing in Publication Data
A catalogue record for this book is available from the British Library

Library of Congress Cataloging in Publication Data
Ney, Alyssa.
    Metaphysics : an introduction / Alyssa Ney. — 1st [edition].
        pages cm
    Includes bibliographical references.
    1. Metaphysics. I. Title.
    BD111.N49 2014
    110—dc23   2014002666

ISBN: 978-0-415-64074-9 (hbk)
ISBN: 978-0-415-64075-6 (pbk)
ISBN: 978-1-315-77175-5 (ebk)

Typeset in Akzidenz Grotesk and Eurostile
by Keystroke, Station Road, Codsall, Wolverhampton

FSC
www.fsc.org
MIX
Paper from
responsible sources
FSC® C013604

Printed and bound by CPI Group (UK) Ltd, Croydon, CR0 4YY

This book is dedicated to the memory of my father, Garrett William Ney.

Contents

Figures and Tables

FIGURES

TABLES

Preface

The distinctive goal of the metaphysician is to understand the structure of reality: what kinds of entities exist and what are their most fundamental and general features and relations. Unlike the natural and social sciences that seek to describe some special class of entities and what they are like – the physical things or the living things, particular civilizations or cultures – metaphysicians ask the most general questions about how things are, what our universe is like.

We will have more to say in the chapters that come about what are the main issues in metaphysics today and what exactly is the relationship between metaphysics and those other ways we have of studying what the world is like, science and theology. In this preface, our aim is to orient the reader with a basic overview of the presentation and supply some suggestions for further resources that will complement the use of this textbook.

This book presents an introduction to contemporary analytical metaphysics aiming to be accessible to students encountering the topic for the first time and yet challenging and interesting to more advanced students who may have already seen some of these topics in a first year philosophy course. To say this book presents an introduction to contemporary *analytical* metaphysics is to signal that the emphasis of this book will be in stating views and arguments clearly and with logical precision. As a result, in many places this book will make use of the tools of modern symbolic logic. Ideally a student using this book will already have had a course introducing the basics of first order predicate logic. For those who have not already had such a course, a preparatory chapter is provided which should bring one up to speed. This chapter may also be useful as a review to students who have already seen this material, or may be skimmed to find the notation that is used throughout the remainder of the text.

This textbook contains several features that have been included to help the introductory student who may be encountering many of these concepts for the first time. This includes a glossary at the end of the book as well as a list of suggested readings accompanying each chapter. The aim of the glossary, it should be noted, is not to provide philosophical analyses of terms or views. These are in many cases up for debate in contemporary metaphysics. The aim of the glossary is merely to give a gloss of the relevant term or view that will be helpful to orient a reader. Terms in the text that have glossary entries are marked in **boldface type.**

In addition to the suggested readings at the end of each chapter, there are also several excellent general resources that are available. Students planning to write papers on any of the topics in this book would do well to consult the following websites and handbooks:

http://plato. stanford.edu/

http://www.iep. utm.edu/

http://onlinelibrary. wiley.com/journal/ 10.1111/(ISSN) 1747-9991

- The *Stanford Encyclopedia of Philosophy* and the *Internet Encyclopedia of Philosophy* are two free, online encyclopedias. All articles are written by professional philosophers.
- www.philpapers.org is a free website cataloging published and unpublished articles and books in philosophy. In addition to including a searchable database of works in philosophy, this website also provides useful bibliographies on a variety of topics.
- The journal *Philosophy Compass* publishes survey articles on many topics in contemporary philosophy aimed at an advanced undergraduate/beginning graduate student audience.

In addition to these online resources, two recent books in metaphysics provide useful introductions to many of the topics we discuss here and beyond:

- The *Oxford Handbook of Metaphysics*, edited by Michael Loux and Dean Zimmerman.
- Blackwell's *Contemporary Debates in Metaphysics*, edited by John Hawthorne, Theodore Sider, and Dean Zimmerman.

The website accompanying this textbook provides links to many of the articles discussed in these chapters as well as selections from the further reading lists.

Although much of this introduction concerns contemporary metaphysics, the topics and debates that are most discussed today and the various methodologies that are most common now, it is often useful to recognize the contribution of philosophers and scientists of the past. This book adopts the convention of noting the years of birth and death for all deceased philosophers discussed in the main body of the text. If no dates are provided, one should assume that this philosopher is still living and writing.

Acknowledgments

I wish to thank several people who have helped to make this book actual. First, I would like to thank Tony Bruce of Routledge who first raised the idea to me of writing this text. I thank Tony for his encouragement and seeing the project through. I would also like to thank Alexandra McGregor of Routledge for her patience and sage advice as these chapters were written and reviewed. Thanks to Allan Hazelett (Reader in Philosophy, University of Edinburgh) for contributing the material on race and social ontology, which added so much to the book. I am extremely grateful to all of the very generous anonymous reviewers who took the time to provide so many useful comments on drafts of these chapters. I wish to thank as well Karen Bennett, Sam Cowling, Daniel Nolan, and Alison Peterman for their comments on the text. I am really fortunate to work in a field with so many brilliant and generous colleagues. Thanks to my metaphysics students at the University of Rochester for their feedback on earlier drafts, and to the teachers who first got me passionate about metaphysics and released me from the spell of logical positivism, especially Jose Benardete from whom I took my first metaphysics course, Ted Sider, and Jaegwon Kim. I was not the first and will certainly not be the last student to realize that so many of the questions she had thought were questions for her physics classes were metaphysical questions and that the philosophy department was where I belonged! I am grateful to John Komdat for his work on the website accompanying the text. Finally, I'd like to thank Michael Goldberg for providing a warm place with the coffee, chocolate, and encouragement I needed to finally finish this book.

Visual Tour of *Metaphysics: An Introduction*

LEARNING POINTS

At the beginning of each chapter, a number of Learning Points are set out so that the student understands clearly what is to be covered in the forthcoming chapter.

EMBOLDENED GLOSSARY TERMS

A Glossary at the back of the book helps with new terms and their definitions. Where these terms are used for the first time in the book they can be found in **bold** and in the margin.

EXERCISES

Each chapter includes Exercises that students can undertake inside or outside the class. These give students an opportunity to assess their understanding of the material under consideration.

ANNOTATED READING

At the end of each chapter there are Suggestions for Further Reading with annotations explaining their context.

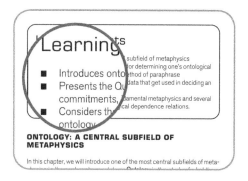

Preparatory Background

Logic for Metaphysics

Learning Points

- Introduces the concept of an argument and tools for assessing arguments as valid or invalid, sound or unsound
- Gives students tools for recognizing incomplete arguments (enthymemes) and applying the principle of charity
- Presents basic notation and valid inference forms in propositional and first-order predicate logic.

ARGUMENTS

In metaphysics, as in most other branches of philosophy and the sciences, we are interested in finding the truth about certain topics. For this reason, it would be nice to have a reasonable, reliable method to arrive at the truth. We aren't going to find what is true by random guessing or stabs in the dark. And in philosophy, we don't think that the best method to find the truth is to simply trust what one has always believed, those views one was raised with (though common sense should be respected to some extent). Nor do we think there is a group of elders who have the truth so that the correct method of discovery is just to seek them out and find what they have said.[1] Instead what we do is seek out arguments for various positions, a series of statements rationally supporting a particular position that can allow us to see for ourselves why a position is correct. It is because philosophers want a trustworthy method for arriving at the truth that much of our time is spent seeking out good arguments.

The word 'argument' has a specific meaning in philosophy that is different from its ordinary usage. When we say 'argument,' we don't mean two people yelling at each other. Also, we should emphasize since this is a common confusion, that when we say 'argument,' we don't simply mean one person's position or view. Rather an **argument** is typically a series of statements presenting reasons in defense of some claim. Most arguments have two components. First, they have **premises**. These are the statements that are being presented as the reasons for accepting a certain claim. Second,

Argument: a series of statements in which someone is presenting reasons in defense of some claim.

Premise: a statement offered as part of an argument as a reason for accepting a certain claim.

Conclusion: the part of an argument that is being argued for, for which reasons are being offered.

they have a **conclusion**. This is the claim that is being argued for, the statement for which reasons are being given. Here are examples of some metaphysical arguments you might have seen in your first philosophy class:

The Argument from Design (for **theism**: the thesis that God exists)

Theism: the thesis that God exists.

The complexity and organization of the universe shows that it must have been designed. But there cannot be something which is designed without there being a designer. So, the universe must have a designer. Therefore, God exists.

Atheism: the thesis that God does not exist.

The Problem of Evil (for **atheism**: the thesis that God does not exist)

If there were a God, he would not allow evil to exist in this world. But there is evil in this world. Therefore, God does not exist.

Each set of statements constitutes an argument because there is a claim being defended, a conclusion, and reasons being offered in defense of that claim, the premises. To better reveal the structure of an argument, throughout this book we will often display arguments in the following form, numbering the premises and conclusion. We will call this **numbered premise form**. Here is how we might present the Argument from Design in numbered premise form:

Numbered premise form: a way of stating arguments so that each premise as well as the conclusion are given a number and presented each on their own line.

The Argument from Design

1. The complexity and organization of the universe shows that it must have been designed.
2. But there cannot be something designed without there being a designer.
3. So, the universe must have a designer.

Therefore,

4. God exists.

And similarly for the Problem of Evil:

The Problem of Evil

1. If there were a God, he would not allow evil to exist in this world.
2. But there is evil in this world.

Therefore,

3. God does not exist.

When we present arguments this way, it allows us to refer easily back to the premises, and if we are interested in criticizing the argument, to single out which ones are questionable or in need of more defense. In the two examples we have just now considered, it is quite easy to figure out which are the premises and which is the conclusion. Sometimes in a text it is more difficult to figure out which is which, or to figure out in which order one should state the premises. The following exercises will help you work through some more challenging cases.

One tool that will help you get these arguments into numbered premise form is to look for the sorts of words that typically signal a premise or a conclusion.

- *Words and phrases that tend to indicate premises*: since, for, because, due to the fact that, . . .
- *Words and phrases that tend to indicate conclusions*: hence, thus, so, therefore, it must be the case that, . . .

You will then want to organize the premises in such a way that they naturally lead to the conclusion.

EXERCISE 0.1

Recognizing Premises and Conclusions

The following paragraphs present the kinds of arguments that were presented in the United States in 2009 for and against nationalized health care. Decide which are the premises and which is the conclusion in each case, and state the argument in numbered premise form. Note that the conclusion may not be presented last in the argument.

A. Americans should reject nationalized health care. This is because a system with nationalized health care is one in which someone's parents or baby will have to stand in front of the government's death panel for bureaucrats to decide whether they are worthy of health care. Any system like that is downright evil.
B. If we don't nationalize health care there may be those, especially the young and healthy, who will take the risk and go without coverage. And if we don't nationalize health care, there will be companies that refuse to give their workers coverage. When people go without coverage, the rest of the country pays for them. So, if the young and the healthy or employees go without coverage, then the rest of the country will have to pay more in taxes. No one should have to pay more taxes. Therefore, we should nationalize health care.

VALIDITY

What we would like in philosophy is to find good arguments that present us with compelling reasons to believe their conclusions. This comes down to two issues. First, we want to find arguments that have premises that are independently reasonable to believe. Second, we want to find arguments whose premises logically imply their conclusions.

What we are going to do in the first part of this chapter is provide you with tools that will allow you to articulate clearly in what way a certain argument is a good argument or a bad argument other than just by simply stating, "That argument is good," "I like that argument," or "That's a bad argument," "I don't like that argument." When debating important topics at a high level, we want to be more articulate than that and these next few sections will give you the vocabulary to be so.[2]

The first important feature we look for in a good argument is that it be a valid argument. 'Validity' is a technical term referring to a logical feature of an argument. By definition, an argument is (**deductively**[3]) **valid** just in case there is no way for its premises to all be true while its conclusion is false. In other words, in a valid argument, if the premises are all true, then the conclusion must also be true. In valid arguments, we say the conclusion "follows deductively" from the premises. An argument is (**deductively**) **invalid** if it *is* possible for all of the premises of the argument to be true while the conclusion is false. In an invalid argument, the truth of the premises does not guarantee truth of the conclusion.

When we speak about validity, I will emphasize again, this is a logical feature of an argument. It is all about whether the conclusion can be said to logically follow from the premises. It is not about whether the premises of an argument are as a matter of fact true. It is only about whether *if* the premises were true, the conclusion would *also* have to be true. The question about the truth of the premises is of course important and it is something we will discuss in the next section. It is just not what we care about when we are interested in validity. Let's run through a few examples of arguments to illustrate this definition of validity.

Deductively valid: an argument is deductively valid when there is no possible way for the premises of the argument to all be true while its conclusion is false. The premises of the argument logically imply its conclusion.

Deductively invalid: an argument is deductively invalid when it is possible for the premises of the argument to all be true while its conclusion is false.

Argument 1

1. If the universe were to end tomorrow, we would never know if there exist alien life forms.
2. The universe will not end tomorrow.

Therefore,

3. We will get to know if there exist alien life forms.

What should we say about this argument? Is this a valid argument? To assess this, all we need to do is ask ourselves the following question: *Is it possible for there to be a situation in which the premises of this argument are all true and yet its conclusion is false?* This is what you should ask yourself every time you are asked to assess the validity of an argument. This is all that matters. If it turns out there is a possible scenario, one we can imagine without contradiction, in which the premises are all true and yet the conclusion is false, then we know automatically this is an *invalid* argument. We are not talking about a likely situation, just one we can understand that doesn't commit us to something of the form P and not-P (this is all we mean by a **contradiction**). If the premises could all be true while the conclusion is false, then the conclusion doesn't follow logically from the premises. And so, by definition, the argument is invalid.

So what we should do to assess Argument 1's validity is try to see if we can understand how the following situation could obtain without a contradiction:

Contradiction: any sentence or statement of the form P and not-P.

TRUE	If the universe were to end tomorrow, we would never know if there exist alien life forms.
TRUE	The universe will not end tomorrow.
FALSE	We will get to know if there exist alien life forms.

Can we tell a story in which this is the case? Could it be that the first two statements are both true and yet the third is false? Yes, this is easy to see. We start by supposing that (1) is true. We haven't yet discovered alien life forms, and so if the universe were to end tomorrow, we would never know if there are any. Then we imagine it is also true that the universe does not end tomorrow. This doesn't rule out the conclusion being false: that even though the universe doesn't end tomorrow, we still never get to learn whether there are alien life forms. Perhaps we never learn this because the universe ends next week rather than tomorrow. Since there is a coherent situation in which both premises are true and yet the conclusion is false, the argument is invalid.

In general, when you provide an example to show that the premises of an argument are true, while the conclusion is false, what you are doing is providing a **counterexample** to the argument.

Let's try this with another case:

Counterexample: an example that shows an argument is invalid, by providing a way in which the premises of the argument could be true while a conclusion is false; or an example that shows a statement is false, by providing a way in which it could be false.

Argument 2

1. All events have a cause.
2. The Big Bang is an event.

Therefore,

3. The Big Bang has a cause.

What should we say about the validity of this argument? Remember: validity is a logical property of an argument. It is not about whether the premises of an argument are in fact true, but whether they as a matter of logic deductively entail their conclusion. So to assess this argument's validity, we should set aside any skepticism we might have about the *actual* truth of the premises themselves. We just want to know in the *possible* (though perhaps not actual) scenario where the premises are true, could the conclusion be false.

So, is this a valid argument? To settle this again all we need to do is see whether there is a possible situation in which the premises are all true and the conclusion is false. And again, by 'possible,' we mean *logically possible.* We are asking is this a situation we can imagine, one that involves no contradiction, in which the premises are all true and the conclusion false.

Here, it turns out: no. There is no possible situation in which the premises of this argument are both true and yet this conclusion is false.

 All events have a cause.
The Big Bang is an event.
The Big Bang has a cause.

Once we fix the premises and make them true, the conclusion has to be true too. If *all* events have a cause and the Big Bang is an event, then the Big Bang must have a cause too. To assume the conclusion is false is to assume the Big Bang does not have cause. So, a situation in which the premises are true and the conclusion is false is one in which the Big Bang both is and is not an event – a contradiction. Since there is no possible situation in which the premises are true and the conclusion is false, the above argument is *valid.* This doesn't mean the above argument is good in every way. There may be some other negative things to say about it. For example, one might be skeptical of the actual truth of one or more of its premises. But at least in terms of its logic, this is a good argument; it is valid.

Table 0.1 illustrates one key point that you should draw from this section: the question of an argument's validity is independent of the actual truth or falsity of its premises and conclusion. There can be invalid arguments with all actually true premises and an actually true conclusion. There can be valid arguments with all actually false premises and an actually false conclusion. All that matters for validity is the logical connection *between* the premises and the conclusion, and we assess that by considering what follows in possible situations.

This table shows the four possible cases for combinations of premises and conclusion. As you can see, there is only one combination that can

Table 0.1 Examples of Valid and Invalid Arguments

Premises: All true Conclusion: True	Premises: All true Conclusion: False
Valid Argument	*Valid Argument*
1. If Paris is in France, then it is in Europe. 2. Paris is in France. Therefore, 3. Paris is in Europe.	*It is not possible to have a valid argument with true premises and a false conclusion*
Invalid Argument	*Invalid Argument*
1. If Paris is in France, then it is in Europe. 2. Paris is in Europe. Therefore, 3. Paris is in France.	1. If Paris is in Spain, then it is in Europe. 2. Paris is in Europe. Therefore, 3. Paris is in Spain.

Premises: At least one false
Conclusion: True

Valid Argument

1. If Paris is in China, then it is in Europe.
2. Paris is in China.
Therefore,
3. Paris is in Europe.

Invalid Argument

1. If Paris is in France, then it is in Asia.
2. Paris is in Asia.
Therefore,
3. Paris is in France.

Premises: At least one false
Conclusion: False

Valid Argument

1. If Paris is in Spain, then it is in Asia.
2. Paris is in Spain.
Therefore,
3. Paris is in Asia.

Invalid Argument

1. If Paris is in Spain, then it is in Asia.
2. Paris is in Asia.
Therefore,
3. Paris is in Spain.

---

never occur. You will never find a valid argument in which the premises are actually true and the conclusion is actually false. This follows from the definition of validity: a valid argument is one in which there is no possible way for the premises to all be true while the conclusion is false.

EXERCISE 0.2

Testing Arguments for Validity

Are the following arguments valid or invalid?

A. All lawyers like basketball. Barack Obama is a lawyer. Therefore, Barack Obama likes basketball.
B. Some snakes eat mice. Mice are mammals. Therefore, some snakes eat some mammals.
C. If the Pope is a bachelor, then the Pope lives in an apartment. The Dalai Lama is a bachelor. So, the Dalai Lama lives in an apartment.
D. All birds can fly. Penguins are birds. But penguins cannot fly. Therefore some birds can't fly.

SOUNDNESS

If there were just one thing philosophers were looking for when they seek out good arguments, most would probably say what they are looking for is soundness. An argument is **sound** just in case it has two features. First, it must be a valid argument, in the sense just defined. Second, all of its premises must actually be true. When an argument is sound, it presents

Sound: an argument is sound just in case it has all true premises and is deductively valid.

good reason to believe its conclusion. This is because by knowing it is sound, we know (i) that *if* its premises are true, its conclusion must be true as well, and (ii) that its premises are, as a matter of fact, true.

In the last section on validity, we considered two arguments. We can now evaluate whether these are sound arguments. The first we considered, about the universe ending tomorrow and the aliens, fails to be sound because it is invalid. The second, about the Big Bang, one might think also fails to be sound, but not because it is invalid. Rather one might think the second argument is unsound because it has at least one false premise. Here is an example of a sound argument:

Argument 3

1. Greece is a member of the European Union.
2. All members of the European Union lie north of the Equator.

Therefore,

3. Greece lies north of the Equator.

This is a sound argument because it satisfies both conditions: (i) it is valid, and (ii) it has all true premises. We can check to see that it is valid by using the method in the previous section. We see if we can coherently imagine a situation in which all of its premises are true while its conclusion is false:

 TRUE   Greece is a member of the European Union.
TRUE   All members of the European Union lie north of the Equator.
FALSE   Greece lies north of the Equator.

We can't do that though. To imagine that would involve imagining a contradiction obtaining, Greece being both north of the Equator and not north of the Equator. So, the argument is valid. Since its premises are both *actually* true, it is also sound.

We are most of the time interested in whether arguments for or against a position are sound. So, in general when you are asked to assess an argument in this course, you should first look for the following:

■ Are all of the premises of this argument true? If not, which do you think are false and why?
■ Does the conclusion follow from the premises? That is, is the argument valid?

If the answers to these questions are 'yes,' then the argument is sound. The premises are true and the conclusion logically follows from them. So, one has reason to believe the conclusion is true as well.

EXERCISE 0.3

Assessing Arguments for Soundness

Go back to Exercise 0.2 at the end of the previous section and assess these arguments for soundness.

CRITICIZING ARGUMENTS

Once one understands what we are looking for in metaphysics (sound arguments for the positions that are of interest to us), one can also see how to rationally evaluate these arguments. One always has two options for criticizing an opponent's argument. One can either (i) challenge one of the argument's premises, or, one can (ii) challenge the validity of the argument. Let's briefly discuss each of these in turn.

First, let's again consider the Argument from Design presented in the first section:

The Argument from Design

1. The complexity and organization of the universe shows that it must have been designed.
2. But there cannot be something which is designed without there being a designer.
3. So, the universe must have a designer.

Therefore,

4. God exists.

We now have the tools to criticize this argument, if this is something we are interested in doing. We can either criticize premise (1) and argue that the complexity and organization of the universe have either (a) no bearing on whether it was designed, or (b) perhaps shows instead that the universe lacked a designer (perhaps a designer would prefer a simple universe over one with so much complexity). Alternatively, one might instead criticize premise (2) and argue that the fact that something is designed doesn't imply the existence of a designer. This would be to get into a debate about what it means to say that something is designed. Either way, if one wants to deny this argument is sound because premise (1) or (2) is false, one would need to present a compelling reason to think the premise in question is indeed false. Since (3) is just supposed to follow from (1) and (2) on the way to the conclusion (4), we call it a **minor conclusion**, as opposed to (4)

Minor conclusion: a statement that is argued for on the way to arguing for an argument's major conclusion.

Major conclusion:
the final conclusion of
an argument.

which we call the **major conclusion** of the argument. If (3) is the premise that seems the most problematic, then what one should really take issue with is either (1), (2), or the validity of the inference that is supposed to take one from (1) and (2) to (3).

There are two inferences that are made in this argument. First, there is the move from (1) and (2) to (3). Then there is the move from (3) to the final, major conclusion (4). Both are places one may try to criticize the argument. Here, what one should do is check both steps for validity. First, is it possible for (1) and (2) to be true, while (3) is false? Probably not. (1) and (2) do seem to logically imply (3). So, it is not the validity of that step that is mistaken here. On the other hand, it is open for one to challenge the validity of the inference from (3) to (4). One might think there is no contradiction that results from assuming that (3) is true, the universe has a designer, and yet (4) is false, God doesn't exist. Perhaps the universe was designed by someone other than God. This situation would constitute a counterexample to the argument.

Either way, if the argument fails to make all valid inferences, or the argument has premises that are false, the argument will fail to be sound. In this case, it fails to provide a compelling reason to believe its conclusion. Note that one may criticize an argument in this way even if one as a matter of fact believes its conclusion. Not every argument for a true conclusion has to be a good argument.

EXERCISE 0.4

Criticizing Arguments

Consider the following argument for the conclusion that God exists.

The Cosmological Argument

1. Everything that happens in the universe must have a cause.
2. Nothing can be a cause of itself.
3. So, there must exist a first cause.
4. If there is a first cause, then this first cause is God.
5. Therefore, God exists.

Identify which premises are supposed to follow from earlier premises in the argument (as minor or major conclusions). Label the independent premises (i.e., those that are neither major nor minor conclusions). If there are reasons to be skeptical about the truth of any of the independent premises, then state these reasons. Then, evaluate whether the inferences that are made to minor and major conclusions all appear valid. Is the argument sound? Why or why not?

THE PRINCIPLE OF CHARITY AND ENTHYMEMES

One thing to keep in the back of your mind as you go about evaluating arguments in metaphysics is that all of us are trying to work together as part of a common enterprise to discover the truth. And so, it is a convention of philosophical debate that one applies what is called the **principle of charity**. What this means is that when it is reasonable, one should try to interpret one's opponent's claims as true and her arguments as valid. For example, if you are reading a text or having a philosophical discussion and someone makes a claim that could easily be interpreted in several ways, some of which are true and some of which are obviously false, the principle of charity recommends that you choose the true way to interpret the author.

Principle of charity: a convention of philosophical debate to, when reasonable, try to interpret one's opponent's claims as true and her arguments as valid.

Another thing you will find is that some of the time when an author presents an argument in a text they will present their argument only incompletely. That is, they will present what is called an **enthymeme**. An enthymeme is an argument that is incomplete and invalid as stated, yet although the premises as stated do not logically entail the conclusion, one still has reason to believe the argument the author intended *is* valid. In the case of an enthymeme, an author leaves out some premises because they are simply too obvious to state. Stating them would perhaps bore the reader, or insult his or her intelligence. So, she leaves them out. The principle of charity compels us in such cases, where it is obvious the author intended these missing premises, and the argument needs them in order to be valid, to fill them in for her.

Enthymeme: an argument that is incomplete as stated and invalid, although it is easy to supply the missing premises that the argument would need to be valid. In the case of an enthymeme, the author left out the missing premises for fear of boring the reader or insulting his or her intelligence.

Here is one example of an enthymeme. Suppose you read in a text an author saying the following:

Argument against Abortion

Anytime one ends the life of a person, it is murder. Abortion ends the life of a fetus. So, abortion is murder. Therefore, abortion is wrong.

One might at first try to state the argument this way in numbered premise form:

Argument against Abortion

1. Anytime one ends the life of a person, it is murder.
2. Abortion ends the life of a fetus.
3. So, abortion is murder.

Therefore,

4. Abortion is wrong.

One might then criticize the argument for being invalid. For there are two inferences made in this argument: the first is the move from (1) and (2) to the minor conclusion (3):

Inference 1

1. Anytime one ends the life of a person, it is murder.
2. Abortion ends the life of a fetus.
3. So, abortion is murder. (Minor conclusion)

The second is the inference from (3) to (4):

Inference 2

3. Abortion is murder.

Therefore,

4. Abortion is wrong. (Major conclusion)

Neither of these inferences is deductively valid. In the first case, (1) and (2) could be true, but (3) false because although ending the life of a *person* is murder and abortion ends the life of a fetus, abortion doesn't count as murder because a fetus is not a person. The second inference is not valid because it could be the case that abortion is murder and yet abortion is not wrong, because murder is not wrong. (Imagine a world very different from ours where the presence of human life is such a plague that murder is altogether a good thing. Such a world might be very different from ours, but there is no contradiction in the possibility.)

At this point, one may just conclude that this argument against abortion is invalid, and so unsound, and so does not present a compelling reason to think abortion is wrong. However, this response would miss something. Here's why. There is a very simple way to fill in both inferences in this argument using supplementary premises that it is reasonable to think the author assumed. And so a better thing to do would be to grant the author the obvious intermediate steps she intends that would make the argument valid. Then we can make sure we have given the argument the best shot we can.

What are the missing links that will give us a valid argument from the premises to the conclusion? How about this:

Argument against Abortion

1. Anytime one ends the life of a person, it is murder.
2. Abortion ends the life of a fetus.

    *2.5 A fetus is a person.   (fixes the validity of Inference 1)

3. So, abortion is murder.

    *3.5 Murder is wrong.   (fixes the validity of Inference 2)

Therefore,

4. Abortion is wrong.

We are allowed, indeed compelled by the principle of charity, to supply the author with premises (2.5) and (3.5) only because it is obvious that these are claims the author intended. This is why we say her original argument is an enthymeme. It is invalid as stated, but it can easily be made into a valid argument by supplying premises that are obvious she intended, and may only have left out because they were so obvious to her.

Note that just because it is often reasonable to reconstruct an author's argument in such a way as to make it valid, this does not mean that we have to accept any argument we ever come across in a text. We still have tools with which to disagree. For although now we can see the above argument is valid, there are several premises whose truth one may take issue with. And this includes the originally unstated premises (2.5 and 3.5) that we added to make the argument valid. All are fair game and open for rational disagreement.

Applying the principle of charity and recognizing enthymemes is a skill that one develops over time as one grapples with more and more philosophical arguments. The following exercises will help you develop this skill.

EXERCISE 0.5

Supplying Missing Premises

Some call the ancient Greek philosopher Thales (624 BC–c. 546 BC) the first philosopher. Thales is famous for arguing that everything is water. Consider the following texts containing arguments against Thales's thesis. Provide the missing premises that will make the arguments valid.

A. There is no water on Saturn. Therefore, not everything is water.
B. There were things that existed in the first seconds immediately after the Big Bang. Water did not come into being until hundreds of thousands of years after the Big Bang. So, not everything is water.

PROPOSITIONAL LOGIC

We've seen that deciding validity is an important tool in assessing the strength of an argument. But sometimes, when an argument has many premises or its inferences are complicated, it is difficult to assess whether or not an argument is valid using the method we introduced in the section on validity. For this reason, philosophers have developed systems of formal logic, rigorous methods for deciding which forms of argument are or are not valid.[4] Here we will just cover a few basics that will give you tools to tell which argument forms can be trusted to yield valid arguments. These are argument forms that recur throughout the discussions in this book.

First, let's clarify what is meant by an argument form. When we talk about the *form* of an argument, we are talking about the kind of shape or structure an argument has, independent of its specific subject matter. For example, consider the following two arguments:

Argument 4

1. If Sally is human, then she is mortal.
2. Sally is human.

Therefore,

3. She is mortal.

Argument 5

1. If determinism is true, then no one has free will.
2. Determinism is true.

Therefore,

3. No one has free will.

These arguments concern very different topics; their subject matter is distinct. And yet, they have something in common: their form. To see this most clearly, logicians will replace the premises and conclusion of an argument with symbols. In the system of logic we are considering now, propositional logic, one chooses upper or lower case letters to represent individual statements or propositions. For example, let's introduce the following symbols to represent the basic propositions that make up the premises and conclusions of Arguments 4 and 5.

H: Sally is human.
M: Sally is mortal.
D: Determinism is true.
N: No one has free will.

Logical connectives: symbols used to build complex propositions out of simpler ones.

In propositional logic, the premises and conclusion of an argument will be represented by either single letters (for the basic or 'atomic' propositions) or complex symbols formed out of single letters and some linking symbols, the **logical connectives**. The logical connectives are what are used to build complex propositions out of simpler ones.

The logical connectives typically recognized in propositional logic are: 'and,' 'if ... then,' 'or,' 'not,' and 'if and only if'; they are often replaced by symbols. The chart in Table 0.2 lists some symbols that are often used to represent these words in logical notation.

Table 0.2 The Logical Connectives

English	Logical symbolism
And Sally is human and Sally is mortal.	∧, & H ∧ M H & M
Or (inclusive or, meaning: either a, b, or both a and b) Either Sally is human or Sally is mortal.	∨ H ∨ M
If . . . then If Sally is human, then she is mortal.	→, ⊃ H → M H ⊃ M
Not Sally is not human.	~, ¬ ~ H ¬ H
If and only if Sally is human if and only if she is mortal.	↔, ≡ H ↔ M H ≡ M

In this book, we will always use '∧' to symbolize 'and,' '∨' for 'or,' '⊃' for 'if . . . then,' '¬' for 'not,' and '≡' for 'if and only if.'

Using this notation, we can now symbolize Arguments 4 and 5:

Argument 4

1. H ⊃ M
2. H

Therefore,

3. M

Argument 5

1. D ⊃ N
2. D

Therefore,

3. N

Once we symbolize the arguments, their logical structure is more clearly revealed and we can see they share the same logical form.

EXERCISE 0.6

Translations in Propositional Logic

Using the key below, symbolize the following sentences in logical notation.

Key:

I: The universe is infinite.
U: The future is unknown.
O: The future is open.
F: Humans have free will.

A.   Either the universe is infinite or the universe is not infinite.
B.   If humans have free will and the future is open, then the future is unknown.
C.   Humans have free will if and only if the future is open.
D.   It is not the case that either the universe is infinite or the future is open.

As we saw, using the representational tools of propositional logic, we can see more easily that Arguments 4 and 5 have the same logical form. The form of both of the above arguments is called **modus ponens**.

Modus ponens:
the logical form:

If A, then B
A
Therefore,
B,

where A and B are
any propositions.

Modus Ponens

1.   If A, then B
2.   A

Therefore,

3.   B

or, using the notation of propositional logic:

1.   A ⊃ B
2.   A

Therefore,

3.   B

It doesn't matter which order the premises are written in. Modus ponens is one form of argument that logicians nearly always regard as valid.

Three more commonly seen valid argument forms are the following. Note in each case, A and B may stand for any proposition whatsoever, no matter how complex.

Simplification

1. A ∧ B   1. A ∧ B

Therefore,   *or*   Therefore,

2. A   2. B

Modus Tollens

1. A ⊃ B
2. ¬B

Therefore,

3. ¬A

Disjunctive Syllogism

1. A ∨ B   1. A ∨ B
2. ¬A   2. ¬B

Therefore,   *or*   Therefore,

3. B   3. A

All of these are valid forms of inference. If you find an argument that uses one of these argument forms, you can be sure it is valid.

EXERCISE 0.7

Recognizing Valid Argument Forms in Propositional Logic

First symbolize the arguments below using the notation of propositional logic and the key from the previous exercise. Then decide whether the argument's logical form is (a) modus ponens, (b) simplification, (c) modus tollens, (d) disjunctive syllogism, or (e) none of the above.

A.   Either the future is open or the universe is not infinite. The future
     is not open. Therefore, the universe is not infinite.
B.   If humans have free will, then the future is open. The future is
     not open. Therefore, humans don't have free will.
C.   If humans have free will, then the future is open. The future is
     open. Therefore, humans have free will.
D.   If humans have free will, then the future is open. Humans have
     free will. Therefore, the future is open.
E.   The future is open and it is unknown. So, the future is unknown.

FIRST-ORDER PREDICATE LOGIC

In the previous section we considered some valid forms of inference in
propositional logic. Building upon the foundation of propositional logic,
logicians have built more powerful logics, logics that recognize more valid
argument forms than propositional logic alone. These logics delve deeper
into the structure of our statements, and will be indispensable to representing the views and arguments one encounters in contemporary metaphysics.

   For the remainder of this chapter, we will consider first-order predicate
logic, initially developed by Gottlob Frege (1848–1925). This will afford us
some tools that will be helpful for our discussion of ontology in the next
three chapters. In later chapters, we will build on this foundation, adding
modal and tense operators. But let's start simple. Consider the following
argument:

Argument 6

   1.   Alex respects everyone who loves the Beatles.
   2.   Betty loves the Beatles.

Therefore,

   3.   Alex respects Betty.

If we just used the tools of propositional logic from the previous section,
we would not be able to prove that this is a valid argument. We could not
see it as having anything but the following form:

   1.   A
   2.   B

Therefore,

   3.   C

And this is not a valid argument form. We would be forced to symbolize it this way because each proposition (1), (2), and (3) is distinct and none contain the sort of parts that would allow us to use the connectives introduced in the previous section.

But the above argument is intuitively valid, and so, to show this using symbolic logic, we need more tools with which to symbolize the argument.[5] First-order predicate logic gives us the relevant tools. The key insight is to recognize that in general we can separate propositions into subjects (or noun phrases) and predicates.

To take a simple case, consider the sentence:

Shaq is tall.

In predicate logic, the symbol for a predicate ('is tall') is always a capital letter. In this case, we will use 'T.' The symbol for the predicate is placed before the symbol for the subject ('Shaq'). We will use 's' to stand for 'Shaq.' The entire sentence or proposition will then be symbolized in predicate logic in the following way:

Ts.

Similarly, 'Ludwig is a philosopher' could be symbolized as:

Pl.

We might also want to symbolize the sentence:

Shaq admires Ludwig.

This would be:

Asl.

Notice again that the symbol for the predicate (in this case, 'admires') always goes in the front. Here our predicate, 'admires,' is a *two-placed predicate* because it takes two noun phrases as inputs. But of course there exist predicates that take more than two inputs. For example, if you've played the game *Clue*, you've probably stated sentences using predicates like:

'__ murdered __ in the __ using the __.'

For example you might say:

Professor Plum murdered Mr. Body in the kitchen using the candlestick.

This can be represented as:

Mpbkc.

One thing that will be especially important in the next chapters is that we are able to represent sentences that make reference to some person(s) or object(s), but without using a name. These are general sentences such as:

■   Somebody is tall.
■   Somebody murdered Mr. Body in the kitchen using the candlestick.

or:

■   Nobody is tall.
■   There is nothing Professor Plum murdered Mr. Body with in the kitchen.

Variables: symbols like x, y, z, etc. used to stand in for other things in a sentence, called the values of the variable.

To represent sentences like this, first-order predicate logic uses **variables** (symbols like x, y, z, etc.) and what is called the **existential quantifier**. The existential quantifier is represented using: ∃. So, for example, consider the sentence:

Somebody is tall.

Existential quantifier: ∃, a symbol of first-order predicate logic. When combined with a **variable**, it can be used to represent a statement to the effect that something exists that is a certain way.

This will be symbolized as:

∃xTx.

This may be read aloud in any of the following ways:

■   There exists an x such that x is tall.
■   There is at least one x such that x is tall.
■   Some x is tall.
■   Something is tall.

Or if we know that our domain of quantification includes only persons (more on domain of quantification momentarily), we may read this as:

■   Somebody is tall.

We can also use a variable and an existential quantifier to translate the sentence:

Somebody murdered Mr. Body in the kitchen using the candlestick,

as:

∃xMxbkc.

We may read this as: "There exists an x such that x murdered Mr. Body in the kitchen with the candlestick."

Or, we can represent the sentence:

> There is something that Professor Plum murdered Mr. Body with in the kitchen,

as:

> ∃xMpbkx.

Note that the variable 'x' replaces the name of the object we are quantifying over, the referent of the quantifier phrase 'something' or 'somebody.' In the first case, the 'somebody' refers to the x that is the murderer, so the variable goes in the first place. In the second sentence, the 'something' refers to the x that is the murder weapon, so the variable goes in the last place.

We can also represent more complex sentences using the existential quantifier. For example, we can symbolize 'Nothing is tall' as:

> ¬∃xTx.

To say that there is something that is tall and friendly, we can use the following translation:

> ∃x (Tx ∧ Fx),

where 'Tx' means x is tall, and 'Fx' means x is friendly.
Or,

> There is at least one baby eagle on that mountain,

Can be symbolized as:

> ∃x ((Bx ∧ Ex) ∧ Mx).

Finally, in some cases, one will find sentences that need more than one variable of quantification. For example, one might want to express in predicate logic the sentence:

> Some cats love some dogs.

This sentence has two quantifier phrases. It says both that *there exists some x* such that x is a cat, but also that *there exists some y* such that y is a dog, and that the cat (the x) loves the dog (the y). So that we do not confuse which variable is referring to the cat and which the dog, we will use distinct variables x and y in the symbolization of this sentence:

> ∃x∃y ((Cx ∧ Dy) ∧ Lxy),

which we may read back into English as, "There exists an x and there exists a y such that x is a cat and y is a dog, and the x loves the y."

Note that in all cases where one uses a variable (x, y, z, and so on) as part of a complete sentence, the variable should always be contained within the **scope** of a quantifier. Either it is right next to the quantifier in the sentence, or there should be parentheses reaching from a quantifier and surrounding the occurrence of that variable. Consider the variables in the following two sentences.

Fx
∃xFx ∧ Gx

In the first sentence, x is not contained within the scope of any quantifier, and so this sentence does not express a complete thought. It says 'x is F,' where 'x' does not have any clear meaning. In the second case, the x in the phrase 'Gx' is not contained within the scope of any quantifier, and so again, the reference of this 'x' is unclear. Is this x that is G supposed to be the same as the x that is F? This isn't clear. To fix this, we may introduce parentheses:

∃x (Fx ∧ Gx).

Now all variables in the sentence lie within the scope of the quantifier '∃' and we can understand this sentence to be saying: "There is something that is both F and G." To say that a variable lies within the scope of a quantifier is to say that it is a **bound variable**. When symbolizing complete sentences in predicate logic, it is important that all variables be bound by quantifiers.

In general, when one makes an existentially quantified claim, one is saying there exists some thing that is a certain way. What kind of thing we have in mind generally depends on the context. The way logicians put it, this depends on the **domain of quantification**, the set of entities over which the quantifiers range. For example, suppose we used 'Bx' to symbolize 'x is blessed,' and then see the sentence:

∃xBx.

What this sentence is supposed to represent depends on the relevant domain of quantification. The domain of quantification may be:

■ the set of all entities that exist whatsoever, so that the sentence may be read as: "Something is blessed,"
■ the set of persons there are, so that the sentence may be read as: "Someone is blessed,"
■ the set of persons in a particular community under discussion, for example, those in this house. Then '∃xBx' would mean: "Someone in this house is blessed."

The relevant domain of quantification is fixed by the context. In later chapters we will see philosophers sometimes making reference to this fact. They will explicitly exploit the fact that our quantifiers may sometimes be restricted, so that they range over a limited set of objects. Or at other times,

---

Scope (of a quantifier): the part of the sentence containing the variables the quantifier is binding. In symbolic logic, the scope of a quantifier is either the part of the sentence immediately after the quantifier phrase (in a simple sentence like '∃xFx'), or the part of the sentence contained in the parentheses that immediately follow the quantifier phrase. (For example, in '∃x(Fx ∧ Gx) ∧ Hx,' the xs in 'Fx' and 'Gx' are contained in the scope of the quantifier. The x in 'Hx' is not.)

Bound variable: a variable that is within the **scope** of some quantifier phrase.

Domain of quantification: the set of objects over which the quantifiers range in a given context, the set of possible values the variables can take.

a philosopher will exploit the fact that in some cases our quantifiers may be "wide open," meaning they range over the largest domain of quantification possible, including any entities whatsoever.

We can now distinguish three types of letter symbols that are used in first-order predicate logic.[6]

■ Predicates, which are symbolized by upper case letters: F, G, H , . . .
■ Names, which are symbolized using lower case letters from the beginning of the alphabet: a, b, c, . . .
■ Variables, which are symbolized using lower case letters from the end of the alphabet: x, y, z, w, u, v, . . .

In addition to the existential quantifier, there is also another quantifier, the **universal quantifier**, which is used to symbolize claims involving 'all' or 'every.' For example,

Everyone is happy,

may be symbolized as:

$\forall$xHx.

We may read this as:

■ For all x, x is happy.
■ Every x is happy.
■ Everyone is happy.

(Note that if the only kinds of entities we ordinarily take to have emotional states like happiness are persons, the relevant domain of quantification is the set of all persons.)

To take another example, 'Everyone is a happy philosopher,' may be translated as:

$\forall$x (Hx $\wedge$ Px)

or, every x is such that it is happy and a philosopher.

How would we symbolize 'All philosophers are happy'? This says something different than saying that everyone whatsoever is both happy and a philosopher ($\forall$x(Hx $\wedge$ Px)). 'All philosophers are happy,' is symbolized using the symbol '$\supset$' for 'if . . . then':

$\forall$x (Px $\supset$ Hx).

We can read this back into English as 'For all x, *if* x is a philosopher, *then* x is happy.' This says the same thing as our original 'All philosophers are happy,' which of course is different than saying 'Some philosophers are happy,' which is expressed in first-order logic as:

Universal quantifier: $\forall$, a symbol of first-order predicate logic. When combined with a **variable**, it can be used to represent a statement to the effect that everything is a certain way.

$\exists x\,(Px \wedge Hx),$

or 'There exists an x such that x is a philosopher and x is happy.'

EXERCISE 0.8

Translating Sentences into First-Order Predicate Logic

Using the key below, translate the following sentences into the language of first-order predicate logic.

Key:

a: Alex
b: Barney
Cx: x is clever
Sx: x is a student
Tx: x is a teacher
Rxy: x respects y

1. Alex is a student.
2. Alex is a clever student.
3. Someone is a student.
4. Someone is a clever student.
5. Alex respects Barney.
6. Alex respects someone.
7. Someone respects Alex.
8. Some teachers respect some students.
9. Everyone is a teacher.
10. All students are clever.

In the next chapter and throughout the book, we will find that the formulation of theses and arguments in the language of first-order predicate logic is often essential. Particularly when we are considering issues of existence, we will be required to formulate statements in predicate logic. Only then can we be clear about what follows from them. To do so, we will need to have under our belts some basic rules of inference involving existentially and universally quantified statements.

There are four basic rules which are summarized in Table 0.3. Some of these rules are a bit complicated, but for our purposes in this book, the rules that will be used most often are Existential Quantifier Introduction (EI) and Universal Quantifier Generalization (UG). So let's just briefly consider some examples using these rules of inference.

Table 0.3 Four Rules of Predicate Logic

Existential Quantifier Introduction (EI)		Universal Quantifier Introduction (UI)	
From anything of the form:	Fa	If one has introduced a new term 'a' as an arbitrary name, and shown for it that:	Fa
One can infer:	∃xFx	Then one can infer:	∀xFx
Existential Quantifier Generalization (EG)		**Universal Quantifier Generalization (UG)**	
If it has been established that:	∃xFx	From anything of the form:	∀xFx
Then one can introduce a new term 'a' into the language to refer to whatever is the object in the domain of quantification that satisfies the description 'is F' and conclude: Fa		One can infer using any name 'a' that refers to something in the relevant domain of quantification that: Fa	

Here is an example of the kind of inference that will be employed in Chapter 2. Suppose one believes the following:

Humility is a virtue.

This will be symbolized in first-order predicate logic as:

Vh.

Using the rule EI then, we can conclude:

∃xVx.

This may be read back as: There exists some x such that x is a virtue.

And, to consider another example, if we have reason to believe the following:

Plato is a philosopher who taught Aristotle.

We may symbolize this as:

Pp ∧ Tpa   (Plato is a philosopher and Plato taught Aristotle.)

And then using EI, we can infer:

∃x(Px ∧ Txa).

In both cases of the application of EI, what we are doing is introducing a variable x to stand in for a particular subject.

Note then that when you have established an existentially quantified sentence, however complicated, that is one where the existential quantifier ∃ is on the outside of any parentheses in the sentence, you now know that there is something in the relevant domain of quantification that has the relevant features. Thus from existentially quantified sentences we can infer that something exists in the domain of quantification that has the relevant features. There is some x that can stand in as the value of this variable that makes the sentence true. For the sentence,

$\exists x\,(Px \wedge Txa)$,

the object that can stand in as the value of the variable to make the sentence true is (as we just saw) Plato.

Before leaving this point, it is worth noting that not all sentences containing existential quantifiers will allow us to infer that there is something that exists that has certain features. In general, even if a sentence contains an existential quantifier, if the quantifier is not outside of all of the parentheses in the sentence, then one is not licensed to conclude that there exists anything with the relevant characteristics. For example, consider these sentences in first-order logic:

$Fa \supset \exists xPx$ (read as: If a is an F, then something is a P.)

$\exists xPx \vee \exists xQx$ (read as: Either something is a P or something is a Q.)

$\neg\exists xPx$ (read as: It is not the case that something is a P.)

None of these sentences imply the existence of anything that is a P. You can tell that immediately because the existential quantifier is not on the outside of the entire sentence.

Finally, we should emphasize a difference between universally quantified and existentially quantified sentences. In general, the way to think about the difference is that existentially quantified sentences tell you that something exists whereas universally quantified sentences (those with a '∀' on the outside of the parentheses) say that everything is a certain way. Universally quantified sentences on their own don't entail the existence of anything. So, for example, if you see a claim like 'All electrons are negatively charged,' we can write this in first-order logic as:

$\forall x(Ex \supset Nx)$.

This sentence on its own doesn't entail that there are any electrons. It just says, if there are electrons, then they are positively charged. The following sentence entails the existence of electrons:

$\exists xEx$.

So does:

$\exists x\,(Ex \wedge Nx)$,

which symbolizes the statement that there exists at least one electron and it is negatively charged. So, if we are looking for claims that imply the existence of something in metaphysics, our attention should turn to those that are existentially quantified as opposed to those that are universally quantified.

Universally quantified sentences have other uses. They are especially useful when one wants to state universal principles. Examples of universal principles one finds in metaphysical debates are:

Nominalism:	Everything is concrete.	$\forall xCx$
Idealism:	Everything is an idea in a mind.	$\forall xIx$
Presentism:	Only present objects exist.	$\forall x(\neg Px \supset \neg \exists y(x{=}y))$
Actualism:	Everything is actual.	$\forall xAx.$

Once one establishes a universal claim like this, one can then use universal generalization (UG) to conclude about particular objects in the domain of quantification that they have the relevant features. For example, idealists usually intend their thesis to be comprehensive, in other words, a claim about the nature of everything whatsoever that exists. This implies that the domain of quantification that is relevant to the idealist is the set of all entities that exist. So if one is an idealist and thus believes that everything that exists (whatsoever) is an idea in a mind, then using universal generalization, one can conclude from:

$\forall xIx,$

and the fact that (say) Barack Obama exists:

$\exists x\ x{=}o$ (There exists some x such that x is identical to Obama),

that:

$Io.$

This may be read back as: Obama is an idea in a mind.

Note that in formulating some of the claims in the last pages, we have made use of the symbol '$=$' to represent the relation of identity. Identity is another two-placed relation like the admiring relation (symbolized above using 'Axy'). It is a relation that is of special interest to metaphysicians and is particularly useful in formulating metaphysical theses. We will have much more to say about identity beginning in the very next chapter.

EXERCISE 0.9

Recognizing Valid Argument Forms in Predicate Logic

In the following examples, state which of the four valid argument forms the arguments instantiate (EI, EG, UI, or UG), or whether the answer is 'None of the above.'

A. Everyone is mortal. Therefore, Barack Obama is mortal.
B. Some humans have free will. Therefore, Barack Obama has free will.
C. Socrates lived in the past. Therefore, there exists something that lived in the past.

SUGGESTIONS FOR FURTHER READING

There are many excellent critical thinking and introductory logic textbooks available that will develop the material introduced in this chapter further. Some excellent critical thinking texts are Richard Feldman's *Reason and Argument* and Thomas McKay's *Reasons, Explanations, and Decisions: Guidelines for Critical Thinking.* Some excellent introductory logic texts are Merrie Bergmann, James Moor, and Jack Nelson's *The Logic Book* and Gary Hardegree's *Symbolic Logic: A First Course.*

NOTES

1 See C.S. Peirce "The Fixation of Belief." We will discuss the role of common sense in metaphysics further in Chapter 1.
2 Most college philosophy departments offer courses in Critical Reasoning and Logic that develop this material further.
3 Deductive validity is the default notion of validity with which philosophers operate. It is controversial whether there is any genuine sense of validity other than deductive validity; however, I put in the qualifier 'deductive' to explicitly contrast this notion with what is sometimes called 'inductive validity.' An inductively valid argument is one in which the premises do not logically imply the conclusion, but the premises make it reasonable to believe the conclusion in some weaker sense of giving evidence for it. For example, from the premise that the sun has risen every day up until now, we may infer the conclusion that the sun will rise tomorrow. This argument is (one might argue) inductively valid but not deductively valid.
4 The method for assessing the validity of arguments introduced in the section on validity is what is referred to as a *semantic* method because it is based on

the *meanings* of the premises and conclusion. In these final sections we will be introducing methods for assessing validity *syntactically*, that is, based on the *forms* of the premises and conclusion, independent of their specific meanings.

5 Of course, we could alternatively use the method introduced in the validity section to show that this is a valid argument.

6 We can now also explain why this logic is called *first-order* logic. In the kind of predicate logic we are discussing here, variables are used to range over entities (people, cats, dogs, cell phones, and so on). They may be used to replace names, as when we move from Ts (Shaq is tall) to ∃x Tx (Someone is tall). In *second-order* logic, variables are also introduced to stand for properties or attributes, ways entities are. They may then replace predicates, for example if we wanted to move from Ts (Shaq is tall) to ∃F Fs (Shaq is some way). The status of second-order logic is controversial. And this controversy is directly related to the metaphysical issue over the status of abstract entities like properties or attributes. We will discuss this debate further in Chapter 2. For now, we will just continue to use first-order logic.

CHAPTER 1

An Introduction to Ontology

Learning Points

- Introduces ontology, a central subfield of metaphysics
- Presents the Quinean method for determining one's ontological commitments, including the method of paraphrase
- Considers the various types of data that get used in deciding an ontology
- Introduces the notion of a fundamental metaphysics and several ways to understand ontological dependence relations.

ONTOLOGY: A CENTRAL SUBFIELD OF METAPHYSICS

Ontology: 1. the study of what there is; 2. a particular theory about the types of entities there are.

In this chapter, we will introduce one of the most central subfields of metaphysics in the past century: ontology. **Ontology** is the study of what there is. In metaphysics, just as in science, one of the main things we want to find out is what kinds of things there are in the world.[1] Although in the various sciences, discussion is usually confined to a particular domain of reality – biology may be concerned with what kinds of living things there are, physics with the subatomic constituents of matter – in metaphysics, we want to know what kinds of things there are in a sense that is even more general.

Suppose physics tells us that the basic constituents of matter are leptons and quarks. The metaphysician will then ask: Are there only these physical objects, or are there also other types of entities? For example, are there, in addition to these electrons and quarks, also some nonphysical entities, like minds? Are there also abstract entities like numbers or qualities? And in addition to objects (abstract and concrete), are there other categories of entities – events, processes, spatiotemporal manifolds? All of these are ontological questions, questions about what types of entities exist.

In the mid-twentieth century, philosophers like W.V.O. Quine (1908–2000), inspired by developments in formal logic, initiated a new method for addressing ontological questions. This method has since become standard in metaphysics and it is the main topic of this chapter.[2] In the following two chapters, we apply this method to two specific debates in metaphysics.

Quine's view is presented in his extremely influential paper from 1948, "On What There Is." In this paper, Quine undertakes two projects. First, he argues that many philosophers before him have been misled in matters of ontology. Metaphysicians of the past have been too quick to believe in all manner of controversial things from abstract entities like numbers and qualities (Virtue, Beauty, the Good) to even nonexistent objects (like Pegasus or the Land of Oz).[3] According to Quine, many of these philosophical errors can be traced to an ignorance of matters of logic. An examination of the logical structure of sentences thus plays a large role in Quine's critique. This negative part of "On What There Is" is followed by a positive part in which Quine develops what he takes to be the correct method to decide which entities one ought to believe in; in other words how to decide one's **ontological commitments**.

> **Ontological commitments**: the types of entities one ought to believe in, given the sentences he or she accepts.

THE PUZZLE OF NONEXISTENT OBJECTS

Quine begins his paper by criticizing what he takes to be a clearly mistaken ontological view – a view according to which there are nonexistent objects. This is a good place for us to begin as well, for seeing the errors with this view will lead us to have a better handle on what is a good method for settling what types of things one should believe in.

First, let's see why anyone would believe there are nonexistent objects. To see the motivation for this surprising view, consider the following two sentences:

> Pegasus does not exist.
> Santa Claus does not exist.

Both of these sentences are true. But if a sentence is true, it must at least be meaningful. And if a sentence is meaningful, then each part of the sentence must itself have a meaning. But then from this it follows that the word 'Pegasus' means something and the phrase 'Santa Claus' means something. But what are their meanings? 'Pegasus' and 'Santa Claus' are names (they aren't adjectives or predicates), and so their meaning must involve what they name. So, 'Pegasus' names something: Pegasus. And 'Santa Claus' names something: Santa Claus. Therefore, there is something that is Pegasus. And there is something that is Santa Claus. So, from the plain fact that the sentences we started with are true (these sentence saying these things *do not* exist), we are forced into believing that these things are, and so we look to be ontologically committed to them. In other words, these are entities in which we should believe given the sentences we take to be true.

This point is traced by Quine all of the way back to Plato (c.428 BC–c.348 BC).[4] It seems that just accepting the claim that something does not exist commits us to its being. As Quine puts it in "On What There Is,"

BOX 1.1

The Use/Mention Distinction

Here you will notice that we have adopted the convention of sometimes placing words or phrases in single quotes. It is standard practice in philosophy to adopt this convention. In doing so, we are respecting a distinction noted by Quine: **the use/mention distinction**. This is a distinction between two ways in which a linguistic item (a word, phrase, or sentence) may appear. A sentence may *use* a linguistic item so that it plays its typical semantic role (naming some object if it is a name, modifying some object if it is an adjective, and so on). Or, a sentence may *mention* the linguistic item, using it to refer to itself. In cases where a linguistic item is being mentioned rather than used, a philosophical convention is to place the relevant word or phrase in single quotes. The following table gives examples in which a word or phrase is being used on the left, and examples in which a word or phrase is being mentioned on the right:

Use	Mention
The book is on the table.	The word 'book' has one syllable.
Santa Claus does not exist.	Nothing exists for the name 'Santa Claus' to refer to.
Please close the cellar door.	'Cellar door' is thought to be the most beautiful sounding word in the English language.

Use/mention distinction: a distinction between two ways in which a word or phrase may appear in a sentence. A sentence may use the linguistic item so that it plays its typical semantic role (naming some object if it is a name, modifying some object if it is an adjective, and so on). Or, a sentence may mention the linguistic item, using it to refer to itself. In cases where a linguistic item is being mentioned rather than used, a philosophical convention is to place the relevant word or phrase in single quotes.

"nonbeing must in some sense be, otherwise what is it that there is not?" (1948, pp. 1–2). What are we talking about when we say that Pegasus and Santa Claus do not exist if not Pegasus and Santa Claus?

At first appearances, this is an absurd conclusion. How could what is nonexistent in some sense be? However, Quine considers a couple of things that a philosopher could say here to make the thesis more intelligible. He conjures two philosophers, whom he names McX and Wyman,[5] to consider two positions as to what these nonexistent things might be:

View 1 (McX): Pegasus, Santa Claus, and other nonexistent entities are not concrete objects existing somewhere in the world, but ideas in the mind. E.g. Pegasus is not a live, physical horse with wings, but the idea of a horse with wings.
View 2 (Wyman): Pegasus, Santa Claus, and other nonexistent entities are "unactualized possibles." They are just like any other entity, except they lack the properties of actuality and existence. E.g. Pegasus is a real, physical horse with wings; just not one that exists in our actual space and time.

Although both of these views may on reflection appear to be natural ways to think about what we are talking about when we talk about nonexistent entities, Quine has objections to both of these views. First, to McX's position, Quine argues it is unsatisfactory to say that Pegasus and Santa Claus are mere ideas in the mind. This is because (recall) the whole issue of nonexistent entities was raised by our initially noting that sentences like 'Pegasus doesn't exist' and 'Santa Claus doesn't exist,' are true. But of course the *ideas of* Pegasus and Santa Claus exist. It is rather Pegasus (the flying horse) and Santa Claus (the jolly man carrying presents) who do not. So, the view of McX must be wrong.

Quine voices several objections to Wyman's view, and these are more subtle. First, let's try to understand better what Wyman's view is. Wyman is appealing to a distinction between objects that are actual and those that are merely possible. In our everyday life, we are used to thinking that there are very many things that are possible: phones that take pictures, life on Mars, flying cars, world peace, but only some of what is possible is actual.

According to Wyman, when we say that Pegasus and Santa Claus don't exist, we aren't saying there aren't such entities. Instead, we are only saying that these entities are among the group of merely possible things, things that are possible but are not actual (more like world peace than phones that take pictures). In doing so, Wyman is understanding existence as a property only of actually existing things. There is a wider class of entities that have *being*, that *are*. Those entities that *exist*, on the other hand, are only those that are actual.

Quine's first objection to the view that nonexistent entities are unactualized possibles involves rejecting the distinction between *being* on the one hand and *existence* on the other. As he puts it:

> Wyman . . . is one of those philosophers who have united in ruining the good old word 'exist'. . . . We have all been prone to say, in our

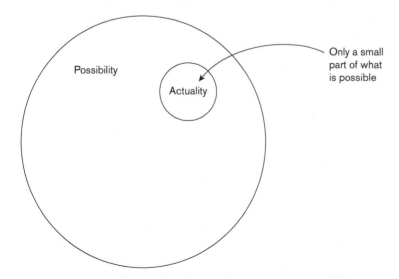

Figure 1.1 Possibility and Actuality

Figure 1.2 Wyman's View

common-sense usage of 'exist', that Pegasus does not exist, meaning simply that there is no such entity at all.

(Quine 1980, p. 3)

What after all is the difference between existing and being? There does not seem to be any. Anything that is exists. Anything that exists is. Existence isn't a special feature some objects have that others lack. At least, as Quine points out, this is how we speakers of English have tended to use the word. Conflating existence with actuality as Wyman does is to distort the meaning of 'existence.'

This simple point, that being and existence are the same, is a point that analytic philosophers since Quine have taken as a postulate. This is also implicit in the way philosophers (both logicians and metaphysicians) treat the existential quantifier, ∃, of first-order logic (see Preparatory Background, final section). '∃x' is taken to mean 'there exists an x such that' or 'there is an x such that.' These are just alternative ways of saying the same thing. The philosopher Peter van Inwagen has boiled down the contemporary view of existence, deriving from Quine, into five theses. The fifth will require more discussion before we can introduce it. The first four theses are:

Thesis 1: *Being is not an activity.* Being isn't something things do like dancing or taking a nap.
Thesis 2: *Being is the same as existence.* There is no such thing as something that is, but does not exist, or vice versa.
Thesis 3: *Existence is univocal.* In other words, the concept of existence has the same meaning whatever kind of entity it is applied to. Chairs and numbers may be different types of entities – one concrete, one abstract – but they do not participate in different kinds of existence. What it

means to say they exist is the same in both cases. The difference between chairs and numbers is not in the way they exist but rather in their properties, what some may call their "natures." Just as when we say, "This coin is round" and "This cricket field is round," we are using the word 'round' in the same, univocal sense, so when we say, "This chair exists," and "This number exists," we are using the word 'exists' in the same univocal sense.

Thesis 4: *The single sense of being or existence is adequately captured by the existential quantifier of first-order predicate logic.* When we say, "There is a table in this room," or "There exists a table in this room," what we are saying may be captured by using the notation of first-order logic, specifically the existential quantifier as in: $\exists x \, (Tx \wedge Rx)$.[6]

So, Quine's first objection to Wyman is that he is distorting the meaning of the word 'exists.' Quine has another critique of Wyman's view.[7] The moral of this critique can be expressed in the form of the famous Quinean slogan: *No entity without identity.* To defend this claim, Quine asks the reader to consider two examples of what we might think are unactualized possibles. Look to the nearest doorway and imagine that there is a fat man in the doorway. Now imagine that there is a bald man in the doorway. Quine asks the following questions:

> Take, for instance, the possible fat man in that doorway; and again, the possible bald man in that doorway. Are they the same possible man, or two possible men? How do we decide? How many possible men are in that doorway? Are there more possible thin ones than fat ones? How many of them are alike? Or would their being alike make them one? Are no *two* possible things alike? . . . Or finally, is the concept of identity simply inapplicable to unactualized possibles?
>
> (Quine 1948, p. 4)

What Quine's slogan "No entity without identity" means is that if something exists, that is, if there is such a thing, then there must be objective facts about what it is identical to and facts about what it is not identical to. Consider any entity that obviously exists, for example, the U.S. basketball player Kobe Bryant. Because Kobe exists, in other words, there is such a person as Kobe Bryant, there are facts about what and whom Kobe is identical to and what and whom Kobe is not identical to. Kobe Bryant *is* identical to the MVP (most valuable player) for the 2009 and 2010 National Basketball Association (NBA) Finals. Kobe Bryant *is not* identical to the current King of Belgium.[8] If it were vague, or if there were no facts about whom Kobe was identical to, if he could be identical to the current King of Belgium, there is just no fact of the matter, then according to Quine's doctrine, we should be skeptical of the very matter of his existence.

This is Quine's second critique of the view that nonexistent entities like Pegasus are unactualized possibles. Quine argues we shouldn't believe there are any unactualized possibles because for unactualized possibles (like the possible fat man in the doorway), there are no determinate, precise

BOX 1.2

Numerical Identity vs. Qualitative Identity

When we discuss identity in this book, please always bear in mind that metaphysicians have something very particular in mind, what is ordinarily called **numerical identity** or **identity in the strict sense**.

When you see someone claiming in metaphysics for some objects a and b that a is identical to b (or a=b), what is usually being said is that a and b are numerically identical. This means that a and b are the same object. We may have two names here ('a' and 'b') but there is only one object. This is why the relation is called 'numerical identity,' because it is identity in the numerical sense of being one.

In ordinary speech we sometimes use the word 'identity' or say some x 'is identical to' some y to express that something weaker than strict identity obtains. For example, we may say "These two cars are identical," or "These two dresses are identical." In such cases, we are not saying the dresses or cars are numerically identical. This would be to say that what appears to be two cars is really only one car; what appears to be two dresses is really only one dress. This would be interesting perhaps, but often in ordinary cases when we say such things we are not ascribing numerical identity to the dresses or cars, but a weaker relation that philosophers call **qualitative identity**. Objects a and b are qualitatively identical just in the case they share all of the same qualities (the same color, the same size, the same shape, and so on). Philosophers will often say that qualitative identity is not identity (in the strict sense of the term). It is a weaker relation than genuine identity

Numerical identity (or **identity in the strict sense**): oneness, the sense of 'a is identical to b' meaning that a and b are the same object, that they are one.

Qualitative identity: the sense of 'a is identical to b' meaning that a and b share all of the same qualities (the same color, same shape, same size, etc.).

answers to identity questions. There simply is no fact about whether there are two possible men in the doorway, just one, or a thousand. There is no fact about whether the possible fat man in the doorway is identical to the possible bald man in the doorway or not. And so we should be skeptical that there are any such things in the first place.

It is conceivable that there are other viable answers to the question of what nonexistent entities could be if there are such things. But to many, Quine's critiques of the two most natural positions on the topic – that of McX and Wyman – have been enough to make one skeptical of the position that nonexistent entities should be part of one's ontology.

EXERCISE 1.1

The Argument for Nonexistent Entities

Put the argument for nonexistent entities presented in the second paragraph of this section in numbered premise form. Before seeing Quine's own response to the argument, which premise or premises of this argument do you think one should consider rejecting (assuming one wanted to reject the conclusion of the argument)?

FINDING ONE'S ONTOLOGICAL COMMITMENTS: QUINE'S METHOD

We have seen that Quine rejects the view that there are nonexistent entities like Pegasus and Santa Claus. Nonetheless, he wants to accept that both of these sentences are true:

> Pegasus does not exist.
> Santa Claus does not exist.

But, according to Quine, just because these sentences are true and just because they mean something, indeed even though the words 'Pegasus' and 'Santa Claus' themselves are meaningful, this does not commit us to believing in such things as Pegasus and Santa Claus. Pegasus and Santa Claus do not exist, and (what is just to say the same thing another way) they lack being. There must be some way in which 'Pegasus' and 'Santa Claus' are meaningful even if they do not name anything.

Quine's view is that once we represent these sentences in the language of first-order predicate logic, it will become clear what the real ontological commitments of these claims are. Quine calls this procedure the process of **regimentation**. We want to regiment the statements we take to be true into a language in which their entailments are clear. When we do this, using 'p' to stand in for 'Pegasus' and 's' to stand in for 'Santa Claus,' we see the structures of these sentences are:

Regimentation: the procedure of representing statements in symbolic logic to make it as clear as possible what follows from those statements.

$$\neg \exists x\, (x = p)$$
$$\neg \exists x\, (x = s)^9$$

These sentences are meaningful. But we can now clearly see that given their structure, they do not entail the existence or being of anything, let alone Pegasus or Santa Claus. Indeed, the presence of the negation sign in the front shows that they explicitly deny the existence of Pegasus or Santa Claus.

BOX 1.3

Semantic Ascent

There is a very interesting move Quine makes in "On What There Is" that is characteristic of much of twentieth century philosophy. This is what is known as **semantic ascent**. This occurs when, in order to address one kind of philosophical question, a philosopher "ascends to the semantic plane," addressing first a question about the meaning of certain key terms in the original question.

In our case, Quine attacks his original question (Are there nonexistent entities?), an ontological, metaphysical question, by addressing the corresponding semantic question (Does a sentence like 'Pegasus does not exist' mean anything, and if so what does it mean?). In doing so, he "ascends" from the "ontological plane" up to the "semantic plane." The hope is that once the semantic issue is cleared up, the original ontological issue will be cleared up as well.

What about the words 'Pegasus' and 'Santa Claus' themselves and the symbols 'p' and 's' we have used in the regimentations? Must they not mean something in order for the whole sentences to be meaningful? Yes, however, one thing Quine emphasizes in "On What There Is" is that we mustn't confuse the demand that words like 'Pegasus' must *mean* something with the demand that they *name* something. Quine proposes the view (following the logician and philosopher Bertrand Russell (1872–1970)) that names are actually disguised descriptions. And so we find the meaning of a name by finding the description it is disguising. For example, Quine considers the view that 'Pegasus' means the same as 'the winged horse that was captured by Bellerophon.'[10] Then, the meaning of 'Pegasus does not exist,' could be expressed as:

$$\neg \, \exists x \, (x \text{ is the winged horse that was captured by Bellerophon})$$

or, using symbols standing in for the predicates 'is winged,' 'is a horse,' and 'was captured by Bellerophon':

$$\neg \exists x \, (((Wx \wedge Hx) \wedge Cx) \wedge \forall y \, (((Wy \wedge Hy) \wedge Cy) \supset y{=}x))$$

This sentence is perfectly meaningful and yet it does not entail the existence of a winged horse. Instead, it explicitly denies that there is such a thing.

Quine's positive view about ontological commitment then is the following. We are only committed to the existence of something when we accept a sentence that quantifies over it. To be precise, we should accept the

BOX 1.4

Names as Definite Descriptions

One might be wondering about the right-hand side of the symbolization here, the clause: $\forall y$ $(((Wy \wedge Hy) \wedge Cy) \rightarrow y=x)$. There is a reason this clause must be included in the symbolization.

We noted that Quine's strategy for showing that names like 'Pegasus' can mean something even if they lack reference appeals to Russell's theory of names as abbreviated descriptions. But Russell's view is actually more specific than that. It is not just that names are descriptions, but that they are definite descriptions. The following table illustrates the distinction between definite and indefinite descriptions:

Definite description	Indefinite description
'the winged horse captured by Bellerophon'	'a winged horse captured by Bellerophon'
'the jolly man from the North Pole who brings presents to children on Christmas'	'a jolly man from the North Pole who brings presents to children on Christmas'
'the teacher of Alexander the Great who wrote the Nicomachean Ethics'	'a teacher of Alexander the Great who wrote the Nicomachean Ethics'

Russell argued that the ordinary names in our language ('Pegasus,' yes, but also names that have referents like 'Barack Obama' or 'George Clooney') are definite descriptions because definite descriptions are like names in that they aim at picking out a unique object.

For example, consider the third set of descriptions in the table above. As it turns out, it is the Greek philosopher Aristotle who satisfies the definite description 'the teacher of Alexander the Great who wrote the Nicomachean Ethics.' And so we might think that 'Aristotle' means the same as 'the teacher of Alexander the Great who wrote the Nicomachean Ethics.' We would not want to say that 'Aristotle' means the same as the indefinite description, 'a teacher of Alexander the Great who wrote the Nicomachean Ethics,' because it is possible that many people could satisfy this description. But if many people satisfied the description, we wouldn't then say that the name 'Aristotle' refers to all of them. This would be a case in which the name is defective since it fails to pick out a unique individual. Russell's point is that it is built into the meanings of 'Pegasus' or 'Aristotle' or 'Barack Obama' that they denote a single individual.

And now finally we can understand why the symbolization of 'The winged horse captured by Bellerophon' includes that final clause: $\forall y (((Wy \wedge Hy) \wedge Cy) \supset y=x)$. Consider this phrase:

$(Wx \wedge Hx) \wedge Cx$.

What this says when read back into English is: x is winged and x is a horse and x was captured by Bellerophon. This is how one symbolizes an indefinite description.

To symbolize a definite description, to make it clear that we are not just talking about *a* winged horse captured by Bellerophon, but that we are talking about *the unique* winged horse captured by Bellerophon, we need to add in an explicit clause stating this uniqueness condition:

$((Wx \wedge Hx) \wedge Cx) \wedge \forall y(((Wy \wedge Hy) \wedge Cy) \supset y=x)$

What this says when read back into English is: x is winged and x is a horse and x was captured by Bellerophon, and for any y, if y is winged and y is a horse and y was captured by Bellerophon, then y is identical to x.

So, we can see what this last clause ensures is that there is no more than one thing that satisfies the description in the first part of the symbolization. And so to symbolize the whole sentence, 'The winged horse captured by Bellerophon does not exist,' we just add our negation sign and the existential quantifier phrase to bind the variable x. This results in:

$\neg \exists x(((Wx \wedge Hx) \wedge Cx) \wedge \forall y (((Wy \wedge Hy) \wedge Cy) \rightarrow y=x))$

One can find further description of Russell's view on definite descriptions in his paper "On Denoting" from 1905.

existence of all and only those entities needed to stand in as the values of bound variables to make these existentially quantified sentences true. To see what this entails, let us consider an example.

Say you take the following sentence to be true, perhaps because you take it to be part of your best theory of the world:

Electrons exist.

To see whether this sentence commits you to the existence of anything according to Quine, we need to regiment it: symbolize it in the language of first-order predicate logic. (In this case of course it is trivial to accomplish this translation. For more complex sentences or those that don't reveal their quantificational structure so clearly as this one, this step will involve more work, but let's just start with this simple case.) When we regiment this sentence using the language of first-order logic, we see it says this:

$\exists x$ (x is an electron)

or, using 'Ex' to stand for 'x is an electron':

$\exists x Ex$

Now, what does Quine's theory of ontological commitment say? Let's see what Quine says in his own words:

To be assumed as an entity is, purely and simply, to be reckoned as the value of a variable. . . . The variables of quantification, 'something', 'nothing', 'everything', range over our whole ontology, whatever it may be; and we are convicted of a particular ontological presupposition if, and only if, the alleged presuppositum has to be reckoned among the entities over which our variables range in order to render one of our affirmations true.

(Quine 1980, p. 13)

To tell whether something (an electron, proton, Pegasus, Santa Claus, and so on) should be "assumed as an entity," we must first translate the sentences we take to be true into quantificational language, into the language of first-order predicate logic. Then we can see what these sentences quantify over.

Returning to the last case, in order for '∃xEx' to be true, there must be something that exists that can stand in as the value of the bound variable 'x.' This means there must be some entity that satisfies the description 'Ex.' Thus, we can see clearly that this sentence commits us to the existence of (at least) one electron.

Let's apply Quine's method to a slightly more complicated sentence:

Some electrons are bonded to protons.

Say this is a sentence you accept. Symbolizing this sentence in first-order logic, we get:

∃x∃y ((Ex ∧ Py) ∧ Bxy),

where 'Py' stands for 'y is a proton' and 'Bxy' stands for 'x is bonded to y.'

Again, to apply Quine's method for determining our ontological commitments, we need to see what needs to exist in order for this sentence to be true. Here, there must be something to stand in as the value of the bound variable 'x' and something to stand in as the value of the bound variable 'y.' This means there must exist some x that is an electron and some y that is a proton and the x must be bonded to the y. So, this sentence ontologically commits us, according to Quine, to at least one electron that is bound to at least one a proton.

It is common to express Quine's method for determining one's ontological commitments as a slogan: *To be is to be the value of a bound variable.* This slogan succinctly expresses Quine's view that to determine one's ontological commitments, one should express the statements one takes to be true in first-order logic, and then read one's ontological commitments off as those entities needed to stand in as values of the bound variables in order to make those sentences true. We can summarize this method in these three steps:

Quine's Method for Determining One's Ontological Commitments

Step 1: Decide which sentences you take to be true.
Step 2: Regiment the sentences by symbolizing them in the language of first-order predicate logic.
Step 3: Commit yourself to all and only those entities needed to stand in as the values of the bound variables in order to make the sentences true.

EXERCISE 1.2

Finding Ontological Commitments

Regiment the following sentences into the language of first-order predicate logic. Determine what Quine would say you would be ontologically committed to, were you to accept the following sentences as true:

1. Some donuts have pink sprinkles.

    a. donuts
    b. sprinkles
    c. pinkness
    d. both a and b
    e. all of the above.

2. All donuts have pink sprinkles.

    a. donuts
    b. sprinkles
    c. pink sprinkles
    d. all of the above
    e. none of the above.

3. Some donuts contain holes.

    a. donuts
    b. holes
    c. perforated donuts
    d. all of the above
    e. none of the above.

THE METHOD OF PARAPHRASE

The three steps above constitute the main parts of the Quinean method. However, there is also a loophole of sorts. What if you take your best theory of the world and after regimentation, you find that it commits you to some entities you find distasteful for one reason or another, some entities you would prefer not to believe in? According to Quine, are you thereby automatically committed to them? Well, not necessarily.

In "On What There Is," Quine imagines he is presented with a biological theory which contains as one of its claims the following:

Some zoological species are cross-fertile.

As we will discuss in more detail shortly, Quine is a naturalist. This means he wants to believe what the best scientific theories tell him. And so, if the best biological theory says some species are cross-fertile, this is something he will accept as true. From here, he symbolizes this sentence in first-order logic to find out what sorts of entities it commits him to. We may use 'Sx' to stand for 'x is a zoological species' and 'Cx' to stand for 'x is cross-fertile' and this leaves us with:

$$\exists x \, (Sx \wedge Cx)$$

When we do this, we can see plainly that the sentence commits us to the existence of species. But what are species? Species are clearly not individual animals like lions or tigers. Lions and tigers are members of species, they belong to species, but are not species themselves. Species are abstract entities, e.g. lionhood (*Panthera leo*) or tigerhood (*Panthera tigris*). Perhaps you might think of them as sets, a kind of mathematical object, that contain individual animals as their members. Quine himself is skeptical of the existence of abstract entities.[11] Quine is happy to accept the existence of individual animals like lions and tigers, but not abstract entities like species.

But what does this mean for his acceptance of the biological claim we just mentioned? Since this sentence, when regimented, reveals itself to require commitment to abstract entities like species, then it looks like Quine must make the choice: accept abstract entities like species or reject the biological theory.

Here is where the loophole comes in. Quine says there is a third alternative:

> When we say that some zoological species are cross-fertile we are committing ourselves to recognizing as entities the several species themselves, abstract though they are. We remain so committed at least until we devise some way of so paraphrasing the statement as to show that the seeming reference to species on the part of our bound variable was an avoidable manner of speaking.
>
> (Quine 1948, p. 13)

Quine gives himself a way to accept the biological theory while at the same time rejecting the existence of abstract species. He allows that in the process of regimentation (Step 2), one may paraphrase the sentence to avoid quantification over entities one does not wish to countenance.

So, instead of symbolizing 'Some zoological species are cross-fertile' as:

$$\exists x \, (Sx \wedge Cx),$$

which as Quine notes would commit one to the existence of species, one might try to instead regiment it in such a way as to only entail the existence of concrete entities like animals. Here is one attempt based on the understanding that what it means for two species to be cross-fertile is for members of those species to be able to mate with each other and produce offspring.

$$\exists x \exists y \, ((Lx \wedge Ty) \wedge Mxy) \vee \exists x \exists y \, ((Bx \wedge Ey) \wedge Mxy) \vee \exists x \exists y \, ((Zx \wedge Cy) \wedge Mxy) \vee \ldots$$

where:

Lx: x is a lion   Zx: x is a zebra
Tx: x is a tiger   Cx: x is a cobra
Bx: x is a bear   Mxy: x mates with y to produce offspring
Ex: x is an elephant

Read back into English, this sentence says "Either some lions mate with some tigers and produce offspring, or some bears mate with some elephants and produce offspring, or some zebras mate with some cobras and produce offspring, or . . . " where this sentence is continued to include all possible animal pairings.

It is easy to see that according to the rules of first-order logic, this sentence will only commit us to the existence of concrete things: individual animals like lions, tigers, and cobras. In the chapters that follow, we will see this method of paraphrase deployed quite often by philosophers wishing to debate the existence of certain types of entities. Even if one's first attempt to regiment a sentence reveals it to quantify over some kind of entity, it will sometimes be possible to produce an alternative regimentation (a paraphrase) that evades that ontological commitment.

One might be wondering at this point whether anything at all goes, whether, that is, one can always apply the method of paraphrase to argue away a class of entities one finds distasteful as Quine wants to do in the case of species. The answer to this question is 'no.' There are rules here. Notice where the method of paraphrase comes in the Quinean method for determining one's ontological commitments. One has already completed the first three steps:

Step 1: Decide which sentences you take to be true.
Step 2: Regiment the sentences by symbolizing them in the language of first-order formal logic.
Step 3: Commit yourself to all and only those entities needed to stand in as the values of bound variables to make the sentences true.

Then, after worrying that one does not want to believe in the entities one comes to in Step 3, one goes back to Step 2 and tries to regiment the sentences in another way that doesn't commit one to the problematic entities. But one can't regiment sentences in any way one likes. One must produce a regimentation that has some plausible claim to capturing what was being said by the original sentence one started with. After all, these are sentences one has already accepted as true. If your best theory of the world involves a claim like, 'There are 10-dimensional strings that make up everything else,' there are regimentations of this that are plausible and others that are not. For example, it will be plausible to regiment this as:

∃x (x is a string and x is 10-dimensional and ∀y (if x≠y, then x makes up y)),

but not:

∃x (x is an electron and x is 3-dimensional and ∀y (if x≠y, then x makes up y)).

This second sentence may be expressed in English as, "Some three-dimensional electrons make up everything else." This is not what the sentence we started with said. For a paraphrase to be suitable in an ontological debate, it must plausibly convey what the original sentence was intended to convey.

EXERCISE 1.3

Producing Paraphrases

The logician Alonzo Church (1903–1995) once gave a parody of Quine's method in which he suggested that all sentences seeming to quantify over women could be paraphrased into statements about their husbands. In a sentence seeming to quantify over a woman, one would regiment this instead as quantifying over a man's "secondary presence." In such a way, following Quine's suggestion, it would be possible to eliminate ontological commitment to women altogether, a view he jokingly referred to as 'ontological misogyny.' As Church puts it, "the misogynist is led by his dislike and distrust of women to omit them from his ontology. Women are not real, he tells himself, and derives great comfort from the thought – there *are* no such things."[12] Let's assume that Church wants to accept the truth of the following sentence:

Some U.S. Senators are women.

What is the paraphrase that Church's theory would recommend?

In addition, explain what exactly makes Church's example so absurd, and how Quine would distinguish Church's case from his example involving zoological species. What makes that a more acceptable use of the method of paraphrase?

http://www.jfsowa.
com/ontology/
church.htm

BOX 1.5

A Case for Events

A good illustration of Quine's method in twentieth century metaphysics involves the philosopher Donald Davidson's argument for the existence of events. Davidson argued for events by claiming that it is only by quantifying over events that we arrive at a satisfactory account of the logical structure of sentences about actions.

To see the argument, consider the following sentence:

(1) John danced in the bathroom at midnight.

One natural symbolization of this sentence in first-order predicate logic is:

Djbm,

using the three-place predicate 'Dxyz' for 'x danced in location y at time z.'

Using three instances of Existential Generalization (EG), we may deduce from this:

$\exists x \exists y \exists z Dxyz.$

We can thus see the truth of the original sentence as committing one to a person (the dancer), a location and a time.

But several philosophers, for example, Anthony Kenny in *Action, Emotion, and Will*, noticed problems with this symbolization. One problem is that 'John danced in the bathroom at midnight' would seem to entail:

(2) John danced in the bathroom.

But this raises the question of how to symbolize (2) so there is such a logical entailment. We might see the logical form of (2) as correctly represented by:

Djb,

using the two-place predicate 'Dxy' for 'x danced in y.' But if this is correct, then (1) does not logically entail (2). Another option would be to represent (2) using the same three-place predicate as (1). The sentence would then be seen as involving an implicit, unvoiced reference to a time. The correct symbolization of (2) would then be:

$\exists x Djbx$

This will make it so that (1) entails (2), but then why think the correct predicate to use to represent (1) and (2) is only three-placed? After all, we might have instead started with the sentence:

(3) John danced the tango in the bathroom at midnight.

And then we would have said the correct predicate to use to symbolize these sentences would be the four-place 'Dxyzw,' for 'x danced the y in z at w.'

Moreover, what of the sentence:

(4) John danced provocatively in the bathroom at midnight.

This too seems to entail (1) and (2), but how could we incorporate the adverb 'provocatively' into our symbolizations to show this?

In his paper "The Logical Form of Action Sentences," Davidson argues that there is a simple way to represent action sentences that does not raise these issues. His solution not only allows us to see the logical relationship between (1), (2), (3), and (4) (that (3) and (4) entail (1) and (2), and (2) entails (1)). It also does not force us to decide arbitrarily how many places our "dancing" predicate should have, and permits a natural representation of adverbs. His solution is to view all action sentences as quantifying over events. On this view, (1) would best be paraphrased as:

$$\exists x\, (((Ixj \wedge Dx) \wedge Bx) \wedge Mx)$$

where 'Ixj' stands for 'x involved John,' 'Dx' stands for 'x was a dancing,' 'Bx' stands for 'x was in the bathroom,' and 'Mx' stands for x was at midnight. According to the rules of first-order logic, this entails:

$$\exists x\, ((Ixj \wedge Dx) \wedge Bx),$$

which Davidson would propose as the correct symbolization of (2). And both of these are entailed by:

$$\exists x((((Ixj \wedge Dx) \wedge Tx) \wedge Bx) \wedge Mx),$$

which would be a natural way to represent the logical structure of (3). The sentence (4) may then be represented as:

$$\exists x((((Ixj \wedge Dx) \wedge Px) \wedge Bx) \wedge Mx).$$

The adverb 'provocatively' can now naturally be seen as modifying the dancing, as it should. To solve all of the problems involved in understanding the logical structure of action sentences, we only need to quantify over events.

Following Quine's view that one is ontologically committed to all and only those entities needed to stand in as the value of the bound variables to make one's sentences true, we thus see how a consideration of the logical structure of action sentences may motivate ontological commitment to events. Today, belief in events is a common view in philosophy. Indeed, in later chapters, we will see the commitment to events being a central part of metaphysicians' views in the philosophy of time and causation.

> **BOX 1.6**
>
> # Ontology and Meta-ontology
>
> When we study **meta**-ontology, we are examining how to conduct ontology itself. A view in ontology is a view about what exists. A view in meta-ontology is a view about what one is doing or ought to be doing when one is engaged in an ontological debate.

Meta-ontology: the study of what one is doing, or what one should be doing, when one is engaged in an ontological debate.

With this discussion of paraphrase complete, this covers Quine's theory of ontological commitment. We now have a useful method for determining one's ontological commitments. Above, we considered the first four theses of Quinean meta-ontology according to van Inwagen.

We can now state the fifth and final thesis. As van Inwagen notes, this thesis doesn't admit of a short and snappy formulation, but here it is in his (van Inwagen's) words:

> The parties to such a dispute should examine, or be willing in principle to examine, the ontological implications of *everything they want to affirm*. And this examination should consist in various attempts to render the things they want to affirm into the quantifier-variable idiom (in sufficient depth that all the inferences they want to make from the things they want to affirm are logically valid). The 'ontological implications' of the things they affirm will be precisely the class of closed sentences[13] starting with an existential quantifier phrase ... that are the logical consequences of the renderings into the quantifier-variable idiom of those things they want to affirm. Parties to the dispute who are unwilling to accept some ontological implication of a rendering of some thesis they have affirmed into the quantifier-variable idiom must find some other way of rendering that thesis into the quantifier-variable idiom (must find a paraphrase) that they are willing to accept and which does not have the unwanted implication.
>
> (van Inwagen 2009, p. 506)

In the next two chapters we will discuss two central issues in ontology concerning the status of abstract entities and the status of material objects. We will see these theses in action there.

OCKHAM'S RAZOR

Now that we have introduced the Quinean method for determining one's ontological commitments, we would like to go ahead and put this method to work. Step 1 of the method requires us to first decide which sentences we take to be true. But what is the correct way to find the sentences one takes to be true? Metaphysicians have a host of different views on this topic. One common view is that expressed by Quine himself towards the end of his paper:

> Our acceptance of an ontology is, I think, similar in principle to our acceptance of a scientific theory, say a system of physics: we adopt, at least insofar as we are reasonable, the simplest conceptual scheme into which the disordered fragments of raw experience can be fitted and arranged.
>
> (Quine 1980, p. 17)

According to Quine, what we are looking for in ontology is similar to what we are looking for in science. We are looking for an overall theory of the world – a set of true sentences that can capture a set of data. Just as in the search for good scientific theories one norm that guides us is the preference for theories that are *simple*, the same is true in ontology. We prefer theories that can state what the world is like using the smallest set of assumptions, positing the fewest number of entities.

When Quine says that one should start with the "simplest conceptual scheme" and thus we should prefer theories that entail the fewest number of entities, he is advocating the philosophical principle known as **Ockham's Razor**. This principle, named after the medieval English philosopher William of Ockham (c.1287–1347), states that entities should not be multiplied beyond necessity. One's ontology should be as simple, as parsimonious, as is possible while still explaining everything that needs explaining. Ockham's Razor is often expressed in Latin as:

Entia non sunt multiplicanda praeter necessitatem.

Ockham's Razor: the principle that one should not multiply one's ontological commitments beyond necessity.

In ontology as well as in science, one should prefer theories that explain one's data using the fewest kinds of assumed entities. Quine expresses this preference for what we might call a **sparse** (vs. an **abundant**) **ontology** by saying he has a "taste for desert landscapes."[14] The preference for parsimonious ontologies is a preference that is independent of Quine's general method for determining one's ontological commitments described in the previous sections. One might use that method and instead have a preference for abundant as opposed to sparse ontologies. One might have a preference for the landscape of the rainforest with its lush variety of things over the austere landscape of the desert. Then one would arrive at a different set of sentences in Step 1 of the Quinean methodology, but one could still proceed from there as Quine recommends, regimenting one's theory of the world into the language of first-order logic. That said, it should be noted that Quine's preference for ontological parsimony is not an arbitrary preference, like having a taste for coffee rather than tea in the morning. Rather, many philosophers (and scientists as well) have thought that ontological simplicity is relevant to truth, that a simpler theory, a theory positing fewer entities, is more likely to be true than a theory which posits more

Sparse ontology: an ontology that posits a relatively small number of types of entities.

Abundant ontology: an ontology that posits a relatively large number of types of entities.

entities. No argument for this conclusion has yet gained widespread acceptance. One natural thought is that the universe is more likely to be simpler rather than complex. But of course this just pushes back the debate to why a simpler universe is more likely.[15] Others have suggested that it is in general more rational to believe in fewer kinds of entities because then there is less for one to be wrong about.

BOX 1.7

Fewer Types of Entities vs. Fewer Individual Entities (Token Entities)

Note that in ontology, what we are generally concerned with is how many kinds or types of entities we posit. We are less concerned with the number of *individual* or *token* entities we posit. The difference may be seen by developing Quine's analogy.

There may be little difference between deserts and rainforests in terms of how many individual objects there are in each. Think of the vast quantity of grains of sand in the Mojave Desert. There may be as many grains of sand in a desert as individual items in a rainforest. The interesting difference between deserts and rainforests isn't so much the number of individual things there are, but instead the number of *kinds* or *types* of things there are. The climate of a rainforest sustains thousands of different species of plants and animals. This is what we mean by the difference between sparse and abundant ontologies. Sparse ontologies contain fewer types of things than abundant ontologies.

WHERE SHOULD METAPHYSICAL INQUIRY BEGIN? SOME STARTING POINTS

For now, let's just say one agrees with Quine that in the study of ontology, one should aim at the simplest theory of the world, a theory that commits one to the fewest kinds of entities. The next question is how to discover this simple theory. There are several salient options for where to begin:

■ Common or ordinary beliefs in your community
■ Current scientific theory
■ Religious texts
■ Some combination of the above.

Where should one's ontological, and really more broadly metaphysical, inquiry begin?

Many philosophers start with some combination of ordinary beliefs, science, and religion to begin their metaphysical inquiry. But others reject one or more of these sources of potential information, considering them irrelevant to philosophical inquiry.

For example, whether or not you think religious texts have any place in an attempt to discover what there is depends on your religious views. In this book, we will not attempt to enter the fray over religious matters like the existence of God or the possibility of reincarnation, although these are both metaphysical issues. On these matters, we will remain neutral and not much in this book will turn on them.[16]

When it comes to scientific theory, there is a general consensus that current science provides at least one essential input to metaphysical inquiry. The main point of contention concerns how much say science has in metaphysics. Some philosophers, naturalists, argue that the only source of objective knowledge about what the world is like must come from science. Quine defines **naturalism** as "the recognition that it is within science itself, and not in some prior philosophy, that reality is to be identified and described" (1981, p. 21). The naturalist thinks it is wrong to begin metaphysical inquiry by reflecting on what we happen to believe or what any other source tells us, whether it be our community, religion, our family, or just plain common sense. We should base metaphysics on science alone. The goal of ontology is then to state our best current scientific theories as clearly as possible, regiment them in the language of first-order logic, and read off their entailments.

> **Naturalism**: the view that it is within science itself that reality is to be identified and described.

One currently popular position, **physicalism**, is even more restrictive in what it sees as the starting point for metaphysical inquiry. Physicalism is typically taken to be the view that it is only from physics itself, not from any other scientific, religious, or folk–scientific theory, that we should start an objective inquiry to find out what exists in our world and what it is like. Physics on its own can provide a complete description of the types of things that exist in our world and what these things are like. To the extent that other scientific theories like biology or psychology provide some guide as to what our world is like, their claims must be grounded in some way in the claims of physics.

> **Physicalism**: the view that physics alone can provide a complete description of what there is in our world and what it is like.

Although naturalism and physicalism at first glance may seem to rule out input from other sources into metaphysical inquiry, this is not entirely the case. Ultimately for the naturalist or physicalist, science will be the ultimate arbiter of what exists, however many naturalists and physicalists see part of the most interesting work in metaphysics as resulting from the question of how many of the things we ordinarily take to be true can be consistent with the picture of the world we get from our best scientific, or more narrowly, physical, theories. Science may be the ultimate decider of what does and does not exist, but what does this entail for the types of things in which we ordinary believe? Can they find a place in the world science describes or must they be eliminated?

The central issue in the philosophy of mind, the mind–body problem, is just this kind of metaphysical issue. The mind–body problem is usually understood today as the question of how the existence of a mental life, the fact that we have thoughts about the world, that we are conscious, can be reconciled with the fact that we are physical beings, made of simple matter of the sort physics describes. How could thinking and consciousness arise from mere physical stuff?[17]

Many of the topics we will engage in later chapters also share this structure. Science in general or physics in particular presents us with a certain view. The question is then how this can be reconciled with other things we ordinarily take to be facts: that we have free will, that time passes, that some things that aren't actual are still possible, or even simply that there are things like ordinary, material objects: tables, chairs, planets, stars, and human beings.

This brings us finally to the question of the place of ordinary or commonly held beliefs in metaphysical inquiry. As we have seen, the naturalist and physicalist think that science is what ultimately gets to decide what exists. And there are some naturalists who take a particularly hard line here arguing that the perhaps naive, pre-scientific beliefs we use in our day-to-day lives have no place whatsoever in metaphysics. As the naturalist philosophers James Ladyman and Don Ross argued in a recent book, common sense and pre-philosophical intuitions have been shown again and again to be wrong – about the fundamental makeup of matter, our place in the universe, and so on. They shouldn't carry any weight at all in an objective inquiry into what exists. And one doesn't have to be a staunch naturalist like Ladyman and Ross to reject the role of common sense in metaphysical inquiry. In his book *Material Beings*, Peter van Inwagen argues that there isn't even a body of opinions that we could identify as common sense that could reasonably guide metaphysical inquiry. According to van Inwagen, common sense is what tells you to taste your food before you salt it or to cut the cards before you deal them; it doesn't have anything to say about the metaphysical makeup of the world (1990, p. 103).

But this viewpoint is not universally shared. Many philosophers think that commonly held beliefs, reports of our intuitions, and other pre-theoretical data do have a place in metaphysical inquiry. Such beliefs are commonly held for a reason, one may think – because they are true. Just as staunchly as naturalists may take contemporary science to be the ultimate arbiter of what there is, other metaphysicians will claim that common opinion holds a central place in metaphysics. Here, for example, is an excerpt from a recent interview with the metaphysician Kit Fine:

http://www.3am
magazine.com/3am/
metaphysical-kit/

> I'm firmly of the opinion that real progress in philosophy can only come from taking common sense seriously. A departure from common sense is usually an indication that a mistake has been made. If you like, common sense is the data of philosophy and a philosopher should no more ignore common sense than a scientist should ignore the results of observation.

There is additional good reason for thinking one cannot ignore common sense altogether in metaphysics. For metaphysics is about issues that matter to us (or it should be!) and if we throw away common sense altogether, we will lose what we cared about talking about in the first place. One might argue that common sense is what tells us that time passes, that we have more certain knowledge of the past than the future, that the number two is even and doesn't have a shape or color, that there exist at least some material objects like tables, chairs, and people. The main debate today concerns how large a role such beliefs should have, and their defeasibility, in other words, how much common sense may be overturned by the results of our best scientific theories or philosophical argument, but it is a less widespread position that common sense has no role to play in metaphysics whatsoever.

FUNDAMENTAL METAPHYSICS AND ONTOLOGICAL DEPENDENCE

So we have several possible starting points for uncovering ontological truth. There is one final issue that we must raise before moving ahead and entering some central ontological debates.

So far we have presented a method for deciding an *overall* ontology, a view about the kinds of entities that exist, and this will form an important, central part of our overall metaphysics. (Recall, an ontology is just a part of a total metaphysics. It will say what kinds of entities there are, but there are other metaphysical issues as well such as what are these entities like, what kinds of properties do they have, do they exist against a space–time background or endure through time? Do they exhibit patterns of causal relations or is it just one little thing happening after another out?) Some metaphysicians will insist that what we really want is not just a theory of what kind of things there are and what these things are like, but more specifically a **fundamental metaphysical theory.**

When metaphysicians talk about a theory being a fundamental theory, what they have in mind is a theory that aspires to completeness in the sense that every fact about the world is either a part of that theory or can be accounted for completely in terms of that theory. There may be some facts that are not fundamental, in the sense that they are not formulated wholly in terms that appear in this fundamental theory, but if the fundamental theory is successful, then it can supply a complete account of all of these nonfundamental facts as well.[18]

Many would argue that in metaphysics what we want is a fundamental theory in just this sense. And so to the extent that we care about ontology, what kinds of entities there are, we should really care about possessing a fundamental ontology, an ontology that forms part of a complete theory of the world.

To illustrate what is meant by a fundamental metaphysics and a fundamental ontology, we may consider a simple example. Suppose it became reasonable to believe that a complete theory of the world could be formulated purely in terms of the following kinds of facts:

- Facts about the existence of a certain number of physical particles.
- Facts about these particles' initial locations in three-dimensional space and their stable identity through time.

Fundamental metaphysical theory: a theory that aims at completeness in the sense that every fact about the world is either a part of that theory or it can be given an explanation completely in terms of that theory.

■ Facts about these particles' intrinsic features which include only their masses, charges, and velocities.

■ A list of dynamical laws (a physics) that specify how these particles will move at future times given their initial locations, velocities, masses, and charges.

If this is it, this is our fundamental metaphysics, then our fundamental ontology will include these fundamental particles (having the features they do, behaving the way they do according to the laws) and nothing else.[19] There remains the question of whether there are any additional nonfundamental facts.

For example, it might be a fact in this world that the movement of one charged particle towards another charged particle at a certain time *causes* the second charged particle to move away at a later time. This causal fact wouldn't be fundamental, since facts about causal relations are not contained in our list of the fundamental facts in this theory. But if this causal fact could be completely accounted for in terms of facts that are on our list, then this additional fact is no threat to the claim that the facts on the list constitute a fundamental theory. Causal facts would then be nonfundamental metaphysical facts that are true and completely accounted for in terms of the fundamental metaphysical theory, even though they themselves are not fundamental metaphysical facts.

Just as causal facts may be nonfundamental, other kinds of facts could also be nonfundamental. There could, for example, be nonfundamental ontological facts,[20] facts about the existence of certain kinds of entities that are not contained in the fundamental theory and yet can be explained in terms of the facts of that theory. Perhaps, for example, the fact that there is a hydrogen atom in a certain place at a certain time can be completely accounted for in terms of facts about the locations of certain kinds of particles and the laws. If so, then, this would be a nonfundamental ontological fact – not the sort of fact our fundamental metaphysical theory includes, but something that can be accounted for completely by this fundamental metaphysical theory.

Grounding: the relation that one set of facts bears to another set of facts when the one metaphysically explains the other.

In recent years, metaphysicians have introduced the concept of **grounding** to denote the relation that one set of facts bears to another set of facts they explain. So when we say the nonfundamental facts are grounded in the fundamental facts, we are saying that there is a complete account or explanation of these nonfundamental facts in terms of the fundamental facts. There is currently a lot of discussion of what sorts of facts grounding facts are (e.g., are they themselves fundamental or nonfundamental) and what it takes in a given case to establish a grounding fact. But we will not enter these debates here.

Ontological dependence: when one entity depends on another for its continued existence.

When we talk about grounding relations, metaphysicians usually have in mind relations between the nonfundamental and the fundamental. However, there is another sort of relation that will be important in what follows and so it is worth being explicit and disentangling this sort of relation from the notion of a grounding relation. This is the sort of relation the metaphysician Elizabeth Barnes has referred to as an **ontological dependence** relation. An entity a bears an ontological dependence relation to an

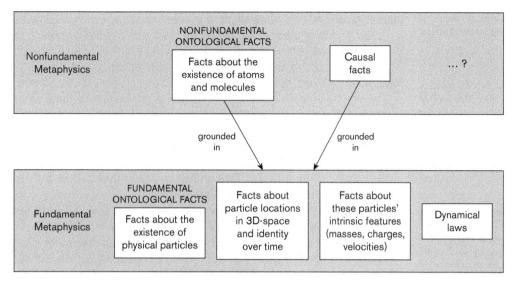

Figure 1.3 Fundamental and Nonfundamental Metaphysics: A Toy Theory

entity b roughly when the entity a requires b for its continued existence. Barnes gives the following example to capture the notion. The example uses the metaphysical concept of a simple which (as we will see in Chapter 3) one can think of as an entity that itself has no parts, much like the elementary particles of fundamental physics.

> The basic distinction is just this: if God took away everything distinct from, for example, a table, she would by that very act have to take away the table. She has taken away the simples that compose the table, and so the table goes with them. The table is ontologically dependent. In contrast, if she took away everything distinct from one of the simples, nothing in that very action commits her to taking the simple, as well. One of the simples can get by without the others (and without the table) in a way the table cannot get by without the simples. The simples are ontologically independent.
>
> (Barnes 2012, pp. 881–882)

This example illustrates how one kind of entity (a table) may be ontologically dependent on another kind of entity (some simples, or physical particles), which themselves ontologically depend on no others.

The notion of ontological dependence here is familiar and intuitive. It is the sense in which a house depends on the bricks of which it is made, an organism depends on its cells, a university depends on its buildings, students, and faculty, a painting depends on the arrangement of some splashes of paint, and so on. Some of the most interesting work in metaphysics concerns the nature of the various ontological dependence relations entities bear to other entities. We will just mention a few here which we will discuss further in the chapters that follow.

Mereological (part/whole) **relations**: these are the sorts of relations objects bear to one another when one object is a part of another object, or some one object has the others as parts. For example, when a brick is a part of a house, this is an example of a mereological relation.

> Mereological relations: part/whole relations.

Realization relations: this is the sort of relation objects bear to one another when one or more objects play the role of implementing some other object. The classic philosophical example of a realization relation is the relation between a piece of computer hardware (say a particular iPhone) and a computer program or software (say the running of a chess program). The iPhone (or some of its parts) realizes the chess program. The hardware, through its physical operations, is able to implement the playing of the chess program.

> Realization: one object or objects realize another when the former plays the role of implementing the latter, e.g. when some hardware components implement a particular program.

Supervenience: is a relation between two sets of facts that is sometimes thought to be an ontological dependence relation. We say facts about one class of entities (the As) supervene on facts about another class of entities (the Bs) when there can be no change in the A-facts without there being a change in the B-facts.[21] For example, one might think that the facts about a given painting (say, van Gogh's *The Starry Night*) and what it is like intrinsically supervene on the facts about paint on a canvas. For example, there can be no change in whether the painting depicts a crescent moon without a corresponding change in the color and arrangement of paint on the canvas. For there to be a change in the painting, there must be a change in the physical distribution of paint.

> Supervenience: one set of facts about a class of entities (the As) supervenes on another set of facts about a class of entities (the Bs) when there can be no change in the A-facts without a corresponding change in the B-facts.

In many cases the way one goes about showing that a set of nonfundamental facts can be explained or accounted for completely in terms of a set of fundamental facts is by revealing an ontological dependence relation. For example, in Barnes's table example, the nonfundamental facts about the existence of a table may be completely accounted for by appealing to facts about the existence of physical simples and a relation of ontological dependence obtaining between the table and the simples. However, as Barnes emphasizes, to say that one class of entities ontologically depends on another is not by itself to express a claim about fundamentality. The fundamental/nonfundamental distinction is not the same as the ontologically independent/dependent distinction. In some cases (like that of the table and its constituent simples) the two distinctions may map on to each other, but this is not so in all cases.

To see this, we need only consider the cases we used above to illustrate the various ontological dependence relations. Houses, bricks, iPhones, chess programs, paintings, and paint: it is conceivable and, to many, plausible that none of these are elements of a fundamental metaphysics. Moreover, as we will see in later chapters, it is sometimes possible to see ontological dependence relations obtaining between some entities both of which turn out to be fundamental. Revealing an ontological dependence relation may settle an interesting question of the metaphysical relation between two or more entities. But it in itself will not suffice to show that either of these entities is fundamental or not.

To return to Quine's method for determining one's ontological commitments, that method as it is officially stated is neutral about this issue of fundamental vs. nonfundamental ontology. It is plausible to think that Quine himself, however, was interested in the discovery of a fundamental metaphysics, and thus a fundamental ontological theory. When Quine examines the procedure for determining an ontology, as we saw, he asks us to consider what is our best theory of the world. If our best theory is one aspiring to completeness, in accounting for all phenomena we may or may not encounter, then this will indeed be a fundamental theory. And this is how we will proceed in what follows, examining what our ontological commitments should be in light of what we have reason to believe is the best, ultimate, fundamental theory of the world.

EXERCISE 1.4

Relations of Ontological Dependence

Which if any of the three kinds of ontological dependence relation would you argue obtains in the cases below – a mereological (part/whole) relation, realization relation, a supervenience relation:

A. A collection of buildings, students, and faculty on the one hand, and a university on the other.
B. The physical facts about a murder and facts about its moral status (as being wrong or morally justified).
C. Cells and a human liver.

SUGGESTIONS FOR FURTHER READING

In addition to the articles discussed above, in particular the Quine and van Inwagen pieces that spell out the standard Quinean line on determining one's ontological commitments, there are several interesting criticisms of this view. Two notable critiques are William Alston's "Ontological Commitments" and Richard Routley's "On What There is Not." We will examine further critiques in the next chapter. The recent volume *Metametaphysics*, edited by David Chalmers, David Manley, and Ryan Wasserman, contains many articles defending, criticizing, and examining the historical origins of Quine's method. Peter Hylton's recent book on Quine is also a useful resource.

There has been a groundswell of recent work on fundamentality, grounding, and ontological dependence. On ontological dependence relations, Karen Bennett's "Construction Area (No Hard Hat Required)" and *Making Things Up* are excellent resources. A good place to begin on grounding is Kelly Trogdon's "An Introduction to Grounding." Kit Fine's "The Question of Realism" and Theodore Sider's *Writing the Book of the World* (especially chapters 6 and 7) are also recommended recent texts on fundamentality and grounding, but it should be noted they mark a significant step up in terms of level of difficulty.

NOTES

1   In this book, we will most of the time use the word 'world' to mean the entire universe, not just what exists on planet Earth. We will address the meaning of 'world' more fully in the chapter on modality and possible worlds (Chapter 7).

2   This is not to say this method is uncontroversial or that no alternatives to it exist. We will discuss alternatives to the Quinean method throughout this textbook. However, since the Quinean method is the most familiar and commonly used method in ontology today, it will be a good starting point for us.

3   Here, and throughout most of the text, we will use the words 'thing,' 'object,' and 'entity' interchangeably.

4   This is traced to the discussion of being and nonbeing in Plato's dialogue *The Sophist*, which was thought to be written in approximately 360 BC.

5   'McX' is thought to be a veiled reference to the English, idealist philosopher J.M.E. McTaggart (1866–1925). 'Wyman' is thought to be a veiled reference to the Austrian philosopher Alexius Meinong (1853–1920), a philosopher who explicitly held the view that anything we can think of must have some being and that existence is a mere property of an object, a property any object can have or lack.

6   Van Inwagen presents these theses in two articles: "Meta-ontology" and "Being, Existence, and Ontological Commitment."

7   There is a third critique as well: that Wyman's view violates the norm of Ockham's Razor (1948, p. 4). We will discuss Ockham's Razor in a later section.

8   This is King Philippe, who ascended the throne in July 2013.

9   The symbol '¬' stands for 'It is not the case that.' '=' stands for the identity relation. See the final two sections (Propositional Logic and First Order Predicate Logic) of the Preparatory Background on logic.

10   Quine actually considers two views about the meaning of names like 'Pegasus' in "On What There Is." One is that mentioned above, that names are disguised descriptions. Another alternative he considers is that names are disguised predicates. Here, the meaning of 'Pegasus does not exist,' would be the same as 'There is no thing that pegasizes' or '¬∃xPx.'

11   We will say much more about this skepticism and the abstract/concrete distinction in the next chapter.

12   In a lecture presented at Harvard University in 1958.

13   A closed sentence is a sentence in which all variables are bound by quantifiers.

14   "On What There Is," p. 4.

15   See the discussion in Alan Baker, "Simplicity."

16 A good anthology covering metaphysical issues in the philosophy of religion is Louis Pojman and Michael Rea's *Philosophy of Religion: An Anthology*.

17 Jaegwon Kim's textbook, *The Philosophy of Mind*, is a particularly good introduction to the mind–body problem and other central issues in the metaphysics of mind.

18 Note that this sense in which metaphysicians are after a fundamental or complete theory of the world is closely connected to the sense in which some scientific theories aspire to be complete, or "theories of everything." We will have the opportunity to explore the relations between fundamental metaphysical theories and fundamental scientific theories more in Chapter 4.

19 In the next chapter we will question this claim, whether a fundamental theory like this would only ontologically commit us to particles. But let's assume this is so for now.

20 This is controversial. Kit Fine (2009), for example, argues that only the fundamental facts about what exists are genuinely ontological.

21 See Jaegwon Kim's "Concepts of Supervenience." It is controversial whether supervenience is an ontological dependence relation; even Kim himself is now skeptical of this (see his *Philosophy of Mind*). But historically, philosophers have been interested in uncovering supervenience relations as they at least seem to be indicators that there is an ontological dependence relation lurking.

CHAPTER 2

Abstract Entities

Learning Points

- Applies the Quinean method to investigate the ontological status of abstract entities
- Introduces the abstract/concrete distinction
- Examines the One Over Many argument for the existence of universals
- Presents truthmaker theory, a rival method for determining one's ontological commitments
- Introduces the indispensability argument and the current debate over the existence of mathematical entities.

MORE THAN A MATERIAL WORLD?

In the last chapter we introduced the Quinean ontological method. This method allows us to decide the answers to questions about which kinds of entities exist. It advises us first to determine which sentences we take to be true, then to regiment these sentences into the language of first-order predicate logic, then finally to read off commitment only to those entities needed to stand in as the values of bound variables in order for those sentences to be true.

In this chapter, we will apply this method to a topic that has occupied metaphysicians since the earliest days of western philosophy in ancient Greece. This is the question of the existence of abstract entities. For the purposes of this chapter, let us take for granted the existence of the concrete, familiar, material objects of our world, those objects like tables and chairs, rivers and mountains, stars and galaxies, persons and other animals, objects that have particular features like shape and size, that occupy spatial locations, objects that we can see, that we can touch or imagine touching.

We will assume for now that these concrete things exist. The question for us is then, in addition to these concrete, material objects, what else exists? For example, consider the mathematical claims you take to be true.

Doesn't mathematics tell us that there are such things as prime numbers, such things as even and odd numbers? Doesn't 144 have at least one square root? Aren't there fractions, at least some of which are less than one and greater than zero? If these claims are true, if we believe mathematics is a true theory, then Quine's method seems to entail that we are committed to the existence of numbers. And if we believe numbers exist, then we must believe that there exist at least some abstract objects. The prime numbers, the evens and odds, the fractions, and the rest are certainly not concrete entities. They are not the kinds of things that occupy spatial locations; we can't see or touch them; they don't have features like shape and size, at least not in the straightforward sense that tables and rivers do. Indeed we can ask the same question about all of the objects of mathematics, the perfect spheres of geometry, the vectors and groups of algebra, the sets of set theory. Do they exist? And if not, are we forced to say that mathematics is simply false?

We will address the ontological status of mathematical entities later in this chapter. First, we will look into a more general argument for the existence of abstract entities, one that applies not only to mathematical entities but to abstract entities of other kinds as well. The sort of abstract entities on which we will focus attention initially are properties. In addition to concrete, material objects like tables and chairs, many have thought there also exist abstract entities that are the *properties* of these tables and chairs: their shapes, sizes, and colors. Or that there exist at least some fundamental physical properties. After all, isn't it the job of our fundamental physical theories to tell us which these are: mass, charge, spin, quark color? Others have argued we should believe that there are certain special properties that we value as human beings and that good people ought to strive after such as humility, honesty, wisdom, and the other virtues. If we believe any of this, and thus become committed to properties likes colors, shapes, masses, or virtues, then we seem committed to the thought that our world is made up of more than the concrete, material objects. Instead, we must expand our ontology by letting in abstracta (abstract entities) as well. Let's start by trying to get a bit clearer on what we mean by an **abstract** entity.

Abstract: a classification of entities, examples include properties and mathematical objects.

BOX 2.1

Propositions

One additional category of abstract entity which we will not explicitly discuss much in this chapter is that of propositions. When philosophers and logicians discuss propositions, they will distinguish them from the sentences that express them. Propositions are often regarded as the contents of sentences; they are what those sentences mean. And like sentences, they may be true or false. For example, consider these two sentences:

Everyone is in a good mood today.
Tutti sono di buon umore oggi.

These are two different sentences. One is an English sentence; the other is Italian. But they both express the same proposition. We may pick out the proposition expressed using a 'that'-clause. It is the proposition that everyone is in a good mood today.

While sentences may be thought to be concrete entities – they may be identified with concrete strings of letters on a page, or concrete sounds uttered by a speaker – the propositions sentences express are typically viewed as abstract. We will consider the metaphysics of propositions later in Chapter 7.

THE ABSTRACT/CONCRETE DISTINCTION

There are two main ways in which philosophers understand what is meant by an abstract as opposed to a concrete entity. The first we have already seen. Abstract entities are sometimes distinguished by their lack of certain features. For example, while **concrete** entities have observable properties like shapes and sizes, colors and smells, abstract entities like numbers seem to lack these features. In addition, while concrete entities are thought to all have spatial locations, abstract entities do not occupy space. They are rather often thought of as **transcendent** entities, located outside of space and perhaps time as well. Finally, it is sometimes thought that only concrete entities have causal influence on surrounding objects. Abstract entities lack such causal influence. You can bang your hand on a chair and this will cause you pain or a bruise, but you can't bang your hand on the number three.

This way of classifying entities as concrete or abstract works nicely for some clear cases, the exemplars of concreteness or abstractness.

However, in general, although we might say that these features on the left-hand side of Table 2.1 generally are *marks of* concreteness, they are neither necessary nor sufficient conditions of concreteness. To see this, consider the cases in Table 2.2.

These cases all make trouble for the proposed way of distinguishing concrete from abstract entities. For what we find is that for each case, we get a mix of 'yes' and 'no' answers. Most philosophers tend to think of the first cases, elementary particles, space, time, and space–time, as cases of concrete entities, and the cases of properties, whether these be general properties like red or green or particular instances of these properties, as abstract. But it can't be because of the sort of distinguishing features

Concrete: a classification of entities that is not abstract, examples include material objects like tables, planets, and rocks.

Transcendent: a transcendent entity is one that is not located in space or time.

Table 2.1 Distinguishing Features of Concrete and Abstract Entities

Tables and vices	Rivers	Stars	Numbers	The virtues
Do they have shape?	yes	yes	no	no
Do they have size?	yes	yes	no	no
Do they have color?	yes	yes	no	no
Do they occupy space? Do they have spatial locations?	yes	yes	no	no
Do they causally interact with anything?	yes	yes	no	no

Table 2.2 Trickier Cases

	Electrons and other elementary particles	Space, time, and space–time	Colors like red and green	Particular colors of individual objects
Do they have shape?	no	depends	no	yes
Do they have size?	yes	yes	no	yes
Do they have color?	no	no	yes	yes
Do they occupy space? Do they have spatial locations?	yes	no	depends on your view about properties	yes
Do they causally interact with anything?	yes	perhaps	depends	perhaps

catalogued above. The proposal works well for distinguishing observable entities from unobservable entities. But once we recognize that there may be concrete entities that are unobservable and abstract objects that are observable, it seems it may be best to find another way to make the distinction between abstract and concrete entities.

An alternative is to view abstract entities as those that are *abstractions from* concrete objects. Here is an example. Consider the table nearest to you right now. This is a clear example of a concrete object. Now consider the color of the table by doing the following. Imagine removing all other features of this particular table, its height, its shape, the material of which it is made, and just leaving this one property of the table, its color. This process of stripping away all other features of the object just to leave this one feature (in this case, its color) is what we mean by 'abstraction.' The table's color is an abstraction then from the table itself. We might also, by abstraction, come to other properties of the table: its shape, its height, its smoothness, and so on.

Let's think through just one more example to see how numbers too may in this way be thought of as abstract entities. Geographers tell us that Japan is made up of 6,852 islands. Consider all of these islands. There are four large ones: Honshu, Hokkaido, Kyushu, and Shikoku. That leaves 6,848 smaller ones. We may think of all of these islands together in all of their complicated detail, or we may abstract away from all of this detail and just consider this one feature, their number: 6,852. When we do this, we abstract away the particular shapes and sizes of all of the islands, their greenness or brownness, their patterns of settlement, their distances from one another. When we do this, we are just left with their number, they are a collection of 6,852 objects. In this way, we may view not just properties like brownness or smoothness, but also numbers as abstract entities, as abstractions from concrete objects. Concrete objects may then be thought of as objects that are not the result of abstraction from any other object.

There are two ways to understand this process of abstraction: one is psychological and conveys only how we come to know about abstract objects. The psychological process of **abstraction** is the process of considering an object while ignoring some of its features. There is also another, metaphysical way to think of abstraction. In this sense, abstraction is not something we do in our minds, but a metaphysical relation that obtains between a target object and another that lacks some of the former's features (the abstraction). In the remainder of this chapter, this will be our preferred way of making the abstract/concrete distinction. Abstract objects are those that are abstractions from other objects.[1]

Abstraction:
1. a psychological process of considering an object while ignoring some of its features; for example ignoring all other features of a table (its color, material, texture) to just consider its size;
2. the metaphysical relation of one entity being an abstraction from another, an entity just like the latter except lacking some of its features.

EXERCISE 2.1

Abstract or Concrete?

Set aside the issue of whether we are justified in believing in the following things. *If* such things were to exist, would you consider them concrete entities or abstract entities? Why?

A. aesthetic features like beauty
B. the Big Bang
C. the center of the Earth
D. dreams
E. electromagnetic fields
F. the fictional characters, Romeo and Juliet
G. God.

UNIVERSALS AND THE ONE OVER MANY ARGUMENT

Let's now turn our attention to the ontological status of properties: the shapes and colors, masses and charges, virtues and vices. We will return to focus on mathematical entities at the end of this chapter. Should we include properties in our ontology? Should we believe not just that there are round tables, but that, in addition, there is an abstract entity: roundness? Should we believe not just that there are electrons, but that, in addition, there is an abstract entity: negative charge?

Properties like roundness and negative charge would be interesting kinds of entities if they existed, not just because they are abstract, but because they may be examples of a kind of entity that is especially puzzling. They seem to be examples of **universals**: entities that are repeatable, capable of being instantiated at multiple locations at once by several different entities. Think about roundness. How many things in the area around you right now are round? The rim of a coffee mug? A doorknob? The button on someone's iPhone? There are many, many rounds things in any given place at a given time. And if we think that in addition to these round things, there is also an abstract entity, roundness, then this entity will be a universal since it is capable of being instantiated in all of these many different places at once. To say that a property is **instantiated** is to say that it is had by an entity. Properties that are instantiated at many different locations (universals) are interesting because when they are instantiated they appear to be wholly present at each of these locations. It isn't that it is a part of roundness that is present here in this coffee mug and another part of roundness that is present there in the doorknob, as I might have part of my body (my torso) leaning against a chair and another part of my body (my feet) propped up on a desk. When roundness is multiply instantiated at a given time it is wholly present in all of these different locations at one and the same time. All of it is there in that mug. And all of it is again there in that doorknob, at the same time.

So, we have another distinction, that between universals (entities that may be multiply instantiated) and **particulars** (entities that may not). As Aristotle says in *De Interpretatione*:

> Now of actual things some are universal, others particular. I call universal that which is by its nature predicated of a number of things, and particular that which is not; man, for instance is a universal, Callias a particular.

Plato (c.428 BC–c.348 BC) and Aristotle (384–322 BC) both believed in universals, but they conceived of them in different ways. Plato believed in universal entities called the **Forms**. These were the fundamental entities in Plato's ontology. Some examples of the Platonic Forms are features like Beauty, Justice, and the Good. Plato believed these universals had several interesting features in addition to being repeatable. They are (i) transcendent, in the sense that they exist outside of space and time. They are (ii) ideal which means that they are perfections. The Form of Beauty is entirely beautiful, not at all ugly. The Form of Justice is entirely just, not even slightly unjust. This is in contrast to those things in our spatiotemporal realm that may instantiate Beauty or Justice, concrete things like people, works of art, or political institutions. These things are never perfectly beautiful or perfectly just. According to Plato, although people and political institutions

Universal: a type of entity that is repeatable, that may be instantiated at multiple locations at once by distinct entities.

Instantiation: the relation between a property and an entity that has that property.

Particular: any entity that may not be multiply instantiated.

Forms: the universals that constitute the fundamental entities of Plato's ontology.

may *instantiate* the Forms of Beauty or Justice, they always instantiate a little of the opposite Form as well. Even the most beautiful works of art, the most just political institutions are just a little bit unbeautiful or unjust. Finally, Plato held that the Forms were the kind of entities that (iii) could only be known through the pure intellect, never through sense perception or observation. Although ordinary, perceptible objects may instantiate Beauty or Justice, these are not perceptible features of them, features of them you

---

BOX 2.2

A Priori vs. A Posteriori Ways of Knowing

When Plato argues that the Forms are known only through the use of the intellect, not through sense perception, he is making a distinction which philosophers today would call the distinction between **a priori** and **a posteriori** (or **empirical**) ways of knowing. To say a fact is known a priori is to say that it is known in a way that does not involve observation or sense experience. It can be known just by reflection in one's mind (using a method that is *prior to* experience). When you do a proof in a geometry class, for example, you are using a priori methods to deduce certain facts from other facts. When you reflect on the nature of certain concepts or the meanings of certain terms to deduce facts, this also involves the use of a priori methods. For example, if I tell you that my brother is a bachelor, then using a purely a priori method, just by reflecting on what it is to be a bachelor, you can come to know that my brother is unmarried.

By contrast, to say a fact is known a posteriori or through empirical means is to say that it is learnt through some process of observation or sense experience. For example, there are many ways of coming to know about the color of the Nile River. You can travel to Africa and see it for yourself. You can view a picture of the Nile online or in a travel book. You can have somebody who has visited it describe it to you. All of these are a posteriori ways of knowing. They involve some kind of empirical observation, whether a direct observation of the thing or fact in question or an indirect observation by way of observation of a record or testimony. Either way, the fact is acquired through the senses, through something that is seen or heard (the object itself, a record, a report).

In Plato's view, you may observe things that are beautiful, institutions that are just. But one never observes Beauty or Justice itself. The Forms cannot be seen or touched or heard, they can only be understood through the intellect.

A priori method: a way of knowing a fact or proposition that does not involve observation or sensory experience.

A posteriori method: an empirical way of knowing a fact or proposition, one that involves observation or sensory experience.

Empiricism: the view that our knowledge and understanding of our world comes entirely from experience.

may see. What we are able to see is only a shadow of the Form. To come to understand and know of the Form itself, perfect as it is, requires the use of the pure intellect.

Aristotle, on the other hand, took universals out of the transcendental realm and viewed them as existing in the concrete objects that instantiate them. This is to say that Aristotle viewed universals as **immanent** as opposed to transcendent, instantiated in space and time, and located where the objects are that instantiate them. David Armstrong is a contemporary metaphysician who endorses an Aristotelian theory of properties as universals. According to Armstrong, properties are abstract, universal (repeatable), in space and time (they are wholly located at each of their instances), and knowable by observation or ordinary empirical means. For Aristotelians, we learn about which universals there are in the same ways we learn about the particular entities there are. If one is a naturalist, as many Aristotelians are, one will think one learns about which universals there are by consulting our best scientific theories.

Realism about universals is the view that there are such things as universals. **Platonism** about universals is the more specific view that there are such things as universals and they have some or all of the features Plato thought they had. Realism or Platonism about universals is usually contrasted with **nominalism**, a position that denies the existence of universals.[2] Realism is also historically contrasted with **conceptualism**, an intermediate position between realism/Platonism and nominalism. The conceptualist rejects nominalism and says that universals do exist. However she claims that universals are entities that depend on our minds' grasp of them, our abstracting them (in the psychological sense) away from concrete objects. Thus, according to the conceptualist, universals exist but are mind-dependent entities. In general, those calling themselves 'realists' about some class of entities will usually insist that the entities with which they are concerned are mind-independent entities; that the entities in question exist and they would exist even if there were never any humans around to think about them. Even for Plato, who thought that the only way one can come to know about the Forms is through the intellect, these entities are robustly mind-independent. The only way *we* can come to know about and understand the Forms is through the pure operation of the intellect, but the Forms would exist even if there was never anybody around to think about them.

The classic argument found over and over again in the history of philosophy for realism about universals is what is known as the **One Over Many**. It is the overall form of this argument that we will be most interested in evaluating, but let's start by considering one particular example. In "On What There Is," Quine explicitly attacks a particular example of the One Over Many, one he attributes to his character McX:

One Over Many (McX's version)

1. There are red houses, red roses, and red sunsets.

Therefore,

Immanent: an entity that is located in space and time, where it is instantiated.

Realism about universals: the view that universals exist and they are mind-independent entities.

Platonism: 1. the view that there are such things as the Platonic Forms; 2. the view that there are such things as abstract, mathematical entities.

Nominalism: 1. the view that there are no such things as abstract entities; 2. the view that there are no such things as universals; 3. the view that there are no such things as mathematical entities.

Conceptualism: the view that universals exist, however they are entities that depend on our mind's grasp of them.

One Over Many: an argument for realism about universals that starts from a premise about some similarities between a group of objects and concludes that there is a universal (a one) that runs through these individual objects (the many).

> 2. These houses, roses, and sunsets have something in common: the universal redness.

(Quine 1948, p. 10)

What makes this an example of a One Over Many is that the first premise of the argument is a simple statement about a group of objects that bear some similarity. In this case, we have three kinds of objects (houses, roses, sunsets) that are all red. In addition, for this to be a One Over Many, in the conclusion we infer that there is a universal (a one) that runs through these objects (the many) and is what they have in common. From the fact that several objects, a "many," have some similarity, it is inferred that there is a "one" that runs through the many and accounts for the similarity.

As we have noted, this form of argument is old. One finds it even in Plato's *Republic*, which is believed to have been written in 360 BC. There, in *Republic* Book 10, one finds the inference from the fact that there is a multiplicity of objects similar in some way to the fact that there is a Form (a Platonic universal) accounting for this similarity:

> We are in the habit, I take it, of positing a single idea or form in the case of the various multiplicities to which we give the same name. Do you understand?
> I do.
> In the present case, then, let us take any multiplicity you please; for example, there are many couches and tables.
> Of course.
> But these utensils imply, I suppose, only two ideas or forms, one of a couch and one of a table.

(Plato, *Republic* Book 10, 596a–b)

This use of the inference, where a universal is generated for every term ('couch,' 'table,' but also 'red' and 'round') we use for a multiplicity of objects, will easily generate an enormous quantity of universals. If one had some sympathies with the principle of Ockham's Razor, one might have concerns. For this reason, some have suggested that the One Over Many be interpreted more narrowly.[3]

The One Over Many, we may assume, always takes roughly the following form:

> *Premise*: There exists some x that is F and there exists some y that is F (where it is assumed the x and the y are distinct entities, i.e. $x \neq y$).

Therefore,

> *Conclusion*: There is a universal F-ness that the x and the y both instantiate.

In McX's version of the argument, there are three objects noted to be similar, but strictly speaking all that is needed is that there is more than one in the first premise (a many).

There are two ways then in which one might use this form of argument to generate a theory of universals. The first way, which is more in line with the passage from Plato, is to allow instances of this argument for every case in which we are disposed to apply a common term to each of a group of objects. In other words, we may allow instances of this argument for any general term we may plug in for 'F.' Here are some examples:

One Over Many (Red)

1.   There are red houses and red roses.

Therefore,

2.   There is a universal, redness, that the houses and roses instantiate.

One Over Many (Chair)

1.   There are two chairs in this room.

Therefore,

2.   There is a universal, chairness, that the chairs instantiate.

One Over Many (In This Room)

1.   There are people in this room and coffee mugs in this room.

Therefore,

2.   There is a universal, in-this-room-ness, that the people and mugs instantiate.

One Over Many (Mass One Kilogram)

1.   There are flowerpots and handweights that have mass of one kilogram.

Therefore,

2.   There is a universal, mass of one kilogram, that these flowerpots and handweights instantiate.

If Plato is willing to countenance universals in any case where there is a multiplicity of objects falling under some common term, all of the above would be legitimate instances of the One Over Many. And what will result is what metaphysicians call an **abundant theory of universals**. An abundant theory of universals is a version of realism that posits a relatively large number of distinct universals. Here we are considering an extreme case in which there is a universal corresponding to any term that is correctly applied to a multiplicity of entities.

Abundant theory of universals (or properties): a version of realism about universals (or properties) that posits a relatively large number of distinct universals (or properties); in the extreme case, a universal (or property) corresponding to any term that is applied to a multiplicity of entities.

However, there is an alternative view. Some may think we should restrict the allowable instances of the One Over Many. For example, Armstrong has argued that we should restrict instances of the One Over Many to cases in which the objects in the first premise are genuinely similar in a certain respect. This will lead to a **sparse theory of universals.**[4] A sparse theory of universals is a version of realism that posits a relatively small number of distinct universals. On an extreme version, and actually this is the kind that Armstrong himself proposes, there are only universals corresponding to the types of entities recognized by our best physical theories. As Armstrong and others have argued, it is only really our most fundamental physical theories that allow us to discern the genuine similarities among objects, the fundamental properties there are in reality. So, for someone with a sparse theory like this, the only legitimate instance of the One Over Many above would probably be the last one, One Over Many (Mass One Kilogram).

More moderate versions of realism are available. For example, a common position is that there are more genuine similarities in nature than just those described by our best, most fundamental physical theories (as extreme sparse theorists believe), but at the same time, not just any term we can apply to a class of things denotes a genuine similarity in nature (as extreme abundant theorists think). For example, one might think objects may be genuinely similar in virtue of being red – all red things have what it takes to appear the same way to human observers with normally functioning perceptual systems. Perhaps one might think as well that objects may be genuinely similar in virtue of being chairs – all chairs have the ability of letting at least some people sit on them. Unless one had a very permissive, abundant theory, however, most metaphysicians would deny that the phrase 'in this room' corresponds to a genuine similarity in nature. All manners of very different things may be in a given room (shape and size permitting) and so One Over Many (In This Room) is not a legitimate instance of the argument.

Sparse theory of universals (or properties): a version of realism about universals (or properties) that posits a relatively small number of distinct universals (or properties); in the extreme case, there are only universals (or properties) corresponding to types recognized by our fundamental physical theories.

EXERCISE 2.2

Generating Instances of the One Over Many

Generate an original instance of the One Over Many in which the "F" you use is a term or phrase corresponding to a genuine similarity in nature. Next, think about the universal that is assumed by the conclusion of this argument. Does this universal seem to have each of the three features ascribed to universals according to Plato's theory of Forms? Why or why not?

Today, metaphysicians have a variety of views about the range of allowable instances of the One Over Many. In the next section we consider why one might think there are no allowable instances of this argument whatsoever. This will also allow us to see what reason there might be to prefer a less abundant theory of universals, aside from Ockham's Razor.

APPLYING QUINE'S METHOD

The One Over Many is one example of a traditional way in which meta-physicians have argued for the existence of universals. But in the last chapter, we introduced a rigorous method for determining the entities to which one is ontologically committed. It would be good therefore to consider what someone who wanted to apply that method would have to say about the One Over Many.

Although Quine's main aim in "On What There Is" is not to deny the existence of universals, only to reveal the proper way to carry out debates on ontology, he does discuss the One Over Many in that paper, arguing that it is an invalid form of argument.

Indeed it is quite easy to see that the One Over Many as it is usually presented is an invalid argument. That is to say, in all of the examples above, the conclusion (2) does not follow from the premise (1). The most straight-forward way to show this is by regimenting the premise and conclusion of a One Over Many into the language of first-order predicate logic. Because the last form of the One Over Many we considered above is one all realists about universals we have considered (from the most sparse theorists to the most abundant theorists) will take as legitimate, let's go ahead and regiment that argument.

Let's use the following key:

Mx: x has mass of one kilogram
Px: x is a flowerpot
Wx: x is a handweight

Then premise (1) may be symbolized as:

1_R. $\exists x(Mx \land Px) \land \exists y (My \land Wy)$.

From this, using the rules of first-order predicate logic, we know we are only committed to the existence of those objects needed to stand in as the values of the bound variables x and y. But these will both be concrete particulars: a flowerpot and a handweight. Once we see the logical form of (1), we can see it does not commit us at all to the existence of a universal, mass one kilogram, that these concrete things have in common. (2) simply does not follow. Using the additional symbols:

Ixy: x instantiates y
m: the universal, mass one kilogram,

a regimentation of (2) would yield:

2_R. $\exists z (z=m \land (\exists x(Px \land Ixz) \land \exists y(Wy \land Iyz)))$.

The rules of first-order logic do not permit us to move from (1_R) to anything like (2_R).

Realists like Armstrong have rejected this point, insisting that on a proper understanding of the One Over Many, it is a valid argument. When there is a genuine similarity in nature, there must be some entity that explains or grounds this similarity. Although it might indeed be the case that (2) doesn't follow from (1) as a matter of simple predicate logic, (1) expresses a fact that, according to Armstrong, needs explaining. So, (2) is best taken not as following from (1) as a matter of simple predicate logic, but rather as a consequence of a more specifically metaphysical principle about what sorts of facts need explaining. In effect, realists like Armstrong would argue that the statement of the argument above is really an enthymeme. (1) does not entail (2) on the basis of logic alone. But there are some tacit premises the realist about universals is deploying that resemblances like this need explanation. Let's restate the One Over Many with the tacit premises made explicit:

1.   There are flowerpots and handweights that have mass of one kilogram.

    *. If some flowerpots and handweights both have mass one kilogram, then they are genuinely similar in some way.

    **. If a group of objects is genuinely similar in some way, then there must be a common entity they all instantiate, a universal, that explains or grounds the similarity.

Therefore,

2.   There is a universal, mass of one kilogram, that these flowerpots and handweights instantiate.

The particularly controversial premise here, the one Quine himself would certainly not accept, is the additional premise **. In "On What There Is," Quine makes the following claim talking about the instance of the One Over Many we started with (McX's version):

> That the houses and roses and sunsets are all of them red may be taken as ultimate and irreducible, and it may be held that McX is no better off, in point of real explanatory power, for all the occult entities which he posits under such names as 'redness.'
>
> (Quine 1980, p. 10)

Let's set aside the jab Quine makes at the defender of universals by calling these abstract entities she believes in 'occult.'[5] Here we see a genuine disagreement between Quine and the realist about universals. The disagreement may be seen to just be over whether or not we should believe in universals. The side who accepts the One Over Many says 'yes' and will be a realist. The side who denies it may say 'no' and remain a nominalist. But what is going on here isn't merely or even primarily a debate about universals. Rather, what we are seeing is more a debate over the correct ontological method.

Armstrong and others who like arguments like the One Over Many are disagreeing with Quine about something more than just the existence of universals. They are disagreeing with Quine about whether or not the correct method for deciding one's ontological commitments is just regimenting one's statements into the language of first-order predicate logic and seeing what follows. Armstrong can accept that the existence of universals doesn't follow from (1) or more precisely (1_R) as a matter of pure logic. Rather, for Armstrong, sentences like (1) commit us to universals because they require metaphysical explanation, grounding. They require an account of what there is in nature that explains this similarity. If this is right, then we are not *just* committed to the existence of the objects needed to stand in as the values of bound variables in the sentences we take to be true. When Quine says the fact that a set of objects are all a certain way may be "ultimate" and "irreducible," he is denying that any such metaphysical explanation is required.

This commitment is the consequence of a more specific meta-ontological position of Armstrong's: **truthmaker theory**. This theory is based around the truthmaker principle:

> **Truthmaker theory**: the theory that truths have truthmakers, some entities or sets of entities that make them true.

(TM) Every truth has a truthmaker. In other words, for every truth, there is some entity or entities that make it true.

Truthmaker theory has become very popular over the past twenty years, and we will see it come up again before too long when we address the philosophy of time. For now, we can just note that when a truthmaker theorist looks at a sentence he or she takes to be true, for example, 'Some houses

---

BOX 2.3

Metaphysical Explanation

We briefly touched on metaphysical explanation in the last section of Chapter 1. As we saw there, another word for metaphysical explanation is 'ground.' A **metaphysical explanation** is an explanation of a fact that says what there is in the world that accounts for that fact's being the case. It tells us what there is in reality or what reality is like, that makes that fact obtain.

> **Metaphysical explanation**: see **grounding**

are red,' or 'This flowerpot has mass one kilogram,' he or she will claim that there must be some entities that make this sentence true. In a case like this, many truthmaker theorists following a long tradition in philosophy will say the truthmaker is a complex entity that consists of individual objects instantiating properties.[6] For Armstrong, truthmakers are states of affairs (Armstrong, *A World of States of Affairs*).[7] Whether all truths require truth-makers and whether truthmakers must be entities made up of particulars and universals are two contentious issues debated today.

BOX 2.4

Second-Order Predicate Logic

What if we did not take the correct logic to be simply first-order predicate logic, but instead used a different logic, second-order predicate logic? Then, would the inference from (1) to (2) follow as a simple matter of logic?

It seems that it would. Recall that in first-order predicate logic, if one sees something of the form:

Ma,   or,
a is M,

one is allowed to conclude:

$\exists x\, Mx$,   or,
There exists an x such that x is M.

Just as in first-order predicate logic there are quantifiers that range over the objects in one's ontology, in second-order predicate logic, there are quantifiers that range over the attributes. In second-order predicate logic, if one sees something of the form:

Ma,

then one may conclude:

$\exists F\, Fa$,   or,
There exists an F such that a is F.

In English, this says that there exists some way that a is. And if we start with a sentence like

$\exists x\, Mx$,

we may conclude using this rule of existential quantifier introduction in second-order logic,

∃F∃xFx.
There exists some thing that is some way.

When we apply this rule to the first premise of the argument, regimented into logic,

(1_R) ∃x(Mx ∧ Px) ∧ ∃y (My ∧ Wy)

we may now replace each occurrence of 'Mx' with a new predicate variable, 'Fx,' and conclude:

∃F(∃x(Fx ∧ Px) ∧ ∃y (Fy ∧ Wy))

And this appears to be an alternative way to get us to the conclusion we desired, (2). We are here quantifying over a way these objects are. And this way is: having mass one kilogram. So, the One Over Many does appear to go through if we assume second-order logic and the view that quantification over a variable brings with it ontological commitment to something that can stand in as the value of that variable. However, there are several things to say about this.

First, Quine himself was extremely skeptical of the use of second-order logic. Quine believed that second-order logic had problems in itself, as a system of logic. In particular, while systems of first-order logic have the logical property of completeness, second-order logic is incomplete.[a] In addition, Quine worried about the ontological presuppositions of second-order logic. Maybe it is true that there are such things as properties, but this shouldn't follow from matters of logic alone. First-order logic doesn't make specific assumptions about what are the kinds of entities quantified over. Logic gives us a framework for expressing which arguments are valid, but it is metaphysical investigation that should be used to find out what kinds of things exist. By contrast, with second-order logic, it seems already built into the rules of the logic itself that there are such things as properties or attributes. Quine thinks it is inappropriate that such issues should get decided already as a matter of logic (see Hylton's book *Quine*, pp. 256–257).

Additionally, the interpretation we have been giving to the quantifiers in second-order logic is not the only one available. Logicians do not all agree with Quine that existential quantification in general expresses ontological commitment to an entity capable of standing in as the value of the relevant bound variable. For example, the logician George Boolos, in a paper "To Be is to be a Value of a Variable (or to be Some Values of Some Variables)" argues for an alternative way of construing higher order quantification, as a device allowing us to refer to (first-order) entities plurally.

Even if we set aside these worries, it is still important to note that those metaphysicians like David Armstrong who use the One Over Many to argue for the existence of universals do not merely think that (2) follows from (1) as a matter of logic. This might be the case if we use second-order logic. But Armstrong thinks that there is a deeper point in the argument, namely that universals are needed to ground or explain certain facts including the similarities between particulars. Realists do not standardly appeal to second-order logic to argue for their view.

Note

a To say a logical system is complete is to say that every valid argument expressible in that system is able to be proved in that system.

EXERCISE 2.3

Paraphrasing Away Commitments to Universals

As we have seen, a Quinean will not be compelled by the One Over Many argument because her method for determining ontological commitments does not require her to posit entities corresponding to the predicate terms in her language, only those needed to stand in as the value of the bound variables in order to make the sentences she accepts true. Some metaphysicians have argued, however, that there are sentences the Quinean ought to accept that do commit her to universals. Here is an example raised by the metaphysician Frank Jackson:

Red is more similar to pink than it is to blue.

Symbolizing this in the language of first-order predicate logic, we get:

Srpb,

using the following symbols:

Sxyz: x is more similar to y than to z
r: the color red
p: the color pink
b: the color blue.

And this entails, using three instances of the rule of existential generalization (EG):

$\exists x \exists y \exists z Sxyz.$

Jackson's claim is that if we accept the original sentence, we appear committed by Quine's own lights to these three colors, universals. That is, we are so committed unless we are able to produce an acceptable paraphrase of this sentence that does not commit us to red, pink, and blue.

It seems there are two options here for the Quinean who wanted to both defend her ontological method and deny the existence of universals: either to (a) produce an alternative regimentation of the original sentence, a paraphrase, that plausibly conveys what the original sentence was being used to convey and yet does not entail the existence of colors, or (b) argue to the effect that the original sentence is really false. What would an attempt at a paraphrase look like here? Is this a promising way for the Quinean to defend her position? Or should she instead try to argue that the original sentence is actually false? What are the costs of that?[8]

NOMINALISM AND OTHER OPTIONS

We have now seen several varieties of realism about universals, a view often motivated by the One Over Many. We have seen how a Quinean may reject the One Over Many. But one then has to ask: If one rejects the existence of universals, then what view are we left with when it comes to the properties we want to ascribe to things?

We have already briefly discussed nominalism, in the form that Quine offers in "On What There Is." Quine rejects the claim that predicates like 'is red' or 'is beautiful' apply to objects in virtue of the instantiation of universals. He simply claims that the fact that these predicates apply in some cases is irreducible, which is to say it doesn't require any metaphysical explanation. This, as it happens, is only one version of the view today called 'nominalism.' It is a version that some have called **ostrich nominalism** since it refuses to answer the question in virtue of what metaphysically objects are similar or appear to instantiate certain properties. Like an ostrich sticking its head in the sand, the nominalist in this case just avoids the question. Probably a more friendly name for this position is **predicate nominalism**. What the view really amounts to is the claim that there are no such things as properties. The term 'nominalism' comes from the Latin 'nomen' for name. There exist only predicates (words), no universals or properties to which they correspond.

Another version of nominalism that is perhaps more popular is what is called **class** or **set nominalism**.[9] Class nominalism has been attractive to philosophers who, for one reason or another, are skeptical of the existence of universals (perhaps because they are entities that may be wholly present in many places at once), but are not similarly skeptical of classes and so will appeal to classes to give an account of what properties are.

Classes and sets, unlike universals, are particulars. They are entities postulated by set theory, a branch of mathematics. Sets or classes are entities that have members (except for the empty set, Ø, that is the only set that has no members). They are tools used by logicians to identify the extensions of predicates, the objects satisfied by a predicate. For example, the extension of 'is red' is the class of all of the red things. The extension of 'is beautiful' is the class of all of the beautiful things. The view of the class nominalist is that when we use a word like 'red,' we are never referring to a universal, but instead we are referring simply to the extension of the predicate, the class containing all and only the red things. Similarly, 'beauty' refers to the class of all and only the beautiful things. For the class nominalist, properties are classes, the classes of entities that have them.

There are a few things to note about this view. First, if one was skeptical about the existence of universals because they were abstract entities, then one will not be any happier with this version of nominalism. Since properties are now being identified with abstract objects, sets, or classes, a class nominalist is still committed to abstract objects. However, one might think, especially if one is convinced by the indispensability argument we will discuss in the next section, that we have more reason to believe in this sort

Ostrich nominalism: a version of nominalism that denies the existence of properties and refuses to answer the question of what it is in virtue of which objects are similar or appear to have certain features.

Predicate nominalism: a view denying the existence of properties. Predicates may be satisfied or not satisfied by objects, but there need be no property that exists to explain this fact.

Class nominalism: the view that properties are to be identified with the classes of objects that instantiate them.

Set nominalism: see **class nominalism**

of abstract entity than the universals that are motivated by the One Over Many argument. This is something Quine himself came to believe.

Next, one should note that there is an important objection to class nominalism. This is the **Objection from Coextension**. Isn't it possible that there exist two or more properties that are instantiated by exactly the same group of things? For example, suppose a skilled and dedicated collector fancies a particular shade of blue. Call it 'sky blue.' The collector searches the world and succeeds in collecting all of the sky blue objects there are. He places them in a museum, the SBM (Sky Blue Museum). He paints every surface in the SBM sky blue and then locks the door forever. It will then turn out that the class of objects that are sky blue is exactly the same as the class of objects that are in this museum. That is, the predicates 'is sky blue' and 'is in the SBM' will have exactly the same extension, apply to exactly the same objects. But if class nominalism is true, then properties are identified with their classes, the classes of objects that satisfy them. And then it would follow that 'is sky blue' and 'is in the SBM' refer to the same properties. But these phrases refer to distinct properties. One is a color. The other is a location. So class nominalism must be wrong.[10]

The class nominalist has a response to this objection.[11] She may say that properties are not identical to classes of things that *actually* instantiate a property. Rather they are identical with classes that include both the things that *actually* and the things that *possibly* instantiate the property. It might be the case that actually all of the sky blue objects are in this one museum. However, it could have been the case that they were not, that the collector was unsuccessful or never born in the first place and so the sky blue objects were scattered all over the world. When we look at properties this way, as classes containing all and only the objects that actually or possibly instantiate them, our two classes differ. For although the two classes will overlap in all of their members at the world where the collector is successful (because all of the actual sky blue things are contained in the SBM), they will have different members at other possible worlds. There are possible sky blue things that never get placed in the museum; things that it may be impossible to get into the museum. This solution to the problem of coextension is appealing since it captures the intuitive reason we have for thinking that even if all of the sky blue objects are in the SBM, being sky blue isn't the same as being in the SBM – because something *could* have been sky blue and *not* been in the museum.

This response helps with the problem of properties that actually happen to be instantiated by the same class of objects. Though, as many have noted, there is still a challenge accounting for properties that may be shared not just by all actual objects, but by all actual and possible objects. For example, all and only triangles have the following two properties: trilaterality (having exactly three sides) and triangularity (having exactly three angles). This is true not just of all actual triangles. This is true of all possible triangles, whatever triangles there possibly ever could have been. So the class of all actual and possible triangular things is identical to the class of all actual and possible trilateral things. But again it seems these are two distinct properties. And so we should not identify properties with classes. It is possible

Objection from Coextension: an argument against class nominalism that there are more properties than those that may be recognized by the class nominalist, since two predicates may have the same extension and yet refer to two distinct properties.

for the class nominalist at this point to just bite the bullet and claim that these are not really distinct properties after all, if we cannot even imagine them failing to be instantiated together. But the realist about universals will likely not find this response compelling.

A final thing to note about class nominalism – one might wonder if the class nominalist has any way of making a similar distinction between a sparse ontology of properties and an abundant one, as we saw the realist about universals doing above. David Lewis is one metaphysician who is not particularly moved by the One Over Many argument, but is sympathetic to Armstrong's view that there is a preferred rather small class of attributes that make for the objective resemblances of objects in our world. Or, another way of seeing the motivation for a sparse ontology of properties: Lewis is sympathetic to the idea that there may be a small number of basic properties in virtue of which it is possible to explain the behavior of all things at this world. One who accepts a sparse theory of universals, like Armstrong, can say that it is in virtue of this small class of universals (perhaps just fundamental physical universals like masses, charges, and spins) that all other features of our world can be explained. If one rejects the existence of universals altogether, is there another way to have a sparse theory of properties? Remember, properties for the class nominalist are not entities objects instantiate in virtue of which they are similar. Rather they are just abstract classes of objects. The main reason to think a class nominalist theory of properties can only be an abundant theory, one with lots and lots of properties and not just a small number, is because set theory yields the existence of classes corresponding to all ways we may carve up the concrete objects there are in the world.

Lewis has argued that it is important to have a sparse account of properties. But one does not need a theory of universals to do it. Appealing to a small basic number of universals as Armstrong does is one option, but another option is to simply believe that certain classes of objects are distinguished in some way from other classes of objects. Lewis calls this feature that distinguishes certain classes from others '*naturalness*.' The classes/properties that are *natural* are those in which each member is similar to each other in some unique way. In addition, it is in terms of these natural properties (natural classes), that one can give a complete account of the behavior of all things in our world. Most of the properties we talk about every day, properties like being a chair or being a student or being famous, are not natural properties. These are not properties whose members are all objectively similar in some one way. These are not properties that will appear in our final scientific theory of the universe, the theory that has the resources to explain everything. But, if one is inspired by the need to account for similarities between objects, and make a distinction between those properties that make for genuine resemblance between objects and those properties that do not, Lewis has shown how the class nominalist can do it: by appealing to a distinction between natural and non-natural properties.

In addition to class nominalism, there is another position on the nature of properties that also rejects the existence of universals. Like realism, this view grants the existence of mind-independent properties as abstract entities that are more than classes of concrete particular objects. But like nominalism, this view denies that there are any universals – any entities that may be instantiated in multiple locations at the same time. This position is known as **trope theory** or the **theory of abstract particulars**. It is a position that is most often associated with the philosopher D.C. Williams (1899–1983). The trope theory says that properties like shapes and sizes are not, as Plato and Aristotle thought, entities capable of multiple instantiation. Rather each object that instantiates a property instantiates its own particular color or own particular shape. These properties are abstract (you may think of them as abstractions from more concrete entities as we discussed above) and yet they are particular (they are not capable of being multiply instantiated). Another word for these abstract particulars is **trope**.

There are several appealing features of a trope theory as opposed to a theory of universals or class nominalism. One attraction is if you thought that there was something problematic about the very idea of a universal, about the idea of something that could have a kind of presence through instantiation in many places at once, then the trope theory gives one a way to avoid this commitment while still accepting the existence of properties. Second, Williams argues that we have more reason to believe in the existence of tropes than in the existence of universals since tropes are what we encounter first in the world. What we observe most directly are tropes, this particular redness here, that blueness there, not the corresponding universals. In addition, trope theory allows one a more parsimonious ontology than one that has two categories, one for particulars and one for universals, and so it should be preferred to realism about universals for this reason.

To see this last point, we should note that the way the trope theory is usually defended is not just as the claim that there are such things as tropes, abstract particular properties, or even as the claim that the only kinds of properties there are are tropes. Rather, trope theory is usually defended as the more ambitious claim that the only kinds of things there are whatsoever are tropes. Ultimately everything there is is just a trope or a more or less complicated relation between tropes (another trope). Tropes are the "alphabet of being."[12]

For example, trope theorists argue that what we ordinarily regard as concrete particulars like tables, chairs, and people, are best regarded as collections of tropes. A table is just a collection of tropes, a particular shape, size, color, texture, and so on. In this way, we needn't believe in two categories, universals and particulars that instantiate them, but just one category of being: abstract particulars. Williams suggests that the trope theorist can build up universals too. Universals are complicated collections of tropes. The universal redness, for example, will be composed of all of the red tropes. Whether what results is a genuine universal in the sense the realist about universals intends is questionable. However, in this way at least the trope theorist can secure referents for terms like 'redness' or 'roundness.'

Trope theory: the theory that properties are tropes, or abstract particulars.

Theory of abstract particulars: see trope theory

Trope: an abstract particular, e.g. the shape of the Empire State Building.

EXERCISE 2.4

Four Theories of Properties

We have now seen four theories of properties: realism about universals (in its several forms), predicate nominalism, class nominalism, and trope theory. Which view of the four seems most attractive to you? In a paragraph, explain this theory's appeal.

MATHEMATICAL OBJECTS

We have focused so far on a particular kind of abstract object, properties. However, one might think that numbers and other mathematical objects constitute a distinct kind of abstract entity, one that there is independent reason for taking with ontological seriousness.

Plato regarded numbers as kinds of universals, Forms, alongside the other kinds of universals: Beauty, Wisdom, and the rest. And one can easily formulate a version of the One Over Many that will get us to a conclusion about the existence of numbers. For example,

1. There are two moons of Mars, two houses of the British parliament, and two lions guarding the New York Public Library.

Therefore,

2. These moons, houses, and lions have something in common: the universal two (or duality).

Again, Quine will use the resources of first-order predicate logic in order to show how (1) does not commit us to the existence of a number two. It only commits us to moons, houses, and lions (lion statues). And the defender of universals may use meta-ontological considerations about metaphysical explanation (grounding) or truthmaking in order to defend her use of this argument. In this section, we will consider a quite different way to argue for the existence of numbers and other mathematical objects, a way that has been more influential over the past decades. This is via the **indispensability argument.**

The indispensability argument is historically associated with Quine and Hilary Putnam. It is an argument for realism about mathematical entities. Realism about mathematical entities is very often called **Platonism** in the philosophy of mathematics literature. We may state the indispensability argument in the following form with two premises:

Indispensability argument: an argument for realism (Platonism) about mathematical entities from the premises that (1) we should be committed to all and only the entities that are indispensable to our best scientific theories, and (2) the claim that mathematical entities are indispensable to our best scientific theories.

Platonism: 1. the view that there are such things as the Platonic **Forms**; 2. the view that there are such things as abstract, mathematical entities.

1. We ought to have ontological commitment to all that is indispensable to our best scientific theories.
2. Mathematical entities are indispensable to our best scientific theories.

Therefore,

3. We ought to have ontological commitment to mathematical entities.[13]

The first premise follows from a commitment to naturalism. A naturalist, recall, is someone who believes that one should use our best scientific theories in order to settle questions of ontology. The second premise is a substantive claim about our best scientific theories. It is not a philosophical point per se. It is a claim about the content of these theories, that they make essential reference to mathematical entities. Mathematics is a pervasive element of all of the sciences, from fundamental physics to the other natural sciences, such as chemistry, biology, and neuroscience, and even today the social sciences, such as economics and political science. Indeed, one might even think, and this is what it means to say mathematical entities are *indispensable* to our best scientific theories, that these theories could not even be accurately stated without reference to mathematical entities. Quantification over mathematical entities cannot be paraphrased away without doing damage to the explanatory success of these scientific theories.

What is especially interesting about the indispensability argument is that it gives one a way to see numbers and classes, indeed all of the mathematical tools used by our best scientific theories, as on a par with other entities that are far less controversial. Nominalists (those who deny the existence of abstracta, including mathematical entities) often motivate their position by noting that we cannot observe mathematical entities and so lack reason to believe in them. But what the defender of the indispensability argument can note is neither do we observe many of the entities posited by our best scientific theories – we can't see or touch electrons or magnetic fields, arguably, we don't observe stock markets or recessions either – but still we are justified in adding them to our ontology because of the role they play in these extremely successful theories (physics, economics).

One influential way of responding to the argument has been to question its first premise. The problem is not so much with naturalism as a general doctrine about using science to guide metaphysics, but rather with the statement of the position given here that says that one should have ontological commitment to *all* that is indispensable to science. One might argue that some kinds of representations used in science are not intended to have ontological import. In interpreting our scientific theories in order to draw out their ontological implications, we shouldn't blithely adopt commitment to everything the theories seem to refer.

Penelope Maddy uses an analogy with the state of the atomic theory of matter in the mid-nineteenth century to motivate this point. At this time, the physics community had substantial justification for the atomic theory of matter, though many remained skeptical of the existence of atoms. As she elaborates:

> [A]lthough atomic theory was well-confirmed by almost any philosopher's standard as early as 1860, some scientists remained skeptical until the turn of the century – when certain ingenious experiments provided so-called "direct verification" – and even the supporters of atoms felt this early skepticism to be scientifically justified. This is not to say that the skeptics necessarily recommended the removal of atoms from, say, chemical theory; they did, however, hold that only the directly verifiable consequences of atomic theory should be believed, whatever the explanatory power or the fruitfulness or the systematic advantages of thinking in terms of atoms. . . . If we remain true to our naturalistic principles, we must allow a distinction to be drawn between the parts of a theory that are true and the parts that are merely useful.
> (Maddy 1992, pp. 280–281)

Maddy is not suggesting that the metaphysician hold off altogether in drawing metaphysical conclusions from scientific theories. Eventually the physics community as a whole came to endorse the existence of atoms, and we should follow their lead. Indeed, Maddy seems to think (given the last sentence in the passage above) that even when the physics community was reluctant to endorse the existence of atoms, they still had no problem endorsing other metaphysical ramifications of the atomic theory. So the issue is, even if we are naturalists, should we endorse the first premise of the indispensability argument? Scientists themselves do not always take all indispensable elements of their best theories to have ontological significance. (Surely the atoms were an indispensable element of the atomic theory of matter.) Maddy's point is that naturalism itself seems incompatible with according ontological significance to all parts of scientific theories, as the first premise of the indispensability argument assumes.

Another sort of case many have used to challenge the first premise of the indispensability argument is the widespread use of idealization in science. **Idealizations** are false assumptions introduced into a theory in order to make it simpler to use. For example, in thermodynamics, we find the ideal gas law (assuming the existence of particles that do not interact), and in mechanics, physicists routinely make the assumption that there are frictionless surfaces. But nobody believes there are such things as ideal gases or frictionless surfaces. These are assumptions made to make problem-solving simpler, laws easier to state. Idealizations are rampant not only in physics, but throughout the natural and social sciences. This suggests that the way to draw ontological conclusions from our scientific theories may be more complicated than the first premise of the indispensability argument suggests.

Another way one might respond to this argument involves challenging the second premise that mathematical representations are indispensable to our best scientific theories. To challenge the argument in this way, one

Idealization: a false assumption introduced into a theory in order to make it simpler to use.

would have to provide good reason to think that one could still express the claims of our best scientific theories without using the framework of mathematics. This is a project that Hartry Field undertook for one part of physics in his 1980 book *Science Without Numbers*. Field's project was to reformulate an important part of science, Newtonian physics, in a way that didn't quantify over any mathematical entities. Field wanted to show that a lot of what physicists wish to express using mathematics could be expressed using reference to space–time. Field's project is thus an example of the method of paraphrase discussed in Chapter 1. Field's work is brave and interesting, however whether he has succeeded in showing that reference to mathematical entities is dispensable is controversial. To show that mathematics is not indispensable to science, one would have to extend his project beyond the case of Newtonian physics to the rest of science, or show why in principle there is good reason to think Field's method will extend to those cases. This is something that has so far not been shown, but what Field did accomplish gives some nominalists hope.

Taking a step back from the indispensability argument, we will close this chapter by considering a more general problem that mathematics is thought to raise for metaphysics. This was best expressed by the philosopher Paul Benacerraf in his influential paper "Mathematical Truth." Benacerraf argued that in deciding the ontological implications for mathematics, we are pulled in two directions by two competing desires. Take any mathematical truth, for example, that two is an even number. First, one would like to have a semantics for this mathematical truth, an account of what this proposition means and what makes it true. In addition, one would also like to have a plausible **epistemology** for this truth, an account that explains how we know it. But, Benacerraf argued, when one tries to achieve an attractive semantics for mathematical truths, one is forced to accept a mathematical ontology that yields a very unattractive epistemology. On the other hand, if one tries to achieve a plausible epistemology for mathematical truths, then one is unable to achieve a plausible **semantic theory**. There is thus a choice one has to make, and this choice directly relates to the question of realism (Platonism) versus nominalism about mathematical entities. This is what is known as Benacerraf's dilemma. Like any **dilemma**, we are faced with a choice between two options, each of which yields some unattractive consequences.

Let's first try to understand the challenge that results when one tries to give a plausible semantic theory for a mathematical truth. Benacerraf asks us to consider the following two sentences:

(1) There are at least three large cities older than New York.
(2) There are at least three perfect numbers greater than 17.[14]

It looks as if these sentences share the same logical form and that they are both true. But what makes these sentences true? One way to find their truth conditions is to regiment them in first-order logic and read off from there what needs to be the case if these sentences are going to be true. When we do this, it looks like both commit us to the existence of certain kinds of entities.

Epistemology: the theory of knowledge and justification.

Semantic theory: an account of a proposition's or set of propositions' meanings and truth conditions.

Dilemma: a choice between two options, each of which yields unattractive consequences.

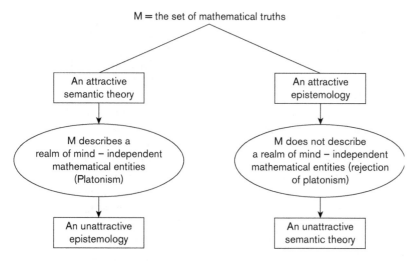

Figure 2.1 Benacerraf's Dilemma

(1_R) $\exists x \exists y \exists z$ $(((Lx \wedge Cx) \wedge Oxn) \wedge (((Ly \wedge Cy) \wedge Oyn) \wedge (((Lz \wedge Cz) \wedge Ozn)) \wedge ((x \neq y \wedge y \neq z) \wedge x \neq z)))$

(2_R) $\exists x \exists y \exists z$ $(((Px \wedge Nx) \wedge Gxs) \wedge (((Py \wedge Ny) \wedge Gys) \wedge (((Pz \wedge Nz) \wedge Gzs)) \wedge ((x \neq y \wedge y \neq z) \wedge x \neq z)))$

In the first case, we are committed to the existence of at least three cities. In the second case, we are committed to the existence of at least three numbers. Benacerraf's conclusion is, if we want to fit mathematical truths like (2) into a plausible semantic theory, one we already use to understand a wide range of claims, then we are forced to be Platonists, realists about mathematical entities.

Having a plausible semantics for mathematical truths would be nice, but Benacerraf argues that since this will involve endorsing Platonism, the consequence is that one cannot then have a plausible epistemology for mathematical truths. For in general, the way we come to know about the existence of objects is by their causal interaction with us. We know there are more than three cities older than New York because we have visited, been told about, or read about these cities. All of these ways of gaining knowledge involve causal interactions, some less direct than others. But if Platonism is true, then mathematical sentences quantify over mathematical objects. And if there are such things as mathematical objects, then presumably these are not objects located in space, objects we can see and otherwise causally interact with. If such things exist, they are, as Plato thought, transcendent entities. An epistemology of mathematics, a theory of how we come to know the truths of mathematics, then cannot depend on our causal interactions with them. We are left then with a question about what could be a plausible epistemology of mathematics.

Benacerraf notes that there is one promising way to provide an epistemology for mathematical truths. One might think that mathematical truths are known because we prove them. Mathematical knowledge doesn't come from our being causally connected somehow with a set of objects like the natural numbers or algebraic groups, but instead by our fitting certain sentences into a system containing a basic set of axioms or postulates and deriving other sentences using the system's methods of proof. Viewing the epistemology of mathematics this way, we are not disposed to view mathematics as a set of sentences about some class of mind-independent objects, but rather as a set of sentences that have their truth conditions determined just by facts about what follows from what deductively. But if this is correct, one cannot take a view about the semantics of mathematical statements that is similar to the semantics we use to understand the truth of other ordinary statements. To return to the example above, we will not understand the truth conditions of (2) as very similar at all to those of (1), because (2) will not be a sentence that refers to a class of three or more objects. It will instead be about what can be proven in a formal system. This is a problem since it forces us to give up the standard semantic theory for the case of mathematical truths. We are forced to adopt a nonunified semantic theory for our language, one theory for mathematical claims, a distinct one for other claims. Moreover, the resulting account of in virtue of what mathematical propositions are true seems implausible as a semantic theory. That there are at least three perfect numbers is known perhaps because we can prove it, but the fact that we can prove it is not what makes it true. Proof is one thing; truth is something else.[15]

EXERCISE 2.5

The Indispensability Argument

State an example from a scientific theory that would help to support the indispensability argument for mathematical Platonism. What is the best strategy for the nominalist to use to respond to this example?

SUGGESTIONS FOR FURTHER READING

On universals and nominalism, David Armstrong has written several influential texts including the two-volume, *Universals and Scientific Realism*, and the shorter *Universals: An Opinionated Introduction*. Several classic texts on the nature and existence of properties can be found in the volume edited by D.H. Mellor and Alex Oliver called *Properties*. On the distinction between natural and non-natural properties, see David Lewis's *On the Plurality Worlds* and his influential article, "New Work for a Theory of Universals." For a helpful discussion of nominalism, its motivations and the arguments against the position, see Zoltan Szabó's paper, "Nominalism." On the indispensability argument in the philosophy of mathematics, the classic statement of the argument appears in Hilary Putnam's *Philosophy of Logic*. One may also consult Mark Colyvan's book, *The Indispensability of Mathematics*. Alan Baker's "Are There Genuine Mathematical Explanations of Physical Phenomena?" provides some good examples of mathematics as it is used in science to support the indispensability argument. For a selection of classic texts in philosophy of mathematics including the debate about Platonism, the collection *Philosophy of Mathematics*, edited by Paul Benacerraf and Hilary Putnam, is recommended.

NOTES

1 This definition also allows us to make room for abstracta that are abstractions from other abstract objects. For example, primeness is an abstract feature of the number three. The property of being a shape is an abstract feature of the property roundness.

2 As we'll see at the end of this chapter, metaphysicians also use these terms to denote similar views about the existence of mathematical entities.

3 Plato commentators (for example, see Julia Annas, *An Introduction to Plato's Republic*, chapter 9) note that elsewhere (even in the *Republic*), Plato doesn't seem to think there is a Form corresponding to *every* multiplicity whatsoever. Instead the number of different Forms is far more restricted.

4 The sparse/abundant distinction is due to the metaphysician David Lewis (1941–2001) who introduced it in his *On the Plurality of Worlds*. See also Jonathan Schaffer's "Two Conceptions of Sparse Properties."

5 What do *you* think Quine means by this?

6 See for example, Bertrand Russell's *The Problems of Philosophy*, chapter 11.

7 A sidenote: as we know, redness is not one of the universals recognized by Armstrong's sparse ontology. And so it won't be the instantiation of a universal redness that makes 'Some houses are red' true. But in this case, there will be some more fundamental features of the house (or the particles that compose it) that do correspond to universals and that explain the truth of this sentence. Ultimately it might turn out that the truthmaker for this sentence is a very complex state of affairs involving many elementary particles instantiating a few fundamental physical universals. The important point for us is that Armstrong will argue the truth of the sentence requires the instantiation of universals by particulars.

8 Frank Jackson examines this case in his paper, "Statements about Universals."

9 For the purposes of this chapter, we will use 'set' and 'class' interchangeably. Both are abstract entities introduced in the part of mathematics called 'set theory.' One feature distinguishing classes from sets that has made the former particularly attractive to some mathematicians and logicians, is that classes cannot be members of other classes. For an accessible introduction to the basics of set theory, see the first chapter of David Papineau's *Philosophical Devices*.

10 D.C. Williams discusses another example in "On the Elements of Being." It looks like the class of featherless bipeds is the same as the class of things

that have a sense of humor. But even if the extensions of 'is a featherless biped' and 'has a sense of humor' are the same, this does not mean we should identify the properties.

11 You will find this response in David Lewis's *On the Plurality of Worlds*, chapter 1. We will discuss this response more in Chapter 7.

12 One trope theorist who rejects the claim that everything there is reduces to tropes is John Heil (2012).

13 This is the version presented in Mark Colyvan's *The Indispensability of Mathematics*.

14 A perfect number is a positive number that is equal to the sum of its positive divisors. For example 6 ($= 1 + 2 + 3$) and 28 ($= 1 + 2 + 4 + 7 + 14$).

15 Or so some would think. There is one theory in the foundations of mathematics, intuitionism, that would say otherwise.

CHAPTER 3

Material Objects

Learning Points

■ Evaluates the notion of a material object
■ Introduces Leibniz's law and some related principles about identity
■ Presents the paradoxes of material constitution and the Special Composition Question
■ Examines the problem of metaphysical vagueness.

WHAT IS A "MATERIAL" OBJECT?

In Chapter 2, we asked whether in addition to all of the concrete material objects (objects like tables and chairs, rivers and mountains, stars and galaxies, persons and other animals), we should also believe in the existence of abstract objects: universals, sets, or numbers. In this chapter, we will take a step back and ask about these material objects themselves.

What do we mean by 'concrete material object'? By 'object' we just mean something that exists. Although it is difficult to give a perfectly satisfactory definition of 'concrete,' we saw that one may distinguish the concrete objects as those that cannot be understood as abstractions from something else. It is now time to consider what is meant by 'material.'

One common understanding of 'material' is that which occupies space and persists through time. René Descartes (1596–1650), in the seventeenth century, defined material substances as those that are extended in space. Today, we tend to allow that something may be material even if it strictly speaking lacks spatial extension but rather is point-sized. This includes the fundamental particles of physics, such as electrons and quarks. This is why we say what is material "occupies space" as opposed to "is spatially extended." When it comes to the question of persistence over time, we will discuss in a later chapter the possibility of time slices of individuals, temporal parts of objects that have zero extension in time. Given the possibility of material objects like this that exist for only a moment, we might also require of material objects only that they have location in time, not that they necessarily persist for longer than a moment.

In addition to these spatiotemporal criteria, it is possible that there are other features that determine what makes an object material. Isaac Newton (1643–1727) defined mass as the quantity of matter in an object. This suggests another criterion: that material objects are those that possess some non-zero mass. There *are* fundamental particles introduced by physics such as the photon that have zero mass. One might think that these provide counterexamples to mass as a criterion for materiality. (It used to be thought that neutrinos were massless as well, but this has now been rejected.) However, physics makes a distinction between those particles that are material, or constitute the matter of the world, and those that instead govern the interactions, and are force carriers. The photon is a force carrier particle; it is what carries the electromagnetic force. So we may hold onto this part of our characterization. Let's then say for the purposes of this chapter that material objects are those that are located in space and time (though they might not have extension in space or duration in time) and have mass. The metaphysician Jessica Wilson has argued that these scientific criteria should also be supplemented with an a priori, metaphysical one, a "No Fundamental Mentality" requirement.[1] If something is a material object, it doesn't have any fundamental mental features. In other words, if it has any mental features, these features are explained in more fundamental (physical) terms. Either way, we should recognize that what it is to be a material object is at least partly an empirical matter and something we may revise as our physical theories change.[2]

Many metaphysicians today are realists about at least some concrete material objects.[3] The question is: which ones to accept? A common position is that there are at least those objects described by the Standard Model of contemporary particle physics: leptons (a category including electrons and neutrinos) and quarks. After that, there is much disagreement about what else exists; in particular, whether in addition to these basic concrete objects there exists anything else, any complex objects composed out of the basic ones. (There is also disagreement over whether in addition to the concrete *material* objects there are also immaterial concrete objects like souls or minds. This is a metaphysical debate we will not enter in this book, but one that you will find discussed in any text in the philosophy of mind.) Many philosophers hold the view that there exist concrete, material objects corresponding to any way there is of composing simple, material objects into complex ones. But in contemporary metaphysics, we find also ingenious arguments for other views. This includes the surprising view, defended by Peter van Inwagen, that the only concrete objects that exist are fundamental particles and organisms. According to van Inwagen, there exist electrons, flowers, and human beings, but no tables or chairs, mountains or rocks! Even more radically, we find philosophers (for example, Peter Unger) arguing that not only do mountains and rocks fail to exist, but there are no human beings either. Indeed, one of Unger's most famous papers bears the title, "I do not exist."

We will start this chapter by thinking about some classic paradoxes concerning concrete material objects. We will then discuss two issues that arise when we assume a fundamental level of basic material particles: the

Problem of the Many and the Special Composition Question. Both have generated a lot of discussion among metaphysicians over the past several decades and show us that the existence of complex material objects like ourselves isn't a trivial matter.

THE PARADOXES OF MATERIAL CONSTITUTION

In this section we will discuss two paradoxes involving material objects. Let's set aside the issue of whether or not there is a fundamental layer of basic concrete material objects, and just focus on the ones with which we are most familiar from everyday life: artifacts (tables and chairs, ships and computers), organisms (human beings, cats, trees), and other medium-to-large-sized, natural, inanimate objects (rocks, mountains, planets).

Perhaps you have already heard of the Ship of Theseus. The story goes: Theseus had a large wooden ship that he sailed from Crete to Athens. After some time, the ship needed repairs as its planks started to rot. Gradually the Athenians replaced the planks of Theseus's ship with new planks. After many years, all of the wood of the original ship was replaced with new planks. By this time, the ship contained not a single plank of the original wood. But the original planks were not destroyed. Instead as each was replaced, the original planks were stored and finally used to assemble all of the original planks into the form of the original ship. Soon, two ships stood side by side.

Let's call the original Ship of Theseus that arrived in Athens from Crete 'S_1.' Without assuming whether it is or is not identical to S_1, call the ship that resulted from the gradual replacement of rotten planks with new planks 'S_2.' And call the ship that was assembled from the old, rotten planks 'S_3' (Figure 3.1).

Now we can ask: which of the two ships resting next to each other on the shore of Athens is the original Ship of Theseus? We seem to have four options.

Option 1: $S_1=S_2$ but $S_1 \neq S_3$ (Only the repaired ship is identical to the original ship.)

Option 2: $S_1=S_3$ but $S_1 \neq S_2$ (Only the ship constructed of the original planks is identical to the original ship.)

Option 3: $S_1=S_2$ and $S_1=S_3$ (Both ships are identical to the original Ship of Theseus.)

Option 4: $S_1 \neq S_2$ and $S_1 \neq S_3$ (Neither ship is identical to the original ship.)

We will look at each option and see what there is to be said for it. But first let's just dwell for a moment on the use of the identity sign '='. When this symbol is used to make a metaphysical claim, it is important that one always reads it as saying "is identical to." In mathematics, one uses the same symbol to express equalities. There you will read '=' as 'equals' as in: 'Three plus two equals five.' In metaphysics, '=' refers to the metaphysical relation of numerical identity.[4] When we say "a=b," this expresses the claim that a and

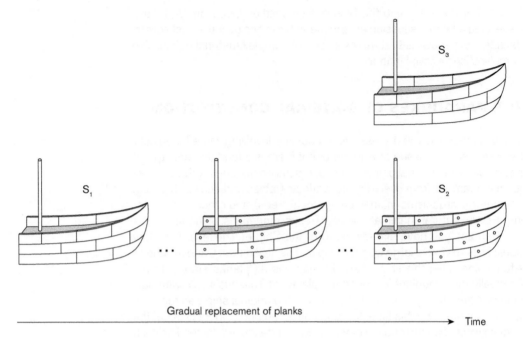

Gradual replacement of planks

Time

Figure 3.1 The Ship of Theseus

b are the same entity. If this identity claim is true, then even though we may have two names 'a' and 'b,' these two names are referring only to one thing. For example:

Mark Twain = Samuel Clemens
Jay-Z = Shawn Carter
Mt. Everest = Sagarmāthā

These statements all express true identity claims in the strict sense we are concerned with here. When we say there is an identity, we are not just asserting the entities are similar in some way (what we called in Chapter 2 qualitative identity). Rather we are saying they are literally the same thing. There are not two people, Jay-Z on the one hand and Shawn Carter on the other. There is only one person to whom we refer using either name.

So, let us return to the case of the Ship of Theseus. The first answer to our question, which ship is identical to the original ship, is that it is only S_2, the ship that resulted from the gradual replacement of parts. Here are some thoughts that motivate this answer. First, think about what happens after the first plank on the original ship has become rotten and gets replaced. Call the resulting ship, which is just like the original ship except for the replacement of one plank: 'S_1*.' Surely we want to say that S_1* is identical to S_1, that it is the same as the original ship. After all, the only difference between S_1 and S_1* is one plank. Surely S_1 can undergo a small repair and maintain its identity. If you've ever owned a car, you've probably at some point had to replace a tire or a fender. One doesn't usually think that making such a repair causes your car to cease to exist and a new, numerically distinct car to suddenly appear. Rather, we usually think the car after the repair is identical to the car before the repair. It's the same car; it just has a new part. If we grant this, then we can imagine a succession of ships, $S_1{}^*$, $S_1{}^{**}$, $S_1{}^{***}$, and so on, where each ship in the sequence differs from the one before it only by one plank. And just as we may say over time, as you make small repairs to your car, it doesn't cease to be your car, but maintains its identity over time, so we can say that Theseus's ship doesn't cease to be Theseus's ship as small repairs are made to it, but it maintains *its* identity over time. We can thus conclude of the sequence leading from S_1 to S_2 (the ship that results from the final small repair) that the identity relation holds at each step:

$$S_1 = S_1{}^* = S_1{}^{**} = S_1{}^{***} = \ldots = S_1{}^{***}\ldots{}^* = S_2.$$

From here, it is just a short step to get us to the claim that $S_1 = S_2$. To establish this, we only have to note that the identity relation is transitive:

Transitivity: the identity relation is transitive.

In other words, $\forall x \forall y \forall z ((x=y \wedge y=z) \supset x=z)$.

BOX 3.1

Equivalence Relations

Actually, the identity relation has three important features:

Reflexivity: the identity relation is reflexive. In other words, $\forall x$ $x=x$.

Symmetry: the identity relation is symmetric. In other words, $\forall x \forall y (x=y \supset y=x)$.

Transitivity: the identity relation is transitive. In other words, $\forall x \forall y \forall z ((x=y \wedge y=z) \supset x=z)$.

Any relation that has these three features (reflexivity, symmetry, and transitivity) is what logicians call an **equivalence relation**. Identity is one equivalence relation. Others include:

- being the same size as
- being the same shape as
- is a member of the same family as.

Equivalence relation: a relation that is reflexive, symmetric, and transitive.

Since there is a chain of identities linking S_1 to S_2, we may conclude that $S_1=S_2$ by the following argument:

1. $S_1=S_1^*$ (starting assumption)
2. $S_1^*=S_1^{**}$ (starting assumption)
3. $S_1=S_1^{**}$ (from premises (1) and (2) and the transitivity of identity)
4. $S_1^{**}=S_1^{***}$ (starting assumption)
5. $S_1=S_1^{***}$ (from premises (3) and (4) and the transitivity of identity)

. . .

. . .

n-2. $S_1=S_1^{***\ldots*}$ (from premises (n-4) and (n-3) and the transitivity of identity)

n-1. $S_1^{***\ldots*}=S_2$ (starting assumption)

Therefore,

n. $S_1=S_2$ (from premises (n-2) and (n-1) and the transitivity of identity)

This is the reasoning motivating the claim that $S_1=S_2$.

This defense is compelling, but there is also reason to say that the original ship is identical to the ship built of the original materials, S_3. The simple reason is that S_1 and S_3 are made of the same constituents; not just qualitatively similar constituents, planks that look the same, but numerically identical constituents, the very same planks. If we adopt a plausible-looking principle that says "Same constituents, same object," then we will be forced to say that $S_1=S_3$.

Given that there is something to be said both in favor of the claim that $S_1=S_2$ and that $S_1=S_3$, one might think that perhaps Option 3 is the best response to the puzzle of the Ship of Theseus. There is a good motivation for thinking that S_1 and S_2 are identical, due to the continuity one finds through the gradual transition from S_1 and S_2, which just amounts to a changing of parts. There is also a good motivation for thinking that S_1 and S_3 are identical, since they are composed of identical parts. We might thus conclude that both identity statements are true. However, this claim is problematic. Indeed, it is probably the most problematic of the four options. The reason is that, as we have noted (see Box 3.1), identity is an equivalence relation. And this means that if $S_1=S_2$ and $S_1=S_3$, then, by the symmetry and transitivity of identity, $S_2=S_3$. Here is the argument:

1. $S_1=S_2$ (initial assumption)
2. $S_1=S_3$ (initial assumption)
3. $S_2=S_1$ (from premise (1) and the symmetry of identity)

Therefore,

4. $S_2=S_3$ (from premises (2) and (3) and the transitivity of identity)

But S_2 is not identical to S_3. Remember what it would mean to say $S_2=S_3$. This would be to say that there are not two ships, S_2 and S_3, but just one. But of course S_2 and S_3 are distinct ships. They are sitting at different locations. They are made of different materials. Therefore, there is not just one ship there, but two. And so, we cannot accept Option 3.

There is actually an important metaphysical principle that is tacitly being appealed to in this last point. This is the principle of **Leibniz's Law**, also known as the **Indiscernibility of Identicals**. It is named after the philosopher and mathematician Gottfried Leibniz (1646–1716). Leibniz's law says that if there is something that has a property that something else lacks, then these things are not identical. If they were the *same* thing, then they would have to share all of the same properties. The very same thing cannot both have and lack a property. (This would be a contradiction.) More precisely, we may state Leibniz's law in either of the following two ways (using the resources of second-order predicate logic):

Leibniz's law: the metaphysical principle that necessarily, if a and b are identical, then they must share all of the same properties.

Indiscernibility of Identicals: see **Leibniz's law**

$$\forall x \forall y \forall F ((Fx \wedge \neg Fy) \supset x \neq y)$$
$$\forall x \forall y \forall F (x=y \supset (Fx \equiv Fy))$$

Sometimes you will see Leibniz's law (and other metaphysical principles) expressed using the box symbol, '□,' attached to it:

$$\Box \forall x \forall y \forall F ((Fx \wedge \neg Fy) \supset x \neq y)$$
$$\Box \forall x \forall y \forall F (x=y \supset (Fx \equiv Fy))$$

This is because metaphysical principles like Leibniz's law are often taken to express facts not just about what contingently happens, but rather necessary truths about what things must be like no matter how the world happens to turn out.[5] The box should be read aloud as 'Necessarily.'

BOX 3.2

The Indiscernibility of Identicals and the Identity of Indiscernibles

Leibniz's law or the Indiscernability of Identicals should not be confused with a more controversial principle that is also associated with Leibniz: **the Identity of Indiscernibles**. The Identity of Indiscernibles says that necessarily, if a and b are qualitative duplicates (i.e. qualitatively identical), then they are the same object (i.e. numerically identical). This principle is expressed by the logical formulas (in second-order logic):

Identity of Indiscernibles: a metaphysical principle stating that necessarily, if any objects are qualitative duplicates, then they are identical.

$\Box \forall x \forall y \forall F ((Fx \equiv Fy) \supset x{=}y)$
$\Box \forall x \forall y (x{\neq}y \supset \exists F(Fx \wedge \neg Fy))$

If any objects share the same features, then they are identical. And, if any objects are not identical, then there must be some feature that one object has that the other lacks.

Leibniz's law itself is not controversial. For most metaphysicians, Leibniz's law just expresses some basic consequences of what is meant by numerical identity. However, when a philosopher endorses the Identity of Indiscernibles, they are making a substantive metaphysical claim: that there could not be two distinct objects that share all of the same features.

The philosopher Max Black (1909–1988) once proposed the following counterexample to the Identity of Indiscernibles:

> Isn't it logically possible that the universe should have contained nothing but two exactly similar spheres? We might suppose that each was made of chemically pure iron, had a diameter of one mile, that they had the same temperature, colour, and so on, and that nothing else existed. Then every quality and relational characteristic of the one would also be a property of the other. Now if what I am describing is logically possible, it is not impossible for two things to have all their properties in common.
>
> (Black 1952, p. 156)

The case of Black's spheres certainly seems to involve no contradiction, and thus it would seem to be logically possible. Since the Identity of Indiscernibles is supposed to express a necessary truth about identity, the logical possibility of these spheres would seem to show that the principle is false ... or at least much more controversial than its converse, Leibniz's law!

EXERCISE 3.1

Leibniz's Law

A. Suppose someone presented the following argument for the claim that Superman is not identical to Clark Kent:

> Superman and Clark Kent cannot be the same person because Clark Kent wears glasses and Superman does not.

Also Superman is faster than a speeding bullet and Clark Kent is not. Therefore, by Leibniz's law, Superman and Clark Kent are not identical. They must be different people.

How would you respond to this argument? Does the case of Superman and Clark Kent violate Leibniz's law?

B. Suppose someone presented the following argument for the claim that Paul McCartney and Stephen Hawking are the same person (are identical):

Paul McCartney and Stephen Hawking are the same person. They were both born in England in 1942. They are both white men. They both have short, brown hair. They have both been married at least twice. Therefore, by Leibniz's law, they must be identical.

How would you respond to this argument?

Applying Leibniz's law back to the case at hand, we may be sure that $S_2 \neq S_3$ because S_2 and S_3 differ with respect to many properties. They differ with respect to their materials, their location, and so on. And so, since they are discernible (they have different properties), they cannot be identical.

Now one might try another move and, noting that neither S_2 nor S_3 has a better claim to being the original ship, instead say that both S_2 and S_3 are new ships. This is another possibility. It is Option 4. Here, we may allow there are important similarities between the ship that originally arrived in Athens and the ships that exist now, but say that strictly speaking the original ship no longer exists. It has been replaced with two new ships.

This last option is appealing since it does not force us to choose between S_2 and S_3 to say which has a better claim to being S_1. And it presents us with a more plausible option than Option 3, which required us to say that what appeared to be two ships sitting next to each other was really just one ship. However, there is still something unsatisfying about this last option in that it forces us to deny that either ship is the original Ship of Theseus. And, given that there doesn't seem to be any other plausible candidate, we are forced to say that the Ship of Theseus has now ceased to exist.[6] What's more, note that the whole trouble here for S_2 having a claim to being the Ship of Theseus is caused by the assembly of S_3. If nobody had collected the original planks and assembled S_3, then there would be no threat to claiming that $S_1 = S_2$. But how could facts about the identity of S_2 be affected by a process happening somewhere else?

This is why the Ship of Theseus presents a puzzle to metaphysicians. One has to choose between Options 1, 2, and 4. Does one want to bite the bullet and accept that the Ship of Theseus no longer exists today and there are only two new ships, S_2 and S_3? Or is there some way to undermine the motivation we have presented for saying either that S_2 or that S_3 is a good candidate for being the original Ship of Theseus?

EXERCISE 3.2

The Ship of Theseus

What is your preferred solution to this puzzle: Option 1, 2, or 4? Defend it against the remaining options.

A second classic puzzle about concrete, material objects is the puzzle of the Statue and the Clay. A sculptor takes a lump of clay (call this object 'Lump') and makes a statue of the warrior Goliath (call this object 'Goliath'). Suppose that at noon, there is only the lump of clay, but at midnight, the statue Goliath is finished and placed alone on a pedestal. At midnight, should we say there are two objects on this pedestal or only one? It might strike you at first as obvious that there is only one object there. But if this is correct, then this means that Lump = Goliath. And it seems this cannot be right since, using Leibniz's law and the fact that Lump has several properties that Goliath lacks, we can deduce that Lump ≠ Goliath.

What are these properties? Some are *temporal properties*. For example, Lump has the property of existing at noon. Goliath lacks this property. Goliath has the property of having been created after 8pm on the day in question. Lump lacks this feature. Lump and Goliath differ as well in their **modal properties**. These are properties having to do with what is possible or necessary, with what could or must happen to these objects if certain conditions were to obtain. While Lump has the property of being able to survive being squashed and rolled into a ball, the statue Goliath lacks this

Modal properties: properties having to do with what is possible, impossible, necessary, or contingent.

Goliath

Lump

Time

Noon   Midnight

Figure 3.2 The Statue and the Clay

property. If Goliath were squashed and rolled into a ball, it would cease to exist. There would no longer be such a thing as the statue Goliath. In addition, it seems that Goliath has the property of necessarily being a statue, whereas Lump lacks this property. It isn't *necessarily* a statue; it could have existed even if it were never shaped into a statue. It could have always just been a lump of clay. And so even though Goliath and Lump share a lot of properties (they are both located in the same place, on the pedestal; they are both shaped like the ancient warrior Goliath; they are both composed of the same atoms), by Leibniz's law we seem forced to say they are distinct. While at midnight, it might look like there is only one object on the pedestal, there are really two objects there, both Lump and Goliath.

Furthermore, if we consider facts about the identity of the statue and the lump, again we seem led to the conclusion that these objects are not identical. For consider the lump at noon. Call this object L_1. Now consider the lump at midnight. Call this object L_2. It seems obvious that $L_1=L_2$. Assuming the sculptor used all of the original clay to create the statue, we seem forced to say that the lump of clay at midnight is the very same lump as that he started with in the morning. After all simply molding and shaping an object shouldn't make it cease to exist! As we noted above, lumps can survive molding. At the same time, it is just as obvious that $L_1 \neq$ Goliath. After all Goliath is a statue and at noon there is no statue. So L_1 can't be Goliath. But then if $L_1=L_2$ and $L_1 \neq$ Goliath, then by the fact that identity is an equivalence relation, we must conclude that $L_2 \neq$ Goliath. We can show this using an argument that employs the method of reductio ad absurdum (or reductio).

Argument that the Lump at midnight (L_2) is not identical to the statue (Goliath)

1. Assume for reductio that $L_2=$Goliath.
2. $L_1=L_2$ (initial assumption)
3. $L_1 \neq$ Goliath   (initial assumption)
4. $L_1=$Goliath   (by premises (1) and (2) and the transitivity of identity)

Therefore,

5. $L_2 \neq$ Goliath   (by premises (3) and (4) and reductio ad absurdum)

So, the lump at midnight cannot be the same object as Goliath.

The resulting view is the **Two Object View** defended by the philosopher David Wiggins in his book *Sameness and Substance*. This is the view that in general, material objects are distinct from the matter from which they are made. We have illustrated the main arguments for this view using the example of the Statue and the Clay, but any concrete objects whatsoever that are constructed out of some materials will raise the same issue. We could raise the same issue about a table and the wood of which it is made, your body and its constituting lump of organic material, and so on. The Two

Two Object View: the view that material objects are numerically distinct from the matter of which they are made.

BOX 3.3

Reductio Ad Absurdum

Reductio ad absurdum (or simply, **reductio**) is a method of argument often used by philosophers. To apply this method, one assumes the negation of the claim one wishes to prove and then shows that this assumption leads to a contradiction (both P and ¬P). This, one might say, reduces the negation of the claim to an absurdity, thus showing that one's initial claim is true.

Object View is interesting, as it seems to contradict a seemingly plausible principle about material objects, the principle that no two material objects can be at the same place at the same time.

One way of avoiding the Two Object View might be to give up on the claim that $L_1 \neq$ Goliath. We might concede that Goliath is a statue of a mythical warrior, and at noon, the lump doesn't look like a statue of a mythical warrior, but really it is. Like the Two Object View, this view has some strange consequences. For it certainly seems that at noon the sculptor could have had a change of heart or got thirsty and instead used the clay to create a coffee mug. This seems to show that the object Lump could have been used to create a coffee mug instead of a statue. But then if Lump=Goliath, they are numerically the same object, then we would be forced to say that the statue Goliath could have been a coffee mug. This seems wrong.

We return to consider other solutions to this puzzle at the end of the present chapter and in Chapter 6 on persistence.

EXERCISE 3.3

The Statue and the Clay

What do you think is the most plausible response to the puzzle of the Statue and the Clay?

THE PROBLEM OF THE MANY

Both of the preceding philosophical puzzles about material objects arose out of changes that might occur over a period of time: a ship deteriorating over many years and slowly having its parts replaced, a lump of clay being shaped over the course of a day into a statue of a mythical warrior. These puzzles forced us to confront issues about **diachronic identity**, that is identity over time. This last puzzle we will discuss isn't a puzzle about diachronic identity, but rather concerns what is the case at a single time. In other words, it is a puzzle about **synchronic identity**. It concerns the relation between ordinary material objects and the collection of particles that might be said to constitute them. For this reason it is called the **Problem of the Many**. The Problem of the Many was introduced by Peter Unger in an article with that name from 1980.

The problem is one that arises for any familiar material object we may consider, but let's focus on the way it arises for the case of human bodies. Take a moment to examine your own body. At first, it may seem to you that there are clear facts about what is a part of your body and what is not. Take a look at a hand. It is easy with your eyes to trace the outlines of this hand and in this way mark the boundaries between what is a part of your body and what is part of the surrounding environment. But now imagine zooming in closer on your body with a microscope. If you did this, things would appear differently. You could see the cells making up your skin. Zoom in further with a scanning tunneling microscope and you might observe the individual atoms and molecules making up these cells. At this level of magnification, the boundary between your body and the surrounding environment would become much less clear. If we had microscopes powerful enough, we could even see down to the level of electrons, protons, and neutrons making up these atoms, and perhaps even to the quarks making up these protons and neutrons. But we don't need to worry about that. Let's stay at the level of atoms. There are a finite number of atoms that make up your body. Let's suppose this number is (what is supposed to be average) 7×10^{27}.[7] Call the collection of all of these 7×10^{27} atoms 'C.' C is structured in such a way as to make up a human body, you. What Unger points out is that there are also many other collections of atoms just slightly different from C that also seem capable of constituting a human body just like yours. And these other collections are located in almost the same place as C. For example, consider a collection of $7 \times 10^{27} - 1$ atoms, the collection of atoms that includes all of the members of C except for one particular carbon atom at the tip of your little finger. Call this collection 'C-.' This collection of atoms also seems to have what it takes to make up a human body. After all, we could imagine a case in which that atom was never a part of you and we wouldn't be forced to conclude in that case that you lacked a body. Similarly we can imagine a distinct collection of atoms C--. This collection is just like C except that it fails to include a single hydrogen atom on the inside of your ear. Again, it seems that C-- has everything it takes to constitute a human body. Unger's point is that there are very many collections of atoms located very close to where your body is located and each of these collections has, it would seem, an equally good claim to constitute a human body. And so we seem forced to admit that even here in the same location at which you are sitting, there are a great many other human bodies that look a great deal like you, but still, because they are composed of slightly different atoms, by Leibniz's law, they are not identical to you.

Diachronic identity: identity over time.

Synchronic identity: identity at a time.

Problem of the Many: a philosophical problem about the existence and identity of material objects introduced by the philosopher Peter Unger in 1980. The problem stems from the fact that ordinary material objects (like persons, rocks, tables, and stars) seem not to have well-defined physical boundaries. There are several precisely defined objects with determinate boundaries that may be associated with any ordinary material object. This raises the question of which if any of these precisely defined objects it is identical to.

This problem is easily extended to the case of any complex, material object we are familiar with in our day-to-day life. Just as there are many human bodies in roughly the same place you are sitting, so there are many chairs in the location under you, many phones, many tables, and so on. Unger's own solution to this puzzle is to deny that there are any complex material objects in the first place. If any collection of atoms has what it takes to make up a human body or a chair, then too many things would have what it takes, so Unger suggests we should revoke our ontological commitment to familiar material objects like human bodies or tables or chairs. If the one commits you to the many, then maybe we shouldn't have believed in the one in the first place.

But perhaps there is a way to distinguish one of these collections of atoms as special, as the one that *really* makes up your body. One thing you might try to argue is that of all of these many collections of atoms, C, C-, C--, and so on, there is one that is the largest – namely C. There is one that includes all of the atoms contained in any of the other collections. One might then identify your body with C, and say that C-, C--, and so on all fail to be bodies, because it is part of the concept of a body that it is the largest such entity of any such sequence. This would be to take the property of

Maximal property: a property F is maximal if large parts of an F are not themselves Fs.

being a body to be what Theodore Sider has called a **maximal property**. Sider suggests just such a move in the following passage:

> Ordinary sortal predicates[8] typically express maximal properties, where a property, F, is maximal, roughly, if large parts of an F are not themselves Fs. A large part of a house – all of the house save a window, say – does not itself count as a house. A large part of a cat – all of it save the tail, say – does not itself count as a cat. Otherwise in the vicinity of every house there would be a multitude of houses; in the vicinity of every cat there would be a multitude of cats.
>
> (Sider 2003, p. 139)

This is a way one might try to evade the Problem of the Many, by an appeal to the maximality of the properties of being a house or being a body.

The trouble with this is that just as we may consider the case of the 7×10^{27} atoms making up your body with an atom here or there subtracted, we may also consider the case of the 7×10^{27} atoms plus one or two that someone might otherwise think are part of the surrounding environment. David Lewis, in his discussion of the Problem of the Many focuses on these other potential objects, those that would result from adding atoms rather than subtracting atoms from some initial collection C:

> think of yourself, or any organism, with parts that gradually come loose in metabolism or excretion or perspiration or shedding of dead skin. In each case, a thing has questionable parts, and therefore is subject to the problem of the many.
>
> (Lewis 1993, p. 165)

Just as we can consider C- and C--, we might consider also C+, and C++. C+ is C with the addition of an atom in a bead of perspiration that is just making its way from the skin. C++ is C with the addition of an atom that was part of some food that has just begun to be digested by your body. Unger would want to say too in this case that C+ and C++ have just as much claim to constitute a human body as does C. If the subtraction of an atom here or there is insignificant, so is a small addition. But if so, then an appeal to maximality doesn't seem to be able to solve the problem. For which is the maximal entity in this case? Is it C? Is it C+ or C++? C is a part of both C+ and C++. But which is the object that makes the person? There seems no way to tell.

EXERCISE 3.4

The Problem of the Many

There seem to be three ways to respond to the Problem of the Many:

A. To deny that any of the collections of atoms make up a human body.
B. To find some way (like Sider) to distinguish one of the collections as special and the only one that constitutes a human body.
C. To accept the consequence that what may seem to only be one human body in a particular case is really many bodies.

Which of these options strikes you as most promising? Is there any other option available?

THE SPECIAL COMPOSITION QUESTION

So far, in our discussion of all of these puzzles, we have made an assumption. This is an assumption that we now need to call into question as it has been the subject of much debate among metaphysicians in recent years. What we have been assuming all along is that individual particles (objects of the kind fundamental physics discovers like electrons, quarks, and so on) combine at least some of the time to form collections of atoms, lumps of clay, hunks of organic material. We have asked about particular collections of atoms, whether they constitute ships or people, but some philosophers think we need an argument that these collections of atoms themselves exist. As Peter van Inwagen notes in his 1990 book *Material Beings*, perhaps individual particles never combine to form composite objects, or perhaps they do sometimes but not always. Maybe, although some particles exist, there is no such thing as the collection of these particles.

In *Material Beings*, the question van Inwagen wants to address is: In what circumstances do some objects compose something? He calls this

'The Special Composition Question.'[9] It is worth emphasizing how it is that our presentation of all of the earlier puzzles and paradoxes made one crucial assumption – that composition occurs at least some of the time. This is most obvious in the case of the first two puzzles (the Ship of Theseus and the Statue and the Clay). There we started by assuming in the first place that there were some planks of wood and that these compose a ship, or we assumed that there was a lump of clay and that at midnight this was sculpted to compose a statue. But even in our presentation of the Problem of the Many, we assumed that composition occurs at least some of the time. After all, we assumed that there were all of these collections of atoms, C, C-, C--, and so on. But to assume there is a *collection* of atoms is to say that the atoms have composed something, if only the collection. And what van Inwagen wants to makes us see is that perhaps there isn't any such thing as the collection of atoms, C, C-, or C--. Perhaps just the atoms exist, and these individual things never come together to form an object that is made of them, what we will refer to as their **mereological sum** or their **fusion**.

Mereological sum: the mereological sum of some objects $x_1, x_2, \ldots, x_n$ is the object that contains $x_1, x_2, \ldots, x_n$ as parts.

Fusion: see **mereological sum**

In order to state the Special Composition Question precisely and accurately, van Inwagen notes that it is necessary to introduce a new kind of logical apparatus, that of plural quantification (1990, pp. 22–26). To see the standard first-order quantificational apparatus is not able to give us a way to draw the distinctions we want, consider how it would have us translate the sentence 'The electrons exist.' We would be forced to translate this as:

$\exists x$ (x is the electrons).[10]

This entails there is such a thing as "the electrons" and hence that composition occurs. Instead we should like a way to speak plurally about the electrons without assuming there is any one thing that they compose referred to by the expression 'the electrons.'

Following van Inwagen then, we will use '$\exists xs$' to mean the same as the English phrase 'there exist some xs.' We will also use plural variables 'the xs' to refer to these xs. This will allow us to speak of them plurally without automatically assuming that there is some thing ($\exists x$) that is the sum or collection of the xs.[11] This would assume already that composition does occur. We can then translate 'The electrons exist' as:

$\exists xs$ (the xs are the electrons).

Special Composition Question: the question for any xs, when is it the case that there is a y such that the xs compose y.

Then, the official formulation of the **Special Composition Question** will be:

For any xs, when is it true that $\exists y$ (the xs compose y)?

We may state this in quasi-English as: For any xs, when is it true that there exists a y such that the xs compose y? Possible answers to this question will all be of the form:

$\forall xs \, \exists y$ (the xs compose y iff the xs . . .)

where the ellipsis (. . .) is filled in by a condition one might argue is required to get any xs to compose something.[12]

Note how general an issue this is. Answers to the Special Composition Question will tell us what it takes for any objects whatsoever to compose something. Some metaphysicians believe there is a particularly interesting class of objects, **simples** or **mereological atoms**. Simples are objects that have no **proper parts**, where some x is a proper part of another object y just in case x is a part of y and x is not identical to y. (Strictly speaking, every object is a part of itself.[13]) An answer to the Special Composition Question will tell us what it takes for any things whatsoever to compose something, whether those things are mereological simples or mereologically complex objects (objects that are composed by objects other than themselves).

It may help to note another way of understanding the Special Composition Question. Although van Inwagen insists this is not the official formulation of the Special Composition Question, he notes that this more "practical" formulation may help to see the issue at stake:

> Suppose one had certain (nonoverlapping)[14] objects, the xs, at one's disposal. What would one have to do − what *could* one do − to get the xs to compose something?
>
> (van Inwagen 1990, p. 31)

Answers to the Special Composition fall under two types: moderate answers and extreme answers. Moderate answers are those that entail that at least some of the time some objects (xs) come together to compose a new thing, but also entail that this does not happen all of the time. Extreme answers to the Special Composition are those that entail either that composition occurs all of the time, for any xs whatsoever we consider, or that composition occurs none of the time (at least no distinct objects ever combine to form a new object; everything trivially composes itself). In the remaining sections of this chapter, we will introduce the various answers that have been proposed so that the reader may assess for him or herself what to think about this issue van Inwagen raises.

MODERATE ANSWERS TO THE SPECIAL COMPOSITION QUESTION

There are many different answers that are available to one who would like to answer the Special Composition Question in a moderate way − by giving an answer that entails that composition occurs only some of the time. Moderate answers are attractive to those who would like a metaphysics of material objects that lines up as much as possible with our pre-theoretic beliefs about when composition does and does not occur. For example, consider all of the objects of various sizes and complexity that exist here on Earth. Ordinarily, before we go too far in thinking about metaphysics, we think that some of these objects combine to compose more complex objects, while others do not. For example, the bricks that are piled neatly

Simple: see **mereological atom**

Mereological atom: an object lacking any proper parts.

Proper part: x is a proper part of y just in case x is a part of y and x is not identical to y.

on top of one another at 10 Downing Street in London, England, do compose something: the official home and office of the UK Prime Minister. On the other hand, the fleas on the fattest dog in Scotland and the Statue of Liberty do not combine together to compose anything. There is no such object that is composed exactly of the fleas on the fattest dog in Scotland and the Statue of Liberty. If we really wanted to, we could invent a name, 'Fleabert,' and insist that this name will be used to denote the object composed of the fleas on the fattest dog in Scotland and the Statue of Liberty. But this would just be a way of playing a game with language. Which objects exist is an objective matter and if there is no such object as 'Fleabert,' then inventing this name will not change that fact. So, one common motivation for seeking out a moderate answer to the Special Composition Question is to find an answer that fits well with our pretheoretical intuitions about which objects exist. The home at 10 Downing Street does exist. Fleabert does not.

One natural attempt at answering the Special Composition Question with a moderate response is provided by the Contact answer. This says:

Contact: ∀xs ∃y (the xs compose y iff the xs are in contact).

The rough idea is: if you have some things, to get them to compose some further object, all one needs to do is bring them next to each other so that they touch.

What is appealing about this answer is that it seems to do well at getting the cases right that are typically used to motivate moderate responses. According to the Contact view, the house at 10 Downing Street exists but Fleabert does not because while the bricks at 10 Downing Street are touching each other, the Statue of Liberty is not in contact with any of the fleas on the fattest dog in Scotland. However, even though there are some cases where the Contact view succeeds, there are other clear cases where it does not.

First, we often think that composition occurs in some cases even though the composing objects are not in contact. For example, the planets Mercury, Venus, Earth, Mars, Jupiter, Saturn, Uranus, and Neptune together compose our Solar System and yet they are not in contact with one another. Indeed they are separated by great distances. Van Inwagen also notes that if we should accept any ordinary cases of composition involving medium-sized objects, it seems it first needs to be the case that the fundamental particles of physics come together to compose relatively basic objects like atoms and molecules. But there isn't good reason to believe that fundamental particles like electrons and quarks compose larger objects like nuclei, atoms, and molecules by coming into contact with one another (1990, p. 34).

In addition, van Inwagen notes that there are clear cases where objects are brought into contact and yet we don't think composition occurs. For example, what happens if you and I shake hands (1990, p. 35)? Now our bodies are in contact and yet there is no reason to think that a new object has come into existence that persists from the moment our hands meet to the moment we let go. But this is a conclusion that is entailed by the Contact view. Thus, it seems we must find some other way of answering the Special Composition Question.

In his book, van Inwagen considers several other moderate answers to the Special Composition Question that he will ultimately reject. These are:

Fastening: ∀xs ∃y (the xs compose y iff the xs are fastened to one another, where the xs are fastened when among the many sequences in which forces of arbitrary directions and magnitudes might be applied, at most a few of them would be capable of separating them without breaking or permanently deforming them).

Cohesion: ∀xs ∃y (the xs compose y iff the xs cohere, where the xs cohere when they cannot be pulled apart or moved in relation to each other without breaking).

Fusion: ∀xs ∃y (the xs compose y iff the xs are fused, where the xs are fused when they are joined together such that there is no boundary).

All of these improve on the Contact account in some ways, in making the relationship that must obtain between the xs in order for them to compose something more stable. However each suffers from new counterexamples.

EXERCISE 3.5

Moderate Answers to the Special Composition Question

For each of Fastening, Cohesion, and Fusion, give one example of a case of composition that would motivate this answer (a case in which composition occurs and the relevant condition is satisfied) and one case that would serve as a counterexample to this answer. The counterexample may either be (i) a case in which the condition is satisfied but composition does not occur, or (ii) a case in which composition does occur but the condition is not satisfied.

Given the difficulty of stating a satisfactory moderate answer to the Special Composition Question, at least one metaphysician, Ned Markosian, has proposed that we instead seriously consider the possibility that there is no good answer to the Special Composition Question. Markosian takes it to be obvious that composition only occurs in some cases and not always, but takes van Inwagen's discussion in *Material Beings* to support the claim that one can't formulate a true and interesting answer to this question. His conclusion is that when composition occurs, this is just a brute fact. There is no metaphysical account one can point to that would distinguish the

cases in which composition occurs from the cases in which it does not.
The house at 10 Downing Street exists and Fleabert does not, but there is
nothing more to be said about these bricks or those fleas and that statue
that could explain why this is so. And so the only way one could give a true
answer to van Inwagen's question would be either to say (trivially) that
composition occurs when it occurs or to list one after the other all of the
cases where composition does as a matter of fact occur. Markosian calls
his position **Brutal Composition**. More precisely, it is the claim that there is
no true, interesting, and finite answer to the Special Composition Question.

Before we can properly evaluate whether Markosian is right, we should
try to see what other answers to the Special Composition Question have
been proposed. Then, if at the end of all of this, we see reason to think any
answer we attempt to give will fail, we might (reluctantly) come to accept
that the facts about composition are brute.

According to van Inwagen, there is something in virtue of which certain
xs come together to compose a new object, but this isn't to be understood
in terms of the xs' spatial positions relative to one another. All of the
accounts that make whether composition occurs rest on objects' relative
spatial positions fall prey to counterexamples. Nonetheless, van Inwagen
is certain that at least one mereologically complex material object exists,
himself, and so there must be something about the objects that compose
him that makes composition occur.

Van Inwagen believes that what makes some mereological atoms
compose him is that they participate in a kind of complex activity, the sort
of complex activity that allows them to constitute a life (1990, p. 82). So,
van Inwagen's proposed answer to the Special Composition is:

PvI: ∀xs ∃y (the xs compose y iff the activity of the xs constitutes a life).

What it is for the activity of some xs to constitute a life is something that
van Inwagen takes to be an empirical matter, something that will be settled
by biology and what biologists say is required for some objects to constitute
a life. Van Inwagen takes lives to only include those of concrete biological
organisms. These arise through the unimaginably complex self-maintaining
behavior of a group of constituents. These groups persist over time by
taking in new constituents by ingestion or respiration, and by expelling old
constituents.

At this point, I am sure the reader will notice that this view entails quite
a surprising ontology. It follows from van Inwagen's answer to the Special
Composition Question and the assumption that there are some mereological simples that the only material objects that exist are mereological
simples and living creatures. Human beings exist, electrons exist, but tables
and chairs, planets and solar systems do not because they are neither
simples nor lives. Certainly this result is surprising, perhaps too it is counterintuitive if one places weight on the examples usually used to motivate
the search for a moderate answer to the Special Composition Question.
However in philosophy just like in science, we often find that the evidence
points us in the direction of what is initially counterintuitive. That a view

does not agree with our initial intuitions is not a decisive reason against it, but must rather be weighed with all of the other reasons in favor of and against it.

Before moving on to discuss the two extreme answers to the Special Composition Question, it is worth remarking that van Inwagen has gone some way towards trying to show that even though his view may look surprising at first, it does not necessarily need to conflict with the majority of statements we make in our everyday lives. For van Inwagen notes there is a very simple way to paraphrase statements that might look to commit one to the existence of mereologically complex objects that are not living (such as tables and chairs) into statements that do not so commit one (1990, pp. 108–111).

For example, consider the sentence 'There are at least two chairs in this room.' At first glance, this seems to commit us to the existence of chairs, and since chairs are mereologically complex material objects that are not living, this seems to commit us to cases of composition violating van Inwagen's answer to the Special Composition Question. A natural first-order symbolization is:

$\exists x \exists y(((x$ is a chair $\wedge$ x is in this room) $\wedge$ (y is a chair $\wedge$ y is in this room)) $\wedge$ x$\neq$y)

But there is a paraphrase available. This paraphrase allows us to see the original sentence as only committing us to simples (entities in which van Inwagen does believe) arranged in certain ways:

$\exists xs \exists ys$ (((the xs are arranged chairwise $\wedge$ the xs are in this room) $\wedge$ (the ys are arranged chairwise $\wedge$ the ys are in this room)) $\wedge$ the xs $\neq$ the ys)

This regimentation fails to commit one to the existence of chairs. It only commits one to things arranged chairwise. It is not too hard to see how one might extend this analysis to all other sentences that appear at first to quantify over complex yet inanimate material objects. Van Inwagen may replace talk of tables with talk of simples arranged tablewise, talk of planets with talk of simples arranged planetwise, and so on. In this way, van Inwagen need not say that any of our ordinary beliefs or statements are false. They appear to commit one to complex inanimate material objects, but when understood properly, they do not.

EXERCISE 3.6

Van Inwagen's Proposed Answer and the Method of Paraphrase

How would van Inwagen propose we regiment the following sentences into the language of first-order predicate logic so that they are consistent with his answer to the Special Composition Question?

A.   There are planets made of iron.
B.   Some tables are heavier than some chairs.
C.   Some tables are heavier than some people.
D.   It is not the case that some tables are heavier than some planets.

MEREOLOGICAL NIHILISM

We now turn to consider the last two answers to the Special Composition Question. These are the two extreme answers, and it is fair to say these are the most common responses one finds defended in the philosophical literature. Let's begin with **mereological nihilism** (hereafter, nihilism). If one is a nihilist, one answers the Special Composition Question in this way:

Mereological nihilism: the view that there are no mereologically complex objects, only simples.

> *Mereological Nihilism*: ∀xs ∃y (the xs compose y iff the xs are exactly one).

Strictly speaking, the nihilist doesn't say composition never occurs. The nihilist will allow that any simple object is such as to compose itself. But when the xs are two or more, there is never anything that the xs compose. In other words, everything that exists is a mereological atom, a simple.

Extreme though it is, there are reasons to find nihilism compelling. The most obvious point in favor of the position stems from Ockham's Razor. If we are confident that a fundamental scientific theory will give us an account of the world just by appealing to some elementary objects without parts, then these objects will be simples. Since a fundamental scientific theory, when it is finished, by definition is one that will be able to give a complete explanation of everything that happens at our world, Ockham's Razor directs one not to posit in addition to these simples mereologically complex objects composed out of them.

Despite this benefit in ontological parsimony, there are two arguments one typically finds against nihilism. The first is the one that van Inwagen himself uses to reject the view and it has already been alluded to above. Van Inwagen presents the following argument (1990, p. 73):

Van Inwagen's Argument against Mereological Nihilism

1. I exist.
2. I am not a mereological simple.

Therefore,

3. At least one object exists that is not a mereological simple.

Therefore,

4. Nihilism is false.

Nihilists, if they are to maintain their position, must find some way of rejecting this argument. Since the validity of the argument is not questionable, this means finding a way to reject at least one of either premises (1) or (2). When it comes to premise (2), it is difficult to accept that van Inwagen is a material entity of some kind and yet not complex. If van Inwagen is to be identified with any kind of material object, he surely isn't a simple object like an electron or quark, but something that has parts and exists due to the complex behavior of these parts. One possibility is to adopt some form of **mind–body dualism** according to which you and I and van Inwagen are not material objects at all, but rather immaterial minds or souls. This is one way to reject premise (2), but won't be appealing to the naturalist or physicalist philosophers who believe that minds are themselves parts of the material world, arising from complex processes of physical matter. Another option for the nihilist is to deny (1) and say the same thing about van Inwagen as he himself says about tables and chairs. The nihilist can then say while this claim is false:

Mind–body dualism: the view that there are two kinds of substances, minds (mental substances) and bodies (material substances).

Van Inwagen exists,

this claim is true:

There exist some simples arranged van-Inwagen-wise.

That is, for all claims van Inwagen accepts that look to commit him to his own existence, the nihilist can produce paraphrases that show them only to be committed to simples.

This itself is controversial. However, debate on this topic continues.[15]

The second argument that many have found to give a good reason to deny nihilism has to do with the fact that for all we know, there might be no bottom level of reality. After all, how can we be sure right now that there really exist some objects that are as a matter of fact mereological simples? Given today's physics, we may think that electrons and quarks are mereological simples; they don't have any proper parts. But time and again, throughout the history of physics, when physicists thought they had reached some realm of ultimate mereological atoms, it turned out that there was more structure to discover. Indeed, traditionally the word 'atom' refers to what is indivisible (*a-tomos*). In the early nineteenth century, John Dalton introduced the term to refer to what he then thought were the mereological atoms, and the term stuck. We now know however that these objects, what we today call 'atoms,' are not really simple at all. And so, what reason is there to think the basic entities of today's physics are the real mereological atoms?

The problem this causes for nihilism is that if there are no mereological simples, but everything is ultimately mereologically complex all of the way down, then it follows from the nihilist's view that no material objects whatsoever exist. After all, the nihilist's view is that only simples exist. This seems problematic. We might question whether there are ultimately only electrons and quarks or whether there are tables and people too, but surely there are material objects of some kind. If nihilism is right, then maybe this isn't so.

We should note that a similar problem obtains for van Inwagen's view as well.[16] If it turns out that there are no simples and van Inwagen's view is correct, then the only things that will exist are living things. There will be no electrons, quarks, tables, or chairs. The only things that will exist are those things that are alive. Since we know this scenario to be false and yet we don't know whether matter is infinitely divisible, it appears we must conclude that van Inwagen's view is false as well.

MEREOLOGICAL UNIVERSALISM

The last answer to the Special Composition Question we will consider is what is arguably the most common response (although it looks mad to many others!). This is:

> *Mereological Universalism*: ∀xs ∃y (the xs compose y iff the xs are disjoint).

To say the xs are disjoint is to say that they do not spatially overlap (i.e., their spatial locations are entirely distinct). This is a view that has been given an influential defense by David Lewis in his book *On the Plurality of Worlds* (1986). Lewis states the position this way:

> I claim that mereological composition is unrestricted: any old class of things has a mereological sum. Whenever there are some things, no matter how disparate and unrelated, there is something composed of just those things.
>
> (Lewis 1986, p. 211)

This view entails that for any material objects whatsoever (simple or complex), as long as they do not overlap spatially, there is something that these objects compose. Some philosophers, for example, Markosian, argue that this view should be rejected for coming into too much conflict with our background beliefs about when composition occurs and when it doesn't. To return to our earlier examples, there is no such thing as Fleabert; there is no such thing as the object composed of the atoms making up you and me when we shake hands. Mereological universalists (universalists, for short) typically dismiss this sort of worry by insisting that we shouldn't rely so heavily on our pre-theoretic intuitions about when composition occurs and when it doesn't. We shouldn't use our intuitions to guide our reasoning about what sorts of things do and do not exist when we have no reason to believe our intuitions will lead us toward the truth. Would following our intuitions have ever led us to quantum mechanics or general relativity, the most well-confirmed theories we have ever had?

But it is worth pointing out that even if the appeal to intuitions is not in general a reliable method of coming to the truth about what exists, in this particular case, there is something to be said for respecting them. The reason is that what universalists are asking us to believe is that composition occurs no matter which group of material objects we consider. And yet the way we come to understand what it is for some things to compose some other thing in the first place has always involved us drawing distinctions between the cases in which it occurs and the cases in which it does not. But what could it mean to say that every case in which some objects exists is a case of composition? Could we ever even understand such a claim? Doesn't this require giving up on our usual understanding of what 'composition' means? And if so, is this really an answer to the Special Composition Question or just a change in topic?

In addition to these worries about the conflict of the view with our intuitions, there is of course the fact that the position involves a considerable cost in ontological parsimony. The universalist's ontology is enormous and certainly larger than that of any view about material objects we have considered up until now.[17] Still, there is at least one argument that motivates many metaphysicians to endorse it.

This argument relies on the premise that if one doesn't say that composition always occurs (or never occurs, but for now let's set aside nihilism), then one is forced to admit the existence of cases in which whether composition occurs or not is vague. But if it is vague in a given case whether composition occurs, then it is vague how many things there are. After all, when we are considering a case of composition involving multiple xs, if the xs compose y, then there will be an additional object y that is the sum or fusion of the xs. If it is vague whether y, a given fusion, exists, then it is vague how many things there are: the number of xs or the number of xs plus one.

Why would someone with a moderate view (i.e., a view that rejects both universalism and nihilism) have to admit that there are cases where it is vague whether or not composition occurs? The reason is that every moderate answer that has been proposed to the Special Composition Question uses vague concepts. Contact, fastening, cohesion, fusion, involved in a life: all of these are vague notions. And since they are vague, we can conceive of cases where it is indeterminate whether or not an object satisfies them. Let's examine this for the concept of fastening. Recall, by definition, objects are fastened when among the many sequences in which forces of arbitrary directions and magnitudes might be applied, at most a few of them would be capable of separating them without breaking or permanently deforming them. Who is to say what counts as "a few of them"? All of the other notions are vague as well. Indeed van Inwagen concedes that the concept of a life is vague. There are boundary cases in which there is no objective fact about whether some xs constitute a life or not. To see this one only need consider the earliest stages of an organism after conception. At what point does the life begin?

Indeed one of the main reasons why metaphysicians have been skeptical about moderate answers to the Special Composition Question is that these answers all involve vagueness. Of the responses to the Special Composition Question, only the extreme answers (nihilism and universalism) and the Brutal Composition view eliminate vagueness about when composition occurs (and so how many objects exist) by saying that composition always occurs, it never occurs, or it is simply a brute fact when and where it occurs. Since this issue of vagueness is so central to debates about composition and indeed many others in metaphysics, we will devote the next section of this chapter to the topic.

VAGUENESS

It was Lewis who originally appealed to vagueness to raise a problem for moderate answers to the Special Composition Question. We should note that he was not arguing that there is not such a phenomenon of vagueness at our world. Everyone grants that there are many concepts that form part of our ways of thinking about the world and words that form parts of our language that are vague. What Lewis wanted to insist however is that vagueness is merely a phenomenon of our language or our way of conceptualizing the world. There is no vagueness in the world as it is in itself, independently of our ways of thinking or talking about it. While Lewis has no problem with what is typically called **linguistic vagueness**, what he was objecting to was **metaphysical vagueness**:

Linguistic (or **semantic**) **vagueness**: vagueness that is the result of semantic indecision; there not being facts to determine precisely in all cases what our terms apply to.

Metaphysical vagueness: vagueness that results from how the world is objectively, not how we think or talk about it; fundamental indeterminacy in what exists or what features things have.

> The only intelligible account of vagueness locates it in our thought and language. The reason it's vague where the outback begins is not that there's this thing, the outback, with imprecise borders; rather there are many things, with different borders, and nobody's been fool enough to try to enforce a choice of one of them as the official referent of the word 'outback'. Vagueness is semantic indecision.
>
> (Lewis 1986, p. 212)

According to many (though not all) philosophers, metaphysical vagueness does not just fail to exist at our world, it is unintelligible.[18] What could it mean to say that whether or not a certain object exists (in the case we have been considering, an object that is the mereological sum of the xs) is vague? That it only partially or somewhat exists? But what could this mean? If it exists in any way, then it exists.

Another option for how to understand vagueness that is compatible with these worries about metaphysical vagueness, but doesn't understand vagueness as the result of semantic indecision, is a view called **epistemicism**. According to epistemicism, it is determinate what our words mean. Our linguistic behavior and dispositions fix what we mean by 'life,' 'the outback,' and so on. It is just that some facts about the world are unknown to us. Applying epistemicism to the case of composition, one would say we simply can't know in every case whether composition occurs. This doesn't mean there isn't a fact about when composition occurs and when it doesn't. It is just that these facts are sometimes hidden from us. We can tell in the easy cases that composition occurs or it doesn't. But in those borderline cases that Lewis is worried about, we are unable to tell.[19] Whether vagueness is ultimately to be understood as semantic indecision or as a failure on our part to know the right thing to say about borderline cases, many believe it is ultimately a phenomenon having to do with our (human beings') connection to the world. It is not a feature of what the world is like independently of us. And so, if one has trouble understanding how there can be vagueness in the world, then one should either try to improve on the formulation of moderate responses so as to eliminate reference to vague terms, or one should prefer some other response to the Special Composition Question. If one is pessimistic about the moderate responses, then one must try to overcome the obstacles to nihilism or universalism, or learn to live with the view that composition is brutal.

> **Epistemicism**: the view that vagueness is ignorance; it is not a matter of fundamental indeterminacy in the world or indeterminacy in what our words or concepts apply to, but our ignorance about what our words or concepts apply to.

EXERCISE 3.7

Responding to the Special Composition Question

We have now seen several moderate and two extreme answers to the Special Composition Question. What is your preferred answer? How would you defend this response against the worries raised above?

BACK TO THE PARADOXES

We have now considered several different answers to the Special Composition Question. Although we have seen the usual lines of arguments that get brought out in support of or against the various views, I haven't attempted to convince you that you should adopt one of these views over the others. All of the views have costs. Now that all of the views have been described, we can briefly come back to the paradoxes of material constitution with which we began this chapter and see if the various views shed any light on them.

Interestingly, van Inwagen defends his own response to the Special Composition Question by noting that it allows him an easy way to get out of the paradoxes of material constitution. For those involving the persistence or constitution of inanimate material objects, he can say simply that there is no paradox because none of these objects exist. There is no Ship of Theseus; there are no statues, no lumps. The mereological nihilist as well can give a similar response to these paradoxes and say they give one all the more reason to think there are no such things as mereologically complex material objects.

When it comes to paradoxes that don't involve inanimate objects, but instead living ones – for example, we can ask not about the statue and the lump of clay, but about you and the lump of matter that composes you, and the Problem of the Many was already formulated in terms of living human beings – van Inwagen must give a different response. (Though the nihilist is once again in the clear.) In these cases, van Inwagen thinks that the puzzles arise because one is assuming mereological universalism. For example, the Problem of the Many arises only because we begin by assuming there are all these collections of atoms, C, C-, C--, and so on. Since van Inwagen denies that all of these collections of atoms exist, he can deny there are many human beings in the same approximate place at the same approximate time. There is just the one collection of atoms that comes together to actually constitute a life. For van Inwagen, it may be vague what exactly this object is (whether it is C, C-, or . . .), but this doesn't mean there are many human beings in approximately the same spatial location at the same time.

When we apply the puzzle of the Statue and the Clay to the case of a human being and its constituent matter, again van Inwagen will be able to argue that his view has an advantage over the mereological universalist's. To see this, consider the intuitions that drove the paradox.[20] We noted that the statue and lump have different temporal and modal properties. While the lump existed at noon, the statue did not. The lump could survive being squashed. The statue could not survive being squashed. By Leibniz's law, we concluded that the lump and statue must be distinct. To apply these intuitions to the case of a living organism like a person, we might say: while the hunk of matter that composes you existed a hundred years ago (it may not have taken the shape of a human, but it existed), you did not.[21] While this hunk of matter could survive being squashed so that its vital organs stop functioning, you could not survive being squashed so that your vital organs stop functioning. Therefore, applying Leibniz's law, we conclude that there are two objects: you on the one hand, and the hunk of matter that composes you on the other.

Van Inwagen will deny there is any hunk of matter that has these temporal and modal properties. The hunk of matter did not exist before you were born (unless what is unlikely is the case, that the hunk of matter that now makes you up previously made up a different organism). This is because there are no such things, according to van Inwagen, as inanimate hunks of matter. In addition, it is false (at least according to van Inwagen's view) that the hunk of matter that composes you could survive being squashed so that its vital organs stopped functioning. If this happened, then the matter would cease to constitute a life and so it would fail to exist. So one who wanted to defend van Inwagen's view can respond to this paradox of material constitution as well.

When it comes to most of the puzzles of material constitution, perhaps it is really only the other moderate views (besides van Inwagen's) and mereological universalism that seem to face problems. In Chapter 6, we will have reason to return to these paradoxes and see a way mereological universalists typically respond. This will involve a particular view about what it is for objects to persist over time.

SUGGESTIONS FOR FURTHER READING

An excellent volume discussing the paradoxes of material constitution and presenting many different solutions to them is *Material Constitution*, edited by Michael Rea. In addition to the works cited above, *Ordinary Objects* by Amie Thomasson and *The Structure of Objects* by Kathrin Koslicki are also recommended. Both present quite interesting views about the nature of ordinary material objects different than those discussed in this chapter. On the issue of whether there could fail to be any mereologically simple objects, but instead complexity all of the way down, Jonathan Schaffer's "Is There a Fundamental Level?" is recommended, as is the discussion in Theodore Sider's *Writing the Book of the World*, pp. 133–137. Many of the articles in the volume *Metametaphysics*, edited by David Chalmers, David Manley, and Ryan Wasserman consider the question of whether the debate over the Special Composition Question is a substantive issue. For more on vagueness, a good collection of essays is *Vagueness: A Reader*, edited by Rosanna Keefe and Peter Smith. Williamson's book *Vagueness* also provides an excellent overview of several rival positions. Elizabeth Barnes's "Ontic Vagueness: A Guide for the Perplexed" defends the coherence of genuine metaphysical vagueness. Finally, one issue about material objects that has received much discussion recently, but that we do not have the space to explore here, is Jonathan Schaffer's defense of monism, which takes off from the debate over the Special Composition Question. His "Monism: the Priority of the Whole" is a recommended starting point.

NOTES

1   See Wilson's "On Characterizing the Physical."
2   Some philosophers have expressed concern that the notion of a material object we receive from physics is actually more poorly understood than many metaphysicians realize. For discussion, see Barbara Montero's "The Body Problem."

3   This means they believe there exist at least some concrete material objects and that the existence of these objects does not depend on any human being's thinking about them; they are mind-independent in this sense.

4   Please refer back to the discussion of numerical identity or "identity in the strict sense" in Box 1.2.

5   We will talk more about the meaning of the box ($\square$) in Chapter 7.

6   This also introduces the problem of having to answer the question of *when* it was that the Ship of Theseus ceased to exist.

7   In other words, 7,000,000,000,000,000,000,000,000,000,000.

Sortal predicate:
a predicate that classifies
an object as a member of a
certain sort (or kind).

8   A **sortal predicate** is one that classifies an object as a member of a certain sort (or kind). Examples are: 'is a chair,' 'is a planet,' 'is a statue,' and 'is a person.'

9   He distinguishes this from the General Composition Question, a question we will not discuss in this chapter. The General Composition Question asks what is the nature of the composition relation.

10   To fully translate this sentence, we would remove the definite description in the way suggested by Russell (discussed in Chapter 1): $\exists x (Ex \wedge \forall y(Ey \supset y=x))$. This still commits us to a group of things, a one.

11   Van Inwagen also raises the same concerns about the terms 'aggregate,' 'array,' 'group,' and 'multiplicity' (p. 22). He also rejects the option of using quantification over sets to express the Special Composition Question, but for a different reason. To speak of 'the set of' of some things doesn't assume composition has occurred. Composition is the relation whereby concrete objects combine to create concrete objects. But, the assumption of abstract objects like sets isn't necessary to raise the Special Composition Question or formulate an answer to it. We can do this without entering the debate about abstract entities.

12   'iff' is an abbreviation for 'if and only if.'

13   This is according to the formal theory of mereology that many metaphysicians use to understand the notion of parthood, that of Henry S. Leonard and Nelson Goodman (1940).

14   By 'nonoverlapping,' we mean that the objects do not have any parts in common.

15   For recent discussion, see the defense of nihilism in Theodore Sider's paper "Against Parthood."

16   This was noted by Sider in his 1993 paper "Van Inwagen and the Possibility of Gunk." Gunk is a technical term introduced by metaphysicians to refer to a material object that has no mereological simples as parts. Instead it has proper parts such that each of their proper parts in turn have proper parts.

17   Though does it commit us to more *types* of things? Recall from our discussion of Ockham's Razor in Chapter 1, this is the real issue.

18   Sider presents another argument against metaphysical vagueness, influenced by Lewis's, in his book *Four Dimensionalism*, Chapter 4.

19   Epistemicism was defended by the philosopher Timothy Williamson in his 1994 book *Vagueness*.

20   See *Material Beings*, pp. 75–79.

21   When we talk about 'this hunk of matter,' note we are talking about the mereological sum of the atoms that compose you. This is not a plurally-referring term like 'these atoms.'

Critiques of Metaphysics

Learning Points

- Introduces logical positivism
- Presents two critiques of metaphysics from the logical positivist school and replies
- Presents a more recent critique of metaphysics from within naturalism and replies
- Evaluates the relationship between metaphysics and science.

A CONCERN ABOUT METHODOLOGY

So far we have introduced some of the central questions of metaphysics: ontological questions about the existence of abstract and material objects. In later chapters, we'll address other ontological issues such as whether we should believe in the existence of past or future objects and events or only present ones, whether we should believe in addition to natural features and objects, in those that are socially constructed like gender or race. We'll also address questions that are not distinctly ontological, but are metaphysical in that they concern other features of our world such as the nature of causality or whether we have free will.

Perhaps now, since we've already spent time on some very abstract issues and we've seen arguments on both sides of each one, you may have started to wonder whether there is any real way of settling these issues. Could there really be a fact about whether there exist universals or only concrete objects? Could there really be a fact about whether mathematical truths involve the existence of a domain of objects inhabiting some realm outside of space and time, or whether they only require our being capable of proving certain claims and not others? What could settle such issues after all? It seems that philosophers can come up with arguments favoring both sides of every metaphysical debate and these issues are so abstract it is difficult to see how anything we could do could settle these issues. And if there isn't any way to settle them, maybe they aren't about anything of substance at all? The Austrian philosopher Ludwig Wittgenstein (1889–1951) famously suggested that the best way to settle philosophical problems, including these metaphysical ones we've engaged here, was through therapy (1953, p. 255); what is needed is not answers to these questions, but a way to get oneself to stop asking them in the first place.

If you've had these worries yourself, you are not alone. As we will see in this chapter, such a worry about metaphysics was quite prevalent at one time in the early twentieth century. It originated in a philosophical movement called **logical positivism**. This movement originated with a group of philosophers and scientists who met in Vienna in the 1920s and 1930s, the Vienna Circle. We will focus in this chapter especially on the arguments of one prominent member of this circle, the philosopher Rudolf Carnap (1891–1970).

Logical positivism: a movement in philosophy originating in Austria and Germany in the 1920s; a movement critical of metaphysics, arguing that all knowledge of the world must originate in sense experience and logic.

CARNAP'S TWO CRITIQUES OF METAPHYSICS

In his "Elimination of Metaphysics through the Logical Analysis of Language" (1932), Carnap argued that the main problem with metaphysics was the distortions of language that metaphysicians use in order to ask their questions and state their theories. These distortions of language are so severe that in the end Carnap thought all distinctly metaphysical claims were meaningless.

Carnap diagnoses several ways in which these distortions occur. Sometimes this comes about because the metaphysician introduces new words without ever supplying clear meanings for them. Carnap gives the example of 'essence.'[1] Other times the metaphysician uses words that normally have a clear meaning in an unorthodox and unclear way. One of Carnap's main examples here is 'God.' This word could, Carnap notes, be used to denote some physical being. In ancient times, the word was used with such a meaning to refer to physical beings living on Mt. Olympus possessing special powers. However, today the word 'God' has what for Carnap is a purely "metaphysical" usage. It is used with the intention of denoting something that is not a physical being but lies beyond what could be observed.

When Carnap claims that words are being used so that the sentences they compose lack meaning, he is very explicit about the theory of meaning he intends. To illustrate this theory of meaning, Carnap says that for a given sentence S, the following are all reformulations of the same question (1932, p. 62):

Verificationist theory of meaning: the meaning of a statement is given by its conditions of verification.

Under what conditions is S supposed to be true, and under what conditions false?

How is S to be *verified*?

What is the *meaning* of S?

Verificationist theory of truth: a sentence is only capable of truth or falsity if it is capable of being verified or falsified.

Carnap is here endorsing a verificationist theory of truth and of meaning. The **verificationist theory of meaning** says that a sentence's meaning is given by its means of verification. The **verificationist theory of truth** says that a true sentence is one that is or may be verified. If a sentence cannot be verified, then it is meaningless and lacks a truth value. According to the logical positivists, there are two kinds of verification: verification by sense experience or empirical observation (**synthetic** means) and verification by logical methods (by **analytic** means) where the latter includes mathematical reasoning. If a claim cannot be proven either using logic (or mathematics) alone or empirical observation, then it is unverifiable and hence meaningless.

Synthetic: see analytic/synthetic distinction

Analytic: see analytic/synthetic distinction

BOX 4.1

Methods of Verification

Logical positivists differ on what verification must involve in any particular case, but a pillar of logical positivism was the view that there are two basic kinds of verification: by analytic and by synthetic methods.

When it comes to verification by analytic methods, Carnap and the logical positivists held that this sort of verification involved logic alone. In some cases, a statement is true in virtue of the basic concepts involved in the statement, e.g.:

All triangles have three sides.

In other cases, a statement's verification requires a deductive proof. Carnap himself was inspired by the developments in logic by Frege in the late nineteenth century to think that all mathematical truths could be verified on the basis of deduction from the principles of logic alone. This view, that mathematics is in principle reducible to logic, is called **logicism**.

When it comes to synthetic verification, many positivists thought an ideal language contained a basic set of statements that may be verified directly by sensory experience. These are what Carnap called **protocol statements**. For example, a protocol statement might be:

The bell is ringing.

This can be directly verified by hearing the sound of a bell. Still other statements may be verified indirectly, that is through a chain of verification leading ultimately back to protocol statements. For example:

Someone is at the door.

This may be verified indirectly by combining the statement "The bell is ringing" with other background information that the ringing of the bell entails that someone is at the door. Or, if one had already verified the statement that the mailman comes every day at about this time, then the protocol statement "The bell is ringing" could indirectly verify:

The mailman is at the door.

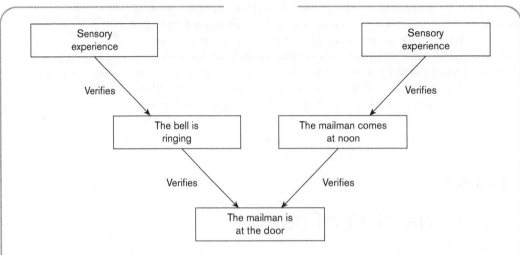

Figure 4.1 A Chain of Verification

This is a claim that may not be directly verified by experience. One might think you cannot directly hear that the mailman is at the door, only that a bell is ringing.[a] Still one can verify this statement through a chain ultimately leading back to what can be directly verified by experience (see Figure 4.1).

In general, the only statements that are meaningful for the verificationist are, on the one hand, the synthetic statements – those that may be directly verified by sensory experience or verified indirectly through a chain of verification leading ultimately back to sensory experience – or, on the other hand, analytic statements, those verified by logic alone.

Note
a Though see Susanna Siegel's *The Contents of Visual Experience* for a rival view.

Logicism: the view that mathematics is reducible to logic.

Protocol statement: a statement that may be directly verified by sense experience.

So often, the problem with metaphysics is that its words lack meanings. In a final case Carnap considers, the problem is one of the form or structure of the metaphysical statement (its syntax). Sometimes, Carnap notes, it is not that the metaphysician uses a word that doesn't have a clear verificationist-style meaning, but instead that she is using a perfectly meaningful expression in a perverse way so as to form a sentence that cannot be evaluated for truth or falsity. In one of the German philosopher Martin Heidegger's (1889–1976) most famous essays, "What is Metaphysics?" he offers the view that it is only by contemplating nothingness that the nature of being can really be understood. Trying to say more about this nothing, Heidegger concludes "*Das Nichts selbst nichtet*" or "The nothing nothings." Carnap takes this claim in for an extended bashing. He argues the meaninglessness of Heidegger's thesis consists in its distorting the logical role of the word 'nothing.'

To see this, note what we are saying when we say something using the word 'nothing,' for example, "Nothing is free." Here, we are not using 'nothing' as a noun phrase that refers to some object that can then be some way or have certain properties. This would be to mistake the sentence's logical form for:

Fn.

But of course this symbolization is incorrect. The role of 'nothing' in a sentence is not to serve as a name, but as a quantifier phrase. The logical form of "Nothing is free" is:

¬∃xFx

Heidegger's claim "The nothing nothings" thus is ill-formed. It cannot even be expressed in logic. It treats a quantifier phrase as if it were a referring term. One might try to symbolize it as:

Nn

if one likes, but this is a distortion of logic. There is no way to symbolize it using correct logical notation. We must conclude then, Carnap says, that Heidegger's sentence is meaningless.

According to Carnap, the trouble with metaphysicians' use of language whether through distortions of logic or meaning, is that such distortions yield sentences incapable of verification. How could one verify if the nothing nothings or a person has an essence or an invisible God exists? Insofar as such questions are unverifiable, they are meaningless.

EXERCISE 4.1

The Verificationist Theory of Meaning

Which of the following claims would count as meaningless according to the verificationist theory of meaning? Explain how they would be verified, or if they are unverifiable, explain why this is.

A. There are prime numbers greater than 3.
B. There are numbers.
C. There are two elevators in the Empire State Building.
D. The universe began before the Big Bang.
E. There is intelligent life on other planets.
F. The God of *Genesis* exists.
G. Dinosaurs once roamed the Earth.

In "Empiricism, Semantics, and Ontology" (1950), Carnap addresses metaphysical statements that wouldn't obviously fall prey to the earlier critique: ontological statements like 'There are material objects,' 'There are universals,' or 'There are numbers.' Let's say that the metaphysician has stripped her language of dubious terms, terms that she cannot supply with clear meanings. And she does her best to make statements that are expressible in clear logical form. Indeed contemporary metaphysicians do their best to ensure that their statements and theories are always formulated in the clearest terms possible. Nonetheless, Carnap thought there would still be problems for metaphysics.

To see Carnap's objection, we must start with his notion of a framework. It is always from within a framework that meaningful questions may be asked. It is from within a framework that statements may be evaluated for truth or falsity. When Carnap talks about a **framework**, he has in mind a linguistic framework. Frameworks involve two things:

Framework (Carnapian): a linguistic system including rules of grammar and meaning.

1. A list of the expressions for the language and syntactic rules, i.e., rules for how these expressions may be combined to form grammatical sentences.

For example, if we are considering the framework of mathematics, say basic arithmetic, the expressions will be numerals like '1,' '2,' and so on, as well as symbols for addition, '+,' '=,' etc. There will be rules that say you may combine these terms in certain ways to yield grammatical sentences, for example '1+1=2,' and not in other ways such as '1+=2.'

The second component of a framework for Carnap is:

2. Rules that allow one to evaluate whether or not a given sentence in the language is true or false.

As we saw above, Carnap and the logical positivists endorsed a very specific view about what kinds of rules these could be. These are summarized by the verificationist theory of meaning: a sentence's meaning is given by its rules of verification. Returning to our case of arithmetic, the sentence '1+1=2' is true just in case the rules of arithmetic allow one to verify this sentence. In an axiomatized mathematics, this is accomplished via the method of proof. And again, there are two broad kinds of verification: verification by analytic methods, which includes logical or mathematical deduction, and verification by synthetic methods, that is, methods that involve empirical observation. In a linguistic framework like that of arithmetic, the semantic rules are entirely analytic. Other frameworks Carnap considers, such as those containing material object terms like 'desk' or 'chair' or 'electron,' will include semantic rules that are synthetic. In this kind of framework, questions will be settled by means of empirical observation.

Internal question: see **internal/external distinction**

Internal statement: see **internal/external distinction**

Given this concept of a framework, Carnap says that all questions we may ask or statements we may make may be viewed as internal or external. An **internal question** is one that is asked and evaluated from within a specific linguistic framework. And an **internal statement** is one that is stated and interpreted from within a linguistic framework. Put this way, we can see that only internal questions and statements are meaningful because only in the context of a framework can we presuppose that there are certain terms and rules for combining them in such a way to form statements capable of being true or false. **External questions** and **external statements** are those interpreted from outside a particular linguistic framework. As such, they are meaningless and not capable of truth and falsity.

External question: see **internal/external distinction**

External statement: see **internal/external distinction**

Carnap asks whether we should view the questions asked by metaphysicians, in particular, ontological questions, as internal or external questions. Ontological questions are questions like 'Are there numbers?' or 'Do material objects exist?' These questions as we have seen can only be meaningful if they are asked as internal questions. The trouble, Carnap argues, is that even if these questions may be evaluated as having answers within a framework with clear syntactic and semantic rules, these ontological questions will always turn out to be hopelessly trivial. As such, they cannot be attributed the significance the metaphysician intends for them. These questions are trivial because once one chooses to use a given linguistic framework, the answers to ontological questions are always obvious. Carnap uses the following example to illustrate this point.

Let's say one decides to use the framework of arithmetic in order to understand the following two statements and decide whether they are true:

There are prime numbers greater than 1,000,000.
There are numbers.

In order to know whether the first is true, one has to do some arithmetic. One will need to verify the first statement using the analytic methods of the arithmetical framework. One has to actually prove some things. By contrast, one finds that the second sentence is true automatically once one chooses to adopt the arithmetical framework. In choosing the framework, we've chosen to use words like '1' and '2' and it is trivial that these terms will refer to numbers.

To use another example, suppose one chooses to adopt a language that uses terms for material objects. Consider the following two statements:

There are two elevators in the Empire State Building.
There are material objects.

Again, once we presuppose the linguistic framework of material objects, once we, in Carnap's terminology, decide to interpret these statements *internally*, we find that although the first statement is substantive, the second is trivial. To evaluate the truth of the first, we have to apply (in this case) synthetic methods. We will have to engage in some empirical observation, trek out to Manhattan or at least look things up online in order to see whether this claim is true. By contrast, once we have decided to adopt this linguistic framework containing terms for material objects, the second statement, and this is the distinctively ontological one, one that would only be questioned by a philosopher, is trivially true.

So, ontological statements turn out all to be trivial when considered as internal statements. Is there any way to make sense of them so that they are not trivial? We have already noted that if one views them as external statements, they will be meaningless. Yet Carnap concedes there is a good question one can ask in the ballpark of such questions as 'Are there numbers?' or 'Are there material objects?', namely whether or not it would be wise to adopt a linguistic system in which such claims come out as true. This is one example of an external question, a question that is asked not from within the linguistic system in question, but from the outside, a question that is about the linguistic system in question as a whole. Such questions will be deemed meaningless by Carnap. They do not have answers that may be evaluated as true or false (nor do they earn objective verification) since such verdicts can only be reached from within a linguistic system, presupposing the system's syntactic and semantic rules. As such, Carnap says in this way they are pseudo-questions. Carnap summarizes his attitude towards ontological statements ultimately in the following way:

> An alleged statement of the reality of [a] system of entities is a pseudo-statement without cognitive content. To be sure, we have to face at this point an important question, but it is a practical, not a theoretical question; it is a question of whether or not to accept the new linguistic forms. The acceptance cannot be judged as being either true or false because it is not an assertion. It can only be judged as being more or less expedient, fruitful, conducive to the aim for which the language is intended.
>
> (Carnap 1950, p. 214)

This isn't too distant a verdict from that reached in the earlier 1932 paper:

> The (pseudo)statements of metaphysics do not serve for the *description of states of affairs*, neither existing ones . . . nor non-existing ones . . . They serve for the *expression of the general attitude of a person towards life* . . . What is here essential for our considerations is only the fact that art is an adequate, metaphysics an inadequate means for the expression of the basic attitude. Of course, there need be no intrinsic objection to one's using any means of expression one likes. But in the case of metaphysics we find this situation: through the form of its works it pretends to be something that it is not. The form in question is that of a system of statements which are apparently related as premises and conclusions, that is, the form of a theory. In this way the fiction of theoretical content is generated, whereas, as we have seen, there is no such content.
>
> (Carnap 1932, pp. 78–79)

Ontological questions like 'Are there numbers' may be construed in such a way as to "face an important question." But this is a practical question about which linguistic frameworks we should adopt. The answer 'Yes, there are numbers' or 'No, there are not numbers' is not something that should be viewed as true or false, certainly not as pertaining to what there is in reality. It is only a practical decision that can be more or less useful to the communicative task at hand.

It should be clear that with this argument in "Empiricism, Semantics, and Ontology," Carnap is not endorsing nominalism or nihilism. He is not saying that abstract entities or material objects do not exist. For Carnap, it is just as much of a pseudo-statement for the philosopher to say that material objects or numbers do not exist as much as it is to say that they do. To focus on the case of numbers, nominalist paraphrases of sentences that look to commit us to abstracta, of the kind for example undertaken by Hartry Field (see Chapter 2), may be motivated. (Although Carnap himself embraced the use of mathematical frameworks.) We might think it is better to replace our current scientific language, which uses mathematical terms and concepts, with a new scientific language that does not use such terms. But even if the nominalist could do this and preserve our scientific theories, this would not mean he has shown that numbers are not real. He will only have shown something about languages – that we don't need to use a mathematical language to do science.

RESPONSES TO CARNAP'S ARGUMENTS

There are three standard responses that have been given to Carnap's arguments and more generally the logical positivists' critique of metaphysics. It is fair to say, given the vitality of metaphysics today, that most philosophers now find at least one if not all of these responses compelling.

Certainly the most contentious part of Carnap's arguments both in "Elimination of Metaphysics through the Logical Analysis of Language" and "Empiricism, Semantics, and Ontology" is the verificationist theory of meaning that both arguments presuppose. Let's grant for the sake of argument that at least some metaphysical statements are incapable of being verified by any means whatsoever. Must that entail that these statements are meaningless?

Consider for example some of the statements involved in the realism/nominalism debate. The realist says, 'There are universals.' The nominalist says, 'There are no universals.' Is it really the case that these statements are meaningless? A metaphysician could say it is at least clear that these statements contradict each other. One says something does exist; the other says that same thing does not. Mustn't these sentences at least mean something if they are to contradict each other?

We could also point to examples of statements that are uncontroversially meaningless. For example I might say, 'Te flob schwubs jip,' or 'Zee gromple.' Surely these are cases of statements that truly are meaningless. Should we really lump 'There are universals' into a class with sentences like that?

Moreover, even if we set aside these cases, consider all of the ramifications of the verificationist theory of meaning. There are all sorts of sentences, not just distinctly metaphysical, but also religious and scientific sentences that, if we accept the verificationist theory of meaning, we will be forced to also reject as meaningless. Could we ever verify whether there is a God (in the sense that many people today care about)? Whether there is life after death? Whether there are other worlds causally disconnected from our own (as many current cosmological theories suggest)? It is one thing to say that a claim is meaningful. It is another thing altogether to say it is something we are capable of verifying. To equate these two issues (semantic and epistemological) is a confusion. Or so most contemporary philosophers believe. The verificationist theory of meaning has long been out of the mainstream for this reason.

A second critique that has often been offered against these arguments is that they are self-undermining. Carnap wanted arguments that would show the claims of the metaphysicians are meaningless, but his arguments if they work are too powerful; they would show not only that the claims of metaphysicians are meaningless but that his own claims too are meaningless. And if Carnap's own claims are meaningless, how are we to believe what they say? To see this, consider some of Carnap's own claims:

> 'An alleged statement of the reality of a system of entities is a pseudo-statement without cognitive content' (1950, p. 214), and

> 'The meaning of a statement lies in the method of its verification' (1932, p. 76).

According to Carnap himself, if such claims are going to be true then they must be verifiable by either analytic (logical) or synthetic (empirical) means. But how is this supposed to work? These don't look like mere truths of logic or truths capable of verification by any observation we could undertake. These look themselves like philosophical claims to be evaluated along the lines of the philosophical claims Carnap is criticizing. In "Empiricism, Semantics, and Ontology," we are presented with a third option. Perhaps Carnap's claims are not intended to be interpreted as internal statements, as statements evaluable within a linguistic system with rules for sentence formation and verification. Perhaps, instead, he intends for us to interpret them only as external statements and themselves meaningless. But then if they are meaningless, what is the point of writing them?

A.J. Ayer (1910–1989), a British philosopher who did much to popularize and defend the views of the logical positivists, has suggested that Carnap might have taken this last position. Wittgenstein, whose *Tractatus Logico-Philosophicus* Carnap and the Vienna Circle much admired, claimed at the end of that work:

> My propositions serve as elucidations in the following way: anyone who understands me eventually recognizes them as nonsensical, when he has used them – as steps – to climb up beyond them. (He must, so to speak, throw away the ladder after he has climbed up it.)
>
> He must transcend these propositions, and then he will see the world aright.
>
> (Wittgenstein 1922, p. 189)

Ayer suggests that Carnap and the other logical positivists intended their statements as a prescription for how to view philosophy. Philosophy should aim not to make statements that can be verified, but instead to elucidate the statements that can be verified (and those that cannot). Whether this idea of elucidation without meaning is coherent is an issue in itself.

Rather than pursue it, let's instead move on to a third critique that has been made of these arguments, in particular the charge that metaphysics is meaningless and in that way defective with respect to claims that are made in other domains. In his paper, "Two Dogmas of Empiricism" (1951), aimed directly at Carnap and his circle, Quine aimed to show that the claims of metaphysics are no more problematic than the claims of science, at least in the respects Carnap targeted. We have already discussed the first "dogma" of Quine's title; this is the distinction between analytic and synthetic statements (statements that are verified by exclusively analytic, logical means, and statements that are verified through empirical means). The other "dogma" to which Quine's title refers is a claim of Carnap's that all meaningful claims can ultimately be reduced to claims about perceptual experience. This second claim, the reductionism, was seen above (see Box 4.1) in our discussion of protocol statements. For Carnap, all verification and hence all meaning, for the class of synthetic statements ultimately leads back to what can be directly verified by means of sensory experience.

Quine argued that there is no clear way to make a distinction between statements that are analytic on the one hand and those that are synthetic on the other. One might think that there is an easy separation. For example, in logic or mathematics all claims get verified analytically; in sciences like physics or biology, all claims get verified synthetically, but Quine suggests this isn't so. Here is a famous passage from "Two Dogmas of Empiricism":

> The totality of our so-called knowledge or beliefs . . . is a man-made fabric which impinges on experience only along the edges. Or, to change the figure, total science is like a field of force whose boundary conditions are experience. A conflict with experience at the periphery occasions readjustments in the interior of the field. Truth values have to be redistributed over some of our statements. . . . But the total field is so undetermined by its boundary conditions, experience, that there is much latitude of choice as to what statements to re-evaluate in the light of any single contrary experience. No particular experiences are linked with any particular statements in the interior of the field, except indirectly through considerations of equilibrium affecting the field as a whole.
>
> If this view is right, it is misleading to speak of the empirical content of an individual statement – especially if it be a statement at all remote from the experiential periphery of the field. Furthermore it becomes folly to seek a boundary between synthetic statements, which hold contingently on experience, and analytic statements which hold come what may. *Any statement can be held true come what may, if we make drastic enough adjustments elsewhere in the system.* Even a statement very close to the periphery can be held true in the face of recalcitrant

experience by pleading hallucination or by amending certain statements of the kind called logical laws. Conversely, by the same token, *no statement is immune to revision.* Revision even of the logical law of the excluded middle has been proposed as a means of simplifying quantum mechanics; and what difference is there in principle between such a shift and the shift whereby Kepler superseded Ptolemy, or Einstein Newton, or Darwin Aristotle?

(Quine 1951a, pp. 39–40)

In this passage, Quine proposes we view our total system of beliefs as like a web. Each belief is connected to others by various support relations: one belief may give us reason to hold onto others; if we reject that belief, this may give us reason to reject others. But we can see that Quine wants to replace Carnap's picture of a chain of verification ultimately leading back to a basic set of beliefs verified directly by experience with a picture where no belief is ultimate. There is no place where the chain ends. In this web of belief, Quine suggests that some beliefs lie closer to the outside, the periphery; others lie closer to the center. Those at the outside of the web bear more direct connection to our sense experience, our empirical evidence. For example, beliefs like, "The sky is blue," or "The bell is ringing," lie closer to the outside of the web. They are the sorts of beliefs that are most directly confirmed or undermined by what we observe. On the other hand, beliefs like "Triangles have three sides," or to give Quine's example, the law of the excluded middle (for any proposition p: p∨¬p), lie closer to the center of the web of belief. These propositions are more insulated from what we observe and are not directly supported or undermined by empirical evidence.

Typically, propositions like that the bell is ringing are held to be synthetic and verified directly by observation. Those like the law of excluded

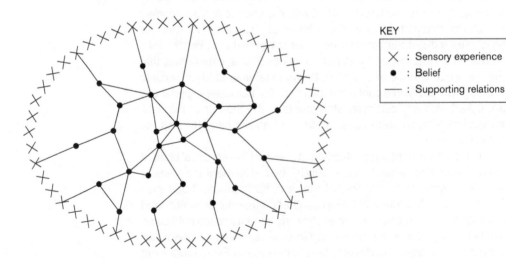

KEY

× : Sensory experience
● : Belief
— : Supporting relations

Figure 4.2 Quine's Web of Belief

middle are held to be analytic, true by logic alone. However, what Quine wants to emphasize is that this distinction is not real. Even belief in the proposition that the bell is ringing may (reasonably) be rejected in the face of seemingly-confirming empirical observation. For example, your sense experience might involve a certain sound, but you might have reason to believe you are under the spell of a hallucinatory drug. Maybe you are the victim of some kind of massive deception, as in the movies *The Matrix* or *Inception*. In these cases, it may seem to you as if the bell is ringing, but still this may be wrong, something you would wish to reject. Beliefs like this may lie, in Quine's picture, more towards the outside of the web. Sensory experience is more directly connected to beliefs like this than (say) the law of excluded middle. But even the most synthetic-seeming beliefs are not solely ever verified on the basis of empirical observation alone. Even they depend for their confirmation on considerations involving one's overall belief system.

Similarly, those beliefs located closest to the center of the web are the most distant from sensory evidence and might thus be thought incapable of being undermined by empirical observation. The law of excluded middle is something all students learn to prove in their first course in logic. The proof is simple and so this proposition may seem to be an example of an analytic truth if anything is. But as Quine points out, one might on the basis of empirical observation find reason to reject this. For example, we learn from quantum mechanics that there are states in which particles' features may not be determinate. For example, consider the proposition that a certain electron is in the left-hand side of a box at a particular time t. According to the law of excluded middle, this proposition must be either true or false: Either the electron is in the left-hand side of the box at t or it is not in the left-hand side of the box at time t. But quantum mechanics tells us this is not so. There are certain states electrons can be in, superpositions of position, in which it is neither true that an electron is in the left-hand side of the box, nor is it false. So, says Quine, even a statement one might have thought of as a paradigm of analyticity may be undermined by experience.

What Quine hopes to show using this image of the web of belief is that Carnap is wrong to think that just because in metaphysics our statements are not immediately confirmed by empirical observation, nor are they verified purely as a matter of logic, this means they are defective in some way; that they are meaningless. Quine's point is that nothing we believe is really confirmed solely by empirical observation or by means of logic alone. This is the case even in science.

> Ontological questions, under this view, are on a par with questions of natural science. Consider the question whether to countenance classes as entities. This, as I have argued elsewhere, is the question whether to quantify with respect to variables which take classes as values. Now Carnap has maintained that this is a question not of matters of fact but of choosing a convenient language form, a convenient conceptual scheme or framework for science. With this I agree, but only on the proviso that the same be conceded regarding scientific hypotheses

generally. Carnap has recognized that he is able to preserve a double standard for ontological questions and scientific hypotheses only by assuming an absolute distinction between the analytic and the synthetic; and I need not say again that this is a distinction which I reject.

(Quine 1951a, p. 43)

Note that here Quine is not rejecting Carnap's view that in answering ontological questions like "Are there classes?" or "Are there material objects?" we must answer external questions. What we are doing is not just deciding the answers to these questions using logical or empirical methods. Rather we are, as Carnap put it, settling a pragmatic question, making a practical choice about which overall system of beliefs we want to adopt. Quine accepts all of this, but he suggests that this is always how we decide what we believe. Indeed this is the case in science too. So if ontological claims fall prey to verificationist worries, then so would scientific claims. But scientific claims aren't meaningless or problematic. So, neither are ontological claims.

EXERCISE 4.2

The Web of Belief

Order the following beliefs from 1 to 6, with '1' indicating the belief that is closest to the center of the web.

- The belief that apples have seeds.
- The belief that 1+1=2.
- The belief that apples taste sweet.
- The belief that apples are fruit.
- The belief that everything is either a fruit or not a fruit.
- The belief that electrons exist.

PRESENT DAY WORRIES ABOUT METAPHYSICAL METHOD

Today, as we saw, the verificationism lying at the core of the logical positivists' critiques of metaphysics is very widely rejected. Many would argue it is simply a confusion to think that for a statement to be meaningful or true, it is necessary that anyone be able to actually verify it. Truth or meaning is one thing, verification is another. Be that as it may, this point doesn't completely eliminate worries related to the verification of metaphysical claims. Rejecting the verificationist theory of meaning, one might concede that statements about the existence of universals or numbers, or metaphysical views like mereological universalism and nihilism are meaningful, but still worry. Even if these claims are meaningful, still isn't it legitimate to be concerned that they don't seem capable of verification? None of these claims are logical truths. They are substantive claims about the types of entities that exist at our world. And yet at the same time, they seem completely incapable of empirical/synthetic verification. Whether there were universals or numbers or not, whether there were chairs or only simples arranged chairwise, everything would look exactly the same to us. But if we can't verify these claims, then how could we ever know whether they are true or not? Verificationism about truth or meaning may be confused, but verificationism about knowledge is another matter. How could we possibly ever know the truths of metaphysics if we cannot verify them analytically or empirically?

This is the sort of post-positivist worry about metaphysics that is presented in the 2007 book by James Ladyman and Don Ross called *Every Thing Must Go*. In this book, Ladyman and Ross argue that while science is capable of making true *and* justified claims about the way the world is, metaphysics, at least insofar as it proceeds detached from science, is not. Ladyman and Ross, although they explicitly associate themselves with Carnap and the logical positivists, do not want to reject all metaphysics as meaningless because they reject the verificationist theory of meaning. They view metaphysical claims as meaningful but worry that the methods metaphysicians have used for coming to discover truth is problematic.

Their main worry about much of contemporary metaphysics is that instead of basing their arguments in scientific statements that possess empirical justification, metaphysicians argue for their positions using a priori intuitions about how the world must be or what seems right to them. Ladyman and Ross argue that it is implausible to think that nature has endowed us with any special way of uncovering objective truth by intuition alone. It is not possible to discover what the world is like fundamentally just by reflecting on what seems right. Indeed our intuitions have been proven again and again over the history of ideas to get things wrong. To counter this reliance on intuitions, Ladyman and Ross propose a new prescription for how to do metaphysics in such a way that it can discover objective truths about the world. This they call 'metaphysics naturalized.'

The proposal is that metaphysicians follow what they call the **Principle of Naturalistic Closure**:

> Any new metaphysical claim that is to be taken seriously at time *t* should be motivated by, and only by, the service it would perform, if true, in showing how two or more specific scientific hypotheses, at least one of which is drawn from fundamental physics, jointly explain more than the sum of what is explained by the two hypotheses taken separately.
>
> (Ladyman and Ross 2007, p. 37)

This is an extremely strict rule in that it would severely limit the sorts of claims metaphysicians could make, if they are to be viewed seriously.

Principle of naturalistic closure: the principle that any metaphysical claim to be taken seriously at a time should be motivated by the service it would perform in showing how two or more scientific hypotheses, at least one of which is drawn from fundamental physics, jointly explain more than what is explained by the hypotheses taken separately.

Metaphysics would be limited to the task of merely unifying claims made in the sciences. For example, one might show the constitutive relation between the states described by sciences like biology or psychology and the atoms and molecules of physics.[2] This may be an interesting task, but is it a specifically metaphysical one? And are these the only sorts of issues we can hope to settle in metaphysics? Ladyman and Ross think that this is the only way for the claims of metaphysics to have legitimacy and avoid the use of intuitions – by drawing on a basic set of information that has been confirmed by the methods of science. Today, however, many metaphysicians happily embrace the label of being 'naturalistic metaphysicians,' metaphysicians who use science to inform their metaphysics. But this doesn't mean they view their task as merely linking together claims made in different sciences.

THE RELATIONSHIP BETWEEN METAPHYSICS AND SCIENCE: A PROPOSAL

Ladyman and Ross's critique of metaphysics has stirred up a lively debate about the proper methodology for metaphysics and its relation to science. Since the crux of their critique focuses on the methods metaphysicians use to justify their claims, most replies have focused on clarifying and defending the methodology of current metaphysics. For example, Laurie Paul, in a 2012 article "Metaphysics as Modeling: The Handmaiden's Tale" (alluding ironically to the frequent remark that philosophy is the "handmaiden of the sciences") argues like Quine that the methodology of metaphysics is really not that different from the methodology of science itself. So if one wants to be critical of the methods used by metaphysicians to establish their claims, then one must be critical as well of the methods scientists use to establish theirs.

It is worth noting that unlike Quine however, Paul does not think this commits us to a merely pragmatic view of metaphysics: that metaphysics just gives us a body of claims it would be useful to accept. Just as we ordinarily think scientific claims may be confirmed and are true (rather than merely useful for one purpose or other), so too may those of metaphysics be confirmed and true. The question is how in metaphysics and in science this truth gets discovered.

Model: a theoretical structure involving a basic set of representational devices accounting for a set of data.

Paul argues that in both metaphysics and science, the central task of the theorist is to construct **models**. Models are theoretical structures involving a set of basic representational devices (new terms and concepts, and principles involving these concepts) that can account for a set of data including but not limited to those observations we may make. In both science and metaphysics, different models may adequately represent the domain under consideration. For example, in physics, a theorist may use a model using the concept of a field to represent the kinds of entities there are (as in electromagnetic theory). Another theorist may use a model that involves only the representation of particles. Similarly in metaphysics one theorist may use a model that represents the world in terms of the concepts of particular and universal. Another may use a model that rejects the concept of a universal and conceives everything as a more or less complex collection of tropes. Different models may succeed to better or worse degrees at capturing the empirical data.

Yet Paul emphasizes that it is an oversimplification to see science as confirming the statements that make up its models simply on the basis of empirical verification.[3] Empirical methods may take us as far as a certain point. But there will always be rival models equally capable of explaining the empirical data. The scientist must supplement empirical criteria with the use of theoretical criteria like simplicity, unificatory power, internal and external consistency, and fruitfulness (ability to generate further hypotheses) to decide between models.[4] Thus when the philosopher looks at rival metaphysical theories and assesses them on the basis of criteria like which is simpler, which is consistent with other things she believes, and so on, she is not applying a kind of methodology that is different from that used by scientists themselves.

Paul also emphasizes that intuitions are used just as much in science as in metaphysics in order to construct and evaluate models. A critic might ask what can be learned from thinking about the Ship of Theseus or the case of Lump and Goliath, but cases like this are used in science just as much as in metaphysics. There are a series of famous thought experiments used by Isaac Newton to justify his basic physical principles.[5] The founders of quantum theory similarly used a series of thought experiments in order to justify their theories, the most famous of which is Schrödinger's cat. And we will see in the next chapter the sort of thought experiment Einstein used to argue for his special theory of relativity. **Thought experiments** are more or less detailed descriptions of fictional cases from which the scientist or philosopher draws out consequences in order to assess a given theory. Since these cases are fictional, these consequences are not discovered on the basis of observation. In science and metaphysics empirical data is of course used to construct models and evaluate models. If a model contradicts what we observe, then this is a reason to throw it out. But since the empirical data only constrains the choice of models up to a point, there is a significant role for a priori methods in both science and metaphysics. This involves, first, the evaluation of rival models according to their success at accommodating the theoretical virtues and, second, the use of thought experiments. According to Paul, the main difference between science and metaphysics does not lie in a difference in methodology.

This is not to say that there is no difference between metaphysics and science. According to many, metaphysics engages a kind of question more fundamental than the kind of question addressed in science. And so there is a difference in subject matter. For example, in physics we may ask what kind of space or space–time there is at our world: one that is flat and Euclidean, or one that is curved and non-Euclidean. In metaphysics we may ask whether there *is* such an entity as space or space–time at all or whether all that exists are relations between material objects. In physics one might ask what kinds of basic particles there are. In metaphysics, we may ask what is the best way to think of these particles, as concrete entities instantiating

Thought experiment: a fictional case used in order to draw out consequences of use to the building of a scientific or philosophical theory.

universals or bundles of tropes. If so, then the difference between meta-physics and science consists in their subject matter, not their methodology. There is no significant difference in methodology.

Paul's proposal for the relationship between metaphysics and science is not the only possible way to see metaphysics as constituting a legitimate research program (and one that is significantly less constrained than that proposed by Ladyman and Ross). However, her proposal certainly reflects the way many contemporary metaphysicians view what they are doing. One controversy that remains is whether metaphysics indeed aims at a more fundamental set of truths than those discovered by science (as Paul argues) or whether metaphysics and science (and perhaps religion as well, if we reject naturalism) are better seen as operating jointly to discover what are a common set of fundamental truths. This is a subtle issue on which we will remain neutral for the body of this text.

EXERCISE 4.3

The Handmaiden to the Sciences

What do you think it would mean for metaphysics to be the handmaiden to the sciences? Do you think this is a good metaphor for metaphysics, that is, something metaphysics should aspire to be? Or do you agree with Paul that there is a distinctive role for metaphysics? If so, what is that role?

SUGGESTIONS FOR FURTHER READING

In addition to the papers of Carnap cited above, one can find more classic works of the logical positivists in the volume *Logical Positivism* edited by A.J. Ayer. Ayer's own *Language, Truth, and Logic* was a very influential popularization and development of the views of the logical positivists as well. In addition to Quine's critique of the logical positivists in his "Two Dogmas of Empiricism," his paper "On Carnap's Views on Ontology" is also worth a look. Matti Eklund, Huw Price, and Scott Soames's articles in the volume *Metametaphysics*, edited by Chalmers, Manley and Wasserman, also provide good overviews of the dispute between Carnap and Quine.

In addition to the contemporary critique of metaphysics of Ladyman and Ross, other neo-Carnapian critiques have recently been given by Eli Hirsch (see his *Quantifer Variance and Realism: Essays in Metaontology*) and Thomas Hofweber in the *Metametaphysics* volume. John Hawthorne and Theodore Sider respond to Hirsch's critique in their contributions to the *Metametaphysics* volume.

The July 2012 issue of the journal *Philosophical Studies* was a special issue devoted to the relationship between metaphysics and science and contained many articles on that topic in addition to the one by Laurie Paul discussed above. For another proposal about the relationship between metaphysics and science, see Steven French and Kerry McKenzie's article, "Thinking Outside the Toolbox."

NOTES

1 We will discuss the topic of essence in Chapter 7 on modality.
2 Though would even statements about atoms and molecules constitute parts of *fundamental* physics? Note how strict Ladyman and Ross's rule is.
3 Here especially, one may note strong similarities between Paul's critique of Ladyman and Ross and Quine's critique of Carnap and the logical positivists.
4 For discussion of these virtues, see Thomas Kuhn's "Objectivity, Value Judgment, and Theory Choice."
5 See Sklar, *Space, Time, and Spacetime* for an overview of some of these.

CHAPTER 5

Time

Learning Points

- Examines an argument that relativity theory may undermine a common view about the passage of time and the distinction between the future and the past
- Introduces and evaluates several rival ontologies of time
- Introduces the distinction between the A- and B-theories of time
- Evaluates the prospects for the logical possibility of time travel.

TIME'S PASSAGE

A basic and perfectly ordinary fact about time would seem to be that it passes. But what do we mean when we say this?

Consider the most important and meaningful events in your life up to now: your birth, your first day of school, a moment when you overcame a great challenge, the time you first bonded with your closest friend, perhaps the loss of a loved one. Whichever these important events are, they are all events lying in your past. At one time they were present, at one time you were living them, you were a part of them. But now they are over. Time has passed. Time and you yourself have in a sense moved beyond these events. It is important to you that they happened, these are events that have shaped you and who you are. Some of what happened in the past may be forgotten. Although these events took place, you no longer possess memories of them. But we don't want to deny that there are facts about what happened in the past. In some sense, these events are no longer happening. They are no longer real. But they *did* happen. They *were* real.

Now consider what lies ahead, those events in your future. We can be certain the future will include all manner of uninteresting events: the sun's rising tomorrow, your next meal. There are some more significant events we can be certain your future will include as well, including your death. Still, there is a lot of uncertainty about the future, more so than there is about the past. Can you be sure what you will be doing five years from now?

Whether you will be a success? Can you be sure who the important people in your life will be ten years from now? Where you will be living? These are events most of us don't think we can be certain about; not because we have forgotten them, but because we haven't lived them yet. They haven't yet happened. They are events we can only plan for or hope to be certain ways, because they are events that only occur in the future. Time has not caught up to them. Unlike events in the past and present, it is very natural to think that there is not yet any fact about what the future will be like. We may have reasonable beliefs, even certainty, about some events in the future (like the sun's rising), but since the future has not yet come to pass, there aren't yet any determinate facts about what will come to pass. Philosophers refer to this as the **openness of the future**: the future is open in a way the past and present are not.

> **Openness of the future**: the view that there are not any determinate facts about the future.

This is part of what we ordinarily have in mind when we think that time passes. There are events in the past, those that have already happened. These are fixed; the past is closed. Then there is what is happening now. And finally there is what has not yet happened – the future is open. Time's passage consists in new events coming to be and becoming present, and those events that are present slipping into the past. (And those that are already past slipping even further into the past.) We ordinarily think time's passage is **objective** or absolute. It doesn't depend on your own personal perspective. Time doesn't pass differently for different people. And it is not subject to anyone's control. Indeed, we ordinarily think time would pass in just the same way as it actually does even if humans never existed. Once an event has happened, it has happened and it belongs in the objective past. In addition, we think we have better epistemological access to events that lie in the past or present than to those that have not yet happened (future events). Events in the present may be known because they are currently happening. Through records, we may be able to discover what happened in the past. But because future events have not yet occurred, it is generally more difficult to gain knowledge of them. Finally, we ordinarily think that time's passage has ontological implications. Those people in the past who have died and those objects that have been completely destroyed do not exist, although they once did. You exist, but your great great great grandmother does not. The European Union exists, but the Ottoman Empire does not. Similarly no wholly future people or objects yet exist. You may have hopes, make plans, or suffer fears about what objects may exist in the future – future offspring, wars, jobs. But it is part of our ordinary way of thinking about the future that these things do not exist. They are not yet real.[1]

> **Objective**: not depending on any individual's perspective, absolute.

Digging deeper, however, we find that there are good reasons to mistrust this ordinary conception of time and its passage. First, there is a compelling argument inspired by current scientific theory aiming to show that there can be no absolute or objective sense in which time passes. Second, there are compelling arguments for the view that the past and the future must be as real as the present. We discuss these arguments in the following sections.

THE ARGUMENT AGAINST THE ORDINARY VIEW FROM SPECIAL RELATIVITY

In a 1967 article, "Time and Physical Geometry," the philosopher Hilary Putnam used scientific considerations to reject the objectivity of time's passage, arguing it is inconsistent with Albert Einstein's 1905 Theory of Special Relativity. Since then, many philosophers of time have thought this presents a decisive argument against the ordinary view.

Let's start by considering a thought experiment Einstein himself liked to use to argue for Special Relativity and demonstrate its consequences. A train is passing through a station at constant velocity **v.**; Patrick is a passenger on the train. Emily is standing on the embankment watching Patrick's train pass by. While Patrick's train is passing through the station, two strikes of lightning occur. Both strikes are visible to both Patrick and Emily. Lightning strike A occurs in the distance back from where Patrick's train came. Strike B occurs in the distance ahead, in the direction where Patrick's train is heading. The strikes occur at an equal spatial distance from Emily's location.

Suppose Emily sees the strikes at the same time. Then assuming that light always moves at a constant speed, she can infer that strike A is simultaneous with strike B. The strikes are at equal distances away from her, so if light from each of them travels at the same constant speed and she sees the two flashes at the same time, she will reason that they occurred at the same time, that they were simultaneous. Here is a question Einstein considers: *Will Patrick, the passenger on the train, agree with Emily that A occurred at the same time as B, that A and B are simultaneous events?*[2]

According to Einstein, unlike Emily, Patrick will say that the lightning strikes do not occur at the same time. And this raises the question of which happens first according to Patrick. Before reading on, take a moment to think about this. Will Patrick think that lightning strike A, the one at the location behind him happens first, or lightning strike B, the one in the place he is heading toward, will happen first?

To answer this question, we again need to be explicit about how it is that Patrick and Emily are in the position to know when the lightning strikes occur at all. The obvious answer is that they see them and from seeing

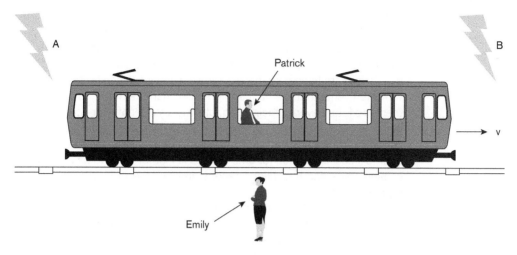

Figure 5.1 Patrick and Emily

them they can infer using the speed of light the times at which the strikes occurred. Emily judges that the strikes occurred simultaneously because light from both strikes reaches her at the same time. Patrick will think that strike A happened earlier than strike B only if light from A reaches his eyes before the light from B. So is this what happens? The answer is "no." Since the train Patrick is riding is moving towards the place where B occurs and away from the place where A occurs, Patrick will see the light from strike B before he sees the light from strike A. Again, a crucial assumption here is that the speed of light is always the same. And it appears the same to all observers whether they are moving away from or towards a light source. So unlike Emily, Patrick will reason that A and B are not simultaneous. Patrick will think that B happened earlier than A, because he sees B before he sees A.

But who is right? One might at first think Emily must be right and Patrick must be wrong. After all, Emily is the one at rest, standing stationary on the embankment. And so, she might seem to have the ultimate authority over which event happened first. However one thing physicists have shown us, and this was long before Einstein came up with his theory of relativity, is that there is no such thing as absolute rest.[3] Just as Emily believes it is she who is at rest and Patrick who is moving with velocity **v**, from Patrick's perspective, it is he who is at rest and Emily who is moving with velocity **-v**.

Since there is no objective fact about who is at rest, in this case there is no objective fact about who is right about whether A and B are simultaneous. There are only relative facts about simultaneity. Relative to Emily, lightning strikes A and B are simultaneous. Relative to Patrick, A happens after B. But there is no objective fact about who is right when A happens with respect to B.

How does this fact about the relativity of simultaneity relate to our central object of concern, the objectivity of the passage of time? The answer is that if simultaneity is relative, then the passage of time is relative too. And this is because if facts about simultaneity are relative, then there are no objective facts about which events are present, which events are future, and which events are past. To be present is just to be simultaneous with the events that are happening here and now. To be past is to be simultaneous with the events that are happening earlier than the here and now. And if there are future events, their being future is a matter of their occurring later than the here and now. If simultaneity is relative, then so are facts about which events are present, past, and future. This undermines the objectivity of time's passage, since for time to pass is just for there to be new events coming to be and becoming present, and those events that are present slipping into the past.

In Einstein's train scenario, the difference in speed between the protagonists is not so great, and so there will not be a very large disagreement about which events are past, present, and future, and how far into the past or future a given event occurs. Disagreements magnify however when one considers cases of observers moving with great velocities relative to each other. If, for example, we imagine Patrick on a rocketship moving at a speed very close to the speed of light[4] relative to Emily on Earth, their disagreements will be much more radical.

ONTOLOGIES OF TIME

The relativity of simultaneity is thought to have implications for facts about what exists. And so we are now in a position to consider some views in the ontology of time. We will consider four views about which sorts of objects and events exist, setting aside a nihilist option claiming that no objects or events exist in time. Note that all four views agree about the reality of the present. The main question in the ontology of time is whether any future or past objects and events exist in addition to those in the present (see Table 5.1).

Only two views on this list are consistent with the common view with which we started. These are **presentism**, the view that only presently existing objects and events are real, and the **growing block theory**, the view that only past and present objects and events are real. These positions are different ways of capturing how most of us start thinking about time before we start getting deeper into physics or philosophy.[5] According to both

Presentism: the view that only presently existing objects and events are real.

Growing block theory: the view that past and present objects and events are real; future objects and events are not.

Table 5.1 Ontologies of Time: Which Objects and Events Exist?

	Past objects and events?	Present objects and events?	Future objects and events?
Eternalism	Yes	Yes	Yes
Presentism	No	Yes	No
The growing block theory	Yes	Yes	No
The shrinking block theory	No	Yes	Yes

theories, future events are not real because they have not happened yet. Present events are real as they are now happening. Presentists and growing block theorists only disagree over the existence of past objects and events. Growing block theorists tend to think that time's passage consists in more being added to the big block that constitutes reality, what exists, what the facts are. Presentists disagree and argue that the past is just as unreal as the future. All that exists is the sliver of time that is present. Although there might be epistemological differences between the future and the past – we can know a lot about the past, and we know much less about the future – this does not correspond to a metaphysical difference. When we consider what there is, according to the presentist, Abraham Lincoln exists no more than future unborn children.[6]

The last position listed in Table 5.1, the **shrinking block theory**, is a rarely held position. According to this view, present and future objects and events are all that exist. The past is unreal. One who is sympathetic to this position pictures reality as a block that steadily shrinks as more and more events come to pass. What is now happening and what is set to come is out there, but as events happen they drop away into oblivion. It is fun to think of the reasons one might come to believe this view. The reasons would have to be quite distinct from those that motivate the growing block theory. The growing block theorist thinks that the future is open in an important sense, in that it does not exist. Thus, perhaps, it is ours to make. On the shrinking block theory, what fails to be real is the past. Perhaps there is some intuitive motivation for this view that arises out of the thoughts we have sometimes that we are "running out of time," that the available instants available in a day, a week, a year are becoming fewer and fewer. But so far, presentism and the growing block theory have had many more defenders.

Eternalism, the view that past, present, and future events all exist and are equally real, is the only one of the above views that fails to capture the intuitive idea that time's passage has ontological consequences. According to the eternalist, past and future objects are real in just the same sense as present objects. The eternalist thinks of other times as like other places. Everyone believes the Eiffel Tower exists in the same way as the building in which you are currently sitting. Unlike the building you are in now, the Eiffel Tower is not *here*, it isn't at your spatial location, but this does not make it any less real. Similarly, the eternalist says that past and future events are just as real as current events. They don't exist *now*, they aren't at one's temporal location. But this does not make them any less real. D.C. Williams calls eternalism 'the Theory of the Manifold.'[7]

Returning to the issue of Special Relativity, we can now see how Einstein's theory has given many philosophers reason to reject all of the other ontologies of time in favor of eternalism.

The Argument for Eternalism from Special Relativity

1. If either presentism or the growing or shrinking block theories are true, then which objects or events are real depends on which are past, present, or future. (from the definitions of these positions)

Shrinking block theory: the view that present and future objects and events are real; past objects and events are not.

Eternalism: the view that past, present, and future objects and events are equally real.

2. But which objects and events are past, present, or future depends on facts about which events are simultaneous with the here and now. (from the definitions of 'past,' 'present,' and 'future')
3. If the special theory of relativity is true, then which events are simultaneous with the here and now is a matter of one's perspective. (consequence of Special Relativity)
4. The special theory of relativity is true.
5. So, which events are simultaneous with the here and now is a matter of one's perspective. (by premises (3), (4), and modus ponens)
6. So which objects and events are past, present, or future is a matter of one's perspective. (from premises (2) and (5))
7. So if either presentism or the growing or shrinking block theories are true, then which objects or events are real is a matter of one's perspective. (from (1) and (6))
8. But what is real is not a matter of one's perspective. (assumption: what is real is an objective matter)

Therefore,

9. Neither presentism nor the growing or shrinking block theories are true.

And this leaves eternalism as the only standing ontology of time since it is the only theory that does not make reality depend upon subjective facts about what is past, present, or future.

One might ask for more support of premise (8), that existence or reality is an objective matter. But how could it be that an entity e was real relative to one person, say Emily, and unreal according to another, Patrick? If Emily is correct, then e exists. Patrick may not believe in e, but if e is out there to be believed in or not believed in, then it exists.

Eternalism is the only ontology of time that avoids making existence subjective, since it makes no distinction in reality between past, present, and future events and objects. And so eternalism is the ontology thought to be implied by the special theory of relativity.

Indeed one of the consequences of the special theory of relativity one learns in a modern physics course is that we shouldn't think of reality as consisting of objects spread out in a three-dimensional space that persists from one instance to the next through time. Instead objects and events take place in one unified four-dimensional manifold of space–time. The space–time of Special Relativity is what is called 'Minkowski space–time,' following the mathematician who suggested it to Einstein. Minkowski space–time has the following important features:

■ It is a four-dimensional manifold. In other words, in order to completely specify a location in Minkowski space–time, one has to give four numbers: (x, y, z, t).
■ There is no preferred, objective partition of this manifold into slices of time. (Different observers moving at different relative speeds will each

slice up space–time into spaces and times in different, equally correct ways.)

■ There are objective facts about the distance between space–time points, but no additional objective facts about spatial distances and temporal durations. (Facts about spatial distances and temporal durations are always relative to a particular observer's way of carving up space–time.)

To illustrate this third point, we may return to our two lightning strikes. Each strike takes place at a distinct location in Minkowski space–time. What the third point implies is that there is an objective fact about the spatiotemporal distance between these strikes (Figure 5.2).

In Minkowski space–time, the only objective fact about their distance is their spatiotemporal distance, what is called the 'space–time interval.' And this is a consequence of the second fact, the fact that there is no preferred way of slicing this block up into spaces and times. If one insists on there being additional, objective facts about which events happen at the same time (as in Figure 5.3), space–time will have a different structure

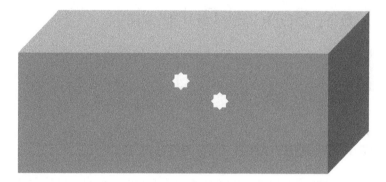

Figure 5.2 Minkowski Space–Time and the Lightning Strikes

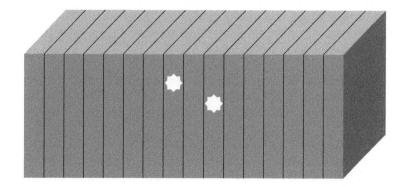

Figure 5.3 A Space–Time Containing Objective Facts about Which Events Are Simultaneous with Which

than Relativity entails. There will then be objective facts about the temporal and spatial relations between these events. For example, when the space–time manifold is broken up in the way suggested in Figure 5.3, there appears to be an objective fact that one lightning strike happens before the other. One lies on an earlier slice of space–time and so there is an objective fact that they are not simultaneous.

However, what Special Relativity appears to tell us is that the slicing up depicted in Figure 5.3 is not part of the objective structure of our world. Just as one observer may slice things up in one way, another observer moving at a different velocity will slice things up in another way. The objective structure of space–time allowed by modern physics is better captured by Figure 5.2 than Figure 5.3 and, as we have just seen, this has consequences for which ontology of time we ought to accept.

EXERCISE 5.2

The Argument for Eternalism from Special Relativity

If you were a presentist, how might you go about trying to challenge the argument against this position from Special Relativity? Be sure to single out a specific premise or inference step in this argument.

THE A-THEORY AND THE B-THEORY

When one views the universe as the eternalist does, one believes that future events are as real as present and past ones, and so in a certain genuine sense the future is already set. The future is set in the sense that there is a fact about what takes place in the future.[8] To say this and be clear about what we are saying, it is helpful to explicitly distinguish two senses of 'is' and 'exists,' (1) a tenseless or eternal sense and (2) a tensed sense. Consider the following sentences:

(1) Abraham Lincoln, unlike Sherlock Holmes, exists. Abraham Lincoln is a real person like Barack Obama.
(2) Abraham Lincoln did exist, but he doesn't exist.

At first glance, these claims look to contradict each other. The presentist will deny that (1) is true, but will agree with (2). The eternalist, on the other hand, will want to say that both (1) and (2) are true, and deny that there is a contradiction between them. The reason they don't contradict each other, according to the eternalist, is that we must recognize two senses of 'exist' and 'is.'[9]

The sense of 'is' and 'exists' used in (1) is the tenseless or eternal sense. Something exists in the tenseless or eternal sense of the word just in case it exists at some time or other, or, if there is a realm of existence outside of time, then it exists in that realm.[10] Sentence (2), on the other hand, uses 'exists' in a tensed sense. Here, 'exists' means *exists now*. Since the eternalist believes there are objects and events that exist in the timeless sense that do not exist now, she is free to endorse both (1) and (2) without contradiction. The presentist, who thinks that existence is limited to what exists now, will reject this distinction between two senses of 'is' or 'exists.' For her 'exists' means the same as 'exists now.'

One might then view the eternalist's position this way. First there is existence in the tenseless, eternal sense. There is what just plain exists – the whole, four-dimensional block. But there are also facts about what exists in the block at certain points, facts about what exists now or earlier or later than now.

At this point one might ask, doesn't the eternalist, following Special Relativity, believe that facts about what exists in the past, present, and future are all relative to one's motion? The majority of eternalists agree with this. They think facts about what is past, present, and future are subjective. They are not objective. And so what exists in a tensed sense of 'exists' is subjective. But the fundamental facts about what exists are not subjective. These are the facts about what exists in the tenseless, objective sense of the word. And that is what matters for ontological purposes.

Many eternalists also argue that tensed facts about what is past, present, and future have another important feature. They are subjective and yet they are reducible to, in other words, ultimately explainable in terms of more fundamental tenseless facts. This marks an important disagreement between the majority of eternalists and presentists. To see this, we will need to introduce another major distinction in the philosophy of time.

This distinction traces back to a 1908 paper by the English philosopher J.M.E. McTaggart. McTaggart distinguished between the A-series and B-series of time. Both are series in which events are ordered according to their relative times.

First, the A-series. The **A-series** orders events in terms of their being past, present, and future (their tensed, **A-features**). We may picture the A-series as a long timeline with those events that are farthest in the past all of the way at one end, and those events farthest in the future all of the way at the other end. (If time is infinite, then we may imagine the A-series as an infinite line with no end or beginning.) Here are some statements we may make assigning objects and events places in the A-series:

■ Washington is the capital of the United States *now*.
■ In the *present* day, people check the time using their phones.
■ We *will* go to the shore next summer.
■ The Sun *will* begin to die approximately 5 billion years in the *future*.

Events' locations in the A-series change as time passes. What is in the future now, will be in the present eventually. And what takes place now, will

A-series: an ordering of events in terms of their being past (or more past), present, or future (or more future).

A-features: tensed features of events such as their happening in the past, present, or future.

B-series: an ordering of events in terms of their dates and times and permanent relations of being earlier than, later than, and simultaneous with each other.

B-features: tenseless yet temporal features of events, e.g. one event's happening five years before or after another.

eventually be in the past. We may call those facts that attribute a location in the A-series to objects and events (such as those listed above): A-facts.

The **B-series** is another temporal ordering, but here events are ordered in terms of their dates and times, as well as their relations of being earlier, later than, or simultaneous with other events. They are ordered according to their **B-features**, tenseless features indicating their relative temporal relations to one another. For example one might make the following statements relating certain events to a particular year, 2014:

- Washington is the capital of the United States in the year *2014*.
- In *2014*, people check the time using their phones.
- We go to the shore in the summer of the year after *2014*.
- The Sun begins to die approximately *5 billion years after 2014*.

Although events' locations in the A-series change, events' locations in the B-series do not. As time passes, it remains a fact that Washington is the capital of the United States in the year 2014. Even in the year 3014, it will remain the case that Washington is the capital of the United States in 2014. Note in all of the above statements, we are using our verbs – 'is,' 'check,' 'go,' and so on –tenselessly. To parse them, it may be helpful to imagine an observer who stands outside of time and is able to view the whole B-series at once. This observer is then able to make statements about when certain events occur, and what are these events' temporal relations to one another. Those facts that attribute locations in the B-series to objects and events are the B-facts. Unlike A-facts, B-facts do not change. And, as we have just seen, these are tenseless facts in the sense that they use tenseless verbs, and are true eternally from an objective perspective. Nonetheless although B-facts are tenseless, they are facts about time since facts about the dates and time of events and their occurring earlier or later than each other are events about these events' locations in time.

Except for those nihilists who deny the reality of time altogether,[11] metaphysicians agree that there are two kinds of facts about time: A-facts and B-facts. The big debate concerns which of these two kinds of facts are more fundamental, the A-facts or the B-facts.

B-theory of time: the view that the A-facts of time are reducible to the B-facts.

There are two main views on this issue. Most (though not all!) eternalists are B-theorists. The **B-theory of time** states that all A-facts (facts about what is past, present, and future) are reducible to, in other words, ultimately accountable in terms of, or grounded in, the B-facts. Another way to put the B-theorist's position is this: all tensed facts are reducible to tenseless facts. Let's consider a couple of examples to illustrate the B-theorist's position. Pretend that today's date is May 9, 2014. A B-theorist would say that the fact expressed by the following sentence:

(1A) Washington is the capital of the United States now,

is ultimately grounded in the fact expressed by this sentence:

(1B) Washington is the capital of the United States on May 9, 2014.

A fact about what happens now, an A-fact, is in this way explainable in terms of a fact about what happens on May 9, 2014, a B-fact. And so while the first sentence looks to express a fact that changes, it really just expresses a tenseless fact that is fixed, something that never changes. Likewise,

(2A) We will go to the shore next summer,

will, according to the B-theorist, reduce to the fact expressed by:

(2B) We go to the shore in the summer in the year after May 9, 2014,[12]

assuming again that (2A) was asserted on that date, May 9, 2014.

The opposing view to the B-theory is the **A-theory of time**. The simplest way to understand the A-theory is as a rejection of the B-theory. The B-theorist says that A-facts are reducible to B-facts. The A-theorist denies this and says that A-facts are not reducible to B-facts. A-facts are irreducible facts about time. A-facts cannot be reducible to B-facts since A-facts may change.

A-theory of time: the view that the A-facts are not reducible to the B-facts.

EXERCISE 5.3

B-theoretic Reductions of A-facts

All of the following sentences express A-facts. Given the time at which you are doing this exercise, what would a B-theorist's reduction of these facts look like?

A. Dinosaurs once roamed the Earth.
B. At one time, Philadelphia was the capital of the United States, but the capital of the United States is now Washington, DC.
C. In the future, there will be human outposts on Mars.
D. The bell rang five minutes ago.

The motivation for the A-theory can be stated simply. A-facts are facts that change. An event that is future will eventually become present. An event that is present will eventually become past. But B-facts never change. If World War I occurs later than the Trojan War, it is always the case that it is later than the Trojan War. If the Rio Olympics occur in July and August of 2016, then they always occur in July and August of 2016. This is characteristic of B-facts. Since A-facts change, but B-facts do not, the

A-theorist argues that A-facts cannot be reduced to B-facts. And since to accommodate the genuine, objective sense in which time passes, one needs A-facts, there must exist A-facts in addition to the tenseless B-facts.

In his article on the subject, McTaggart endorses what is an even stronger claim. McTaggart argues not only that facts about past, present, and future are not reducible to B-facts, but that indeed the A-facts are more fundamental than the B-facts. For McTaggart, if there were no A-facts, no facts about which events are past, present, and future, then there would be no such thing as time – time would be unreal. The reason for this is that time essentially involves change. For time to be real, something must change. But McTaggart thought change is only possible if there is an objective A-series. If there were just the B-facts, facts about the absolute and relative locations of events in the B-series, there wouldn't be any change. McTaggart illustrates this point using a specific example of an event, the death of Queen Anne.

McTaggart asks how, if the only facts about time are facts about the B-series, there could be change. Since an event's place in the B-series is fixed and permanent, events never change their B-features. If the death of Queen Anne occurs in 1714, then it (tenselessly) always occurs in 1714. If the death of Queen Anne occurs before the American Revolution, then it (tenselessly) always occurs before the American Revolution. Events don't change in their nontemporal features either. As he puts it, Queen Anne's death is always a death. The event doesn't exist for a little while, then gains the feature of being a death. The death of Queen Anne is never not a death. If it was a painful death, it was always a painful death. If it occurred in Kensington Palace, then it always occurred in Kensington Palace. McTaggart thus concludes: if there is only a B-series, there can be no change. Change requires the existence of an irreducible A-series. For the only way for events to change is change in their A-properties. In the case of the death of Queen Anne, this event once was future and then present, but now it is past. At the time McTaggart was writing, it was nearly 200 years in the past. It is now 300 years in the past. Because one needs the A-series for there to be genuine change, and, according to McTaggart, there needs to be genuine change if time is to be real, it follows for him that the existence of any temporal series including the B-series requires the A-series.

Because many philosophers have followed McTaggart in this reasoning, the B-theory of time is often pejoratively referred to as a static theory of time. Without an irreducible A-series, it is thought, nothing changes.

This a legitimate concern about the B-theory. But the B-theorist may respond that this argument has left out consideration of one way in which there can be change in the universe. Yes, events don't ever change according to the B-theory. But events are not the only component of the B-theorist's ontology. The B-theorist may also believe in the existence of *objects* and say that objects do change. For at one time (or space–time point) an object may have a certain property. Then at another time (or space–time point) that same object may lack that property. To use McTaggart's example again, perhaps the *event* that is Queen Anne's death may not change in any of its features. But Queen Anne herself does change.

After all, she is alive in 1713 and dead in 1714. Since Queen Anne herself has different properties at different times, there is change after all on the B-theory.

In this way, the B-theorist is able to respond to the worry that her picture is one of a static universe without change. Her response is that since objects in the universe have different features at different locations in the four-dimensional block that is the universe, the view does accommodate change. However, A-theorists have historically been dissatisfied with this response. They may concede that there is a sense in which the B-theorist can accommodate change on her picture, but it is not the genuine kind of change that we know occurs as time passes. This is the change that constitutes the A-series: events from the future coming to be present and then passing away into the past. It is a kind of change we experience and we are aware of.[13] We know from our own experience of ourselves in time that this objective passage exists, and the B-theorist misses this kind of change altogether. The B-theorist may offer back the response that the experience that there is this kind of change is an illusion, and the kind of object–change she offers is the only kind that genuinely exists. This is a point on which philosophers of time continue to disagree.

I have said up until now that *most* eternalists are B-theorists.[14] This combination of eternalism and the B-theory is often called the **block universe view**. However, it is not the case that they are all B-theorists. In fact, there is a way to endorse the A-theory while at the same time holding eternalism. The result is what is often called the **moving spotlight view** (Figure 5.4).

Block universe view: the combination of the B-theory of time and eternalism.

Moving spotlight view: a view that combines eternalism with the A-theory of time.

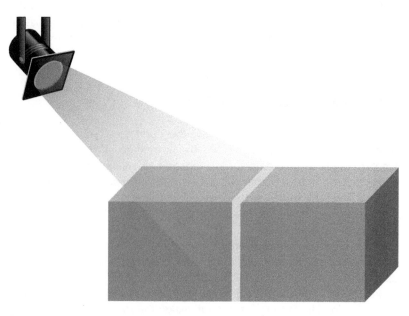

Figure 5.4 The Moving Spotlight View

Here the Minkowski space–time block is supplemented with an additional set of facts about what exists now. We can visualize this moving now as a spotlight that shines over different regions of space–time as time passes. Insofar as it assumes an objective passage of time, this view also falls afoul of the argument of the preceding section.

The moving spotlight view has been unpopular for a number of reasons. Probably the most common worry about the view concerns a general sense the content of the position is unclear.[15] Consider what this view says. Since it is an eternalist picture, past and future objects and events exist in the same sense as present events. Still, the view makes room for a real, objective passage of time by claiming that present objects and events instantiate A-properties that past and future objects and events lack: their presentness. Present events are happening now. But what is this feature that distinguishes present events and objects from ones in the past and future? The view invokes the metaphor of a spotlight. This leads us to think that although past objects and events are just as real as present ones, they are somehow dimmer than events in the present. Or alternatively, events and objects in the present have a special glow about them that past and future objects and events lack. But of course all of this is just metaphor. We want to know the truth about the distinction between the present and other times. At some point, one who wants to defend the moving spotlight view is going to have to move beyond metaphor.

Indeed it is for this reason that most A-theorists today are presentists. Only the presentist has a clear answer to the question of what makes for the distinction between the present and all other times. Only the presentist has a clear account of what objective passage of time amounts to. The distinction between present and non-present objects and events is a distinction in existence. Only present objects and events exist. And the passage of time is precisely a change in which objects and events exist. It is old (past) objects and events passing out of existence and new (what were future) objects and events coming to be.

THE TRUTHMAKER OBJECTION

There are two main packages of views then: first, the combination of the A-theory and presentism, which has the advantage of making sense of time's passage as we ordinarily experience it and, second, the combination of the B-theory and eternalism, which seems the most easy to reconcile with Special Relativity. In this section, we will consider one more reason why some philosophers have worried about presentism and the A-theory.[16] This is the truthmaker objection.

The objection starts from an appeal to the truthmaker theory we encountered in Chapter 2. Truthmaker theorists believe that when a sentence or proposition is true, there must be something in the world that makes it true. The truth of a sentence or proposition cannot be a brute fact. This is the idea that motivates the **truthmaker theory**: all truths have truthmakers. So, for example, consider the following sentence:

Truthmaker theory: the theory that truths have truthmakers, some entities or sets of entities that make them true.

(1) There are three pandas in the San Diego Zoo.

If this sentence is true, then there must be some thing or things in the world that make it true – these are the sentence's truthmakers. The sentence's truth must be connected with reality in some way, the kinds of objects there are in the world and how they are. Truth cannot "float free" of reality.

Typically, truthmaker theorists think there are particular kinds of entities that may serve as truthmakers. The truthmakers for a sentence consist of the objects the sentence is about having the right sort of categorical features and standing in the right relations to make the sentence true. For example, sentence (1)'s truthmaker will involve three pandas being located within the boundaries of the San Diego Zoo.

BOX 5.1

Categorical vs. Non-categorical Features

When metaphysicians appeal to **categorical features**, they have in mind features that just concern what that object is like at a certain time in those actual circumstances. In other words, an object's categorical features do not concern how the object is (a) relative to other objects, (b) in other possible situations, or (c) at other times. For example, one might describe a particular tennis ball as being spherical or made of rubber. In either case, this would be to ascribe it certain categorical features. Here are some non-categorical features we might ascribe to it:

Categorical features: features that just concern what an object is like actually in itself at a certain time.

- being the only yellow object in the room
- possibly being used in the Australian Open
- having the ability to bounce
- having been created in a plant in 2010.

None of these three features concern merely how the object actually is at a given time. The first involves a comparison between the ball and other objects. The next two concern facts about what might be the case in other situations. The fourth involves facts about the ball at other times. So, examples of non-categorical features are: relational features, modal features, **dispositional features** (features about how an object might behave in various situations), and temporal features.

Dispositional features: features about how an object might behave in various situations.

Or consider:

(2) Paris is west of Vienna.

This sentence is also true. Here the truthmaker consists of two cities, Paris and Vienna, related in such a way that Paris is west of Vienna.

Similarly the following two sentences are false because they lack the required truthmakers:

(3) There are seven pandas in the San Diego Zoo.
(4) Paris is east of Vienna.

Although there are seven pandas in the world, there are not seven pandas located within the boundaries of the San Diego Zoo. So sentence (3) lacks a truthmaker. There exist no objects structured in the way the sentence requires for it to be true. Similarly, for (4) to be true, both Paris and Vienna would have to exist and they would have to be ordered in such a way that Paris is east of Vienna. Since Paris fails to be related to Vienna in this way, there is no truthmaker for this truth.

EXERCISE 5.4

Truthmaker Theory

Provide truthmakers for the following truths.

A. The Eiffel Tower is 324 meters tall.
B. The average Brazilian female is 1.61 meters tall.
C. San Francisco is more populous than Seattle.
D. Glass is fragile.

We have just illustrated the truthmaker principle using examples of sentences that are about presently existing objects. To see the trouble for the presentist, we need to consider examples of past- and future-tensed statements. Consider the following sentences:

(5) Dinosaurs once roamed the Earth.
(6) The 2020 Olympics will be held in Tokyo.

Both (5) and (6) are true. So, according to our truthmaker principle, they must have truthmakers. Intuitively, since (5) is about dinosaurs, the truthmaker for (5) would involve the existence of some dinosaurs (among other things). The truthmaker for (6) would appear to involve the occurrence of the 2020 Olympics. If one is an eternalist and a B-theorist, then there is no problem accounting for the truth of (5) and (6) since these truthmakers exist. For the eternalist, past and future objects and events are just as real as presently existing objects and events.

Let's be a bit more careful for a moment about how the B-theorist will understand (5) and (6). These are tensed sentences and, recall, the A- and B-theorists have different ways of making sense of tensed statements. As we saw in the previous section, the B-theorist thinks that tensed sentences reduce to tenseless sentences. Let's again pretend these sentences are being asserted on May 9, 2014. According to the B-theorist, the fact expressed by (5) is grounded in the fact expressed by (5_B):

(5_B) Dinosaurs roam the Earth at some time earlier than May 9, 2014.

And the fact expressed by (6) is grounded in the fact expressed by (6_B):

(6_B) The 2020 Olympics are held in Tokyo at some time later than May 9, 2014.

(5_B) and (6_B) both express tenseless, B-theoretic truths. For (5_B) to be true, it must be the case that there exists some time earlier than May 9, 2014, and that dinosaurs are roaming the Earth at that time. For (6_B) to be true, it must be the case that there exists some time after May 9, 2014, that this be in the year 2020, and that the Olympics are held in Tokyo at this time. Indeed, we can restate (5_B) and (6_B) using the language of predicate logic to say:

(5_B) $\exists t$ (t is earlier than May 9, 2014 $\wedge$ Dinosaurs roam the Earth at t)

(6_B) $\exists t$ (t is later than May 9, 2014 $\wedge$ (t is in 2020 $\wedge$ the Olympics are held in Tokyo at t))

Thus, we can see that as the B-theorist understands (5) and (6), they require the existence of past and future times to be true. If no future or past times exist, then (5) and (6) cannot be true. But they clearly are true. So, given the B-theory, presentism must be false. This argument generalizes. Pick any truths about the past or the future. Given the B-theory of time, the presentist cannot account for their truth.

But, as we have already seen, presentists aren't B-theorists. They are A-theorists. And so they will not agree that (5) and (6) reduce to (5_B) and (6_B). But then how do A-theorists understand past- and future-tensed truths?

As we have seen, the A-theorist instead thinks the tenses in the sentences are irreducible. And this means that the A-theorist would not agree to use existential quantification over past and future times to represent the logical structure of tensed language. Rather, typically the A-theorist will introduce novel logical notation to capture the phenomenon of tense in symbolic logic.

This tense logic was first developed in the 1950s by the logician Arthur Prior. In tense logic, new operators are introduced that apply to entire sentences.[17] For example, **P** may be used to represent the past tense operator. We will read 'PA' as: In the past, A. **F** may be used to represent the future tense operator. We will read as 'FA' as: In the future, A. Then we may represent (5) and (6) as:

(5_A) **P** (Dinosaurs roam the Earth)

and

(6_A) **F** (The 2016 Olympics take place in Rio)

Now by itself, the use of tense logic does not assume that the A-theory is correct. What is distinctive about the A-theorist rather is that she believes that the facts expressed by sentences like (5_A) and (6_A) are irreducible to facts involving quantification over past and future times. The B-theorist has no objection to symbolizing (5) and (6) in the way the A-theorist suggests, using tense operators. The B-theorist will only say that the tense operators in (5_A) and (6_A) reduce to quantifiers over past and future times.

We can now return to our main point concerning truthmakers. The presentist as an A-theorist will take (5_A) and (6_A) to be the correct ways of understanding (5) and (6) and will claim that these should not in turn be paraphrased as (5_B) and (6_B). But then one wants to know what are the facts that make (5_A) and (6_A) true? What are these sentences' truthmakers? The eternalist who accepts the B-theory can say that it is the existence of other times in which there are dinosaurs and Tokyo Olympic Games that contribute to making these sentences true, but the presentist must deny this. So what *are* the truthmakers for (5_A) and (6_A) according to the presentist?

Some metaphysicians think there is no good answer for the presentist here and take this to be a decisive reason to reject presentism. We may summarize the objection in the form of an argument:

The Truthmaker Objection to Presentism

1. All truths have truthmakers.
2. So, if any sentences about the past and future are true, their truth will require the existence of past and future objects or events.
3. Some sentences about the past and future are true.
4. So, there must exist some past and future objects or events.
5. If presentism is true, no past or future objects or events exist.

Therefore,

6. Presentism is not true.

There are several strategies the presentist may take in responding to the truthmaker objection.

We will consider three distinct strategies for rejecting this argument:

- Reject Premise (1), the truthmaker principle
- Reject the move from the truthmaker principle to Premise (2)
- Reject Premise (3) and claim all statements about the past and future are false.

First, is there any reason the presentist can give to reject the truthmaker principle? We have seen it is motivated by the simple idea that for a sentence to be true, there must be some objects in the world structured in the right way (having the right categorical properties and the right relations) to make it true. However, the principle is not entirely uncontroversial. A common complaint is that the truthmaker principle is too strong. Consider for example:

Unicorns don't exist.

This sentence is true (sorry), but what is its truthmaker? Non-existent unicorns? Unless we are going to pursue the view of Quine's McX or Wyman considered in Chapter 1, we must insist that there are no such things. Indeed the sentence seems to be true precisely because there are no unicorns. It is true because something *doesn't* exist. Its truth doesn't require that something *does* exist, as the truthmaker principle states.

And so the presentist may claim that not all truths have truthmakers. Some sentences can be true without having truthmakers. This then opens up some options for what the presentist might say about statements appearing to be about past and future entities (e.g., (5) and (6)). One option is to say that these are brute truths. (5) and (6) are true, but their truth cannot be explained by more fundamental facts.[18] Another option is to say that (5) and (6) are not brute, but that, nonetheless, their truth doesn't require a truthmaker.

One alternative, interesting maneuver available to the presentist would be to appeal to an analogy between past- and future-tensed truths and truths about fiction. For example, consider the sentence:

Harry Potter is a wizard.

This sentence is true, but it isn't true because there is a person this sentence is about and that person is a wizard. What it takes for the sentence to be true is not that there is some person that has a certain property. Rather this sentence is true because of the existence of a certain fiction or story *that says* there exists a person, Harry Potter, who is a wizard. If so, the logical form of this sentence is not adequately represented as:

Wh

Instead, a better way to represent the truth conditions of this sentence is to symbolize it using a new operator. Like the tense operators introduced above, this will be a **sentential operator**, an operator acting on an entire sentence or proposition. We will write 'F_{HP}' to abbreviate 'In the fiction of Harry Potter . . .'

Sentential operator: a bit of logical notation acting on sentences or propositions to form more complex sentences or propositions.

$$F_{HP} (Wh)$$

The sentence is true just in case it is a fact in the fiction of Harry Potter that Harry Potter is a wizard.[19]

In a similar manner, we may introduce operators relating to truth in other fictions:

'In the fiction of Sherlock Holmes . . .'
'In the fiction of Star Wars . . .'
'In the fiction of the Hunger Games . . .', and so on.

A presentist may then apply this point about the logical structure of statements about fictions to past- and future-tensed truths. According to the presentist, no past or future times exist. However, she might allow that there is a common fiction with which we are familiar that consists in certain past- and future-tensed claims. In this fiction, it is the case that there are past dinosaurs and future Olympic Games. She could then understand an ordinary assertion:

(5) Dinosaurs once roamed the Earth,

as containing a tacit fiction operator of the form:

(5F) According to the fiction of past entities, dinosaurs once roamed the Earth.

Similarly for:

(6) The 2020 Olympics will be held in Tokyo,

this will be thought to express something like:

(6F) According to the fiction of future entities, the 2020 Olympics will be held in Tokyo.

If this is right, then past- and future-tensed sentences don't need truth-makers — objects they are about — to be true. This would be to presuppose their truth made some claim about things that genuinely exist. Instead, they just require facts about what is true according to a certain fiction. We might call this view temporal **fictionalism**, the view that past- and future-tensed truths are to be understood analogously to truths about fictions.

We have now discussed two ways a presentist who rejects the truth-maker principle may respond to the truthmaker objection. The first is to claim that the fact that certain past- and future-tensed claims are true is just a brute fact, not capable of any further explanation. The second is to appeal to fictionalism. A third possibility that has been explored is to say that past- and future-tensed truths are true in virtue of the present time having certain basic non-categorical features. For example, a presentist

Fictionalism: what is required for the truth of sentences in a given domain is to be understood by analogy with truths of fiction.

BOX 5.2

Fictionalism

Fictionalism is a general strategy to which metaphysicians have appealed in order to account for the truth of various sorts of claim where truthmakers for these claims do not seem available. In Chapter 7, we will consider a position called 'modal fictionalism' that takes truths concerning possibility and necessity to involve tacit 'In the fiction . . .' operators. Fictionalism has also been proposed to make sense of mathematical claims and moral claims.

For example, in the mathematical case, we noted in Chapter 2 that the sentence 'There are at least three perfect numbers greater than 17' appears to quantify over of numbers. Adopting the truth of a sentence like this would appear to commit one to Platonism. However, the mathematical fictionalist may argue that the logical form of this sentence is not properly represented as:

$$\exists x \exists y \exists z \left(\left(\left((Nx \wedge (Px \wedge Gxs)) \wedge (Ny \wedge (Py \wedge Gys)) \right) \wedge (Nz \wedge (Pz \wedge Gzs)) \right) \wedge \left((x \neq y \wedge y \neq z) \wedge x \neq z \right) \right),$$

but rather instead as:

$$F_M \exists x \exists y \exists z \left(\left(\left((Nx \wedge (Px \wedge Gxs)) \wedge (Ny \wedge (Py \wedge Gys)) \right) \wedge (Nz \wedge (Pz \wedge Gzs)) \right) \wedge \left((x \neq y \wedge y \neq z) \wedge x \neq z \right) \right).$$

where 'F_M' is an operator abbreviating 'In the fiction of mathematics . . .' The mathematical fictionalist thus thinks of mathematics as a collection of stories similar to the Harry Potter books or Star Wars. Just as claims in the fiction of Harry Potter may be true even though Harry Potter does not exist, claims in the fiction of mathematics may be true even though numbers and sets do not exist. What makes these claims true is just that the fiction of mathematics, actual mathematics books and articles, say they are true. (Of course there may be interesting disagreements about which books and articles count as definitive sources for what is true in the fiction of mathematics. The same issue arises for what counts as the definitive sources for what is true in the fiction of Harry Potter: just the books or the movies too? Just the books and movies, or the fan fiction too?)

Moral fictionalists deploy a similar strategy to account for the truth of moral claims. Moral fictionalists will deny that there are any features like moral rightness or wrongness that actions may possess. However, they argue that we as humans share in a common fiction that there are such features and that is what allows sentences like, 'That was a morally right action' or 'That was a morally wrong action' to be true.

might say (5) is true in virtue of the universe (that is, everything that exists presently) having the property of previously containing dinosaurs. Similarly, she may say that (6) is true in virtue of the universe having the property of in 2020, having the Olympic Games in Tokyo. Explaining the truth of these claims by appealing to non-categorical features like "previously containing dinosaurs" or "in 2020, having the Olympic Games in Tokyo" is not a maneuver the truthmaker theorist will accept. As we saw, the truthmaker theorist thinks that all truths may be accounted for in terms of the existence of certain entities possessing *categorical* features and standing in certain relations. These features are not categorical features. As such, the truth-maker theorist will likely think the presentist is cheating if she appeals to the universe's having properties like this to "explain" the truth of (5) and (6). But this is one possible option for the presentist, and one which will allow her to point to things in the world to account for the truth of past- and future-tensed claims.[20]

But let's say that the presentist is sympathetic to the truthmaker principle. What can she then say to respond to the objection? One option is to respond to the argument by rejecting the move from the argument's first premise to the second. Recall what these premises said:

1. All truths have truthmakers.
2. So, if any sentences about the past and future are true, their truth will require the existence of past and future objects or events.

The presentist might argue that (5) and (6) do have truthmakers, it is just that these truthmakers do not consist of past or future objects. All of the truthmakers for all truths, including past- and future-tensed truths, are contained in the present time. Two options are commonly explored.

One strategy is to ground the truth of past-tensed sentences in the existence of traces or records that past objects and events have left behind. Perhaps what makes (5) true is not the existence of dinosaurs, but rather the existence of present dinosaur bones scattered over the Earth. Similarly, the truthmakers for future truths may be the present plans and intentions that exist now. What makes (6) true are not future Olympic games, but instead records of meetings of the International Olympic Committee stating that the 2020 Olympics will be held in Tokyo.

The presentist might worry however about having enough traces and records, plans and intentions to serve as truthmakers for all of the past- and future-tensed truths there are. Couldn't there be truths about the past that have left no trace? Perhaps once in 2011 you wore mismatched socks to school, but the socks have since been destroyed, no one photographed this, and the incident has been erased from your memory. Does this mean it is not true that you wore mismatched socks to school that day? The worry is even more striking about future-tensed truths. There are many events in the future of your life, the planet, the universe that will come to pass – many future-tensed truths out there to be known. But so few of these are intended or planned, and even those that are planned may not come to pass. There is thus good reason to look elsewhere for truthmakers for past- and future-tensed truths.

Another option that has been explored is to take the truthmakers for past- and future-tensed truths to be some conditions in the present that necessitate what will happen in the future or what happened in the past. Knowing the present state of the universe and the laws of nature, one might naturally think one could then deduce what all past and future truths are. So then why not take the truthmakers for all past- and future-tensed truths to be the combination of the present state of the universe – all of the objects that now exist and what they are like – plus the laws of nature.

For this to work, there must be some strong constraints on what the laws of nature are like. First, for there to be determinate past and future truths, the laws of nature will have to be deterministic. **Determinism** is the position that the laws are such that given any state of the universe, one can predict with certainty what the state of the universe will be at any other time. There are no chances entering into the laws of nature.[21] In addition, for this response to be compatible with both presentism and truthmaker theory, the facts about the laws of nature must somehow ultimately be explainable in terms of what objects there are instantiating which features at the present time. But are there enough truthmakers at the present time to ground what the laws of nature are? One might think the facts about what the laws are depend on what things are like over extended periods of time.[22]

There is a more fundamental worry however about these attempts to respond to the argument by rejecting the move from premise (1) to premise (2). For both ways of carrying this out, whether by appealing to traces and plans or to present states of the universe and the laws, seem to involve a confusion. This is a confusion we have seen before[23]: the mistake of confusing the metaphysical issue of the truth of sentences like (5) and (6) with the epistemological issue of how we could know whether (5) and (6) are true. The discovery of traces and deduction from the laws may very well be ways we may have of coming to know about the past and future from what we have to go on in the present. But the issue of what makes sentences like (5) and (6) true is a different issue than the issue of how we could know they are true. To see this, let's go back to the original example used to motivate the truthmaker principle:

(1) There are three pandas in the San Diego Zoo.

What makes (1) true is the existence of three pandas (Bai Yun, Gao Gao, and Yun Zi) in the San Diego Zoo. There is a separate issue of how we might know about this truth. I know about it because I read about the pandas at the zoo's website. Maybe you know it because you have visited the zoo and seen the pandas there and now have a memory trace of seeing them. But these are epistemological issues, not issues about what is (1)'s truthmaker. The truth of (1) is grounded in facts about the pandas themselves, not in our ways of knowing about them.

Finally we can discuss a final strategy the presentist may use to respond to the truthmaker objection. This is to deny the argument's third premise and say that there are no truths about either the past or the future. There are only truths about the present because all that exists exists in the present. It may be a serious blow to common sense to deny that there are any truths about the past and the future. But the presentist might argue it is sometimes the case that metaphysical inquiry reveals that common sense was wrong. Since past and future objects and events do not exist, neither (5) nor (6) is true.

One immediate worry about denying the truth of all past- and future-tensed truths is what to say about these pairs of sentences.

Determinism: the position that the laws are such that given any state of the universe, one can use them to predict with certainty what the state of the universe will be at any other time.

(5) Dinosaurs once roamed the Earth.
(5*) Unicorns once roamed the Earth.
(6) The 2020 Olympics will be held in Tokyo.
(6*) The 2020 Olympics will be held on the Moon.

Unlike (5) and (6), their starred counterparts seem clearly wrong. But if we deny (5) and (6) are true, aren't we assigning them the same status as (5*) and (6*)?

In the end, all that is clear is that the eternalist has an easier time accounting for the truth of past- and future-tensed sentences than the presentist does. This is a mark in favor of eternalism, but certainly not a knockdown argument. Presentists may view this as a challenge to which they will have to work out a response.

EXERCISE 5.5

The Truthmaker Objection

Above, we explored several strategies the presentist may use for responding to the truthmaker objection. Which way seems most promising to you? How would you defend this response against the worries presented in the text?

TIME TRAVEL

We have now seen several distinctions in the philosophy of time: between the A-theory and B-theory of time, between presentism and eternalism. The issue about which of these views is correct is interesting on its own. But, as we will see in this section, these distinctions will also help us understand some other more complicated issues related to time. For example, time travel is a favorite motif in popular books and films, but it is often difficult to think about. There are a host of interesting questions related to time travel. Some of these are scientific or technical questions. Is time travel consistent with the laws of nature? Would it be possible to actually build a time machine? These are certainly interesting questions. But what we will consider here are instead the distinctively metaphysical questions that come up even before we ask about these scientific or technical issues.

To start, one might wonder whether time travel is even logically possible or whether the very idea of time travel presents one immediately with a contradiction. D.C. Williams once suggested that time travel, if it doesn't just consist in the banal fact that at each moment we occupy a different moment than the one we did previously, must fundamentally involve a contradiction.[24] For example, consider the novel *The Time Machine* in which the protagonist travels in minutes from nineteenth century Victorian England to the year 802,701 AD. We seem asked to imagine that in minutes, he is millennia from where he began. But this appears to be a contradiction. It is impossible to be both minutes away and millennia away from the same starting point in time. So time travel, in any interesting sense that would mark the time traveler apart from the rest of us, seems to involve a contradiction.

To resolve the contradiction, philosophers like Paul Horwich and David Lewis[25] have appealed to a distinction between two ways in which we speak of durations of time. Suppose the journey in the time machine takes the time traveler ten minutes according to his experience. Then, as Williams suggests, this time travel will seem to imply a contradiction. The time traveler can say as he steps into the time machine, "Ten minutes from now, I will be hundreds of millennia from now." To resolve this contradiction, let's first call the sense in which millennia pass **external time**. This is what Lewis characterizes as "time itself." It is how much time has passed objectively according to the world outside the time traveler. On the other hand, we may refer to the sense of elapsed time in which only ten minutes have passed (according to the experience of the time traveler) as **personal time**. This is the time that is measured by the time traveler him- or herself. It is measured by the ticks of one's wristwatch, the growth of hair on one's head, and the occurrence of other bodily processes. With this distinction in hand, we can resolve the contradiction. When the time traveler steps out of his time machine, ten minutes of his personal time will have elapsed. But millennia in external time will have elapsed. There is no contradiction if we are careful. In general, Lewis suggests we understand time travel as any discrepancy between personal time and external time. In this sense it seems time travel is at least logically possible.

There may be no contradiction in the very idea of time travel, but can the time traveler do anything once he or she arrives in the past? Is it possible to change the past? This had been a vexing issue, but one that may be resolved by deploying the resources of the previous sections. First, let's start by assuming the combination of B-theory and eternalism: the block universe view. If we are asking about travel to the past and assuming there are facts about the past, then the most natural picture to assume in the background is a view in which the past is real and so provides one some locations to travel to.

If the past exists and there are facts about it, then is it possible to change these facts? Well, in a strict sense of "change the past," where we are assuming it was once the case at a particular time t that an event occurred, and then one brought about a change so that at t, the event did not occur, the answer would seem to be: no, you can't change the past. Whatever happened happened. Suppose, for example, that on May 2, 2011, you slipped and fell in the rain. Then, unless you accept the view considered at the end of the last section which denies there are any truths about the past and future, you can't go back to the past and make things so this did not happen.

After all, what if you did succeed in going back to that date and warn yourself so that you do not slip? This would imply a contradiction. This would

External time: distinguished from personal time in David Lewis's account of time travel, it is time itself.

Personal time: distinguished from external time in David Lewis's account of time travel, elapsed time as measured by the normal behavior of physical objects: ticks of a watch, aging processes of human beings, etc.

involve it being the case both that: (a) on May 2, 2011, you slipped and (b) on May 2, 2011, you did not slip. This is a contradiction.

One might concede that whatever one does it is impossible to undo a fact that occurred and make it so that it did not occur. But one might think there is still a way time could be such that you could go back and stop the slipping on May 2, 2011. This would be if time were not a one-dimensional line, as we ordinarily think, but instead two-dimensional.

Think of time as represented by a two-dimensional graph with the x-coordinates corresponding to locations in what we ordinarily think of as one-dimensional external time (1950, 2000, 2011, and so on) and the y-coordinates corresponding to alternative timelines, beginning with the original timeline before anyone time travels (see Figure 5.5).[26] If we look at time two-dimensionally, then we can understand how you might go back to the past and prevent your slipping. When you travel back, you don't change the fact that there was a slipping on May 2, 2011. This slipping still occurs at location x = May 2, 2011, and y = 1. However, what you can do is make it the case that at the location x = May 2, 2011, and y = 2, there is no slipping. That there is a slipping at one location in two-dimensional time and no slipping at a distinct location in two-dimensional time presents no contradiction. But we can now see that even on this two-dimensional model, still, one is incapable of changing the past. The fact remains that you did indeed slip on May 2, 2011, on the original timeline.

It is possible that some of us when thinking about time travel, say in the context of watching a movie like *Back to the Future* where a character does successfully go to the past and change things, may think of time two-dimensionally. We may be imagining there are multiple timelines. But ultimately this isn't a coherent way to imagine changing the past. For if time is two-dimensional, one doesn't ever go back and change the past. If time is two-dimensional in this way, then one doesn't really ever

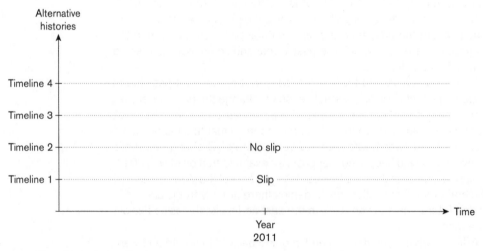

Figure 5.5 Two-Dimensional Time

even go back to one's own past. For on this model, when you go back to prevent your slipping, you are traveling to a different location in time than you were. You don't travel back to (May 2, 2011, 1). You travel to (May 2, 2011, 2). This is a different temporal location altogether. So, when thinking about time and time travel, most philosophers represent time one dimensionally. The two-dimensional model does not seem to help make our thoughts about changing the past more coherent.[27]

No one can undo what has already happened. As we have seen, this would result in a contradiction. But does this mean that if one were able to time travel, one would be frozen, incapable of any action? That one couldn't even step out of the time machine because in doing so one might trample a blade of grass thus generating a contradiction?

No, there is no contradiction in the idea that time travelers may do things in the past, even do an interesting variety of things. As Horwich puts it, even if one cannot change the past, this does not mean one cannot *affect* the past. You can go back to the past and do things. Imagine Smith who in her fascination with Jane Austen decides she will build a time machine, travel to the past and meet her. She can do this. But if this occurs, it will have to have always been the case that she met Jane Austen. There can be no *change* in what happened, no change in the events that lie along the B-series. Nevertheless, the time traveler can certainly be a part of what happened in the past.

EXERCISE 5.6

Time Travel and the A-series?

Would an appeal to an irreducible A-series help to remove the contradiction involved in changing the past? If one believed that in addition to the permanent B-series, there was in addition a set of facts about which of these events are past, which are present, and which are future, would this allow one to change the past, not merely affect it? Explain why or why not.

What about changes in one's earlier life? What if you did something in your teen years you now regret? What if Smith always regretted the fact that she never learned to speak a foreign language in high school? Instead she goofed off in all of her language classes and now as a result is monolingual. Finally, at the age of 40, she finds a time machine and travels back to the year 2000 to convince her younger self to pay more attention in Spanish class. Can she do this? Well, certainly there is no contradiction in Smith's traveling back to the time of her youth and *trying* to convince herself to pay more attention in class. She is certain not to succeed in convincing her younger self, since she can't change what happens and what happens is that she never learns to speak a foreign language. But she can go back and have this conversation with her younger self. If she does this, then, as we have already established, it will always be the case that this happened. But what if she doesn't remember ever having had a conversation with an older version of herself?

There is no changing what happens at any point in the B-series. This would involve a contradiction. However, this leaves open the possibility that Smith did have this conversation with her older self and yet she forgot it. One can go back and affect one's past, that is, play a role in the events that occurred in one's past. However, then it will have always been the case that this is what happened.

We may now finally consider one last case, what is perhaps the most interesting and frustrating one to think about, at least for many authors. Is it possible to go back in time and kill one's younger self?[28] Here again, logic seems to point to the answer "No." If you could go back in time and kill your younger self, then that would mean you did not survive to the moment in personal time at which you supposedly did the killing. So this would mean you both killed yourself and did not kill yourself, the latter because you were alive to complete the killing.

So you can't do it. What's the puzzle? Think about it the following way. It seems you are able to make things quite easy for yourself. You can decide to go back to the time when you were most vulnerable, a time when you were asleep in your crib as a gentle baby, a time at which you know no one else was in your house. Your parents had just crossed the street for an hour to talk to the neighbors. You can make things easier for yourself as well by training. In the months leading up to your time travel, you can train rigorously in what it will take to carry out the murder, practicing with different weapons and techniques. You are able to meditate on the task and deepen your resolve, ensuring that you won't back out at the last moment. You can ensure that when the time comes to commit the act, you are as skilled and remorseless as any assassin. Logic permits you to travel to the past, to enter your childhood bedroom, attack your defenseless baby self. But somehow despite all of this training and how close you are able to come, logic will not permit you in the end to achieve your task. As Lewis notes, in one sense of 'can,' the sense of having the skills it takes, of course you can kill your baby self. However, in another sense of 'can,' the sense of logic, the sense in which what you can do does not imply a contradiction, you cannot kill your younger self. Somehow or other, Lewis points out, you will fail. It seems the power of logic alone must prevent you from succeeding no matter how far you can get.

And this is puzzling. No matter how hard you try, there are some things you cannot do even if you build a time machine and travel to the past. Killing your younger self is one of them.

So far, we have presupposed eternalism and the B-theory. This is indeed the framework in which Williams, Horwich, and Lewis write. Time travel is much more difficult to understand if one presupposes some version of the A-theory with its objective and, on most versions, ontologically loaded sense of time's passage.[29] We have already noted that if one is a presentist, time travel is puzzling since there are no locations in time to travel to other than the one that is immediately next. If one endorses the A-theory, one additionally introduces questions like the following: If I travel to the past, but my friends stay behind and continue to persist into the future, which way does time pass? Where does the objective flow of time go, with me or my friends? If any version of the A-theory is true, there must be some objective fact about when the present is. Does it stay with me or with my friends? Either way, there are problems. If time goes with me and my personal time, then my friends cease to exist when I time travel. (Or on a moving spotlight model, my friends are plunged into darkness). If time continues to pass with my friends' personal time, then by time traveling away from them, I cease to exist. It looks like eternalism and the B-theory is required to even begin to make sense of time travel. However, even then, as we have seen, there are surprising consequences about the limits of one's powers.

SUGGESTIONS FOR FURTHER READING

A good place to begin further reading in the philosophy of time is the collection *The Philosophy of Time*, edited by Robin Le Poidevin and Murray MacBeath.

For the argument against presentism from Special Relativity, see Hilary Putnam's "Time and Physical Geometry." Responses to the problem Special Relativity poses for presentism may be found in Mark Hinchliff's "A Defense of Presentism in a Relativistic Setting," William Lane Craig's *Time and the Metaphysics of Relativity*, and Ned Markosian's "A Defense of Presentism." James Ladyman's "Does Physics Answer Metaphysical Questions" contemplates the possibility that fundamental physical theories moving beyond Special Relativity may not lend support for eternalism.

For a classic defense of the B-theory, see D.C. Williams, "The Myth of Passage." Other contemporary defenses of the B-theory and eternalism may be found in J.J.C. Smart, *Philosophy and Scientific Realism* and the second chapter of Theodore Sider's *Four Dimensionalism*.

For the argument that we have special epistemological reason to favor the A-theory, see William Lane Craig, *The Tensed Theory of Time: A Critical Examination*, chapter 5. See the debate between Dean Zimmerman and Theodore Sider for more on this issue in *Contemporary Debates in Metaphysics*, edited by Theodore Sider, John Hawthorne, and Dean Zimmerman. Simon Keller's "Presentism and Truthmaking" is an excellent discussion of the truthmaker objection. For more on fictionalism, see the essays collected in *Fictionalism in Metaphysics*, edited by Mark Kalderon.

For more on time travel, see Jenann Ismael's "Closed Causal Loops and the Bilking Argument," and the essays collected in *Science Fiction and Philosophy*, edited by Susan Schneider.

NOTES

1 Or to put things more carefully following the discussion of Quine (1948) in Chapter 1, it is not the case that there are any such future people or objects.

2 One can find Einstein's discussion of a case just like this in *Relativity: The Special and General Theory*.

3 For more on this topic, you could consult Lawrence Sklar's textbook, *The Philosophy of Physics*, or his more advanced monograph on the topic, *Space, Time, and Spacetime*.

4 The speed of light is approximately 3×10^8 meters per second, that is, 300,000,000 meters per second.

5 This isn't to say that there aren't many physicists or philosophers who continue to hold these views.

6 His bones exist, yes. However, this is not the same as Abraham Lincoln's existing.

7 The manifold being the four-dimensional block that is space–time.

8 Note that this is a different sense in which the future is set than what one means when one endorses the metaphysical thesis of determinism. Here, the claim is just that there are facts about what happens in the future. Whether these facts come to follow from what happens in the present as the result of deterministic or indeterministic laws (see Chapter 9 on Free Will) is a separate matter altogether.

9 Recall from Chapter 1 that 'exist' and 'is' are interchangeable.

10 For example, one might believe in God or numbers and believe that these entities exist outside of time. If so, one will think they exist in the tenseless sense of 'exists.'

11 McTaggart himself was such a nihilist.

12 This will be understood relative to a particular observer's state of motion. For simplicity, we will leave this tacit in what follows.

13 A-theorists like William Lane Craig and Dean Zimmerman have argued that the belief in the passage of time has a special epistemological status, in others words that we know of the passage of time in a way that is especially direct.

14 Though, as noted above, all B-theorists are eternalists.

15 Another line of attack may be found in Theodore Sider's *Four Dimensionalism*, chapter 2. Roughly, Sider's argument is that since the moving spotlight theorist believes in facts about the past and the future, she has them available for a reduction of tensed facts. It is then puzzling why she should adopt the anti-reductionist, A-theory. For a defense of the moving spotlight view against objections, see Bradford Skow's *Objective Becoming*, chapter 4.

16 For more objections, see Sider, *Four Dimensionalism*, chapter 2. And for replies on behalf of the presentist, see Markosian "A Defense of Presentism."

17 Tense logic was built on the framework of the modal logic that will be introduced in Chapter 7.

18 Simon Keller considers this option in his "Presentism and Truthmaking."

19 For more on these sentential operators, see "Truth in Fiction," by David Lewis.

20 For the complaint that this constitutes "cheating," see Sider, *Four Dimensionalism*, chapter 2.

21 We consider the case for (and against) determinism in Chapter 9.

22 This is what is referred to as **Humeanism about the laws**: the view that the facts about the laws of nature are reducible to facts about regularities in what happens in our universe over time.

23 See the final section in Chapter 2, Mathematical Objects.

24 In "The Myth of Passage."

25 In their papers "On Some Alleged Paradoxes of Time Travel," and "The Paradoxes of Time Travel." I will follow Lewis's terminology in this chapter.

26 Jack Meiland considers two-dimensional time in detail in the paper "A Two-Dimensional Passage Model of Time for Time Travel."

27 The position seems to also be in tension with the physicist's way of representing time as one-dimensional.

28 This is closely related to the "grandfather paradox" – the issue of whether it is possible to go back in time and kill one's grandfather before one's parents were conceived.

29 For a clever way of showing how the presentist A-theorist too may make sense of time travel, see Keller and Nelson's "Presentists Should Believe in Time-Travel."

Humeanism about laws: the view that the facts about the laws of nature are reducible to facts about regularities in what happens in our universe.

CHAPTER 6

Persistence

Learning Points

- Introduces perdurantism as a solution to the paradoxes of material constitution
- Distinguishes the main metaphysical views about persistence
- Examines the debate over the existence of temporal parts.

THE PUZZLE OF CHANGE

In Chapter 3, we discussed some of the classic puzzles of material constitution including the Ship of Theseus and the Statue and the Clay. These puzzles caused us to rethink our commonsense views about material objects given some basic facts about identity, including Leibniz's law.

In the case of the Ship of Theseus, we seemed to have to admit that although both S_2 (the ship whose constitution resulted from slow changes over time with the gradual replacement of planks) and S_3 (the ship constructed from the Ship of Theseus's original, rotten planks) both have good claims to be identical to the original Ship of Theseus, they can't both be the Ship of Theseus since there is more than one of them (and identity is numerical identity). We thus seem forced to choose between the claim that neither is the original ship – the ship has ceased to exist – and the claim that one of the two successor ships (S_2 or S_3) is privileged. But what objectively could make one criterion of identity (sameness of material makeup or continuity over time) privileged over the other?

In the puzzle of the Statue and the Clay, we had what initially appeared to be just one object, a lump of clay in the shape of a statue. However, by reflecting on the nature of statues and lumps, we seemed forced to admit that the statue could not be identical to the clay of which it is composed. (The statue and lump differ in their temporal and modal properties and so, by Leibniz's law, must be distinct.) And so we seemed committed to the existence of two objects wholly located at the same place at the same time: the lump of clay that we called 'Lump' and the statue, Goliath. There is nothing especially exotic about this case. In general, when we consider any case of a material object and the material of which it is made, there will be temporal and modal properties to which one may appeal to show that what may look like one object is really two. We therefore seem to be committed to an abundant multiplicity of objects.

This is how we left things in Chapter 3 more or less,[1] but we are now in a position to consider a new candidate solution to these puzzles. This will allow us to see how we need not choose between identity conditions for our ship. It will allow us to see how both S_2 and S_3 may be later versions of the Ship of Theseus without entailing the identity of S_2 and S_3. We will also finally see a way to avoid the claim that in the case of the Statue and the Clay there are two material objects wholly present in the same place at the same time, while at the same time acknowledging that statues and lumps of clay generally possess different temporal and modal properties. The solution comes in the form of a theory of persistence for material objects. The thought is, if we understand better what it is for an object to persist over time, we can resolve these puzzles of material constitution.

We'll introduce this theory of persistence momentarily and try to evaluate whether it is indeed the panacea it is often claimed to be. But let's pause momentarily to see why persistence through time has long been thought to be such an interesting issue.

Persistence is now thought of as a distinctively metaphysical problem, but this was not always so. Aristotle, in his *Physics*, asked how objects could persist over time. The core of the puzzle is that as objects persist, this involves their becoming different. Sometimes the change is dramatic, as when a tadpole becomes a frog or an ordinary lump of clay gets transformed into a sublime work of art. But even if nothing particularly extraordinary happens to an object, as it persists through time it at least changes in one respect: becoming older. Philosophers before Aristotle, such as Parmenides (c.515 BC), responded to this issue by denying that there could ever be persistence through change. For Parmenides, change was impossible and so everything is as it is always and permanently. In his view, if something that is a certain way could become something that is not that way (for example if what is young could become not young, if what is wise could become not wise), then what is could become what is not, which is impossible. What is always is and never is not.

Aristotle's response to Parmenides was that this argument against the possibility of change suffered from a conflation between two senses of 'is.' One may use 'is' to predicate a feature of an object, as when we say a person is young or that she is wise. Or one may use 'is' to speak of an entity's existence, as when we say the person is, she exists. Once we recognize this distinction between two senses of 'is,' we can see that in allowing that (a) a person that is young may become not young, we are not thereby saying that (b) something that is (exists) becomes something that is not (that does not exist). The latter (b) would indeed imply the destruction of an object rather than its persistence through a change, but this is in no way implied by (a), once we recognize these two senses of 'is.'

There is still the question of how anything may survive a change over a period of time. How could a person that is young survive to become different: something that is not young? Actually, Aristotle recognized several ways changes might occur:

> by change of shape, as a statue; by addition, as things which grow; by taking away, as the Hermes from a stone; by putting together, as a house; by alteration, as things which "turn" in respect of their material substance.

(*Physics*, I.7)

For Aristotle, there must be something that survives through a change. Otherwise, the case will be one of the destruction of one object and coming-into-being of another, rather than the persistence of one continuous object through a change. To explain how there could be continuity through a change, Aristotle proposed the view that substances are complex and consist of two parts: matter and form. For example, in the case of a person, the matter is the flesh and bones, the form is man or woman. In the case of the Eiffel Tower, the matter is iron, the form is that of a tower. This was the core of Aristotle's physics, his theory of the makeup of objects in nature that explains how they are able to change. The view is called **hylomorphism**, from the Greek *hyle* for matter and *morphē* for form. Where there is persistence through a change rather than the destruction of an object, we have continuity of matter through a change in form.

Aristotle's theory has of course been succeeded as a physics. When it comes to understanding the various kinds of changes objects undergo, a lot has been learned in the past 2,400 years. Still, hylomorphic theory remains an almost unseen part of the way we think about material objects, and is still an explicit part of some current metaphysical theories.[2] But even if it is part of a correct total theory of persistence, there are problems for which we need additional conceptual machinery to solve. We need more conceptual tools to take into account the fact that ordinary material objects are at least sometimes able to persist through changes in not just their form but their matter as well. The Ship of Theseus presents one such case. In that thought experiment we imagined the wooden planks of the ship were replaced slowly over time so that eventually none of the original wood remained. To cite another example, scientists tell us that the cells of a human body are constantly in flux. After approximately seven to ten years, a human body recycles all of its cells.

It looks like objects like human beings are able to survive through changes even when their underlying matter fails to provide any continuity to explain this persistence. In this section we will consider some rival metaphysical theories that attempt to explain in what persistence consists. As we will see, one central point of disagreement between these views is whether in order for objects to persist over time, there must be something that exists continuously through the change, as Aristotle assumed when he introduced his matter/form distinction.

Hylomorphism: the Aristotelian view that substances are complex objects made of both matter (*hyle*) and form (*morphē*).

http://www.nytimes.com/2005/08/02/science/02cell.html?pagewanted=all&_r=0

SOME VIEWS ABOUT PERSISTENCE

Typically, when we think about persistence, we presuppose that there is some one object that is present both before and after the change. For example, consider our piece of clay, Lump. We may assume there is a certain time at which Lump came into existence. Call that time 't_0.' As time passes, Lump, that very same object, continues to exist. Perhaps at some later time, t_1, Lump is rolled up into a ball. Then at some time after that, t_2, it gets squashed into the shape of a disk. Finally at time t_3, our sculptor gets a hold of Lump and shapes it into a statue of the mythical warrior Goliath. And so Lump persists for the rest of its existence. Our assumption here is that it is the same object, Lump, that exists at each time from t_0 through t_3 and onward. This suggests the picture of the persistence of Lump over time as shown in Figure 6.1.

The view captured in this figure is what is called **endurantism**. It is the view that objects like Lump persist by surviving from one instant to the next, where what survival comes to is strict, numerical identity. Lump persists from t_0 through t_3 by existing at each time along the way from t_0 to t_3,[3] so that the object (Lump) that exists at t_0 is numerically identical to that which exists at t_3. If 'persists' is a neutral term that may be used to refer to the phenomenon that each of the rival theories in this chapter is trying to explain, we will say that an object *endures* when it persists in the way the endurantist thinks of persistence. We will next consider endurantism's main rival, the view that objects like Lump persist over time not by enduring, but instead by *perduring*.

Perdurantism is the view that objects persist over time by being spread out or extended over it. The perdurantist believes that in addition to having spatial parts, material objects also have temporal parts or stages. Material objects are four dimensional in the sense that they are spread out in time in the same way they are spread out in space. Just as material objects have different parts at different places (left halves and right halves, arms and legs), they have different parts at different times (first halves and last halves, childhoods and "golden years"). According to the perdurantist, objects like persons or lumps of clay persist over time by having parts (stages) at distinct times. If the perdurantist is correct, then we should not view Lump's history in the way portrayed by Figure 6.1, but instead view it as depicted in Figure 6.2.

Endurantism: the view that what persistence amounts to is strict numerical identity over time.

Perdurantism (the worm view): the view that material objects persist by having temporal parts at different times.

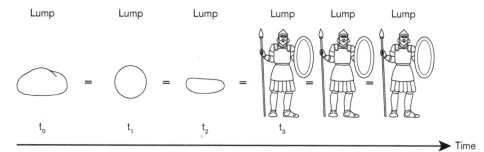

Figure 6.1 The Persistence of Lump (Endurantism)

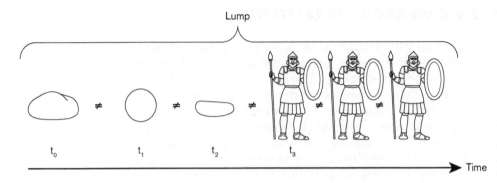

Figure 6.2 The Persistence of Lump (Perdurantism)

The reason is that, strictly speaking, what exists at t_0 for the perdurantist is not identical to what exists at any later time. For what exists at t_0 is only one temporal part of Lump. What exists at t_1 is a later temporal part of Lump. It is not the same part as that which existed at t_0. And so on for all other times. The temporal parts of Lump are no more numerically identical to one another than your right arm is identical to your left arm.

Perdurantism is a view that has become increasingly influential since Quine's presentation of the position in his paper "Identity, Ostension, and Hypostasis" (1950). It is a view, like the eternalism considered in Chapter 5, that is inspired by the idea that we should treat time analogously to space. The eternalist thinks we should treat other times just as we treat other places and view them all as equally real. The perdurantist believes just as people and other material objects have spatial parts, are spread out over different places, we should view them too as having temporal parts, as being spread out over different times.[4]

To distinguish endurantism from perdurantism, endurantists will often emphasize that their view is not merely that objects persist by existing at distinct times, or even that objects exist by being the same object from one moment to the next. The perdurantist after all can agree with this. The perdurantist can agree that it is the same Lump that exists at t_0 and then again at t_1 and then again at t_2 and so on. For the perdurantist this is just like if one hid behind a curtain, first poking a hand out, then a leg, then one's head: we would say at each time it was the same person that appeared momentarily from behind the curtain, even though in another sense all that was revealed each time was a part. What the endurantist needs to say to distinguish her view is that objects persist over time by being **wholly present** at each time at which they exist. For the endurantist, it is not just a part of Lump that is there at t_0 and a part of Lump that is there at t_1. It is all of Lump, the whole object, that is present at each time.

To be **wholly present** at a time: to have all of one's parts exist at that time.

Endurantism is typically combined with a related position about material objects: **three dimensionalism**. This is the view that denies any objects have temporal parts in addition to spatial parts. The view is called 'three dimensionalism' because it views material objects as having extension in just the three spatial dimensions: height, width, and depth. Objects also exist in and

Three dimensionalism: the view that although objects may have spatial parts, they never have temporal parts.

persist through time of course, but the three dimensionalist does not view this persistence as a way of being extended or spread out over time. Rather, objects are only spread out over space. All of their material parts are spatial parts. By contrast, perdurantists (all of them) will reject three dimensionalism in favor of **four dimensionalism**. This is just the view that at least some objects have temporal parts in addition to spatial parts. Perdurantists are all four dimensionalists because this is required by their view about how ordinary material objects persist over time, by having distinct temporal parts at different times. Later we will see one way of being a four dimensionalist without being a perdurantist.

Four dimensionalism: the doctrine of temporal parts, the view that in addition to spatial parts, objects have temporal parts.

EXERCISE 6.1

Time and Space, Analogies and Disanalogies

We have now seen several metaphysical positions that are based on the view that time and space should be treated analogously. What are some features common to time and space? What are some points of difference? Try to think of three of each.

A SOLUTION TO SOME PARADOXES OF MATERIAL CONSTITUTION

Perdurantism is often defended for its ability to help us find solutions to the puzzles of material constitution. So let's now return to our two puzzles of material constitution and see how perdurantists have used these puzzles to motivate their position. First, consider the Ship of Theseus. Earlier, we were tacitly assuming endurantism. The question was framed as a question about which object at a later time, S_2 or S_3, was identical to the original ship, S_1. This assumed that if the Ship of Theseus was to persist, it must be identical to one of these objects at a later time, S_2 or S_3. However, we may now see that if we are perdurantists, we won't think that the ship persists over time by there being a later object that is strictly identical to that earlier existing object, S_1. Instead, we will think that the ship persists by having numerically distinct temporal parts at different times. And so when we ask about S_1, S_2, and S_3, the perdurantist will say that none of these objects is identical to any of the others. Rather, these are three, numerically distinct temporal parts. And then the question is, are there any wholes that have both the original object S_1 and either of S_2 or S_3 as parts. And here we must think back to our views in Chapter 3 about parts and wholes.

If we are mereological universalists, as many four dimensionalists are, then we will think that any non-overlapping material objects whatsoever

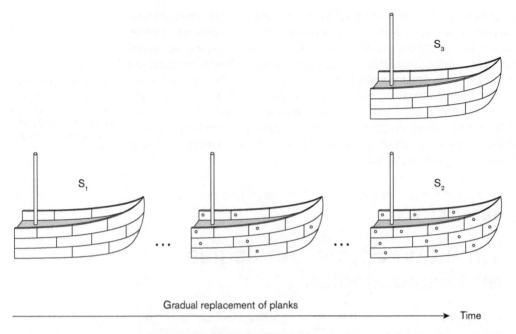

Gradual replacement of planks

⟶ Time

Figure 6.3 The Ship of Theseus

compose some further object. And so, in the case of Figure 6.3, there are at least two temporally extended objects: one that includes S_1 and S_2 as parts, and another that includes S_1 and S_3 as parts.[5] Depending on what is required to be a ship, it is possible to say that both of these temporally extended objects are ships. And if both contain S_1 as parts, then one can say that each is equally worthy of the name 'The Ship of Theseus.' Since there are two ships here, not one, and names are typically understood as terms denoting a single individual (see Box 1.4), we might be careful and say that, strictly speaking, we should introduce two names: 'The Ship of Theseus-A' and 'The Ship of Theseus-B.' But note that we are now able to say everything we wanted to when we considered the problem.

The problem was that first, we didn't want to have to choose between S_2 and S_3 as the better candidate for being the original Ship of Theseus. Both had good claims to be Theseus's ship. And yet we recognized that if we allowed that both $S_1=S_2$ and $S_1=S_3$, then by the symmetry and transitivity of identity, we would be forced to say what is absurd, that $S_2=S_3$. However, if the persistence of the ship does not consist in the strict numerical identity of S_1 with either later object, as the perdurantist thinks, then we don't have to choose between S_2 and S_3 and we are not forced to say the absurd thing.

At this point, one might worry a bit about the perdurantist's solution. For if it is true that both ships contain S_1 as a stage or temporal part, then doesn't this mean that there are really two ships present at the same place at the same time, that there are two ships at the location of S_1 where there certainly would appear to be only one ship?

In a sense, the answer to this question is clearly 'yes.' If one accepts what has been said up until now and concedes that S_1 is a part of two ships, then, yes, both ships are present in the same location at our starting time. But this need not be problematic. For first, it isn't true that either ship is *wholly* present at that place at that time. Instead what is true is that a stage of each ship is present at the same place at that time. Furthermore, this is a stage that each of the two ships have in common. What is happening according to the perdurantist is that the two ships temporally overlap: they share a common temporal part. And the simple reason the perdurantist doesn't find *this* problematic is that it is very similar to other cases we don't find at all problematic, cases of spatial overlap. We have no problem under-standing how two objects may share a common spatial part at a time. My body and my left arm share many common spatial parts, including my left hand and my left wrist. When two roads intersect, they share a common part. Sometimes two roads will overlap for an extended stretch. For example, when one is traveling north out of New York City, there are a few miles where I-95 and I-87 overlap. At this time, one may say truly that one is traveling simultaneously on two highways, both I-95 and I-87. Most people (philosophers and non-philosophers alike) find nothing puzzling about this. Once you press the analogy between space and time in the way the perdurantist wants to, temporal overlap (the sharing of temporal parts) seems no more problematic than spatial overlap (the sharing of spatial parts). It is something we can understand and something that obtains in the case of the Ship of Theseus when our two ships share a common stage, S_1. There are indeed two ships present at S_1 according to the perdurantist. But this need look no more like there are two ships present any more than it need look like there are two roads present at a place where two roads overlap for a certain stretch.

And now we can turn to what the perdurantist wants to say about the case of the statue and the lump of clay of which it is composed. The perdurantist can note that only an endurantist will be forced to say that this is a case in which two material objects are wholly located at the same place at the same time. For at the time Lump constitutes Goliath, it is true these two objects spatially and temporally overlap, but this doesn't mean these two objects are wholly located in the same place at the same time. For the perdurantist will consider both Lump and Goliath to be objects that are extended over both space and time, and although these objects temporally overlap for some of their histories, they share some stages in common, they do not overlap for their entire histories. Goliath does not come into exis-tence until t_3. And so they don't share all of the same parts.

Here again, one might try to insist that even though Lump and Goliath are never wholly present at the same spatiotemporal region (because these objects only partially overlap), that these two objects are still both present at the time Lump constitutes Goliath and so one remains committed in a sense to the Two Object View of David Wiggins (see Chapter 3). But as we saw above in the case of the Ship of Theseus, at no time are two material objects wholly present at the same place. For at the time and place of the overlap, there are not two temporal parts, one belonging to Lump and one belonging to Goliath. Rather there is just one temporal part shared by the two objects. Perdurantism allows us to avoid having to say that there are two objects located in that same place at the same time. And we can concede that the statue and lump are distinct (since by Leibniz's law they differ in modal and temporal properties). They are distinct four-dimensional objects.

EXERCISE 6.2

Coinciding Objects

The perdurantist has an elegant solution to the problem of the Statue and the Clay as we have so far presented it. But some philosophers point out that there are variations on this case that pose more of a difficulty for the perdurantist. Suppose the lump of clay and statue are not created at different times, but instead brought into existence at the same moment. And suppose as well that they are later destroyed at the same moment. What should the perdurantist say about this case? Does this reinstate the appeal of the Two Object View of Wiggins?

THE PROBLEM OF TEMPORARY INTRINSICS

As we have noted, perdurantists take it to be a virtue of their position that they are able to solve what were earlier thought to be problem cases involving material constitution. However, this is not the only argument for the view. The master argument for the view, at least so far as some perdurantists are concerned, comes from considering the **problem of temporary intrinsics**. This problem, a problem for endurantism, was first stated by David Lewis in his *On The Plurality of Worlds* (1986). Lewis calls it the "principal and decisive objection against endurance," and in favor of perdurantism.

To see the problem, note that among the different properties that material objects possess, some of these appear to be intrinsic properties. When we speak of **intrinsic properties**, we mean properties objects have just in virtue of how they are in themselves, not how they are in relation to other things. Lewis takes shapes and sizes to be paradigm cases of intrinsic properties. When we speak of an object being spherical or a cube or we say it has a certain volume, we are not thereby relating it to other objects that exist, as we might if we said the object was a father or married or that it was located on the surface of the moon. As Lewis notes, many of the intrinsic properties that objects possess are had only temporarily by the objects that instantiate them. To use his own case, it happens at certain times that he (Lewis) is standing and thus has a straight shape; it happens at other times that he is sitting and so has a bent shape.

Problem of temporary intrinsics: a problem raised for endurantism by David Lewis, who argued that the endurantist cannot account for change in an object's intrinsic properties.

Intrinsic properties: properties objects have just in virtue of how they are in themselves, not how they are in relation to other things.

But this raises a problem for endurantism.[6] Recall that the endurantist thinks that when an object persists from a time t_1 to a later time t_2, this is because there is one object wholly present at both times t_1 and t_2. Let's consider the case in which Lewis changes his shape by sitting down. Call the object that is wholly present at t_1: L_1. Call the object that is wholly present at t_2: L_2. According to the endurantist, if Lewis persists from t_1 to t_2, if he can persist through this change in shape, then this will be because $L_1=L_2=$Lewis. But if $L_1=L_2$, then it cannot be the case that Lewis is straight at t_1 and bent, i.e., not straight, at t_2. This would entail a violation of Leibniz's law. The same thing cannot both have and lack the same property. So if endurantism is true, then this means that no persisting object can ever undergo a change in its intrinsic properties. This would always involve a violation of Leibniz's law.

Lewis considers a couple of ways an endurantist might try to avoid this problem, although neither of them is, he thinks, satisfactory. One thing an endurantist might do is endorse presentism, the view considered in Chapter 5 that only the present is real. If presentism is true, then we may avoid contradiction by saying that actually nothing is ever both straight and not straight even if endurantism is true and objects change their intrinsic properties. The presentist will say that at t_1, Lewis is straight and not bent. Lewis *will be* bent when he sits down. But he is not bent since only what is present exists. And the presentist can say at t_2, there is also no tension with Leibniz's law, since at this point Lewis is bent and not straight. Lewis *was* straight, but he isn't straight. As it turns out, many endurantists are presentists (even if not primarily for this reason!) and so this is indeed a response to the problem that will be attractive to many an endurantist.

This is not something Lewis himself finds attractive. He says this is a solution that:

> rejects persistence altogether ... in saying that there are no other times ... it goes against what we all believe. No man, unless it be at the moment of his execution, believes that he has no future; still less does anyone believe that he has no past.
>
> (Lewis 1986, p. 204)

The presentist will of course reject the implication that the view goes against what we all believe. She may concede that it is true that there exists no future or past moments. But she does of course allow that many of us *will* live to do many things. (In the future, a different moment will be present.) And she will allow that for all of us that we *did* exist. (Again, these times are now unreal, but were real when we were living them.) And this should be enough to capture what we ordinarily mean when we say we have a future or a past.

A second endurantist response Lewis considers involves maintaining eternalism, but instead reinterpreting how we think of properties like shapes. This endurantist will say that we might have thought that shapes were intrinsic properties, but really these properties hide more fundamental relations. Objects only have shapes relative to times. And so, strictly speaking, Lewis does not ever have the intrinsic property of being straight; there is no such property. Instead, Lewis has the relational property of being straight-at-t_1. He also has the relational property of being bent-at-t_2. He may therefore lack the property of being straight-at-t_2, but this doesn't entail that he lacks the property of being straight-at-t_1, and so there is no conflict with Leibniz's law.

There is much to say about this response and, again, this is a response that has been taken up by endurantists to solve the problem of temporary intrinsics. Lewis himself calls the view "incredible," saying, "if we know what shape is, we know that it is a property not a relation" (1986, p. 204).

There is certainly something to be said on Lewis's behalf. It seems like an object's shape is just a fact about it. It doesn't seem at all to involve a relation to a time, like the property of being late or beginning at noon. But maybe we can concede that shapes are intrinsic properties while at the same time allowing that they may involve relations to times. This is a possibility Sally Haslanger has considered. First let's understand a monadic property as one that is best represented in logical notation as 'Mx,' as opposed to as 'Mxy,' as we typically understand relations. It is a property that an object has on its own, but not in virtue of standing in a relation to another object. Haslanger argues:

> Relations to times are exactly the sort of relations that may plausibly count as intrinsic. For example, consider two balls, b and b*, that are intrinsic duplicates. Plausibly intrinsic duplicates can exist at different times, so suppose b exists at t and b* exists at t*. Now suppose b and b* differ in their relational properties, e.g. b is red at t, but b* is not red at t*, or b is 3 inches in diameter at t but b* is not 3 inches in diameter at t*. Surely, contrary to our original supposition, we should not count the balls as intrinsic duplicates even if they only vary in the relational ways just indicated; but if the balls must be alike in certain relational respects in order to be intrinsic duplicates, then it is plausible to say that their intrinsic nature is not captured by their monadic properties. Conversely, suppose that no temporary properties are monadic (namely, all temporary properties are relations to times), but x and y stand in all the same two-placed relations to their respective times (so where one is red at t, the other is red at t'; where one is 3 inches diameter at t, the other is 3 inches diameter at t', etc.). Is it not plausible that they are intrinsic duplicates?

> (Haslanger 2003, p. 330)

So there is a case to be made, even if one concedes that the endurantist must reinterpret shapes as relations to times, that shapes and sizes and other temporary properties are still, in an important sense, intrinsic properties.

As we have noted, Lewis prefers neither of these responses to the problem of temporary intrinsics. A much more straightforward response in his view is to give up on endurantism altogether and embrace perdurantism. If we are perdurantists, then there is no problem in saying that Lewis is straight at t_1 and not straight at t_2 because what this really comes to for the perdurantist is Lewis having one temporal part that is straight and a distinct temporal part that is not straight. There is thus no violation of Leibniz's law. Shapes are intrinsic properties (and not relations to times), but they are intrinsic properties of temporal parts. Objects like us can persist through change in our intrinsic properties because, according to Lewis, only part of a person exists at any given time and there is no incoherence in an object having one part that has a feature and another part that lacks that feature. My right arm may be bent, while my left arm is straight.

This is a solution to the problem of temporary intrinsics that many are happy with. It doesn't involve relativizing properties to times or denying eternalism. But some four dimensionalists have pointed out that there may be a better way to solve the problem. This is by embracing an alternative four-dimensionalist theory of persistence: what is known as the stage view or **exdurantism**.

The exdurantist, like the perdurantist, believes in the existence of temporal parts. He believes in all of the material objects the perdurantist does. However, he will note, if one wants to capture the idea that *it is Lewis* who is bent at one time and straight at another, the perdurantist does not succeed. Lewis after all is not really ever bent *or* straight on this view. It is only his temporal parts that have these features.

Exdurantism (the stage view): identifies the familiar material objects we ordinarily think of as persisting with temporary stages.

What the exdurantism offers is the view that Lewis is not to be identified with the temporally extended material object that *has* parts that are bent or straight. Instead, according to the exdurantist, Lewis *is* one of these parts that is bent or straight. Lewis is a temporary stage. Which stage the name 'Lewis' refers to will depend on features of the context in which the name is being used. Theodore Sider originally defended this position in a paper titled "All the World's a Stage."

Note that the difference between the perdurantist and exdurantist is not one in ontology. In principle, both the perdurantists and exdurantists can

---

BOX 6.1

The Stage View vs. the Worm View

Exdurantism is called the stage view because it identifies the familiar material objects we ordinarily think of as persisting with temporary stages. People, statues, dogs and cats, stars and planets, these are all stages according to the exdurantist. To distinguish it from the stage view, perdurantism is often called the worm view. This is because the perdurantist thinks of ordinary material objects like people or statues as four-dimensional space–time worms extended not just over space, but over time as well.

Worm theory/perdurantism

Stage theory/exdurantism

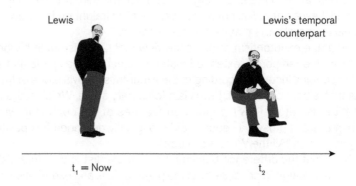

Figure 6.4 The Stage Theory and the Worm Theory

hold the same view about composition. If so, they will believe in all of the same entities and agree about which entities are temporal or spatial parts of which others. The difference between the two views has only to do with which of these entities are the ordinary, familiar objects we ordinarily think about and have names for, like 'David Lewis' or 'the Eiffel Tower' or 'the planet Venus.' The perdurantist thinks that objects like this are temporally extended objects possessing temporal parts. The exdurantist thinks they are all temporary stages.

EXERCISE 6.3

Exdurantism and the Problem of Temporary Intrinsics

Do you agree with the exdurantist that his view provides a better solution to the problem of temporary intrinsics than Lewis's own preferred perdurantism? Is Lewis forced to say when one says "Lewis is straight at t_1," or "Lewis is bent at t_2" that what is said is literally false? Explain your answer.

EXDURANTISM

That it is supposed to do a better job at solving the problem of temporary intrinsics is one reason Sider thinks we should prefer exdurantism to perdurantism or endurantism. Sider also thinks the view does better at explaining what to say about cases in which space–time worms overlap. Recall in the case of the Ship of Theseus, the perdurantist was forced to say that in a real sense there are two ships present at the initial time. S_1 is a part of two ships, the Ship of Theseus-A (that contains S_2 as a later part) and the Ship of Theseus-B (that contains S_3) as a later part. And so if we ask at that time, how many ships are present according to the perdurantist, it would seem the right answer is "Two." However Sider notes, both sides concede (indeed it is an important part of the perdurantist's view) that there is only one stage there, S_1. If ships are not extended space–time worms, but instead temporary stages as the exdurantist argues, then the answer to "How many ships are present?" at that time will be "One." And this seems to be the better answer.

So there are some reasons to think exdurantism might do a better job even than perdurantism at solving the puzzles of change we have discussed in this chapter. One might nonetheless have qualms about exdurantism. Primarily, there is a question about whether it even constitutes a genuine theory of persistence. Persistence seems by definition to involve an object's existing at multiple times. The endurantist and perdurantist offer rival views about what this comes to. But the stage theorist, in identifying familiar objects with temporary stages, would seem to deny that any of the objects we are ordinarily interested in discussing ever persist over time.

In response to this concern, the exdurantist typically adopts the strategy of semantic ascent. Strictly speaking, her metaphysical view does entail that ordinary objects like people, buildings, and planets exist only momentarily. However, she can give a theory that explains why sentences we ordinarily assert that appear to require these objects' existing over extended temporal durations are nonetheless true.

Consider the following example. The planet Venus exists now. Most of us believe that the planet Venus has existed for many millions of years and will continue to exist in the future, at least for the next hundred years. But, if one is an exdurantist, then strictly speaking one has to deny this. Strictly speaking it is false that the planet Venus has existed for millions of years since the planet Venus, according to the exdurantist, is a temporary stage. Nonetheless, the exdurantist is able to offer us a paraphrase of our ordinary claims that appear to assert otherwise. We may say, for example:

(1) The planet Venus will survive for the next hundred years.

Here is how the perdurantist and endurantist will understand what this comes to:

($1_{Perdurantist}$) The planet Venus has a temporal part that exists a hundred years from now.

($1_{Endurantist}$) The same entity, the planet Venus, that exists now will exist a hundred years from now.

The exdurantist thinks both of these claims are false, but what is true is the following:

($1_{Exdurantist}$) There exists a stage a hundred years from now that bears the temporal counterpart relation to the planet Venus.

And this can ground the truth of our original sentence (1).

According to the exdurantist, the planet Venus is a temporary stage. But the exdurantist does think there are other stages in the future and in the past, many of which bear interesting relations to Venus. These other stages are similar in many ways to Venus — have the same size, shape, physical makeup, velocity, a similar position. In addition, these other stages bear causal relations to Venus. The past stages are causally responsible for the way Venus is now. The later stages are affected by what Venus does now. If one were a perdurantist, one would say this is because these earlier and later stages are temporal parts of Venus. The exdurantist says this instead makes these earlier and later stages temporal **counterparts** of Venus. They are not parts of Venus itself, but instead distinct objects that bear salient similarity and causal relations to Venus. And, it is in virtue of the existence and nature of these counterparts that sentences like (1) are true.

Counterpart: a counterpart of one entity x is an entity that bears some salient similarity and causal relations to x.

What goes for the planet Venus goes for other familiar objects as well. According to exdurantism, you are a stage as well. And this means that strictly speaking, your childhood memories concern things that happened to other people, other stages in the past. Still because these other stages bear salient similarity and causal relations to you, they are similar to you in various ways. You are the way you are today because of the way they were then, they are your counterparts. And so if one of these stages took piano lessons, it is in virtue of this fact that the following sentence will be true:

(2) You took piano lessons when you were young.

And if a future counterpart of yours will take a trip to Israel in the next twenty years, then it is in virtue of this fact that the following sentence is true:

(3) You will travel to Israel at some time in the next twenty years.

According to the exdurantist, people are stages, and as stages they only exist for an instant. Still the exdurantist has a particular metaphysical explanation available for sentences we assert that look superficially to require a person's extended existence over a period of time. So, although strictly speaking for the exdurantist, people and other familiar objects are temporary, he will say it is true that they persist. Facts about their persistence are grounded in the existence of counterparts in the future and the past.

EXERCISE 6.4

Exdurantism and Temporal Counterparts

According to the exdurantist, could it be true that any person is 30 years old? How could this be if the exdurantist believes we are all temporary stages?

DEFENDING THREE DIMENSIONALISM

For most of this chapter, we have considered the case in favor of the two four-dimensionalist views, perdurantism and exdurantism. But is there anything to be said for endurantism in its defense? Endurantism is frequently characterized as the commonsense view on the nature of persistence. Before we think too hard about the puzzles of material constitution, about Leibniz's law, and temporary intrinsics, this view may certainly seem plausible: that the me that exists now, just at this time right here, is the same as, is strictly and numerically identical to, the me that existed yesterday and the day before. Many philosophers will concede that common sense counts for something in metaphysics. What we will examine here is whether there is anything more to be said in defense of endurantism.

Indeed there is. What we will do here is outline two interesting ways in which metaphysicians have defended endurantism against its four-dimensionalist rivals. The first way involves calling into question the very notion of a temporal part of a material object. Perdurantists believe that objects persist over time by possessing temporal parts at each time they exist. Exdurantists (stage theorists) identify ordinary, familiar objects like people and planets with temporary parts of larger objects. If one denies material objects ever have temporal parts, one is thereby denying four dimensionalism in either form.

Peter van Inwagen and David Wiggins are two metaphysicians who have denied that it makes sense to think of material objects as possessing temporal parts. To one seeing this debate for the first time, one might be confused how this could be. Isn't the analogy with spatial parts sufficient to make this clear? What could these philosophers not be understanding? Let's consider Wiggins first.

Wiggins, in his *Sameness and Substance Renewed* (2001), insists that four dimensionalism is confused. For Wiggins, it is not even an answer to the question we are interested in about how objects persist over time. The conceptual problem for Wiggins isn't in understanding the notion of a temporal part per se. Rather the problem is in understanding the notion of a temporal part of a material object. Wiggins has no problem conceding that other types of entities, in particular, events, have temporal parts. He argues:

> An event takes time, and will admit the question 'How long did it last?' only in the sense 'How long did it take?'. An event does not persist in the way in which a continuant does – that is *through* time, gaining and losing new parts. A continuant has spatial parts. To find the whole continuant you have only to explore its boundaries at a time. An event has temporal parts. To find the whole event you must trace it through the historical beginning to the historical end.
>
> (Wiggins 2001, p. 31)

This passage is vivid. You may imagine examining any object, your cellphone, your best friend, and asking what are its boundaries, where is she wholly located. If it is easy to see how you might at a time examine one of these objects and feel satisfied that you have located its boundaries, even though you have only examined it at one time, then you understand Wiggins's point. If all of an object's boundaries can be discerned at one time, then it cannot be an object extended in time, for then it would have more parts, and a boundary that you cannot see.

In his paper "Temporal Parts and Identity across Time" (2000), van Inwagen expresses puzzlement as well about attributing temporal parts to material objects. Van Inwagen doesn't claim to have a problem understanding how there could be what he calls a 'person stage.' There could be a person who exists just for a short time and then goes out of existence. What he doesn't understand is how such things could be parts of ordinary people like you or me:

> God could, I suppose, create *ex nihilo*, and annihilate a year later, a human being whose intrinsic properties at any instant during the year of its existence were identical with the intrinsic properties of, say, Descartes at the "corresponding" instant in, say, the year 1625.

BOX 6.2

Extended Simples

Throughout this chapter, we have sometimes spoken of objects *being extended* through space and/or time and objects *having parts* in various places and/or times. It is fine generally, when we are talking about ordinary, material objects, to run these two notions together. However, it is worth briefly mentioning that to say an object is extended (through space or time) is not to say the same thing as to say that it has spatial or temporal parts. To say that something is extended in space or time is to say that it occupies a greater than point-sized location in space or time. Tennis balls, which are spheres with diameter 6.7 cm, are extended. Electrons, when they are assumed to be point particles, are not extended.

To see that there is a genuine distinction here, we may note the conceptual possibility of objects that are (spatially) extended simples. These are entities extended in space, but lacking spatial parts. Ordinarily when we think of objects that are spatially extended, we think of them as having parts. For example, tennis balls are made up of bits of rubber and felt. However, it is conceivable that there be spatially extended objects that lack parts. As Kris McDaniel has pointed out in his essay "Extended Simples" (2007), the strings of string theory appear to be examples of extended simples. These are postulated to be fundamental physical objects, not made of any smaller parts. And yet they are claimed to have spatial extension, extension not just in the familiar three dimensions of our ordinary experience, but in additional "hidden" dimensions as well.

And if God could do that, he could certainly create and annihilate a second human being whose one-year career corresponded in the same way to the 1626-part of Descartes's career. But could God, so to speak, lay these two creations end-to-end . . . Well, he could create, and two years later annihilate, a human being whose two-year career corresponded to the 1625/1626-part of Descartes's career . . . What I cannot see is how, if God did this, it could be that the "two-year-man" would have first and second "halves." More exactly, I don't see how it could be that the first half of a two-year-man's career could be the career of anything, and I don't see how it could be that the second half of the two-year-man's career could be the career of anything. When I examine the story of the creation and annihilation of the two-year-man, I don't find anything that comes to the end of its existence after one year: the only thing "there" (as I see matters), the two-year-man, will not come to an end after one year; he will rather, continue to exist for another year. And, in the same way, when I examine the story, I don't find anything in it that begins to exist halfway through story.

(van Inwagen 2000, p. 446)

This story begins to capture what troubles van Inwagen about the existence of temporal parts. There may be temporarily existing objects and then there are stages in a sense, but this doesn't entail any temporal *parts*. Once there is a larger whole that is a person, then it is hard to see how anything at a time that also appears to be a person is not that whole thing.

EXERCISE 6.5

Van Inwagen's Argument against Four Dimensionalism

Reconstruct van Inwagen's argument in numbered premise form. Which part of this argument would you object to if you wished to defend perdurantism?

So, on the one hand there are conceptual worries about the very thought that objects like people and tables have temporal parts. There are also worries about the four dimensionalist's ability to provide a compelling and coherent account of persistence and change. One thing some three dimensionalists press, something one finds in Wiggins and also the work of Haslanger, is that in denying strict identity over time the four dimensionalist is denying the whole phenomenon of persistence in the first place. For is an object really *persisting* over time if there is not one, numerically the same thing that is present at one time and then also present at a later time? To come back to the discussion in the first section, what the four-dimensionalist theories present us with appears more like the destruction and generation of a succession of temporary objects, rather than the continued persistence of some one object over time. Since temporal parts are confined to instants, they are not strictly identical from one time to the next. And so they do not persist. But then nothing persists according to the four dimensionalist.

We have seen the exdurantist's response to this problem. They semantically ascend and provide an account of the truth conditions of sentences about persistence in terms of the future or past existence of an object's temporal counterparts. Perdurantists also have a response. They think it is in virtue of objects' possessing temporal parts at successive times that they persist. In addition, the perdurantist will note that it is true for her, just as it is for the endurantist, that there is one thing that survives in the strict sense of being identical to itself over time – this is a temporally extended, four-dimensional space–time worm. Whether this is enough to satisfy the endurantist is another matter.

SUGGESTIONS FOR FURTHER READING

For two defenses of four dimensionalism, see Theodore Sider's *Four Dimensionalism* and Mark Heller's *The Ontology of Physical Objects: Four-Dimensional Hunks of Matter.* The collection, *Persistence: Contemporary Readings,* edited by Sally Haslanger and Roxanne Marie Kurtz contains many essential readings. Katherine Hawley's article, "Temporal Parts," in the *Stanford Encyclopedia of Philosophy* is another excellent resource and contains an extensive bibliography. For more on intrinsic properties, see "Defining 'Intrinsic'" by Rae Langton and David Lewis.

NOTES

1   We did see how denying the existence of most of these material objects, as the mereological nihilist or van Inwagen does, will allow us to escape the problems.
2   Most explicitly, this is a key component of the theory proposed in Kathrin Koslicki's *The Structure of Objects.*
3   Perhaps Lump does not have to exist at *each* time along the way from t_0 to t_3 in order to persist from t_0 to t_3. Perhaps objects can have *gappy* histories, flickering in and out along the way. This is a metaphysical issue we will set aside in this chapter.
4   As we noted in Chapter 3, to say something is extended in space is not the same as to say it has parts in different spatial regions. We considered there the possibility of extended simples. Similarly, we should note that to say some thing is extended in time is not the same as to say it has parts at different times. Still, since in most cases what is extended in space or time has parts at different spatial or temporal locations, we will move back and forth between talk of extension and talk of mereological complexity. See Box 6.2.
5   There will additionally be an object that includes all three of S_1, S_2, and S_3 as parts, but since this is not a candidate for being a ship (since at certain times it is the mereological sum of two ship-stages rather than a single ship-stage), we will ignore this object.
6   As we saw in the first section, the fact that objects may come to change their properties is a classic problem recognized by the ancient Greek philosophers. Lewis turns this into a distinctive problem for the endurantist by focusing on the case of objects' changes in their *intrinsic* properties.

CHAPTER 7

Modality

Learning Points

- Introduces the modal notions of necessity, possibility, and contingency
- Introduces the distinction between de re and de dicto modality
- Presents several reductive theories of modality
- Evaluates the prospects for essentialism, a thesis about de re modality.

POSSIBILITY AND NECESSITY: MODES OF TRUTH

Modal claims: those that express facts about what is possible, impossible, necessary, or contingent.

Contingent: what is neither necessary nor impossible.

In this chapter, we examine modal claims. **Modal claims** express facts not about what merely happens to be the case or what things are actually like, but involve the notions of possibility or necessity. They concern what is possible or impossible; what is necessary or contingent (where something is **contingent** if it is neither necessary nor impossible).

We use the concepts of possibility and necessity all of the time. These concepts are key components of many metaphysical claims as well. But on the face of it, it isn't clear what claims involving these notions mean and in virtue of what they may be true or false. Modal claims don't describe how things actually are, so how can they express facts about our world? Wittgenstein famously claimed that the best way to understand necessity was to see necessarily true claims as nonfactual, as not expressing facts about how the world is, but instead stating our conventions about what we are disposed to take as irrefutable. In this chapter, we will encounter some of the more influential ways of understanding modal claims in contemporary metaphysics. Most metaphysicians want to hold on to the factuality of claims about what is necessary and possible. They then attempt to reduce modal statements to statements that are more easily capable of being understood.

BOX 7.1

Modes of Truth

Modal claims concern modes of truth or falsity. A proposition or sentence may be:

possibly true: (e.g., that Abigail Adams was the first president of the United States)

impossible, or necessarily false: (e.g., that 2+2=5)

contingent, or both possibly true and possibly false: (e.g., that George Washington was the first president of the United States)

necessarily true: (e.g., that 2+2=4).

SPECIES OF POSSIBILITY AND NECESSITY

There are several senses of possibility and necessity in which one might be interested. For example, we might ask:

Is it possible to build a vehicle that travels faster than the speed of light?

Philosophers generally recognize at least two senses of the word 'possible' that would give two different answers to this question. One sense is: possible according to the laws of nature, or **nomologically possible** (from the Latin *nomos* for law). If the laws of nature don't rule out that a certain proposition p is the case, then p is nomologically possible. In this sense of 'possible,' the answer to our question is 'no.' It is not possible to build a vehicle that travels faster than the speed of light. This is something that the laws of nature, Special Relativity in particular, rule out.

> **Nomological possibility or necessity**: possibility or necessity according to the laws of nature.

On the other hand, there is another sense of 'possible.' Here, a proposition is possible just in case it doesn't itself entail any contradiction. This is what is often called **logical possibility**. This was the sense of 'possible' we used when we defined the notion of deductive validity and said that an argument is valid just in case it is not possible for its premises to all be true while its conclusion is false. It is logically impossible that 2+2=5 or that there are triangles that have four sides. It is logically impossible as well for there to be any round squares, married bachelors, or dogs that are not dogs.[1] In this sense of 'possible,' cars traveling faster than the speed of light are possible. Even if such technology is incompatible with the laws of nature, and so physics would have to be different for there to be cars traveling faster than light speed at our world, there is no contradiction contained in

> **Logical possibility**: what does not entail any contradiction.

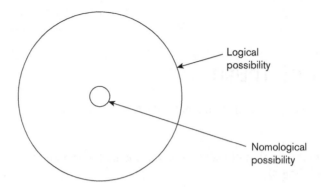

Figure 7.1 Nomological and Logical Possibility

the very idea of a car that can travel at superluminal speeds. This is ruled out by the laws of physics, but not by the laws of logic (and meaning).

We can picture these distinct senses of possibility using the diagram in Figure 7.1, since the propositions that are nomologically possible are a subset of those that are logically possible. Anything that is possible in any sense is at least logically possible. For this reason, it is often referred to as 'possibility in the widest sense of the term.'

EXERCISE 7.1

Nomological and Logical Possibility

For each of the following propositions, decide whether it is nomologically possible, logically possible, both, or neither.

A. Somebody eats a dinosaur for breakfast.
B. There is an object that weighs exactly 5 grams and exactly 7 grams at the same time.
C. There is an electron that is both positively charged and negatively charged at the same time.
D. There exists a unicorn.
E. There exists a cat that is made entirely of silicon.
F. There is a mind that exists without a body.

De dicto modality: concerns the modal status of propositions (or dictums), whether they are possible, necessary, or contingent.

So far we have been talking about the modal status of propositions. Some are necessary, some contingent; some possible, some impossible. This sort of modality is what is called **de dicto modality**. Here we are discussing the status of a proposition or a dictum, hence 'dicto.' But we could also ask about the modal features of objects themselves. We could ask, for example, about whether a certain basketball player has the possibility of being traded to another team. Or we could ask whether a martini is necessarily made of gin. A historically interesting position in metaphysics is that objects have certain properties that hold of them necessarily, so-called **essential properties** or **essences**. For example, if you are a Platonist and believe in entities like numbers, it is natural to think that the number 3 has certain essential features: it is necessarily prime, it is necessarily odd. It also has certain contingent features, such as numbering the moons of Pluto. More controversial is the issue of whether material objects like tables, chairs, or organisms have essential features. Was it only a contingent feature of Socrates that he was wise? Or was Socrates essentially wise? Are penguins essentially birds? Are persons essentially rational, thinking creatures, or could there be a human who was not rational? We'll discuss these issues later in the chapter. For now, we will just distinguish the issues of **de dicto modality**, concerning which propositions are necessary or contingent, possible or impossible, from the issues of **de re modality**, concerning which properties, if any, are had essentially or contingently or possibly by which objects. This is called 'de re' modality from the Latin for 'thing': *res*.

Essential properties (essences): properties that hold of an individual by necessity that make them the kinds of things they are.

De re modality: concerns the modal status of features of individuals, such as whether a certain feature of an individual is essential or contingent.

THE POSSIBLE WORLDS ANALYSIS OF MODALITY

We will begin by trying to understand better the phenomenon of de dicto modality which is to some extent less controversial, and then in the last sections of this chapter we will return to the issue of de re modality.

Let's start with a simple example of a modal truth to see where the main issues in the metaphysics of modality lie. There is a common expression used to discuss something that is unlikely to happen, 'when pigs fly.' Now pigs don't actually fly, but it's possible that they could. They might fly if they had wings. And there is no contradiction contained in the very idea of a pig with wings. That is, the proposition expressed by the following sentence is possibly true (in the sense of logical possibility):

(1) Pigs have wings.

And its being possible means the following is just plain true:

(2) It is possible that pigs have wings.

The central question that bothers metaphysicians is what it could be in virtue of which a sentence like (2) is true. Is there any way to understand (2) in terms that do not involve modal notions? Or does (2) just express a brute fact?

To take another example, we have seen that there are certain features of reality that couldn't be different than they actually are. For example, it is necessary that triangles have three sides. In other words, the proposition expressed by the following sentence seems necessarily true:

(3) Triangles have three sides.

And in virtue of its being necessarily true, the following is just plain true:

(4) Necessarily, triangles have three sides.

But again, what is the content of the 'necessarily' in this sentence? Is there a way to explain the truth of (4) in non-modal terms?

We want to talk about the metaphysics of modality. Following the methodology we have used in this book, it should be no surprise that most metaphysicians first approach the topic of modality by looking at the correct way to symbolize modal truths in first-order logic. There is a branch of logic that was developed in the early twentieth century to represent modal claims and assess the validity of arguments involving them: **modal logic**. Modal logic introduces new sentential operators to represent the possibility or necessity of individual propositions.[2] It was initially developed in the 1920s and 1930s by the philosopher and logician C.I. Lewis (1883–1964) as a form of propositional logic. In the 1940s, Ruth Barcan Marcus (1921–2012) and Rudolf Carnap, working independently, extended Lewis's modal logic to include first-order quantification. Today, the most commonly used notation is the diamond, ◊, for representing possibility and the box, □, for representing necessity. So, for example, we might write:

> **Modal logic**: the branch of logic that represents modal claims.

◊ (Pigs fly)

or

◊ ∃x (Px ∧ Fx),

and

□ (Triangles have three sides)

or

□ ∀x (Tx ⊃ Sx).

If you take a course in modal logic, you will learn new rules that will allow you to prove the validity of arguments using the □ and ◊. You will learn that there is an equivalence between □A and ¬◊¬A for any sentence A. You will also learn that even in the weakest systems of modal logic, if A is a theorem in that system, that is, if A is a logical truth, then so is □A.

EXERCISE 7.2

Symbolizing Modal Claims Using the Box and Diamond

Using the key below, symbolize the following sentences using the notation of modal logic. Remember to bind all variables to quantifier expressions.

Mx: x is married
Bx: x is a bachelor
Dx: x drinks cocktails

A. Married bachelors are impossible.
B. Necessarily, all bachelors are unmarried.
C. There exists someone who is a bachelor, and is necessarily unmarried.
D. It is possible that there exists a bachelor who drinks cocktails.
E. It is a contingent fact that some bachelors drink cocktails.

We won't worry about proving anything in modal logic here. Instead what we will do is try to better understand what makes sentences using these modal operators true or false. In plain first-order predicate logic, we understood the truth conditions for our sentences to be given rather straightforwardly. For example, in a language where the name 'a' is assigned to Alice and 'Fx' stands for the predicate 'x is friendly,' we could understand what it would be for 'Fa' or '∃x¬Fx' to be true. 'Fa' is true just in case Alice is friendly. '∃x¬Fx' is true just in case there exists at least one person who is not friendly. But what does the world have to be like for '◊∃xFx' to be true? If Alice is friendly, this would seem to be enough to make '◊∃xFx' true. If Alice is friendly, then someone is friendly, and so it must be at least possible that someone is friendly. (What is actual can't be impossible.) But what if it turned out that no person who actually existed was friendly? It still seems the modal claim '◊∃xFx' would be true. There isn't any contradiction after all in the very idea of a friendly person. So, we need to have a more general understanding of what it takes to make modal claims asserting possibility true, one that could make '◊∃xFx' true even if no one was actually friendly.

One common way of understanding modal claims today is what is called the **possible worlds analysis of modality**. This view has historical origins tracing back to the work of Leibniz. It can be boiled down to two claims:

'◊A' is true iff there is a possible world in which 'A' is true.[3]
'□A' is true iff 'A' is true at all possible worlds.

Possible worlds analysis of modality: an analysis of claims about possibility and necessity in terms of what is true at various possible worlds (including the actual world).

So, according to the possible worlds analysis of modality, 'It is possible that someone is friendly' will be true just in case there is at least one possible world in which someone is friendly. There doesn't have to be any actually existing friendly person, just some friendly person at some possible world.

Similarly, according to the possible worlds analysis of modality, 'it's necessary that there are no round squares' is true because 'there are no round squares' is true at all possible worlds. There is no possible world that has a round square.

As I said, the possible worlds analysis is a very common way of understanding modal claims today. However, to a metaphysician, this analysis should immediately raise some eyebrows. What are these possible worlds? Are these worlds supposed to be literally existing alternative universes? If so, by saying the possible worlds analysis of modality is extremely common, am I saying that just by accepting the truth of 'Possibly, someone is friendly,' most philosophers thereby commit themselves to the existence of alternative universes?

The short answer is "it depends what you mean by 'universe.'" Some metaphysicians think they have a special way of understanding possible worlds so that they aren't literal universes. This is tricky and controversial, but first let's consider what has for the past thirty years or so been the most provocative and hotly debated view about modality: David Lewis's view that the possible worlds appealed to in the possible worlds analysis of modality are literal universes, just as real as our own universe. This view is called **modal realism**.

Modal realism: the view that in addition to the actual world, there exist other alternative universes, possible worlds, just as real as our own; and that it is in virtue of the nature of these universes that our modal claims are true or false.

Lewis defended this view most famously in his 1986 book *On the Plurality of Worlds*. Here he defines a world as a "maximally connected space–time region." Anything that is spatiotemporally connected to us is a part of our world. And so when he uses the word 'world,' he doesn't mean something as small as our own planet Earth, but instead everything that exists at any space–time distance from us. This will include all of the other planets, and indeed the rest of what we usually call our universe.

Each other world lies in its own space–time. Worlds for him are concrete[4] and exist in the same sense as our world. Cars, planets, and people at these other worlds are no less real than those at our own world. They aren't ideas in our mind or fictions. For this reason, to say that our world is actual and the others are merely possible is just to say that the parts of those other worlds are not contained in our own space–time. For Lewis, 'actual' is an indexical term like 'I' or 'here': what is actual for one depends on one's own perspective. It depends on what is the case in one's own space–time.

There is certainly one thing that is appealing about Lewis's modal realism. This is how clear an analysis of modality it provides. If you want to know what makes it true that it is possible that pigs could fly, his answer is simple. This proposition is true because there literally are flying pigs at some other possible world, some space–time disconnected from our own. And if you want to know what makes it true that necessarily triangles have three sides, again his answer is clear. It is because at every single world, every space–time region, ours and all of the others, there never exists a triangle with anything other than three sides.

Figure 7.2 The Incredulous Stare

Despite its clarity, Lewis recognizes that his view will strike many as far-fetched. In a famous passage in *On the Plurality of Worlds*, Lewis notes the one objection to his view he cannot answer is the "incredulous stare." Nonetheless he insists that however crazy this view may sound, he has excellent reasons to believe it. This is because of the vast amount of theoretical work his concrete possible worlds are able to do. Let's say a little bit about that.

Lewis calls his plurality of worlds a "philosophers' paradise." It is a philosophers' paradise because, he notes, once one believes in the genuine existence of alternative possible worlds, one is able to exploit them in analyses that help us understand scores of otherwise perplexing phenomena. The big three phenomena on which we will focus are: (1) modality, (2) properties, and (3) content. However this is really the tip of the iceberg, because once one has an account of these three, lots of other phenomena that have been interesting and puzzling to philosophers are much easier to understand.

Let's start with modality. We have already seen that modal realism gives us a way to adopt the possible worlds analysis of modality and interpret it literally thus demystifying modal talk. A modal realist is able to understand the box and diamond of modal logic as disguised quantifiers, quantifying over possible universes. If we let our variable w range over possible worlds, then:

'◊A' may be understood in the same way as: ∃w (A is true at w).
'□A' may be understood in the same way as: ∀w (A is true at w).

But there are several other modal notions that belief in possible worlds can help one analyze as well. For example, we think that some propositions are contingent; in other words, it is possible that they are true and also possible that they are not true. For example, we think it is a contingent fact that

Manchester United wears red uniforms. It is possible (because it is actual) that they wear red uniforms. But it is also possible that they didn't wear red, but uniforms of a different color, say, green. Contingency can now be analyzed as:

A is contingent just in case ∃w (A is true at w) and ∃w (A is not true at w).

There are also special sorts of claims, counterfactuals, that Lewis's analysis can help us better understand. Counterfactuals are conditional claims that assert what would have been had things been different. For example, consider:

If the World Trade Center attack hadn't happened, then airport security would have been weaker.

We can use the symbol '□→' to represent this sort of conditional, where:

'A□→B' may be read as: If A were the case, then B would be the case.

Counterfactual:
a conditional asserting what would have been the case had things gone differently than how we suppose they actually go.

Then, supposing A did occur, the **counterfactual** '¬A□→B' may be read as:

If A hadn't happened, then B would be the case.

Lewis, and also the philosopher Robert Stalnaker, proposed analyses of counterfactual conditionals that appealed to what is true at the worlds that are most similar to the actual world. For example:

'¬A□→B' is true iff in all of the most similar possible worlds to the actual world where A doesn't occur, B occurs.

What Lewis and Stalnaker mean by a 'similar' world is a world that as much as possible contains the same kinds of objects instantiating the same kinds of properties and relations (while making the changes required for A to be false at that world). So, 'If the World Trade Center attack hadn't happened, airport security would have been weaker,' will be true on this analysis just in case in all of the worlds most similar to actuality where the World Trade Center attack never occurs, airport security is weaker.

Similarly, we can use one of Lewis's favorite examples:

If kangaroos had no tails, they'd topple over.

If we assume modal realism and the Lewis–Stalnaker analysis of counterfactuals, then for this to be true, it must be the case that in all of the other universes most similar to our own but where kangaroos don't have tails, the kangaroos topple over.

There are lots of other modal notions we won't have time to discuss here that also get clearly illuminated if one is able to assume the existence of possible worlds: dispositions, supervenience, physicalism, to name a few. One can find much more discussion in chapter 1 of *On the Plurality of Worlds* (Lewis 1986).

Another topic that is illuminated if we are permitted to quantify over other possible worlds is that of properties. In Chapter 2, we discussed class nominalism. This is the view that a property is just the class of its instances. So redness is just the class of red things, wisdom is the class of wise things, and so on. This is a view that will be appealing to those metaphysicians who (perhaps due to the indispensability argument) want to believe in classes, but for one reason or another find the existence of universals hard to swallow.

In that earlier chapter we noted a problem for class nominalism: the objection from coextension. Recall, this was the problem that there seemed to be cases in which two distinct properties have the same extension. This would be the case if, for example, the class of red things turned out to be identical to the class of round things. Even if this were so, we wouldn't want to say that the property of being red and the property of being round were the same property. But if one says a property just is the class of its instances, then in this case redness and roundness would turn out to be the same property. This is a place where Lewis's modal realism can help. If we believe in the existence of objects beyond those in our universe, then we can distinguish these properties. For even if it turns out that all of the red things are actually round, it is possible that there are some red things that aren't round. And this just means for Lewis that there are other possible worlds where there are red things that aren't round things. The class nominalist may then identify properties with the set of all of the objects that actually and possibly instantiate them. Thus our two properties are distinguished. The objection from coextension thus seems to be solved for the class nominalist. This response seems unavailable however if one does not believe in merely possible objects − objects that exist only at other possible worlds.

If we believe in possible worlds, we can also give an interesting account of the content of our thoughts and language. For our purposes here, let's just focus on the content of thoughts. Suppose at a given time t you are ignorant about a certain topic. Say you would like to know but don't yet know in what year the nation of Italy was founded. At this point you believe there is such a nation (Italy) and that it was founded in a certain year, but you don't have any belief about which year in particular it was founded. Here we may describe your state of mind in the following way. You believe you exist in one of the set of possible worlds in which a nation of Italy exists. But you can't narrow down the world you live in any further.

Now suppose you decide to find out when Italy was established as a nation. You look online and find out that Italy was founded in 1861. What this lets you do, one might say, is narrow in more closely on the set of worlds that could be actual according to what you believe. More generally, as one comes to form more and more beliefs, what one does is close in more and more narrowly on the set of worlds that could be the actual world.

Since Lewis is a realist about possible worlds, he can say that the content of one's belief literally is a set of possible worlds at which that

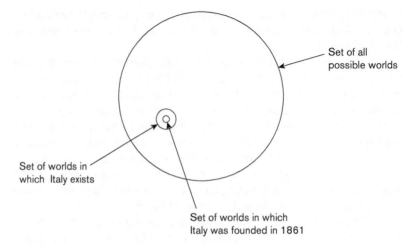

Figure 7.3 The Content of Beliefs as Sets of Possible Worlds

belief is true. The content of the belief that Italy was founded in 1861 is the set of worlds in which Italy was founded in 1861. This belief is true just in case the actual world is a member of this set of worlds. The belief is false just in case the actual world is not a member of this set of worlds. So, in addition to giving us a way to understand (1) modality and (2) the nature of properties, modal realism also gives one (3) an intuitive and clear analysis of mental content.

EXERCISE 7.3

The Content of Beliefs as Sets of Possible Worlds

The theory that the content of a belief is the set of possible worlds at which it is true is initially quite intuitive. It makes sense to many to think that what one is doing as one forms more beliefs is closing in more narrowly on the set of worlds one takes to be the actual world. But there are some difficulties for the view. For example, many take mathematical truths to be necessary. It is a necessary truth that π is an irrational number. There is no possible world in which π is rational.[5] Why would this present a problem for the view that the content of a belief is the set of possible worlds at which it is true? What could a modal realist do to allay the concern?

As I have mentioned, these are only some of the useful theoretical applications of modal realism. Of course it is a bold and controversial claim that there really exist all of these universes distinct from our own, but what

Lewis argues is that the hypothesis of the existence of these worlds lets us do so much explanatory work (in understanding modality, properties, content, and more) that this gives us reason to believe the hypothesis. Like Quine, whose views we considered in the first chapter, Lewis believes that a choice between ontologies should be settled in a way very much analogous to the way choices are made between scientific theories. The metaphysician like the scientist postulates a realm of whatever objects are necessary to achieve explanations that are simple and powerful; he or she seeks out the hypotheses that can explain the most in the fewest possible terms. Lewis makes a good case that just by positing other possible worlds, he can explain an extremely wide range of perplexing theoretical phenomena.

Still, unsurprisingly, most philosophers have not been convinced by Lewis that there really are such things as these other possible universes. And this raises the question of whether there may be an alternative way to understand possible worlds that dials back on the ontological commitments while at the same time manages to achieve all of the explanatory power of Lewis's framework. One strategy is to postulate possible worlds while conceiving them as something other than additional concrete universes. Those who adopt this type of view are called **ersatz modal realists** ('ersatz' means fake). This position, and the challenges it faces, will be the topic of the next section.

Ersatz modal realism: the view that there are possible worlds (worlds that can play a similar role to the concrete worlds of the modal realist), but that these are not additional universes in the same sense as our universe.

BOX 7.2

Modal Realism and the Multiverse

If you are familiar with developments in recent cosmology, you'll notice that Lewis's proposal that there exist a plurality of possible worlds, space–times disconnected from our own with inhabitants just as real as us, bears strong similarities to the sort of multiverse hypotheses defended today in cosmology. Indeed, many think that the most promising account of our early universe, the inflationary hypothesis, straightforwardly entails that there are many universes disconnected from us so that we can never observe them.

There is certainly a similarity between modal realism and the multiverse hypothesis. This is quite interesting given that the reasons Lewis adopted for his hypothesis are philosophical and, many would argue, purely a priori, while the reasons cosmologists have for endorsing their hypothesis are scientific, and many would argue, largely empirical. Still there are real differences between the philosophical proposal of Lewis and these scientific proposals. First, although the alternative universes of contemporary cosmology appear *causally* isolated from one another, they are not genuinely *spatiotemporally* disconnected in the way Lewis's universes are. Moreover, it seems clear that the cosmologist is proposing these extra universes not as alternative possibilities, or ways things might have been, but as additions to how things actually are. These are not mere possibilities according to the inflationary cosmologist, but more parts of actuality. Thus, it is not clear Lewis would be satisfied with them as part of his analysis of modality.

ERSATZ MODAL REALISM

There are many different forms of ersatz modal realism. Alternative versions of the view have been proposed by Peter Forrest, Alvin Plantinga, Robert Stalnaker, and many others. They typically adopt a common strategy; accept the possible worlds analysis of modality (and of counterfactuals, and properties, and content, and so on) but don't think of the worlds figuring in these analyses literally as alternative concrete universes. Instead, they think of these worlds as objects constructed out of things we already believe in as existing at the actual world. The ersatz modal realist will typically construe his or her possible worlds as abstract rather than as concrete entities. In this section we will focus on one very natural way of thinking of these worlds, as linguistic items, sentences (very long sentences) that describe alternative ways things might have been. To find alternative ways philosophers have thought of these ersatz worlds, consult the suggestions for further reading at the end of this chapter.

Because ersatz modal realists construct possible worlds out of things that actually exist, they don't have to believe in anything that is *merely* possible. Ersatz modal realism is thus one way to hold on to **actualism**: the position that everything that exists actually exists. (We will discuss other ways to be an actualist while rejecting ersatz modal realism in the next section.) Actualism contrasts with **possibilism**, the view that there are at least some entities that are merely possible. This is Lewis's position of course since he believes there are some entities that are not actual: all of those things that exist in the space–times disconnected from our own.

The kind of **linguistic ersatzism** (short for 'linguistic ersatz modal realism') we'll discuss here is criticized by Lewis in his book and we'll get to that criticism in a moment but it is worth pointing out first how intuitive the view is. It is not just a way of getting everything Lewis gets without having to buy into the ontological commitments of modal realism; it is also a very natural position on its own. You might ask yourself a second: What does it mean to say that a certain proposition is possible or impossible? For example, what does it mean to say it is possible that there are talking donkeys or impossible that there are round squares? One natural response to these questions is that the former is possible because if you said 'There are talking donkeys' you wouldn't be contradicting yourself despite saying something false, while if you said 'There is a round square,' you would be saying something that involves a contradiction.

Linguistic ersatzism captures this intuition by conceiving of possible worlds as maximal consistent sentences, long conjunctive sentences of the form 'A ∧ B ∧ C ∧ D ∧ . . .' They are maximal in the sense that for any basic or atomic sentence (A, B, C, etc.) in the language in which these sentences are constructed, either it or its negation is contained as a conjunct in that sentence. According to the linguistic ersatzer, a proposition p is possibly true just in case it is true according to some possible world, that is, iff some maximal consistent sentence in the ersatzer's worldmaking language says that p.

Actualism: the view that everything that exists actually exists, nothing is merely possible.

Possibilism: the view that at least some entities are not actual, but merely possible.

Linguistic ersatzism: a form of ersatz modal realism that interprets possible worlds to be sentences or other linguistic entities.

The Linguistic Ersatzer's Way of Understanding the Possible Worlds Analysis of Modality

'◊A' is true iff some maximal consistent sentence in the ersatzer's worldmaking language says that A.

'□A' is true iff every maximal consistent sentence in the ersatzer's worldmaking language says that A.

It is up to the linguistic ersatzer (a) how she wants to think of these sentences, as abstract or concrete, and (b) which language she wants to use to build up her worlds. One thing that will be important is that she has a rich enough language to be able to build up sentences describing all of the possible ways a world might be. An initial obvious problem for the linguistic ersatzer is that she isn't going to be able to use a natural language like English or Japanese to construct her worlds since no natural language has a name for every actual object there is, let alone every possible object there could be.

What we will discuss here is the problem for linguistic ersatzism that Lewis finds most pressing and this is that the view does not, unlike his own view, really provide an analysis of possibility in terms of antecedently understood notions like existence and space–time, but instead presupposes an

---

BOX 7.3

Finding a Worldmaking Language

To find a worldmaking language with enough terms to capture all of what is possible, Lewis suggests that the ersatzer use a language in which all entities of all types function as names for themselves. In *Gulliver's Travels,* Gulliver visits the town of Lagado, where the residents use objects as names for themselves. So, Lewis suggests calling this a 'Lagadonian language.' Using a Lagadonian language, at least the ersatzer will have a name for every actual object or property. This will be enough for some ersatzers. Others may think we need names for not just all of the actual entities but also all of the merely possible entities there could be.[a] This would require more resources than a Lagadonian language has to offer.

Note

a   See Armstrong, *A Combinatorial Theory of Possibility.* Lewis and Armstrong disagree about whether there are genuine possibilities involving alien (i.e. otherworldly, merely possible) properties.

understanding of modality. If this is so, the view cannot solve the problem the metaphysician of modality is aiming at: to explicate what we mean when we say something is possible or impossible, necessary or contingent. To see how linguistic ersatzism fails to analyze but instead presupposes an understanding of possibility, Lewis presents the ersatzer with a dilemma. When she chooses a language in terms of which she will construct her possible worlds, the linguistic ersatzer faces the following choice. On the one hand, she may use what Lewis calls a rich worldmaking language. On the other hand, she may use what Lewis calls a poor worldmaking language. Either way, the ersatzer faces a problem. Let's start with the first option.

To say that the ersatzer is using a rich worldmaking language is to say that her worlds are built up using a language rich enough to state all of the very diverse kind of possibilities we think there are simply and directly. For example, suppose all of the following sentences are possibly true:

(1) There are talking donkeys.
(2) The World Trade Center attack did not occur.
(3) There are unicorns.
(4) Barack Obama is a world-class tennis player.

Suppose these sentences are all actually false, but possibly true. Then, according to the ersatzer, for each of these sentences, there must be a possible world, a maximal consistent sentence in her worldmaking language, that says it is true. If she is using a worldmaking language that is rich, that has enough structure to state these possibilities simply and directly, then there will be maximal consistent sentences in her language with parts that say each of (1)–(4). So, there will be a part of one of these sentences that says there is a talking donkey, a part of another that says Barack Obama is a world-class tennis player, and so on.

So far there is no problem. The trouble comes when we ask what determines which possible worlds there are and which there aren't – what determines which are the maximal *consistent* sentences? Recall the linguistic ersatzer's analysis:

> '◊A' is true iff some maximal *consistent* sentence in the ersatzer's worldmaking language says that A.

> '□A' is true iff every maximal *consistent* sentence in the ersatzer's worldmaking language says that A.

To see the worry, we might ask, is there a possible world according to our ersatzer that says the following:

> (O) Barack Obama is a world-class tennis player and yet Barack Obama has never picked up a racket in his life.

Intuitively, the answer to our question should be 'no.' Being a world-class tennis player requires picking up a racket because that is how one plays tennis, by picking up a racket and swinging at a ball. And no maximal *consistent* sentence will say this since this involves a contradiction.

However, it is going to be challenging for the ersatzer to give an account of what makes this sentence inconsistent in a way that doesn't simply appeal to the notion of possibility. If there were a logical contradiction in this sentence, something of the form $\lceil A \wedge \neg A \rceil$, then the ersatzer could simply apply a rule that nothing with that form ever appears in her language. The trouble is that even though it is impossible to become a world-class tennis player without ever picking up a racket, this is not because there is a logical contradiction contained in this thought. The ersatzer can't build into her account either the claim that the maximal consistent sentences are the ones that are possible. If she does this, she will be giving up on the project of trying to *explain* what it means to say something is possible.

There is a response the ersatzer can make here however. She might argue that all of her worlds also contain a set of what we might term the 'metaphysical truths,' truths such that if we build them into our maximal sentences, they will allow us to eliminate contradictions in a straightforward way because they will entail logical inconsistencies. For example, one might propose, 'For all x, if x is a world-class tennis player, then x has picked up a tennis racket' as one of these metaphysical truths. This would then entail that no maximal consistent sentence in her language will ever say (O). However, there is a question whether this project of discovering all of the metaphysical truths can be carried out. In any case we seem to have postponed the project of analyzing modality until this is done.

This brings us to the other horn of Lewis's dilemma. The linguistic ersatzer also has the option of constructing her ersatz worlds using what Lewis calls a poor worldmaking language. This would be a language consisting of a small set of basic terms that are sufficient to construct all of the possibilities there are. Here the hope would be that the ersatzer can allow for the sentences we considered above to come out as possibly true. ('There are talking donkeys,' 'The World Trade Center attack never occurred,' etc.) But this will not be done by using a worldmaking language in which such claims are expressed simply and directly. The motivation for using a poorer worldmaking language is to avoid the problem we just considered, to give a straightforward account of which sentences in the worldmaking language are consistent and which are inconsistent. The move to a poor worldmaking language is an attempt to give the ersatzer a shot at a reductive analysis of modality, an analysis that gives an account of all modal claims in nonmodal terms.

There are several ways in which one might try to set up a poor worldmaking language. One would be to start with a list of names, 'a_1,' 'a_2,' and so on to refer to all of the fundamental objects in the world (perhaps elementary particles) and then a list of predicates, 'F_1,' 'F_2,' and so on to refer to all of the fundamental properties and relations there are. Then each sentence (each ersatz world) will be a conjunction of basic sentences saying for each fundamental object whether for each property it has that property or not.

Another kind of poor worldmaking language that Lewis considers uses the real numbers to denote locations in space–time. Ersatz worlds are then constructed out of sets of ordered pairs in which the first member is a number naming a space–time location and the second member is a zero or a one depending on whether that location is occupied with matter or not. Here the sentences in the worldmaking language are sets. A maximal world sentence will have members corresponding to each space–time location in that world. So, for example, an ersatz world in this language might be written like: {<0.0001, 0>, <0.0002, 0>, . . ., <1.00001, 1>, <1.0002, 1>, <1.0003, 1>, . . .}.

The advantage of using a poor worldmaking language is that an ersatzer who constructs her worlds in this way does not have to appeal to our pre-theoretic grasp on what is and is not possible in order to say which worlds, which maximal sentences, are consistent and which are not. Depending on her choice of worldmaking language, she can give a simple and straightforward account of what consistency amounts to. In the first language, she can say a consistent sentence is one in which for each name a_i and predicate F_i either $F_i a_i$ or $\neg F_i a_i$ appears as a conjunct in the sentence but not both. Here, consistency reduces to logical consistency. In the second case of a poor worldmaking language we considered, a consistent sentence will be one in which no number denoting a space–time location is paired to both a 0 and a 1. This account again is straightforward and does not presuppose any antecedent grasp of what is and is not possible.

However, there is a different kind of problem for the linguistic ersatzer who appeals to a poor worldmaking language. Recall, the linguistic ersatzer wants to say:

'◊A' is true iff some maximal consistent sentence in the ersatzer's worldmaking language says that A.

'□A' is true iff every maximal consistent sentence in the ersatzer's worldmaking language says that A.

But if this is right and we use one of the above poor worldmaking languages, then none of the facts we considered above will turn out to be possible. Recall, these are:

(1) There are talking donkeys.
(2) The World Trade Center attack did not occur.
(3) There are unicorns.
(4) Barack Obama is a world-class tennis player.

At least in neither case of the poor worldmaking languages we considered above will there be parts of these ersatz worlds that say any of these things. The sentences will talk about fundamental particles and their properties or points of space–time and whether they are occupied or unoccupied. But they will say nothing about donkeys or unicorns or tennis players.

Intuitively, what the ersatzer who likes a poor worldmaking language will want to say here is that even though her worlds don't in so many words say that there are unicorns in the worlds or talking donkeys, still some of these worlds are such as to *entail* facts about the existence of unicorns or talking donkeys, the ones that describe the correct arrangements of fundamental properties instantiated by fundamental objects or the correct patterns of filled space–time. But now what a modal realist will press on is this notion of entailment. Entailment is itself a modal notion. To say a certain pattern of filled space–time entails the existence of a talking donkey means *there couldn't be* such a pattern of filled space–time without the existence of a talking donkey. And so the linguistic ersatzer who uses a poor world-making language to construct her worlds also seems to be presupposing modality in her account.

As with the case of the rich worldmaking language, there is a reply the ersatzer might make. She might hope to be able to provide a list of facts about which patterns of fundamental stuff correspond to which nonfundamental possibilities and just append this list of facts to her analysis. (E.g., such and such pattern of occupied space–time corresponds to a talking donkey, thus and so pattern of occupied space–time corresponds to a unicorn, and so on.) However, again, this will be a substantial undertaking. It is questionable whether anything like this can be carried out and, even if it can, it only postpones the analysis of modality.

Thus, although an ersatz version of modal realism is a live option, such a position does have well-known difficulties and the question of how best to overcome them makes the view much less clear and worked-out than Lewis's own position.

REJECTING THE POSSIBLE WORLDS ANALYSIS

The possible worlds analysis of modality is by now deeply entrenched in metaphysics as well as philosophy more generally. This analysis finds wide use in the philosophy of language, epistemology, ethics, the philosophy of science, and other areas, as philosophers often have reason to appeal to modal notions in their analyses. Philosophers across these sub-disciplines will often slip back and forth unconsciously between talk of what is possible and what exists in some or other possible world, what must be and what is the case in all possible worlds. But we have now seen there are deep metaphysical questions that arise with appeals to possible worlds language. One must either adopt Lewis's modal realism and buy into a controversial ontology of many alternative universes or find some alternative and yet clear way of understanding these possible worlds as constructed out of sentences or other actual entities.

The problems with both alternatives have caused some metaphysicians to insist that all of this possible worlds talk, convenient as it is, must not be the correct way to analyze our modal language. It may be useful, evocative as a *façon de parler*, but it shouldn't be taken as anything more than that, a way of speaking. To find out what we really mean when we say such and such a state of affairs is possible or necessary, we need to pursue an alternative analysis.

Fictionalism: what is
required for the truth of
sentences in a given
domain is to be understood
by analogy with truths of
fiction.

Probably the most popular (at least best known) contemporary alternative to the possible worlds analysis of modality is modal **fictionalism**. We have already encountered fictionalism in Chapter 5.[6] Here again, fictionalism is a way of understanding the truth conditions of a certain domain of claims that appear to carry ontological commitments, while avoiding these ontological commitments. We will consider one version: that of Gideon Rosen (in "Modal Fictionalism").

The primary motivation for the fictionalist is to avoid ontological commitment to alternative possible worlds. There are no concrete alternative universes like Lewis thought. And there are no ersatz worlds either. So, the following must be rejected:

The Possible Worlds Analysis of Modality

A is possible just in case there is a possible world in which A is true.
A is necessary just in case A is true at every possible world.

Still, the fictionalist believes there are lots of true modal claims, claims about what is possible and what is necessary. And the fictionalist does accept possible worlds talk as an evocative and useful way of thinking about what is possible and necessary. Her proposal is that we can use possible worlds talk but that we should replace the Possible Worlds Analysis of Modality with the following fictionalist analysis of modality:

The Fictionalist Analysis of Modality

A is possible just in case according to the fiction that there are possible worlds, there is a possible world in which A is true.

A is necessary just in case according to the fiction that there are possible worlds, A is true at all possible worlds.

Note that for there to be modal truths on this analysis, no possible worlds need exist, only fictions, stories, about the existence of possible worlds. And of course no one questions the existence of such stories. One such fiction, as Rosen cheekily points out, is Lewis's own *On the Plurality of Worlds.*

Many questions have been raised about the adequacy of modal fictionalism as an account of our modal claims. Among the questions some have raised is whether the fictions about possible worlds that exist (including Lewis's book) really say enough to give a complete account of all of the modal truths there are. It is also frequently asked whether it follows from Rosen's account that there were no facts about what was possible or necessary before the publication of Lewis's book in 1986. (He says it doesn't follow.)

EXERCISE 7.4

Rejecting Commitment to Possible Worlds

Why do you suppose Rosen and other philosophers have been skeptical about the existence of possible worlds? What reasons are there for a philosopher to be skeptical about the existence of ersatz possible worlds? Are these reasons for skepticism good reason to reject either modal realism or ersatz modal realism? Which view do you prefer?

Fictionalism is one strategy for understanding possibility and necessity while avoiding commitment to possible worlds (genuine or ersatz). Another strategy, one that before the 1970s and 1980s was dominant, was that alluded to in the beginning of this chapter: **conventionalism**. Conventionalists try to reduce modal claims to facts about what is or is not true according to the conventions of our language. A conventionalist account of modality completely avoids talk of possible worlds. Instead, those sentences that are necessary will be those that are entailed by the meanings of the terms constituting those sentences. For example:

> Triangles have three sides.
> All bachelors are unmarried.

Conventionalism: a position that seeks to reduce modal claims to facts about what follows or does not follow from the conventions of our language.

These are necessary truths because they are entailed by the meanings of the terms, 'triangle,' 'bachelor,' 'unmarried,' etc. Similarly, the following sentences are contingent truths:

> There are no pink donkeys.
> All members of the European Union lie north of the Equator.

Their contingency, according to the conventionalist, consists in the fact that the conventions of our language do not entail by themselves that these sentences are either true or false. It is consistent with the way we use the word 'donkey,' that there be no pink donkeys. It is also consistent with the conventions of our language that there be pink donkeys. The meaning of the word 'donkey' does not settle the matter of whether donkeys are pink or not pink. A sentence is contingent if its truth depends on what the world is like (beyond the facts about how we use our language). On the other hand, consider:

> There exists a round square.

This is a sentence that is necessarily false or impossible. The conventionalist will explain this fact again in the facts about how our language works. Based on the meanings we give to the terms 'round' and 'square,' she will say, something's being a square rules out its being round. And so this sentence is not just false, it is impossible.

The conventionalist's account of modality will be appealing to those who view ascriptions of possibility, necessity, or contingency to not be about what sort of things exist at our world and what they are like, but instead about our language, the kinds of things our language permits us to say or not say. If you just understand how our language works, you will in principle be able to figure out all of the necessary truths, what is possible, and what is impossible.

The reason why conventionalism is especially controversial today can be traced to some arguments developed in the 1970s by the philosophers Saul Kripke (in *Naming and Necessity*) and Hilary Putnam (in "The Meaning of 'Meaning'"). According to the conventionalist, necessary truths are supposed to be truths that are entailed simply by the meanings of our terms. But Kripke and Putnam noted that there were a class of necessary truths, the **necessary a posteriori**, that are not knowable through the meanings of the terms involved in them. These necessary truths had to be empirically discovered. Although these are necessary truths, what makes them true is not facts about our language but facts about our world. Consider:

Necessary a posteriori: truths that are necessary and yet known on the basis of empirical observation.

> Gold has atomic number 79.
> Water is H_2O.

Both of these are necessary truths. Something cannot be gold if the atoms that make it up do not have 79 protons. This is something we have learned about the chemical structure of gold. Similarly, a substance cannot be water if it does not consist of molecules containing two hydrogen atoms and an oxygen atom. But these facts aren't contained in the meanings of the words 'gold' and 'water.' 'Gold' and 'water' are words that were used for centuries and could have continued to be used without our ever discovering modern chemistry. You do not have to understand facts about chemistry in order to understand the meaning of these terms and use them, to understand perfectly well that a certain ring is gold or a certain glass contains water. Given these examples, the necessary truths cannot simply be the truths that hold in virtue of the meaning of our terms and the conventions of our usage. Just by reflecting on the meanings of these terms and how we use them, we never could have discovered these modal facts.

The other kind of claim that threatens conventionalism is the **contingent a priori**. The conventionalist would like to say that contingent truths are those that are not made true merely by the conventions of our language but depend on how the world turns out (independent of how we use our terms). But Kripke raised the following example of what appears to be a contingent claim that we could discover just by reflecting on the meaning of our terms:

Contingent a priori: truths that are neither necessary nor impossible and yet discoverable merely by reflection on the meanings of the terms or concepts involved in them.

> The standard meter stick is one meter long.

The standard meter stick is an object kept in the International Bureau of Weights and Measures (BIPM) in Sèvres, France. This is an object that has been used to define what length it is that our term 'one meter long' refers to. For this reason, it is true just in virtue of the meaning of the terms involved that the standard meter stick is one meter long.

And yet, at the same time, it is a contingent fact about this meter stick that it is the length it is (one meter long). It could have been the case that the standard meter stick, that very object, wasn't used as the standard for the meter at all, but used for some other purpose. It could have been used to hammer a nail and broken in half in which case it wouldn't have been one meter long after all. It is a contingent fact that that object, the standard meter stick, is the length it is. And so, even though the above sentence is true in virtue of how we actually use the term 'one meter long,' it is not a necessary truth.

And so, although conventionalism at first seems to be a good idea, cases like this do appear to suggest that the facts about what is necessary and what is contingent do seem to concern (in at least some cases) something more than the facts about how we as a matter of fact use our terms. The conventionalist will need to find a way to argue against these cases if she wants to reduce modality to facts about language.

EXERCISE 7.5

The Necessary A Posteriori and Contingent A Priori

What other examples of the necessary a posteriori and contingent a priori can you think of? Provide an additional example of each.

ESSENTIALISM AND ANTI-ESSENTIALISM

We can now finally discuss de re modality, what are the modal features if any of objects. Recall this contrasts with the topic of de dicto modality, or which propositions are possible, necessary, or contingent. Here, we'll focus on the most central issue which is the question of **essentialism**. We will use 'essentialism' to denote the view that objects themselves, independently of any ways we may have of thinking about or categorizing them, have essential properties. An essential property is a property of an object such that were that object to fail to have that property, it would cease to exist. It is a property an object must have if it is to exist.

Essentialism is an old view in philosophy that traces back to Aristotle who talks in his *Metaphysics* about objects possessing essences, features

Essentialism: the view that objects themselves, independently of any ways we may categorize them, have certain properties necessarily.

it is in an object's nature to possess. The position survives into the modern period with René Descartes (1596–1650) who famously claimed that the essence of a mind is to think and the essence of a material body is to be extended in space. John Locke (1632–1704) as well discusses objects' *real essences*, those features that make an object the kind of object it is and explain its observable features.

However, by the middle of the twentieth century, with the influence of logical positivism and the transition into naturalistic metaphysics, philosophers became skeptical of the existence of essential properties. Quine's critique of the entire notion of de re modality is perhaps the most famous and so we will discuss this here and why he may be considered perhaps the most influential contemporary 'anti-essentialist.'

In his book *Word and Object* (1960), Quine expresses a puzzlement with the idea of de re modality. He asks us to consider the case of a certain individual (call him 'Jones') who is at the same time both a mathematician and a bicyclist. Surely, Quine suggests, the following claims are both true:

> Mathematicians are necessarily rational and not necessarily two-legged.

> Cyclists are necessarily two-legged and not necessarily rational.

And yet what does this mean for Jones and his essential features? Surely, Quine complains, "there is no semblance of sense in rating some of his attributes as necessary and others as contingent."

Note that Quine doesn't seem to be particularly puzzled with the use of modal operators in general. Relative to a conceptual scheme or way of categorizing an object, it makes perfect sense to say an individual is essentially rational or essentially two-legged. The puzzlement comes when one asserts that objects may have certain essential properties not relative to a given classification but in themselves, independently of how we think of them. We may describe Quine in this way as being particularly puzzled about de re modality and the commitment to essentialism.

We may more clearly see the distinction by considering two ways of regimenting a claim that if one is a mathematician, then necessarily, one is rational. Using the '□' introduced in the second section, 'Mx' for 'x is a mathematician' and 'Rx' for 'x is rational', we may consider these two interpretations:

> (DD) □ ∀x(Mx ⊃ Rx)
> (DR) ∀x(Mx ⊃ □Rx)

The first (DD) is what metaphysicians think of as the de dicto reading. It says it is a necessary truth that all mathematicians are rational. To accept this we need not think that there are any objects possessing essential properties, properties that if the objects failed to have they couldn't exist. Rather we just need to think that it is a necessary truth that all mathematicians are rational. This could be true in virtue of the fact that at every possible world, if something is a mathematician, then it also happens to be rational.

On the other hand, the second claim, (DR), is what is thought of as the de re reading. We can see the difference between the de dicto and de re readings corresponds to a difference in the relative placement of the quantifiers and modal operators. In the de re reading, the quantifier takes wide scope outside of the modal operator. In the de dicto reading, the quantifier takes narrow scope and lies inside the modal operator. It is only the second de re reading that implies the instantiation (given the existence of mathematicians) of essential properties. For what (DR) says is that if a mathematician exists, then this mathematician has the property of being essentially rational. This means in any world in which this object x exists (whether in that world it is a mathematician or not), x has the property of being rational. If one is skeptical of essentialism, then one should also be skeptical about the truth of claims like (DR) in which quantifiers take wide scope outside of modal operators.

ESSENTIALISM TODAY

Essentialism remains a controversial position today, but not all philosophers want to reject it as Quine did. Indeed in one of the masterpieces of contemporary analytic philosophy, *Naming and Necessity* (1980), Saul Kripke argued in defense of essentialism.

One of Kripke's most interesting claims in this regard is what is called **origins essentialism**. This is the claim that the origins of material objects, like tables and chairs as well as those of organisms including human beings, are essential to them. For example, consider the Queen of England, Elizabeth II. Kripke asks his reader to consider whether it is plausible that this person, Queen Elizabeth, could have existed and yet had other parents than she actually had. Could it have been the case, for example, that Queen Elizabeth's parents were Mr. and Mrs. Harry Truman?[7] Kripke thinks not:

Origins essentialism: the view that the origins of material objects and organisms are essential to them.

> Can we imagine a situation in which it would have happened that this very woman [the Queen] came out of Mr. and Mrs. Truman? They might have had a child resembling her in many properties. Perhaps in some possible world Mr. and Mrs. Truman even had a child who actually became the Queen of England and was even passed off as the child of other parents. This still would not be a situation in which *this very woman* whom we call 'Elizabeth II' was the child of Mr. and Mrs. Truman, or so it seems to me. It would be a situation in which there was some other woman who had many of the properties that are in fact true of Elizabeth . . . It seems to me that anything coming from a different origin would not be this object.
>
> (Kripke 1980, pp. 112–113)

Kripke extends this argument not just to human beings and their origins, but also to material objects as well. He asks us to think about a particular wooden table and conjectures we will agree with him that it is not possible to imagine a situation in which literally this same object exists and yet it has its origin in a different piece of wood. If the table were made of a different piece of wood, it would be a different table, not the same table. Thus it has its origin essentially.

As we saw earlier, there are some philosophers, most notably Quine, who would be skeptical of claims like this one of Kripke's. Kripke takes it to be obvious that this very person, the Queen, or that very object, the table, could not have existed without having the same origins. But Quine wonders what could make a claim like this true. Take for instance the case of the Queen. Yes, Quine would say, if we consider this object the Queen in a particular way, relative to a classification as a particular organism say, then we may consider it to be an essential feature of hers that she is the daughter of these particular parents (George VI and Elizabeth, Duchess of York). This is just like the case of Jones. Relative to a particular way of thinking about him, as a mathematician, we are disposed to think of certain of his features as essential. But we may think of the Queen in another way, not worrying so much about her as an organism coming from a particular sperm and egg, but thinking of her simply as the English queen of more than sixty years (say on the occasion of her Diamond Jubilee in 2012). Then we might say it is not essential that today's queen had these particular parents, but only that she had whatever particular features enabled her to live so long as queen.[8]

It is common to find metaphysicians on both sides of the essentialist divide today. For some, Kripke is just simply right that independently of how we think about the Queen, she couldn't have been the very same person if she weren't born of the same parents. For others, Kripke's intuitions are better accounted for in terms of the way we think about these objects in certain contexts.

What is slightly less contentious is the claim that objects have other less robust sorts of essential properties. For example, one might less controversially adopt the view of **sortal essentialism**, that it is essential to objects what kinds of things they are. So, the Queen couldn't exist without being a person. And this table, this very object, couldn't have existed without being a table.

> **Sortal essentialism**: the view that it is essential to objects what kinds of things they are.

Perhaps even less controversial is the claim that objects have their self-identity necessarily. It is true that necessarily every object is identical to itself. Does this mean that every object has at least the essential property of being self-identical? This certainly seems trivial, doesn't it? Or doesn't every object necessarily have the feature of being such that 2+2=4? Do claims like this then make essentialism trivially true? Ruth Barcan Marcus argued for a distinction between a class of "traditional" essentialist theses and other weaker essentialist theses that even the Quinean should accept. What is distinctive about the traditional essentialist theses is that they claim there are certain features that are necessary to some objects but not to all.[9]

Even so, we should distinguish the de dicto and de re interpretations of these claims. Consider the claim that every object is necessarily self-identical. This may be symbolized as:

(=DD) $\Box\forall x\ (x{=}x)$

or as:

(=DR) $\forall x\Box\ (x{=}x)$

The first, de dicto claim, just says it is necessary truth that every object is self-identical. It doesn't posit any essential features of individual objects as the second does. One may read the second, de re claim, as saying: take any object you like, *that object* has the essential feature of being self-identical. A skeptic about de re modality can say that the truth of the claim that everything is necessarily self-identical can be understood as reducing to the truth of (=DD) and thus avoid commitment to any essential properties.

THE RELATION BETWEEN ESSENCE AND NECESSITY

Finally it is worth closing by mentioning that although it has been common in the past several decades to view the question of essentialism as the question of which properties are had necessarily by an object, if it is to exist, there is another tradition, another way of thinking about essence, that does not tie essence to necessity in this way.

Kit Fine argues for detaching the question of an object's essence from questions about necessity in his paper "Essence and Modality." He argues that it is better to think of an essence primarily as capturing what an object is in itself, its being. This will certainly have consequences for an object's necessarily being a certain way, but that it is necessarily some way doesn't make it what it is.

This may help us to see trivial properties such as being such that 2+2=4 as irrelevant to essentialism in any sense of the word. It is true this is a feature any object has necessarily. But this doesn't make it a part of the object's essence, something that captures what that object is. According to Fine, essences should be thought of more as definitions, accounts that define what an object is.

SUGGESTIONS FOR FURTHER READING

For Lewis's and Stalnaker's theories of counterfactual conditionals, see Stalnaker's "A Theory of Conditionals" and Lewis's "Counterfactuals and Comparative Similarity." For more on the debate between the modal realist and the ersatzer, see the papers by Phillip Bricker and Joseph Melia in *Contemporary Debates in Metaphysics*, edited by Theodore Sider, John Hawthorne, and Dean Zimmerman. A widely influential version of ersatzism is described and defended in Alvin Plantinga's *The Nature of Necessity*. Others are defended by David Armstrong in his *A Combinatorial Theory of Possibility*, Peter Forrest's "Ways Worlds Could Be," and Robert Stalnaker's

"Possible Worlds." An anthology containing many of the classic articles in the debate is *The Possible and the Actual*, edited by Michael Loux. For more on essentialism, see Richard Cartwright's "Some Remarks on Essentialism" and Laurie Paul's "In Defense of Essentialism." Marcus's "A Backward Look" paper gives a helpful overview of Quine's evolving distrust of de re modality as well as a critique. For discussion of modal epistemology, how we can know what is possible (or what is necessary), see the essays in Tamar Szabó Gendler and John Hawthorne's collection, *Conceivability and Possibility*.

NOTES

1   Sometimes the term 'logical possibility' is reserved for propositions that do not entail any contradictions on the basis of their logical form alone. In other words, something is logically possible if and only if, on the basis of logic alone, we could not deduce something of the form $\lceil A \wedge \neg A \rceil$ from it. Since you have to additionally assume facts about the meaning of 'triangle' or 'square' to deduce a contradiction from a statement about the existence of a four-sided triangle or a round square, it will not be logically impossible in this narrow sense of 'logical possibility.' Usually, however, the phrase is used in a looser sense where the sentences that are logically possible are those that do not entail contradictions on the basis of their logical form *plus* facts about the meanings the concepts involved.

2   The tense logic of Arthur Prior discussed in Chapter 5 was based on this modal logic of C.I. Lewis.

3   Where the world in question may be the actual world.

4   Lewis is not a great fan of the word 'concrete.' He doesn't think the term has a sharp and well-defined meaning for the reasons we discussed in Chapter 2. He introduces concreteness merely to emphasize that these other worlds are as real as our own and exist in the same sense as our own.

5   To say that a number is irrational is to say that it is unable to be expressed as a fraction of two integers, e.g., ½, ⅔, etc.

6   See Box 5.2.

7   Harry Truman was the president of the United States from 1945 to 1953.

8   See also Penelope Mackie's *How Things Might Have Been* for an alternative account of how we may be misled into thinking that objects and organisms have their origins essentially.

9   In her "Essentialism in Modal Logic."

Causation

CAUSATION IN THE HISTORY OF PHILOSOPHY

Most of us think that our world is full of causes and effects. Things don't just happen randomly, but often, if not most of the time, things are the way they are, events happen, because of other things or events that are their causes. A kitchen window is shattered into a hundred pieces and a rock is found lying outside. A cookie jar is empty and crumbs are found scattered beneath it. These are not random events but have explanations, causal explanations.

Causation is what the philosopher David Hume (1711–1776) called 'the cement of the universe.' It is what ties together the various disparate things that happen. Although much of contemporary metaphysics concerns questions of ontology, since the beginning of our discipline, philosophers have also been interested in questions about the connection between the various objects and events in our world and what are the reasons things are the way they are. If one seeks a complete account of the nature of our universe and what it is like, it doesn't seem sufficient to merely list the types of entities there are: the objects, properties, and events. We want to know as well the nature of the relations between these objects and events, which ones are tied causally to which others and what these causal connections come to.

In Chapter 6 on persistence, we saw that Aristotle appealed to the distinction between matter and form to explain the behavior of material objects, how it is that they are able to survive through changes and in what these changes consist. For Aristotle, ordinary changes consisted in a sub-stance, some matter, coming to take on a new form. But Aristotle too thought that more ingredients were required to provide complete expla-nations of why things are the way they are. A complete explanation should provide an account of an object's so-called efficient cause and also its teleological or final cause.

Final cause: the purpose or goal for which an object exists or why it is the way it is at a given time.

Teleological cause: see final cause

Final or **teleological causes** concern an object or event's *telos*, or purpose. The telos of an object is that for which the object was created, what it was made for, the reason why it exists or is the way it is at a given time. Teleological causes provide an object or event's end purpose or goal. For example, the final cause of a window is to let in light. The final cause of my riding my bike today is to get to school. Today, especially due to the influ-ence of naturalism and general skepticism about purposes in scientific explanations, many metaphysicians tend to deny that objects, especially natural objects, have final causes. Our best scientific theories tend not to appeal to purposes or goals to explain why things happen or why objects are the way they are, and so the naturalist argues, neither should we appeal to teleological causes in metaphysics. Philosophers of a more theistic persuasion tend to be less skeptical about final causes, however the present chapter will focus on the species of causation that is most commonly discussed by metaphysicians on both sides of the naturalist/theist divide. We will set aside final causation, although it is certainly an interesting issue whether objects do indeed possess purposes or final causes that can explain why they are the way they are.

Efficient cause: what brings an object or event into being.

Contemporary discussions of causation typically concern something more like Aristotle's efficient causation. An **efficient cause** of an object or an event explains what in its history brought that object or event into being. Usually, barring exotic cases like time travel, to find an object or event's efficient cause, one looks into the past. The efficient causes of objects are the processes that brought them into being: for artifacts, some kind of manufacturing process, for humans, the coming together of a sperm and an egg. Events' efficient causes are to be found in other events or actions. Two events involving one naughty child may be the efficient cause of both a window shattering and the emptying of a cookie jar.

BOX 8.1

The Relata of Causal Relations

Causation is typically thought to be a relation between entities, but entities of which kind? What types of entities are causes and what types of entities are effects? A common view is that the relata of causal relations are events. For example, we say one event, the assassination of Franz Ferdinand, caused another event, World War I. Or we may point to a particular lightning strike (one event) as the cause of a particular wildfire (another event). There are different views about the nature of events, but the two most common are those associated with Donald Davidson (events are a species of concrete particular that involve changes taking place at particular space–time regions, e.g., a window's breaking at a particular place and time) and Jaegwon Kim (events are just the exemplification of properties by objects at particular times, e.g., a window's having the property of breaking at a particular time).

Some have argued that a better way to think about causation is as a relation between tropes or property instances. Given the similarity between tropes and Kimean events, most don't take this view to be all that different to the standard view that the relata of the causal relation are events.

Others (e.g. David Armstrong) have argued that it is facts, not events, that are causes. Whereas events are things that *happen*, facts are things that *are the case*. Facts, moreover are often thought to be more finely individuated than events. What this means is that where there is only one event, one might think there are two or more corresponding facts. Take, for example, the event that consists of a certain ball going through a particular net at a time t. This one event might be described in several different ways and thus taken to correspond to several different facts:

It being the case that this ball went through this net at time t.
It being the case that a shot was scored at time t.
It being the case that the game-winning shot was scored at time t.

A more controversial position is that the relata of the causal relation are substances rather than events. For example, in certain cases, like that of free actions, some think it is important that particular kinds of substances be causes: human agents. This is the **agent causation** view. However, many remain skeptical about whether it truly makes sense to cite substances as causes (or effects). For consider a case of causation that is especially interesting to defenders of substance or agent causation: a case in which a politician makes a free decision to cast a certain vote thus raising her arm. A defender of events as causes would likely say that the cause in this case was the politician's decision to vote, while a defender of substances as causes would say it was the politician herself that was the (or at least a) cause of her arm's rising. But if this is right, and it was the politician herself, not any particular decision she made or any other event occurring in her mind or body, then why was it that the arm raising occurred at that particular time and not earlier? For, she didn't come into existence suddenly at the time of the arm going up, but presumably existed for many years before that; if it is the substance herself that is the cause and not any particular decision or event on her part, then why doesn't the effect come into existence as soon as the substance exists?

Table 8.1 Distinction between Objects and Events

Objects	Events
a particular window	a window's shattering at time t
a particular rock	a rock's striking a window at time t-1
Michelangelo's *David*	*David*'s having a chip on his toe in 1991
Barack Obama	Barack Obama's taking the oath of office on January 20, 2009

HUME'S EMPIRICISM

In this section, we will consider a puzzle about the nature of causation from a later period in the history of philosophy that continues to inform discussions of the topic today. This puzzle concerns how we could ever learn about causal relations.

This philosophical problem was raised by David Hume. Hume was a defender of **empiricism**. This is the view that our knowledge and understanding of the world comes entirely from experience. Although earlier philosophers, from Plato and Aristotle to Descartes and Leibniz, thought that some of our knowledge of the world is a priori, is available to us prior to experience by pure reasoning, empiricists like Hume were skeptical that we had any ideas or knowledge of the world that does not come from experience.

Hume held a particularly stringent form of empiricism in which all of our ideas, the concepts we have that structure our thoughts and what we can know, are built up out of copies of simple sense impressions. For example, we can form the idea of a blue thing or a square thing, of a loud thing or a soft thing, because we have sense impressions of these kinds. The simple ideas (of blueness or squareness, loudness or softness) are copies our minds make of these basic sense impressions. For Hume, it is not that we cannot form ideas of things we haven't actually seen with our eyes, or heard or smelled or tasted or felt. We can, but any new ideas we form must ultimately be complex ideas built up out of the ideas of things we have already experienced. For example, we can easily come to have the idea of a unicorn, even though no one has ever seen one, by combining the ideas of things we have seen, a horse and a horn. One can easily have the idea of a one-mile-wide golden sphere as well even if one hasn't ever seen one of those, by combining the simple ideas of goldness and roundness and being one mile wide.

If this form of empiricism is appealing to you as it was to Hume, then you might start to worry, as he did, about how one could ever form the idea of a causal relation between objects. Surely we can perceive objects and events and if we want to talk in Hume's way, we can say we form sense impressions of them, but do we ever directly perceive the causal relations *between* objects and events? Is there a sense impression that we form of a causing itself? To take a silly example, say your friend sits across a table from you and quickly drinks a pint of beer.[1] He then becomes red in the face and stumbles around drunk. This is a clear case of causation if anything is: his drinking causes his redness and stumbling. But although you may perceive his drinking and perceive as well his subsequent redness and stumbling, do you perceive the causal link between the drinking and the redness and stumbling? What would that even look like? But then if Hume is right and all of our ideas are built up out of simpler ideas copied from sense impressions we've had, then how is it possible for us to ever have the idea of the causal relation linking the drinking and the redness and stumbling?

Empiricism: the view that our knowledge and understanding of our world comes entirely from experience.

A key part of the trouble the concept of causation makes for the empiricist is that causation is typically thought of as a necessary connection between events. Effects seem to be events that follow as a matter of necessity from their causes. An effect doesn't just follow a cause – it *has to* follow, once the cause occurs. If your friend quickly drinks a pint of beer, then if this drinking is a cause of his subsequent redness and stumbling, it is a sure thing, the universe guarantees, that he will get red and stumble around once he drinks the beer.[2] But although we may perceive the effect to follow the cause, it is hard to see how we may perceive it following the cause *with necessity*, as the cause really making the effect happen rather than simply happening before it.

There is a lively historical debate about what exactly Hume thought here and whether he thought that causes indeed must be events that necessitate their effects. Those philosophers who think that Hume held on to this position have called the view about causation they think he held 'skeptical realism' – this is the view that although causal relations really do exist in our world and they are necessary connections between events, we can't really understand this notion of causation and so the nature of causal relations will always be out of our cognitive reach. We can only predict with likelihood which events will follow which; we can't see the hidden or 'secret' connections between what happens.[3]

A far more common position one finds among historians of philosophy however is that Hume ended up rejecting the idea that causation is a necessary connection between events. Instead he found a way in which our concept of causation may arise out of a combination of simpler ideas derived from sense impressions. Since there is no problem with our observing how one event may follow another, one might use such complex ideas of one event following another to build up to a concept of causation. A natural thought is that one may view our idea that one type of event is the cause of another type of event as constituted by our idea of the *regular succession* of events of these kinds. If an event of a given kind follows another in just one case, we might not view the sequence as indicating a causal link, but if this happens regularly (that is, time after time, again and again), then this would seem to suggest that what we are seeing is a case of causation. Returning to the previous example, we may have observed the quick drinking of a pint of beer to be followed by redness and stumbling not just in this one circumstance, but also in several instances in the past; that redness and stumbling follows drinking with regularity. If so, we may infer from this that quickly drinking pints of beer is a cause of redness and stumbling.

This suggests an empiricist analysis of the concept of causation. An event of type A (say a drinking) is a cause of an event of type B (say a stumbling) just in case events that are As are regularly followed by events that are Bs. This understanding of the concept of causation involves replacing the idea of causation as a necessary connection with the more empiricist-friendly idea of causation as the regular succession of events. This is a simple version of the **regularity theory of causation**. Hume is often thought to be the first regularity theorist of causation.[4] To say that a

Regularity theory of causation: a theory of causation that explains causal relations in terms of the regular occurrence of patterns of events.

particular event a is the cause of another particular event b, on this view, is to say that these events a and b both occur, a is an A-type of event, b is a B-type of event, and A-type events are regularly followed by B-type events.

If this is on the right track, one might wonder why or how it is that anyone ever thought that causes necessitated their effects in the first place. How did we ever get confused into thinking we have the idea of necessary connections between events? Where did this idea come from? To answer this question, Hume proposed that after we see a regular sequence of events – an event of type-B again and again following an event of type-A, our mind comes to be led to have the expectation, when first observing an A-type event, that a B-type event is about to occur. This impression we have, this feeling upon experiencing one event that another is about to occur, is where we get the idea of something like a necessary connection between events. We mistakenly think this impression in our minds corresponds to some external necessitating force between the events themselves.

EXERCISE 8.1

Copying Ideas from Experiences

Do you agree with Hume that we do not directly observe the causal relations between events? What sort of examples might suggest otherwise? Besides causation, what are some other cases of concepts that we seem to have that do not seem to be built up out of ideas copied from sense impressions?

It is rare to find a philosopher today subscribing to the strict form of empiricism we find in Hume, that all of our ideas are built up out of simpler ideas copied from our sense impressions. There are certainly still questions about whether we should take causation to be a necessary connection between events and if not what other conceptions of causation are possible, but the worries about causation as a necessary connection don't arise for exactly the same reasons as they did for Hume. For example, a naturalist might think that we are able to grasp many new kinds of concepts through mathematical and scientific theorizing, and that this generally doesn't involve building concepts out of simpler ideas copied from sense impressions. Yet she might still worry that concepts like necessity don't appear in the natural sciences and so perhaps should be avoided in our best philosophical theories. Other philosophers might be fine with using the concept of a necessary connection between events, but wish for a reductive analysis that can explain these concepts in terms of more fundamental notions that are better understood. We turn now to consider the prospects for such a reductive analysis.

THREE REDUCTIVE THEORIES OF CAUSATION

Reductive theories of causation are theories (like Hume's) that give an explanation of what it is for one event to cause another in noncausal terms.[5] In this section, we will discuss the three most common kinds of reductive theory of causation: regularity theories of causation, counterfactual theories of causation, and probabilistic theories of causation.

There are many forms a regularity theory of causation may take, starting with the simple version discussed by Hume:

> *Simple regularity theory*: an event a of type A causes an event b of type B *just in case* a and b actually occur and A-type events are regularly followed by B-type events.

We can see this is a *reductive* analysis of causation since the explanation, what is on the right side of the 'just in case,' makes no use of causal notions. The simple regularity theory is a good first pass at a regularity theory of causation, but one might worry that mere regular succession isn't enough to make for genuine causation. For example, it is undoubtedly the case that every time your favorite football team has ever won a game, the sun has risen the following day. Your team's winning is regularly followed by the sun's rising. And yet it doesn't follow that the cause of the sun's rising on those days is your team's win.

A natural thing to say in response to a case like this is that causation can't be *mere* regular succession, but must involve something more. The effect must somehow follow the cause not just as a matter of coincidence but rather as a matter of the cause's *entailing* the effect. But what sense of entailment do we want? Logical entailment seems too much to require. (Indeed this would seem to bring us back to the idea of causation as a necessary connection between events.) To see why logical entailment between cause and effect doesn't anyway seem required for causation, consider the following paradigm cases of causation:

> a lightning strike at time t causes a fire at time t'
> a rock thrown at a window at t causes the window to break at t'

In neither case is there a logical entailment between the cause and the effect. If there is a relationship between lightning strikes and fires, or rock-throwings and window-breakings, it is not a logical relationship, but a relation of some other kind.

Instead, many regularity theorists have suggested that causation requires that the effect be entailed by the cause not on its own as a matter of logic, but as a result of the laws of nature. For example, a regularity theory of this kind might look like:

> *Nomic regularity theory*: an event a of type A causes an event b of type B just in case a and b actually occur and the laws of nature imply that A-type events are regularly followed by B-type events.

The laws of nature don't entail that the sun will rise tomorrow, nor do they imply that if your football team wins today, the sun will rise tomorrow. This fix works to rule out the sort of case that is a problem for the simple regularity theory. And, in general, it works to avoid counting cases of succession by coincidence as cases of causation. The nomic regularity theory also seems to nicely capture those cases we ordinarily think of as cases of causation – it does seem to follow as a matter of natural law that drinking leads to redness and stumbling, that dropping objects causes them to fall, that lightning strikes lead to fires, that throwing rocks at windows causes those windows to break, and so on. Many philosophers have endorsed a version of the regularity theory that builds in entailment according to the laws.[6]

Yet in the 1970s, David Lewis pointed out several difficult issues for regularity theories of causation that caused many to reconsider the position. Instead, Lewis proposed a distinct kind of reductive theory of causation, a **counterfactual theory of causation**.[7] Lewis's theory has been extremely influential ever since, not just in philosophy, but in how causation is thought about in psychology and the social sciences as well.[8]

Two of the problems Lewis raised for the regularity theory were the problem of epiphenomena and the problem of preemption.[9] When we speak of **epiphenomena**, we are talking about events that are the results of other events but that have no effects of their own. What Lewis argued was that it could be the case that an event a may satisfy the requirements of a regularity theory of causation to count as a cause of another event b, while a actually isn't a cause of b. This could happen if a were an epiphenomenon traceable to some other event in b's causal history. For example, let's consider again the case of your friend's drinking and this leading to his turning red and stumbling. The causal structure of this situation may be represented as shown in Figure 8.1, with the dots representing events and arrows representing relations of causal influence.

In this case, the drinking (c) is a cause of both the reddening (a) and the stumbling (b). After the drinking, the reddening occurs first and then the stumbling. But the stumbling is not caused by the reddening. Despite this fact, a regularity theory would take the reddening to be a cause of the stumbling. Because the laws of nature entail the drinking will be followed by first a reddening and then a stumbling, the laws entail a reddening will be followed by a stumbling. And this is what the regularity theorist says is sufficient for the reddening to be a cause of the stumbling. But the

Counterfactual theory of causation: a theory that reduces facts about causation to facts about what would have happened in various counterfactual circumstances.

Epiphenomenon: an event that is the result of another event but that has no effects of its own.

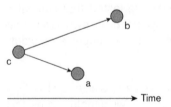

Key:
a : Reddening
b : Stumbling
c : Drinking
→ : Relation of causal influence
  : An event that occurs

Figure 8.1 The Problem of Epiphenomena

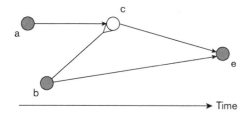

Key:
a : Billy's throw
b : Suzy's throw
c : Billy's rock staying on course to
     strike the window
e : Window breaking
→ : Relation of causal influence
—< : Relation of causal inhibition
● : An event that occurs
○ : An event that does not occur

Figure 8.2 The Problem of Preemption

reddening is an epiphenomenon. It is caused by something earlier in the causal chain (the drinking) but it doesn't have any causes of its own. So the regularity theory has a problem. It counts epiphenomena as causes.

Another problem for regularity theories is the problem of preemption. Suppose two naughty children, Billy and Suzy, are trying to break a window by throwing rocks at it. Billy throws his rock first, aiming carefully and throwing with enough force to break the window. But just as Billy releases the rock from his hand, Suzy throws hers in just such a way as to knock Billy's off its trajectory. Suzy's rock bounces off of Billy's into the window, thus breaking it. In this case, the obvious thing to say is that it was Suzy's throw that was a cause of the window's breaking. Billy's throw could have been a cause, but in fact it wasn't, since it was *preempted* from being a cause of the window's breaking by Suzy's throw. This is represented in Figure 8.2: steps on the causal chain that would have led from Billy's throw to the window's breaking have been inhibited by Suzy's throw.[10]

Let's first see why preemption presents a problem for the regularity theory. What makes this a case of preemption is that the preempted cause, Billy's throw, on its own seems to have what it takes to cause the window's breaking. It occurs, the effect occurs, and events just like Billy's throw are regularly followed, according to the laws, by window-breakings. And so according to the regularity theory, it counts as a cause of the window-breaking. But it is not a cause of the window-breaking. Only Suzy's throw is. Thus, the regularity theory has another problem. It counts preempted causes as causes.

The account Lewis proposed as a replacement to the regularity theory of causation begins with the notion of counterfactual dependence between events. Recall from Chapter 7, a counterfactual is a conditional in which one supposes that something occurred differently than it actually did. Some examples of counterfactuals are:

If kangaroos didn't have tails, they would topple over.
If Paris were in England, then people would speak English there.
If Suzy hadn't thrown her rock, then the window would still have broken.

Lewis proposes to analyze causation in terms of counterfactual dependence where one event e counterfactually depends on another event c just in case had c not occurred, then e would not have occurred either. Note: Lewis analyzes causation *in terms of* counterfactual dependence. He does not analyze causation *as* counterfactual dependence. Lewis's original account of causation from his 1973 paper "Causation" is the following:

> c causes e just in case:
>
> (i)   The events c and e both actually occur, and
> (ii) There is a chain of counterfactual dependence running from c to e.

What it is for there to be a chain of counterfactual dependence running from c to e is for there to be some sequence of events starting with c and terminating with e such that every event in the sequence counterfactually depends on the event that immediately precedes it in the sequence. In some cases, this chain will only involve c and e. In this case, c will be a cause of e in virtue of both c and e occurring and the following counterfactual being true:

> If c hadn't occurred, then e wouldn't have occurred either.

But in other cases, there may be no direct dependence of e on c.

Actually, cases of causal preemption are good cases to use to illustrate why some counterfactual theorists like Lewis think causation should be analyzed in terms of the presence of a chain of counterfactual dependence. We have already noted that the case of Billy and Suzy is a problem for the regularity theory of causation since there is regular nomic succession of rock-tosses like Billy's and window-breakings and yet Billy's throw is not a cause of the window's breaking.

But cases of preemption like this also show why a simple counterfactual theory of causation couldn't be true either; one saying that what is required for causation is that one event e counterfactually depends on another event c. A simple counterfactual theory *would* get it right that Billy's throw is not a cause of the window breaking. The following counterfactual after all is false:

> If Billy hadn't thrown his rock, the window wouldn't have broken.

This is false because if Billy hadn't thrown his rock, Suzy still would have been there to throw hers. And so even if Billy hadn't thrown his rock, the window would have broken. This is a good result for the simple counterfactual theory. But there is also a bad result for this theory. It fails to count Suzy's throw as a cause of the window breaking. For this counterfactual is also false:

> If Suzy hadn't thrown her rock, the window wouldn't have broken.

This counterfactual is false because of the presence of Billy and his throw. If Suzy hadn't thrown her rock, the window still would have broken because of Billy's throw.

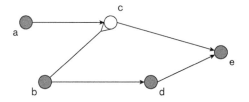

Key:

a   : Billy's throw
b   : Suzy's throw
c   : Billy's rock staying on course to
      strike the window
d   : Suzy's rock staying on course to
      strike the window
e   : Window breaking

Figure 8.3 Billy and Suzy (Detail)

This is one of the main reasons why Lewis complicates the counterfactual theory to make it require not counterfactual dependence between c and e, but instead a chain of counterfactual dependence between c and e. Although there is not direct counterfactual dependence of the window's breaking on Suzy's throw, there is a chain of counterfactual dependence leading from Suzy's throw to the window breaking. We see this chain by adding more detail to the previous figure, as shown in Figure 8.3.

Even though the following counterfactual is false:

If Suzy hadn't thrown her rock, the window wouldn't have broken,

the following counterfactuals are all true:

If Suzy hadn't thrown her rock, then her rock wouldn't have stayed on course to strike the window

(i.e. if b hadn't occurred then d wouldn't have occurred.)

If Suzy's rock hadn't stayed on course in that way, the window wouldn't have broken

(i.e. if d hadn't occurred, then e wouldn't have occurred.)

Since these counterfactuals are true, there is a chain of counterfactual dependence linking b with e. And so Lewis's account counts Suzy's throw as a cause of the window's breaking.

As has been mentioned, many philosophers have been attracted to the idea of a counterfactual theory of causation. The idea is so natural that even Hume (although he proposed another theory) when he states what he means by causation says it is the idea that if c hadn't occurred, e wouldn't have occurred. Still, counterfactual theories are not without their problems and especially in the 1990s and 2000s there was a cottage industry devoted to producing counterexamples to Lewis's theory and offering more sophisticated counterfactual theories of causation to avoid the counterexamples. Indeed the definitive version of Lewis's "Causation" included in his 1986 *Philosophical Papers Volume II* includes a series of postscripts in which he discusses many of these problem cases and proposes a more sophisticated model (one he also ultimately rejected) to repair the damage.[11]

EXERCISE 8.2

Regularity and Counterfactual Theories of Causation

Determine what the following four theories of causation would say about each case: (i) the simple regularity theory, (ii) the nomic regularity theory, (iii) the simple counterfactual theory, (iv) Lewis's counterfactual theory,

A. Every time Tony wears a white shirt, he spills coffee down the front of it. This happens often when he wears shirts of other colors as well, but it happens every time he wears a white shirt. Is Tony's wearing a white shirt a cause of his spilling coffee on himself?

B. White and Scarlet, two assassins, have both been hired to murder Mr. Body. Both are skilled and reliable at carrying out the murders they are hired to perform. On this occasion, White finds their target first. As Body is just about to die of strangulation from White's rope, Scarlet comes into the room and shoots him in the chest, stopping his heart. Was Scarlet's firing her gun a cause of Mr. Body's death?

C. Michael is set to compete in a major ping pong tournament. The night before the finals, he trips and falls, breaking his right hand. As a result, he is only able to use his left hand. This is disappointing, since Michael is right-handed and not used to using his left hand to play ping pong. Miraculously, playing with his left hand only, Michael wins the championship. Is Michael's tripping and falling the night before the finals a cause of his winning the championship?

Alongside regularity and counterfactual theories, there is a third kind of reductive theory of causation that has been influential. Some prefer to analyze causation not in terms of regularities, laws, or counterfactuals, but rather in terms of probabilities. One simple version of a probabilistic theory of causation says that causes are probability-raisers. More precisely, c is a cause of e just in case the occurrence of c raises the probability of e's occurring. Or, the probability of e given that c occurs is higher than the probability of e given that c does not occur.

The probabilistic view has appealed to philosophers for several reasons. First, one might think it is a way of capturing the intuition behind regularity accounts without requiring something so strict as entailment between a cause and an effect. To return to the earlier case, we might think the drinking caused the stumbling even if the laws didn't strictly imply that the stumbling would happen, it only made it much more likely. The probabilistic view is also popular due to the fact that probabilistic or statistical correlation seems to be the concept of causation that is operative in many of the sciences (both the natural and social sciences). In medicine, something is taken to be the cause of a disease if it raises the probability of one's developing the disease. In sociology, something is taken to be a cause if it is a statistically significant factor.

Still, probabilistic theories are not without their difficulties. First, it is not always clear how to apply the concept of probability to events, even events that we very clearly believe have causes. For example, is it really possible to assign any definite probability to your friend's stumbling around given his drinking or not drinking a pint of beer? Even if we could find a way to agree on a definite probability to assign your friend's stumbling around on a particular occasion, this probability assignment would likely depend on a lot of other assumptions we make about the case and thus how we are thinking about it. This is what is known as the **reference class problem**. The probabilities we assign to the occurrence of particular events do not seem to be objective features they possess, but instead seem to be determined by our contingent ways of conceptualizing those events on a given occasion.

Reference class problem: this is the problem that the probability we assign to an event seems to depend on our way of conceptualizing it (placing it against a reference class) on a given occasion. This may vary depending on the context making it difficult to say what is *the* probability of the event.

BOX 8.2

Van Fraassen's Cube Factory

Bas van Fraassen once used a clever case to illustrate the fact that which probabilities it is reasonable to assign to a type of event's occurring depends on how we choose to think the situation (1989, p. 303). Suppose there is a factory designed to produce cubes of various sizes. We want to know the probability on a particular Monday that the factory will make a cube with a particular size. Here is a description of the situation:

This factory is equipped with machinery to make cubes with edges of any length up to 2 cm. For any length up to 2 cm, there is an equal chance on Monday that the factory will manufacture cubes with edges of that length. *What is the probability that on Monday the factory will manufacture cubes with edges 1 cm in length?*

Think about this. Since the factory can make cubes with edges of any size up to 2 cm, and half of the possible lengths up to 2 cm are <1 cm, it would seem the correct answer to this question is ½. The probability that on Monday the factory will manufacture cubes with edges <1 cm in length would seem to be ½.

But here are two other situations we might describe and questions we might ask:

This factory is equipped with machinery to make cubes with sides of any area up to 4 cm². For any area up to 4 cm², there is an equal chance on Monday that the factory will manufacture cubes with sides of that area. *What is the probability that on Monday the factory will manufacture cubes with sides 1 cm² in area?*

This factory is equipped with machinery to make cubes with any volume up to 8 cm³. For any volume up to 8 cm³, there is an equal chance on Monday that the factory will manufacture cubes with that volume. *What is the probability that on Monday the factory will manufacture cubes 1cm³ in volume?*

But now you should be scratching your head. The answers to the second and third questions would appear to be different from the answer to the first. The answer to the second question seems to be ¼. The answer to the third question seems to be ⅛. But the trouble is that each paragraph is describing the same scenario and asking the same question about that scenario. To say that our factory can make cubes with edges up to 2 cm is to say the same thing as to say our factory can make cubes with sides up to 4 cm² in area, and this is to say the same thing as to say our factory can make cubes with volumes up to 8 cm³. And to ask for the probability of the factory producing a cube with edge length 1 cm or less is to ask for the probability of the factory producing a cube with sides of area 1 cm² or less which is again just another way to ask for the probability of the factory producing a cube with volume 1 cm³ or less.

Which probability one assigns to a given situation would seem to depend on the way one describes that situation and the concepts one is applying to consider the case. This is the **reference class problem**. It is called this because it relates to the problem of finding the correct reference class against which to compare the given possibility – in this case, one with cubes with other possible edge lengths, or cubes with other possible side areas, or cubes with other possible volumes.

But causation is supposed to be an objective phenomenon concerning the relations between events. Whether one event is the cause of another doesn't seem to depend on how we think about these events, or whether we think about them at all.

An additional problem probabilistic theories face is that there appear to be cases in which c causes e but the occurrence of c seems definitely to lower, not raise, the probability of e's occurring. Lewis considers a case where we have two systems in place that are capable of triggering a given event e. System A is reliable and will raise the probability of e's occurring to 99 percent. System B is much less reliable and makes the probability of e's occurring 50 percent. Suppose one throws a switch to turn off system A and turn on system B. Later, system B works and, as a result, the event e happens. The throwing of the switch lowered the probability of e's occurrence, but it is still intuitively a cause of e's occurrence. Cases like this suggest that sometimes a cause is something that doesn't raise the probability of an event's occurring. Whether this means the probabilistic theory should be thrown out altogether, revised, or supplemented with additional criteria is an open question in the philosophy of causation.

AN OBJECTION TO REDUCTIVE THEORIES OF CAUSATION

We have now seen three approaches to developing a reductive theory of causation, that is, one that tries to produce an account of causation in noncausal terms: (a) regularity theories that try to analyze facts about causation in terms of facts about regular sequences of events and perhaps laws, (b) counterfactual theories that try to analyze facts about causation in terms of facts about what would have happened under circumstances in which the putative cause did not occur, and (c) probabilistic theories that analyze causation in terms of probabilistic notions. These accounts have been influential and are still very prominent, however some philosophers remain skeptical of the very idea of reducing facts about causation to noncausal facts and it is worth seeing at least one example to get the flavor of these objections.

One set of objections comes from the philosopher Michael Tooley (for example, in his 1990 paper "Causation: Reductionism vs. Realism"). Tooley defends a **primitivist theory of causation** – a theory according to which causal facts are not reducible to any noncausal facts, including facts about regularities, laws, counterfactuals, or probabilities. Tooley himself calls his view 'realism about causation,' but this is of course contentious. Davidson, Lewis, and the others who have developed and endorse reductive theories of causation consider themselves "realists" as well about causation even if they think causal notions are ultimately explainable in more basic terms. 'Primitivism' is thus a more neutral term for Tooley's view.

Primitivist theory of causation: a theory according to which causal facts are not reducible to any noncausal facts, including facts about regularities, laws, counterfactuals, or probabilities.

One of Tooley's cases involves a simple world with only two fundamental laws.[12] The first law of this world is:

(L_1) For any object x, x's having property P at time t causes x to acquire one of property Q or property R at t'.

The second is:

(L_2) For any object x, x's having property S at time t causes x to acquire one of property Q or property R at t'.

Note that these are both indeterministic laws. They don't say with necessity which type of events follow necessarily from which others, but make a weaker claim about what could follow (either Q or R).

Suppose a single object has property P at one time and then later goes on to acquire Q (or R). We may then infer using any of our reductive theories and L_1 that it was this object's having P that caused it to acquire Q (or R).

And similarly, if at one time an object has property S and then later acquires Q (or R), we may infer, using any of our reductive theories and L_2, that it was this object's having S that caused it to acquire Q (or R). The trouble, Tooley points out, arises when there is a situation like the following:

Time t	Time t'
Object a has properties P and S.	Object a has properties Q and R.

Now some real questions arise. The laws entail that the instantiation of P causes the instantiation of Q or R. The laws entail that the instantiation of S causes the instantiation of Q or R. But in this situation, was it the instantiation of P by a that caused a to possess Q? Or was it the instantiation of S by a that caused a to possess Q? And similarly, we can ask about a's instantiation of R at t'. Was it a's possession of P or of S that caused a to have R at t'?

Tooley's point is that the facts about the laws underdetermine the facts of causation in this case.[13] And so the facts about causation cannot be analyzed in terms of nomic regularities. Nor does he think they may be adequately analyzed in terms of counterfactuals. Laws L_1 and L_2 may also supply us with evidence about which counterfactuals are true. This still won't determine which it is, Pa or Sa, that is responsible for Qa, and which of Pa or Sa it is that is responsible for Ra. Thus, Tooley concludes, we ought to see the facts about causation as additional facts irreducible to any facts about regularities or counterfactuals or probabilities. The causal facts are not reducible to any more fundamental facts. Causal facts are "primitive."

EXERCISE 8.3

Tooley's Objection to Reductive Theories of Causation

Select what you take to be the most promising reductive theory of causation. How should a defender of this theory respond to Tooley's alleged counterexample?

PHYSICAL THEORIES OF CAUSATION

So far, we have introduced several different kinds of theories of causation: regularity theories, counterfactual theories, probabilistic, primitivist theories. This leaves out one important class of theories of causation: process theories of causation. Process theories of causation try to give an account of causation in terms of the occurrence of physical processes.

In not all cases are defenders of process theories trying to analyze all cases of causation. Often, process theorists only claim to analyze the kinds of processes involved in physical causation. However, some recent process theorists of causation do attempt to do more than describe the sort of processes involved in physical causation. They go so far as to try to explicate what causation is (in all cases) in terms of physical processes. For this reason, their theories are often called 'physical theories of causation.'

Probably the physical theory of causation that is most discussed today is the one that was proposed in a 2000 book by Phil Dowe called *Physical Causation*. The account there was heavily influenced by previous work of Wesley Salmon (1925–2001) and Hans Reichenbach (1891–1953). Dowe's theory starts with an account of two central causal notions, that of a causal process and that of a causal interaction.

First, Dowe borrows the notion of a **world–line** of an object from Special Relativity. This is the path of any object through space–time. It is in terms of this notion of a world–line and the additional notion of a conserved quantity from physics that Dowe develops a general theory of causation:

World–line: the path of any object through space–time.

> A *causal process* is a world–line of an object which manifests a conserved quantity,

> A *causal interaction* is an intersection of world–lines which involves exchange of a conserved quantity,

> An *exchange* is a case in which at least one incoming and at least one outgoing process manifest a change in the value of the conserved quantity.[14]

Conserved quantities are physical quantities that do not change their total values over time. For example, the principle of conservation of energy says that the total energy of a closed system (one that does not interact with an outside environment) never changes over time. Over time, individual objects may gain or lose energy. But if energy is a conserved quantity, any loss in energy by one object must be made up for in the gain in energy by another object.

Dowe's account is widely taken to be the most sophisticated and well-worked out physical theory of causation currently on the table. Still, it has met with many objections from different parties.

On the one hand, there are those philosophers who are skeptical in general of the project of understanding causation in terms of physical processes. Several metaphysicians have complained that physical theories ignore the many cases of causation involving not a physical process, but the *absence* of a physical process. For example, many believe there are cases of causation by omission such as:

(1) X's failure to water the plants caused the plants to die.

There also appear to be compelling cases of causation of absence:

(2) X's wearing her seatbelt caused her not to be ejected from her seat.

There even seem to be cases in which both the cause and the effect involve the absence of a physical process:

(3) X's failure to send an invitation caused Y's not appearing at the party.

In all of these cases, the causal claims seem to describe not a physical process involving the exchange of a conserved quantity, but the absence of a physical process. In these cases, since the process fails to occur, there can be no exchange of conserved quantities as the process theory seems to require. Usually such cases are presented in support of a counterfactual theory of causation. In all of the above cases, we have corresponding counterfactuals whose truth does not appear to require the occurrence of any physical process:

(1_{CF}) If X had watered the plants, the plants wouldn't have died.

(2_{CF}) If X hadn't worn her seatbelt, she would have been ejected from her seat.

(3_{CF}) If X had sent Y an invitation, Y would have attended the party.

The counterfactual theorist may note that the causal claims (1)–(3) are true in virtue of the truth of these counterfactuals (1_{CF})–(3_{CF}). Since there are genuine cases of causation that physical theories cannot explain, the physical theory must be inadequate as a theory of causation.

EXERCISE 8.4

Causation Involving Absences and Physical Theories of Causation

Defenders of physical process theories typically have two ways of responding to objections appealing to cases of causation involving absences. They have the option of (a) arguing that the case in question is not a genuine case of causation, or (b) arguing that in the relevant case, there is a physical process one can point to that grounds the causal fact. For each of (1)–(3), decide how it is most appropriate for the physical process theorist to respond.

Dowe's theory has also faced objections from those who are in principle sympathetic to the project of developing a physical process theory of causation. Some philosophers of science have worried that Dowe's account doesn't capture the full range of causal processes and interactions that one finds in our best physical theories. For example, modern physics describes some causal interactions that don't involve the crossing of world–lines. Objects typically interact with each other at a distance through the intermediary of fields without their world–lines actually intersecting. This suggests that more work is required to better understand physical causal processes. This is not a surprise. As physics continues to evolve, our physical theories of causation should evolve as well.

TWO PROJECTS IN THE PHILOSOPHY OF CAUSATION

One issue worth considering at this stage is the status of all of these competing accounts of causation with respect to one another. Often regularity, counterfactual, probabilistic, primitivist, and physical theories of causation are presented as if they are competitors to one another, but there are many distinct aims that a theory of causation may be taken to have. With this in mind, it is important to keep in mind when evaluating a theory of causation what exactly that theory is trying to explain. It is possible that some of these theories may actually be compatible with one another if they are trying to give accounts of different phenomena.

For example, it is very clear in Lewis's work on causation that what he is aiming at is an account that captures the truth of the majority of causal claims we assert in ordinary circumstances. His counterfactual theory of causation is thus intended as an **analytic account** of causation, an account of what we mean when we say something of the form ⌈c causes e⌉. Lewis acknowledges the possibility that his account might fail in some cases to track what we might ordinarily say or that there may be some cases (tricky, complicated philosophers' examples) where our intuitions just won't settle what the correct answer will be, but that is OK. What he is aiming for is an account that gets most of what we ordinarily say right and the weird, complicated cases can be left as a matter of "spoils to the victor." Whichever account handles the majority of cases, the cases where our intuitions are clear, gets to decide what it is right to say about the cases where our intuitions fail to deliver an obvious result.

Analytic account: an account of what we mean.

It is widely agreed that counterfactual theories are well placed to address what it is we try to express when we assert causal claims. Most philosophers of causation today are sympathetic to what Carolina Sartorio has called "the difference-making intuition," the idea that causes are those events that make a difference to their effects.[15] If e is counterfactually dependent on c, then this is to say that if c hadn't happened then e wouldn't have happened either. This is one obvious way in which c could make a difference to e. If our ordinary talk about causation assumes causes are difference-makers, then this would also seem to give support to probabilistic theories of causation. For another way for c to make a difference to e is for the occurrence of c to raise the probability of e's occurring.

On the other hand, in *Physical Causation*, Dowe is clear that his account is not trying to be an analytic account, an account that captures what we mean when we make everyday causal assertions, even an account according to which most of the causal claims we make are true. Rather, Dowe is trying to develop an accurate empirical account of causation. What he is trying to do is spell out what causation is in our world according to our best scientific theories. Our best scientific theories can often tell us things that conflict with our ordinary intuitions, things we might frequently assert in everyday circumstances whether we know it or not. And so it is clear that the project Dowe has in mind as he develops his account of causation is distinct from the project Lewis was working on.

It is thus possible that multiple kinds of theories may have a role in the ultimate, complete philosophical account of causation. We might learn from our best scientific theories that there are certain distinctive kinds of physical processes that are characteristic of causation at our world. And yet a distinct account may turn out to be appropriate when we attempt to capture the truth conditions of most of our ordinary causal claims. Many have thought that counterfactual theories of causation are best up to this task. There have certainly been many sophisticated counterfactual theories developed to meet the challenge. But it is still possible that no reductive theory will ultimately suffice to capture what we mean by our causal claims, which is what Tooley's arguments were intended to show.

SUGGESTIONS FOR FURTHER READING

The two main theories of events are found in Jaegwon Kim's "Events as Property Exemplifications" and Donald Davidson's "Events as Particulars." Aristotle's four causes (material, formal, efficient, and final) are presented in his *Physics*, Book II, Chapter 3, and his *Metaphysics*, Book V, Chapter 2. For an interesting defense of teleological causation, see John Hawthorne and Daniel Nolan, "What Would Teleological Causation Be?" Hume's theory of causation can be found in his *Enquiry Concerning Human Understanding*, sections 4–7. For a recent discussion of whether we directly experience causal relations, see Susanna Siegel's *The Contents of Visual Experience*.

An excellent anthology collecting many of the classic papers discussed here including those by Davidson, Lewis, and Tooley, among others, is *Causality*, edited by Ernest Sosa and Michael Tooley. The 2004 anthology *Causation and Counterfactuals*, edited by John Collins, Ned Hall, and L.A. Paul, contains many of the most important recent papers on counterfactual theories of causation, including critiques by David Armstrong and Tim Maudlin and later versions of the counterfactual theory offered by, for example, David Lewis, Laurie Paul, and Stephen Yablo. For physical and probabilistic theories of causation, one may consult the papers by Wesley Salmon in the Sosa and Tooley volume. Predecessors for the type of physical theory found in Dowe's *Physical Causation* may be found in

Reichenbach, *The Direction of Time,* and Salmon, "Causality without Counterfactuals." There are two other important theories of causation that we did not have the space to examine here. One is the INUS-condition account of J.L. Mackie developed in his 1980 book *The Cement of the Universe.* This is a more sophisticated version of the regularity theory. Causes are taken to be "INUS-conditions," conditions that are insufficient but necessary parts of a condition which is itself unnecessary but sufficient for the result. Another kind of account of causation that has become very popular in recent years, especially among philosophers of science, is the interventionist account popularized by James Woodward in his 2003 book, *Making Things Happen.* Interventionism is a sophisticated version of the counterfactual theory which gives an account of what causes what in terms of facts about what the results of various interventions on a system would be.

NOTES

1   It is a pint of Snake Venom by the Scottish company Brewmeister. With a 67.5% ABV, this is the strongest beer in the world.

2   You might worry that *strictly speaking,* just because your friend quickly drinks a pint of Snake Venom, this doesn't absolutely guarantee that he will get red and stumble around. Your friend could have eaten an entire loaf of bread immediately before the pint in an effort to soak up the alcohol he was about drink. He could have also fallen asleep immediately after he drank it and never had the chance to stumble around. In either case, the defender of causation as a necessary connection between events will argue that to find the complete cause of the redness and stumbling, we need to fill in a bit more about the background conditions of the case (e.g., his starting with a fairly empty stomach while remaining awake).

3   Galen Strawson defends the view that Hume was a skeptical realist about causation in his book *The Secret Connexion.*

4   Hume also adds a contiguity constraint to his regularity theory. Causes must be contiguous to their effects, meaning they must occur at a spatial location near or next to their effects.

5   To be really precise, one should make a distinction between theories that try to analyze *type causation,* what it is for one type of event to cause another type of event (e.g., for smoking to cause cancer, marriage to cause happiness) and those theories that try to analyze *token causation,* what is required for a token event to be the cause of another token event (e.g., for Jim's smoking to cause him to develop cancer, the marriage of Jack and Jill to cause their happiness). To keep this chapter manageable, we will restrict our attention in what follows to theories of token causation.

6   One influential version appears in Donald Davidson's paper, "Causal Relations."

7   This theory was first developed in his paper from 1973, "Causation." The account was later modified in the postscripts added to the paper in its 1986 reprinting in Lewis's *Philosophical Papers: Volume II.* Lewis modified his theory a final time in 2000 in his paper "Causation as Influence."

8   For example, the cognitive scientist Judea Pearl's influential book on the topic, *Causality*, explicitly acknowledges the influence of Lewis's theory.

9   It is worth noting that although counterfactual theories of causation are definitely much more common today as a result of Lewis's work, regularity theories have not completely disappeared. Michael Strevens's "Mackie Remixed" is a nice piece offering a nomic regularity theory responsive to Lewis's concerns.

10   For more on the use and interpretation of these diagrams, see Ned Hall and Laurie Paul's, *Causation: A User's Guide*.

11   The book *Causation and Counterfactuals*, edited by John Collins, Ned Hall, and Laurie Paul, collects much of this work.

12   The example has been very slightly modified to allow for ease of presentation.

13   He gives an additional case where the laws include facts about probabilities. E.g., L_1 might be modified to say that an object's having property P raises its probability of later having Q or R. L_2 might be modified to say that an object's having property S raises its probability of later having Q or R. This, Tooley argues, would show that the facts about probabilities underdetermine the facts about causation.

14   Dowe also supplements these definitions with an account of causal connection which we will not get into here.

15   See Sartorio, "Causes as Difference-Makers" for discussion.

CHAPTER 9

Free Will

Learning Points

- Introduces the various conceptions of free will at stake in the contemporary philosophical literature and their connection with other topics that matter to us, including moral responsibility
- Considers the putative conflict between free will and determinism and various ways of resolving the conflict
- Assesses the case for and against determinism
- Considers views rejecting the claim that we possess free will.

WHAT IS FREE WILL?

Until now we have focused on metaphysical issues that concern objects considered in a very general way. We have discussed fundamental issues in ontology, the nature of time, modality, and causation. However there are a host of other issues in metaphysics that are not quite so general but concern some important features of a more narrow class of entities. One metaphysical issue that has been incredibly interesting to philosophers for centuries is whether it is possible for persons to have free will. Are the actions of ordinary human beings like ourselves ever truly up to us? Do we ever have any control over the types of things we do and the kinds of people we are?

Typically, these philosophical questions arise out of worries that there exists some threat to our having free will. Sometimes the threat comes in the form of a God or other deity who, it is suggested, might be controlling our natures and our decisions about what to do. Other times, and this is the problem that will concern us here, the threat comes from the impersonal and universal laws of nature that govern everything that happens. The metaphysical issue then concerns how to reconcile the sense that we are free agents with the existence of God or the laws. Or if this is not possible, the job of the philosopher becomes to assess the important implications this has for the way we must see ourselves and the relationships we have to our environments and other human beings.

So, the main issue in this chapter is whether in any important sense any of our decisions or actions are up to us. This is what it means to say an agent's action or decision is free – it is up to that agent. It comes from her and not someone or something else. The philosopher Robert Kane has argued that there are different species of freedom we may distinguish: what he calls **surface freedom**, on the one hand, and a *deeper* form of freedom, or **ultimate freedom**, on the other.[1] Most metaphysicians who discuss the topic of free will agree that this distinction exists and indeed it is freedom in the deeper sense that we should care about.

Surface freedom: being able to act in such a way that one's desires are satisfied.

Ultimate freedom of the will: having the ability to satisfy one's desires and being the ultimate source of those desires.

To see the distinction, imagine one day you have nothing special to do, no outside responsibilities demanding your time. And imagine on this day you decide to do everything just the way you want to. You wake up and get out of bed only when you want to. You eat and drink all and only what you desire. You perform the activities that make you happy. Perhaps you go and see your favorite sports team play, or you spend the day lying out in the sun reading a book, or you ride your bike out to a favorite spot. In a sense, what you do on this day is maximally free. It would seem there are no constraints on you forcing you to do things you don't want to do. Instead you do exactly what you want. What Kane means by 'surface freedom' is exactly this ability to do what one wants, to satisfy one's desires. And, one might wonder, what could be missing? What more could there be to freedom of the will?

To show that there is a deeper kind of freedom, we must ask what it is in virtue of which you have these desires in the first place. Do these desires have their ultimate source in you, or do they arise from something else outside of your control? To see how that might be, consider a science fiction version of the previous scenario, where on that day indeed you do everything you want to do and these activities make you happy, but these desires and wants have all been programmed into you by some malicious neuroscientist. So the activities of the day really do give you what you want and really do make you happy but they would not be what you want and these activities would not make you happy if you hadn't been programmed in just this way.

This suggests that surface freedom is not sufficient for genuine freedom of the will. Still, one might say, who cares, this is a science fiction case. In reality, I am not controlled by a malicious neuroscientist and my desires are my own.

But we may consider less science fiction versions of the scenario as well. Many philosophers have worried, and perhaps this is something you have worried about as well, that even those of us who are happy, those of us who seem to think they have what they want out of life, lack freedom in an important sense that affects the character and value of their lives. For although there may be no evil neuroscientist controlling what I care about and what makes me happy, my desires and dispositions were shaped by factors beyond my control. The circumstances in which I was raised as a child, the norms of the society in which I live, the education I have had up until now, the books I have read and movies I have watched, all of these things have constrained the type of person I am now, influenced what I desire and what it is that makes me happy. If I weren't subject to these constraints, would I still desire what I do, would these things still make me happy? It is hard to know, but it is also hard to avoid thinking there may be a deeper freedom of the will to be had. This deeper sense of freedom is what we mean when we talk about our being the ultimate source of our will and actions. We are now going to consider a reason to think it is lacking, even if somehow we could know we were not under the control of evil scientists or not shaped in some problematic way by our environments.

THE PROBLEM OF FREE WILL AND DETERMINISM

When metaphysicians today worry about there being a threat to our free will, the main threat they worry about comes from the laws of the universe constraining our choices and actions. This comes from the **epistemic possibility** (possibility given what we know) that the basic laws of the universe are **deterministic**. This means that the laws are such that, given any complete state of the universe at a time and facts about what the laws are, it is possible in principle to deduce what the complete state of the universe will be at any later time. Given any past or present state of the universe, the laws determine what the future holds.

Epistemic possibility: something that is compatible with everything that one knows.

How would determinism in the laws threaten free will? The rough idea is very simple. If determinism is true, then this means that the choices and decisions you make now, indeed everything you have ever done, were determined by states of the universe that occurred long before you were born. In fact, if determinism is true and there was, as cosmology suggests, a Big Bang 13.7 billion years ago, it was already determined then what kind of person you are and what you will be doing right now. None of these facts then about who you are and how you act, it would seem then, are up to you. Given the laws and the facts about this early state of the universe, you couldn't have been any way than how you actually are; you couldn't have done anything else.

This reasoning was articulated very clearly in a famous argument by Peter van Inwagen. This is the Consequence Argument. Its aim is to demonstrate the incompatibility of free will and determinism. Here is one way of presenting this argument:

The Consequence Argument

1.   There is nothing we can do now to change the past.
2.   There is nothing we can do now to change the laws of nature.

Therefore,

3.   There is nothing we can do now to change the past and the laws of nature.
4.   If determinism is true, then our present actions are the necessary consequences of the past and the laws of nature.

Therefore,

5. If determinism is true, then there is nothing we can do now to change the fact that our present actions are the necessary consequences of the past and the laws of nature. (by (4))

Therefore,

6. If determinism is true, then there is nothing we can now do to change the fact that our present actions occur. (by (3) and (5))

Therefore,

7. If determinism is true, then no one has the power to do otherwise than what one actually does. (by (6))
8. Free will requires the power to do otherwise.

Therefore,

9. If determinism is true, then no one has free will. (by (7) and (8))

Van Inwagen's argument appears valid and rests only on a few basic assumptions, all of which seem hard to deny. How could one deny that there is nothing we can do now to change the past or change the laws of nature? Similarly, the steps of the argument from (4) to (7) seem intuitive and difficult to deny.

Van Inwagen's premise (8) is substantive. It involves a particular view about what free will requires. It assumes that for an action to be free, it is not merely enough that it is an action that is consistent with your desires, but also that it was one you were able to refrain from doing. But that seems intuitive too. Think about any putatively free action of yours. Say you had a bowl of cereal for breakfast. You didn't *have to* have that bowl of cereal this morning. You could have had eggs or a smoothie instead. You could have had none of these things and started your day without breakfast at all. But what if it turned out that you couldn't have done otherwise? Something was constraining you so that you had to have that bowl of cereal. Then there is an intuitive pull towards thinking that maybe that action wasn't really free after all. It wasn't really up to you.

What the Consequence Argument aims to show is that if the laws are deterministic, then given past states of the universe and these laws, you really could not have done otherwise. If you ate cereal for breakfast, you had to eat cereal for breakfast. And then, it would seem to follow, this, like all of the rest of your actions, is not really free; it is not really up to you.

Philosophers have not all been persuaded by this argument. But before
we consider the main types of responses one encounters, we should try to
see what one is committed to if one accepts the premises of this argument
and follows van Inwagen where he thinks they lead.

There are two broad positions philosophers take today with respect to
free will: those who think (as van Inwagen does) that free will is incompatible
with determinism in the laws, and those who think free will is compatible
with determinism. Those adopting the former position are called **incom-
patibilistists**; those adopting the latter, **compatibilists**. If one thinks that free
will is incompatible with determinism, then one has another question to
answer that is relevant to the question of whether we have free will: Is
determinism true? And this marks another big division in the philosophy of
free will. There are, on the one hand, those who think we have good reason
to accept determinism. These philosophers end up being skeptics about
free will. They are often called **hard determinists**. This name signifies that
they accept determinism and think it has serious consequences for our
sense that we are free. It contrasts with what is called **soft determinism**. This
is the position of those philosophers who accept determinism but are
compatibilists; that is, who don't think determinism is incompatible with our
having free will. Finally, if you are an incompatibilist, there is another option,
and this is the position van Inwagen favors: **libertarianism**.[2] Libertarians
believe that free will is incompatible with determinism, but instead of
rejecting the existence of free will, they reject determinism. Libertarians
think they know they are free. They know they often or at least some of the
time have the ability to do otherwise, and so, as a consequence, they reject
the claim that the laws of the universe are deterministic. We may represent
these various positions as shown in Figure 9.1.

Since which position you adopt about free will depends so much on
whether you think that the laws are deterministic, let's explore for a bit what
reason there is to think determinism is true. What if anything suggests this
and are we justified in believing it?

Incompatibilism: the
view that free will is
incompatible with
determinism.

Compatibilism: the view
that free will is compatible
with determinism.

Hard determinism:
the view that free will is
incompatible with
determinism and so human
beings lack free will.

Soft determinism: the
view that determinism is
true and it is compatible
with the existence of free
will.

Libertarianism: the view
that free will is incompatible
with determinism and so
determinism is false.

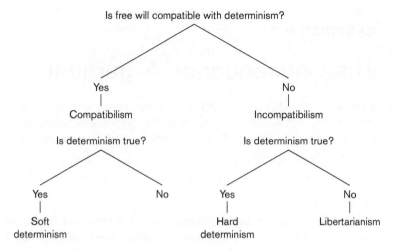

Figure 9.1 Main Views in the Free Will Debate

DETERMINISM

Determinism is a view about the character of the laws of nature. It is a position that became motivated as scientific progress, especially after the development of Newton's mechanical framework, gave us reason to believe there were a set of fundamental, physical laws that govern the entire universe. The thought is that if we could just know where all of the fundamental particles in the universe are located and what their basic features are (their masses, velocities, and so on), we could use these laws to predict everything that will happen for all times into the future. In the early nineteenth century, Pierre-Simon Laplace (1749–1827) was so inspired by the ability of Newton's physics to accurately predict the behavior of physical systems that he imagined the possibility of a supremely powerful intellect, one capable of using this system to predict all future behavior:

> We may regard the present state of the universe as the effect of its past and the cause of its future. An intellect which at a certain moment would know all forces that set nature in motion, and all positions of all items of which nature is composed, if this intellect were also vast enough to submit these data to analysis, it would embrace in a single formula the movements of the greatest bodies of the universe and those of the tiniest atom; for such an intellect nothing would be uncertain and the future just like the past would be present before its eyes.
>
> (Laplace 1951, p. 4)

This hypothetical intellect is now known as Laplace's Demon. If Laplace was this impressed with Newtonian mechanics, it seems he would be all the more impressed with the fundamental physical theories that have succeeded it. The special and general theories of relativity and quantum mechanics both have had empirical successes unrivaled by any previous physical theories. We know neither is a final theory, as relativity and quantum theory will eventually need to be unified into one more encompassing view, but we can eventually hope to discover the fundamental laws. Perhaps once we know these and have the ability to describe an initial state of the universe, one could, given enough computing power, predict everything that will happen with perfect precision, as Laplace imagined.

Now there are some reasons, independent of the issue of free will, for thinking that perhaps determinism isn't correct. For, speaking of quantum mechanics, doesn't that theory tell us that the laws of nature are fundamentally indeterministic and so even if we may be getting closer and closer to discovering the basic laws of the universe, this doesn't mean we are getting closer and closer to having the ability to predict what happens in the future with certainty?

There is a lot to say about the relationship between quantum mechanics and indeterminism. I will limit the discussion to two points, but first let's get just a bit clearer about what is meant by 'indeterminism.' Like determinism, indeterminism is a position about the character of the laws. It is defined simply as the denial of determinism; so it is the view that the laws are such that, given any complete state of the universe at a time and the facts about what the laws are, this *fails to* logically entail what the complete state of the universe will be at any later time. There are a number of reasons why indeterminism might be the case. Here are three possibilities. First, it could be because there aren't any laws of nature in the first place. It could be that the universe is such a disordered jumbled place of random facts that there are no such things as laws in any plausible sense of the word.[3] Second, it could be that there are laws of nature, but they do not cover all of the types of situations that may arise in our universe (perhaps they say how an object will behave when there are no forces acting on it, but do not describe what happens when there are forces). Or, perhaps there are laws of nature, but these are local laws that describe what happens in this or that part of the universe (here on Earth, or here in the part of the universe that we may observe), and there are other parts of the universe for which there are no even local laws that apply. Finally, and this is what many physicists and philosophers think follows from quantum theory, there are universal laws that govern what happens everywhere and in all types of situations, but these laws do not describe what will happen as a matter of necessity. Instead they only describe what will happen as a matter of chance. Let's see whether it is true that quantum mechanics implies the laws are indeterministic in this sense.

The truth is that the interpretation of quantum mechanics is still widely debated even though the theory was developed almost a century ago in the 1920s. The central dynamical laws of quantum mechanics, be they Schrödinger's equation or the relativistic variants thereof, are all purely deterministic laws; they do not make any reference to chances. But some think that Schrödinger's equation cannot be all there is to quantum mechanics and that there must be some additional laws describing the chances that there will be a so-called collapse of the wave function.[4] If this is correct and there must be a probabilistic law governing wave function collapse, then indeed the laws of the universe will be indeterministic. However, this is by no means a settled opinion. One popular interpretation of quantum mechanics that many physicists and philosophers take seriously, the many worlds interpretation, denies that quantum mechanics needs supplementation with any indeterministic law.

Despite the fact that it is contentious whether the fundamental physical laws are deterministic or indeterministic, some have argued that even if the laws are indeterministic, this still doesn't help one avoid the kind of determinism that threatens our having free will. The reason is that the probabilities one finds in the laws of quantum physics have important consequences for the behavior of subatomic matter and radiation, but they have negligible consequences when it concerns the behavior of objects at the scale of the macroscopic.[5] When we consider systems of particles as large as human beings, indeed even as large as the cells making up human beings, the probabilities in the quantum laws "wash out," and it becomes possible to tell for most systems how they will behave at the next time. Strictly speaking, this isn't quite right. If the quantum laws are truly indeterministic, there is always a tiny chance even for a large system the size of (say) a human being that we will observe some unexpected quantum effect. However, the chances of these effects are so tiny, they are so unlikely, that such effects would not suffice to give us the freedom and control we want over the choices we make every day. Or at least this is a common view. In the later section on libertarianism, we will see how some philosophers have tried to exploit quantum indeterminacy, however rarely it may have a noticeable significance in the lives of human beings, to save free will.

COMPATIBILISM

So determinism, even if it is not a settled feature of physics, is a live option and seems to at least obtain at the macroscopic level of human beings and the medium- and large-sized objects with which they interact. If this is right, and we follow van Inwagen's argument where it leads, then it looks like we as people never have control over our decisions and actions. We are never free since everything we think and do is determined by events that took place long before we were born and the laws of nature. But should we follow van Inwagen's argument where it leads? A large number of metaphysicians think we should not – these are the compatibilists about free will – and they have a variety of ways of responding to the Consequence Argument. We will just discuss two such responses here and the impact these responses have for how we should understand free will.

One response that has seemed obvious to some is to question the validity of the move van Inwagen makes from his fifth premise:

> (5) If determinism is true, then there is nothing we can now do to change the fact that our present actions are the necessary consequences of the past and the laws of nature.

to his sixth:

> (6) If determinism is true, then there is nothing we can now do to change the fact that our present actions occur.

The inference to premise (6) follows not just from (5), but also from the earlier premise (3) that there is nothing one can do to change either the past or the laws of nature. Van Inwagen says the inference to (6) from (3) and (5) follows given a "transfer of powerlessness" principle: if you can't do anything about X and you can't do anything about the fact that Y is a necessary consequence of X, then you can't do anything about Y.

This certainly seems intuitive, but David Lewis, in his paper "Are We Free to Break the Laws?" argues that this reasoning fails. To see this, let's hold determinism fixed in the background and just ask what it takes for it to be true that you could change a fact about whether one of your present actions occurs. Earlier, we considered the case of someone, say you, having breakfast this morning. Now ask, is there something you could do to change what you had for breakfast this morning? Now if the breakfast has already passed, then of course there is nothing you can do about it. But the real question, what is relevant to the issue of free will, is whether just at the time when you were about to have the cereal (let's call that time t), you could have made it so you did not have the cereal. So, Lewis asks, what would make it the case that you did not have that cereal this morning? And is it possible that you didn't have the cereal this morning?

Now in any usual sense of the word 'possible,' of course this is possible.[6] It is of course a *possibility* that you did not have cereal this morning, but had (say) a smoothie instead. But you may ask, is it a possibility that you did not have cereal this morning and everything about the world was the same up until the time when you made the decision? Again Lewis says yes: there is certainly no contradiction in your past history being just the same up until time t and then instead of choosing cereal, you chose a smoothie.

Now what is true is that in a situation like that, something would have to give, if determinism were true (which, remember, is the background assumption we are making), then things couldn't have been just the same up until t *and* the laws were the same as those at our world *and* yet you chose a smoothie. But this is not the question. The question is whether there is a possible world in which things are just the same up until t and yet you have a smoothie. And this is possible. What we will have to say is that at that world, there are different laws of nature. But this doesn't mean that anything outrageous happens, that you somehow have special powers to break the laws of nature at this world. The world in which you choose the smoothie is just a world at which the laws are different.

At this point, there is a disagreement that was never resolved between the incompatibilist van Inwagen and the compatibilist Lewis. The incompatibilist in general will think that Lewis is misunderstanding what the issue is in premise (6). For him, the issue is: given determinism, and how things are up until t, and the *actual* laws, we fail to have any power not to have cereal. For Lewis, to understand our freedom, we have to understand that part of what is involved in free action is that in a sense we have the freedom to break the laws, not in the sense of creating exceptions in the actual laws of nature (which is what (2) denies is possible), but rather in the sense of acting such that the laws of the world are different than what they otherwise would have been. Probably a large part of this disagreement stems from a disagreement about what the laws of nature are. Lewis thinks the laws of nature are the sorts of things that are determined by what actually happens at a universe. And so if people act differently at a world, this will entail that the laws at the world are different. Van Inwagen seems to be assuming in the background a different theory of laws, where they could not be ultimately dependent on what people choose to do.

BOX 9.1

Humeanism about Laws

We have now seen the laws of nature play a role in several central debates in metaphysics. So it is worth briefly outlining a few theories about the nature of these laws. One common view about the laws of nature is what is now referred to as **Humeanism about laws**. Humeans believe that the facts about what the laws are are ultimately explainable in terms of or reducible to facts about what happens at a world, that is facts about what kinds of objects and events there are and how they are distributed over space–time. Anti-Humeans think that the facts about what the laws are are not reducible to facts about what happens. Rather the facts about what the laws are are additional facts over and above what happens at a world. The facts about the laws instead *explain* what happens.

Humeanism is named after David Hume because it was he who held there were no necessary connections between distinct entities. Since if laws were fundamental, this would mean there are fundamental, necessary connections between the events that take place; the Humean wants to explain what appear to be necessary connections in terms of more basic facts about what happens just as a matter of fact (not as a matter of necessity).

Lewis sketches his particular Humean theory of laws in his paper "New Work for a Theory of Universals." An exhaustive critique of Humeanism in its various versions, as well as the defense of a rival anti-Humean position, may be found in David Armstrong's *What Is a Law of Nature?*

So this is one issue compatibilists have raised for the Consequence Argument. Perhaps a more frequent criticism that really gets to the heart of the issue of what is involved in freedom of the will is directed at van Inwagen's eighth premise:

(8) Free will requires the power to do otherwise.

Many philosophers have questioned this premise, many raising interesting thought experiments showing us that we have no trouble at all imagining cases where someone makes a decision or acts in a way that is perfectly free and yet it turns out that he was incapable of deciding or acting otherwise. One old example comes from the philosopher John Locke (1632– 1704) who imagined a situation in which a man wakes up in a room that is, unbeknownst to him, locked from the outside. The man decides on his own to stay in the room. The decision and action are both free, and yet the man does not have the ability to do otherwise.

The philosopher Harry Frankfurt, in a paper in 1969, constructed an alternative case that has seemed to many philosophers to be a more compelling illustration of the fact that agents can act freely even if they do not have the ability to do otherwise.[7] This sort of case is now widely referred to as a **Frankfurt case**. Frankfurt cases involve the following features:

- There is an agent who makes a decision at some time t to engage in some action A and then acts on this decision without interference from the outside.
- Unbeknownst to this agent, there is an outside party with an interest in the agent's doing A. The outside party has planted a device in the agent's head ensuring that if the agent does not choose on her own to do A by t, the device will forcibly set the agent's body in motion to bring about A anyway. If the agent does decide to do A by t, then the device does nothing.

Frankfurt case: a case in which intuitively one acts freely and so is morally responsible for an action, and yet one did not have the ability to do otherwise.

For example, suppose there is an assassin Alice who is hired by the mob to murder an important political figure Beatrice. The mob boss who hired Alice, Carlo, finds it very important that the assassination is carried out and does not entirely trust Alice, so Carlo has a device planted in Alice's head while she is unconscious and without Alice's knowledge. The purpose of the device is to ensure that if she should back out of the assassination, the device will make it so that Alice undertakes the assassination anyway. As it happens, Alice carries out the assassination as planned. Of her own accord, she makes the decision to murder Beatrice, the murder takes place, and the secret, implanted device never needs to interfere with Alice's body. Many find this a good example of a free action, although because of the presence of the device, it appears to be a case in which the agent is not able to do otherwise.

What is important and clever about this case, like Locke's, is the fact that even if there are constraints that may have prevented the agent from doing something other than what she chose, those constraints turn out not to be operative. In the actual circumstances they do nothing to influence the agent's action. We have two clear cases in which an agent acts directly on the basis of his or her own decisions. It is thus puzzling why the mere possibility of the agent's action being constrained should affect whether in the situation under consideration, the act (and the decision too) was free.

Now this case by itself is sufficient to undermine the Consequence Argument, since it would show why premise (8) of that argument is false. And so incompatibilists have done a lot to try to show why these Frankfurt cases are confused. We will not get into these challenges here, but please consult the further readings listed at the end of this chapter.

EXERCISE 9.2

Frankfurt Cases

How might one respond to the Frankfurt case described above in order to defend the principle that free will requires the ability to do otherwise?

Instead, let's consider what the compatibilist thinks *is* required for free will if it does not require the ability to do otherwise. At the core of compatibilism lies the idea that even if our actions are in a genuine sense determined by prior states of the universe and the laws of nature, there is still an important distinction between those choices and actions that are truly up to the agent and those that are not. One important concept for the compatibilist is the notion of constraint. Following A.J. Ayer, many compatibilists prefer to understand free will and action as that which is not constrained.[8] What does constraint amount to? Ayer gives several examples to show what he has in mind. Someone may constrain your action by putting a pistol to your head, or by gaining a "habitual ascendancy" over you so that, without force, you do what they want. One may also be constrained by one's own uncontrollable urges. The kleptomaniac is impelled to steal and feels satisfied when she does, but these are not free actions. They are not ones that are under her control. What seems common to these cases is that although the agent is doing something, she is not doing what she ultimately wants. Her action is not in line with her desires, what she prefers to be doing. Ayer's is probably the simplest compatibilist view: an act is free just in case it is not constrained.

The compatibilist thinks we can have free will even if our actions are the results of earlier states of the universe and the laws. For the compatibilist, determinism doesn't stand in the way of freedom, because what is really important to our concept of freedom is that our actions come from us and are in line with what we want rather than constrained. In fact, many compatibilists would argue not only that there isn't tension with determinism in the laws, but that our sense of freedom importantly relies upon the laws being deterministic. For if the laws were *not* deterministic, then there would be no guarantee, given what one wants and what one chooses, that these choices would ultimately allow one to have any control over what happens. We rely on determinism in the laws in order to be able to predict which sorts of behavior will lead to which sorts of consequences.

I call Ayer's a simple form of compatibilism and it is. Recalling our earlier discussion of the distinction between surface freedom and deeper freedom of the will, one might worry that this view doesn't build in enough to capture the sense of freedom we most care about. To say that a given action is unconstrained, where this means it is an action that is in line with what we desire, is compatible with its not having its ultimate source in one's true character. One might propose to the compatibilist that she should adjust her view to call free only those actions in line with what a more self-reflective, rational person would want. For example, say I am the kind of person who desires all of the time to sleep and watch television. These are, as a matter of fact, the actual desires I have, but I also recognize that if I were the person I really wanted to be, there would be other things I would want to do and so these would not be my desires anymore. One might strive for an account of freedom that doesn't count as free those actions that are simply consistent with one's desires, or that stem from one's desires, but those that are consistent with some deeper fact about one's psychology.

There are many ways of modifying Ayer's simple compatibilist account of what freedom is in order to accommodate a deeper sense of freedom. One suggestion made by Frankfurt is to shift from talk of ordinary, first-order desires (desires to do some action A), to talk of second-order desires (desires to desire some action A). I may very well desire to sleep and watch television all day. But this may not be what I desire to desire, and if so, one might think, I am only really free if my actions line up with these higher order desires. Other compatibilists have argued that instead of using desire in an account of free action, one should appeal to the use of reason on the part of the agent in choosing an action. One might worry that in order to really rule out the kleptomaniac's actions as free, one cannot allow that free actions are those that are merely in line with one's desires or what one wants. The kleptomaniac may really want to steal. Instead, what is distinctive about actions that are genuinely free is that they are the types of actions that stem from an agent's rational assessment of an action and choosing what to do based on reasons in favor of that action. This type of reasons–responsive compatibilism has been developed by the philosopher John Martin Fischer.[9]

EXERCISE 9.3

Compatibilist Theories of Freedom

How would you state the conditions required for an action to be free, genuinely up to the agent? Give one example of a free and another example of an action that is not free to show how this account works to get the cases right. Can an action be free in this sense while at the same time being determined by the laws of nature and past states of the universe?

LIBERTARIANISM

There are a good many compatibilists today, those who think that we have free will even if the laws are deterministic. But there aren't enough compatibilists to say by any means that it is the orthodox or even most popular view in philosophy on the topic of free will. Just as there are a good many compatibilists, there are also very many philosophers who endorse libertarianism. These libertarians do not disagree with the compatibilist that we possess free will, but they do disagree about what is required for us to have it. The libertarian thinks it is not merely enough that our actions stem from our desires, or our higher order desires, or our goals or reasons for those actions to be free. For our actions to be free, our actions must not be determined by the laws. And for many this is because, as we saw in van Inwagen's argument, freedom requires the ability to do otherwise. And so, the libertarian holds, determinism must be false.

However, there is an immediate problem that arises if one rejects determinism. This is something that was briefly touched on in the last section. If determinism is false, then this means that given that the world is in a given state at a one time, this does not guarantee that the world will be another determinate way at a later time. And so one might form a specific intention, make a decision to act in a certain way, but if the laws are indeterministic, then one can't thereby guarantee that one's actions will follow in the way one expects them to from these intentions and decisions. The connection between these psychological states and your later behavior and the eventual state of the world that results would seem to be a matter outside of your control. If determinism is false, your actions will not be determined by the laws, yes. But they will not be determined by you either.

This is the main challenge for the libertarian: to explain how your actions may be up to you in the sense that matters for free will if the laws are indeterministic – why your actions are not then just arbitrary or a matter of chance or random or uncontrolled. We will discuss two ways that libertarians have tried to meet this challenge.

Agent causal libertarianism: see **agent causation**

This first is a form of libertarianism that received an influential defense by the metaphysician Roderick Chisholm.[10] This view is called **agent causal** libertarianism or the **agent causation** view. The main idea behind the view is that your actions may be free and not the result of chance or random when they are directly caused by you. Chisholm thought that if your actions were the results of any earlier event or states, even your own psychological states, these actions couldn't truly be yours since then in a sense you wouldn't have ultimate control over them. Once the desire or intention was formed, the action would follow automatically. This is what makes Chisholm an incompatibilist. But he also recognized that it would not do to say that free actions are caused by nothing; that they just arise out of nowhere. In that case it would seem even more obvious that our actions aren't free. The alternative is to say that there is a cause of any free action, but this cause isn't any earlier event or state, even a psychological state. The cause for a free action must lie outside of the causal sequence of events that is governed by the laws of nature. Free actions involve agents acting in a way that transcends the causal chain of events to directly bring about changes in the world.

To some philosophers, Chisholm's reasoning and the agent causal view has been very attractive, even obvious. However, to many it is mysterious. One may ask: What are these agents that somehow lie outside of the order of events in the causal sequence that is the result of the laws? How do they do what they do without exploiting and acting in terms of the laws that govern our universe? It is probably not surprising to you, especially if you've already learned some philosophy of mind, to hear that Chisholm's position is one that is especially popular among mind–body dualists, those like Descartes who think that there is a fundamental distinction between mental substances (minds, souls) and physical substances (bodies, matter) and that we, as persons, are to be identified with mental substances not physical substances. If one views the agent this way, as a nonphysical substance, then it doesn't seem much to also take on board the idea that the agent acts in a way that may transcend the law-governed chain of events.[11]

This doesn't mean one has to reject physicalism to be a libertarian about free will. An alternative position, event causal libertarianism, tries to make sense of freedom in an indeterministic world while holding on to the view that the only kinds of entities that may be causes and effects are events or states of some kind. There is a fundamental metaphysical disagreement then between these two kinds of libertarian over what are the relata of causal relations (see Box 8.1). The event causal libertarian thinks causation always only links events or states of the world, whereas the agent causal libertarian thinks at least sometimes certain kinds of substances can be causes, in particular, agents in cases of free action.

There are many versions of event causal libertarianism available. To give the flavor of what some of these views look like, I will just describe one version that has been much discussed in the free will literature. This is Kane's version of event causal libertarianism. Kane exploits the indeterminism that is thought by some to be a consequence of quantum mechanics to show how some of our actions may be free. His account centers around the discussion of a class of important, life-directing actions, what he calls **self-forming actions**.

Agent causation: the view that human agents are sometimes causes.

Self-forming actions: important actions in the life of a person that decide the kind of person he or she will be.

Kane doesn't think it is necessary or plausible for the libertarian to try to argue that the majority of the actions in our daily lives are free in the deep sense that matters to us for free will. Every day, we do an uncountable number of things, often without thinking very hard about what we are doing. We do things on whims, or out of habit, or out of a sense of duty or a desire to stick to plans we've made or settled on in the past. I wake up, brush my teeth, have breakfast. I practice my instrument, do the reading I've assigned for class, or go to the gym. Some of these actions are important, many are constitutive of the kind of person I am or who I want to be. But, Kane would argue, most of them are not free in any deep sense. And thus it is fine, Kane can concede, that these are actions that are caused by earlier states of the universe (perhaps including earlier psychological states) and determined by the laws.

It is, however, important for Kane, as it is generally for libertarians, that there are some actions that are free in a deep sense and so are not the results of earlier states of the universe and the laws. These are those actions that make one the kind of person that one is; these are the self-forming actions. To illustrate the kind of action Kane has in mind, we may consider a famous case described by Jean-Paul Sartre (1905–1980) in his discussion of the self and free action.[12] Sartre was writing in German-occupied France during World War II. He describes the case of a young student who was involved with the French Resistance movement and wanted very much to join the effort to free his country by fighting. This would require him to be far away from his family. What made this decision especially hard was that at the time, his mother was very sick and required him to take care of her. If the student left to go fight with the Resistance, his mother would certainly become worse and might die. What Sartre was most interested in demonstrating with this example is the fact that although there are most certainly facts about the kinds of people we are, facts, he said, about our *essences*, these are facts that are not determined by something external to us, something set in place before we are born or something transcendent like a God or innate nature. *We* are responsible for our essences, for the kinds of people we are. In fact, this is how Sartre defined the view for which he is most famous: **existentialism**. This, for Sartre, is characterized as the view that existence precedes essence rather than the other way around. It is not that there are facts about the kinds of people we are and then we act in the way we do because it was already determined we are that way. (This would be for our essence to precede our existence.) Rather, we act in a certain way and this makes us the kind of people we are. In the case of the student, he decides to fight for the Resistance and thus becomes this kind of person, the kind of person who would put his political causes above the strong pull of family. It is the student's action that makes him the kind of person he is, not the other way around.

These are the types of actions in which Kane is most interested. Perhaps you have never had to choose between taking care of your sick parent and going off to fight in a war, but Kane (and Sartre too) would argue that at certain points in your life, you have had to make important decisions. There were two or more paths you could have taken and these

Existentialism: the view that it is the kind of things we do that determines our essences, the kind of people we are. We do not possess innate essences that determine who we are and what we will do.

would have led to your becoming a different sort of person. You choose one and this then forms you, forms the kind of person you are, and thus leads to many of the more mundane actions you perform later as a result. If you have never made any of these self-forming actions, then you are not truly free in the sense that should matter to us as persons.

We may now better understand the sort of actions on which Kane thinks an account of free will should focus, but this doesn't yet say anything about how he proposes to solve the libertarian challenge of reconciling freedom with indeterminism. His account has two main parts. First, Kane must articulate in what respect these self-forming actions are not determined by earlier states of the universe and the laws. Second, Kane must explain how actions that are not so determined may nonetheless not be random or arbitrary, but free actions of a rational agent.

On the first issue, Kane points to features that are special about those situations in which agents are making self-forming actions. In these cases, Kane speculates that there may be two or more processes taking place in the brain. In the case of Sartre's student, there may be a well of neural activity that under normal circumstances would lead to the decision and action of going to war and another that under normal circumstances would lead to the student's staying at home and caring for his mother. Since these neural processes lead to incompatible behavior, they can't both ultimately lead to action. One must, as it were, win out. Here is where indeterminism enters the picture. Kane speculates that in cases like this, activity in the brain may be described in the technical sense of the scientist as chaotic. One thing that is characteristic of chaotic processes is their unpredictability. Often their unpredictability can be traced to their turning on a very small detail.[13] This may be a tiny, indeterministic quantum process. In the case of a self-forming action, things could have, given earlier states of the agent's brain, gone one way or the other. The fact that this is an indeterministic process though ensures that whichever action results was not determined in the sense that would be a threat to free will.

What remains then is only for Kane to explain how it could be that such an undetermined act could be free. If the action was not *caused* by earlier mental states of the agent, but things could have gone either way, then in what sense could it truly be free? And here Kane points to the nature of these special cases of self-forming actions. It is not that any action that results from quantum indeterminism is free, but, in these cases, we can see that there are only a small number of actions that could have resulted. Either, if they had obtained, would have had their source in the agent, because both stemmed from these sorts of self-constituting activity.

There is a lot to say about both of these models of libertarian free action: Chisholm's agent causal libertarianism and Kane's event causal version. And, indeed, many objections have been raised to both accounts. But if one wants to understand how at least some of our actions can be free and one finds freedom incompatible with determinism, one has to develop some account. But this is a subtle and difficult project. It has led some incompatibilists, van Inwagen most notably, to claim that free will is and will always remain a mystery. It is extremely difficult to see how freedom could be compatible with determinism, but it may be equally difficult to see how it could be compatible with indeterminism as well.

SKEPTICISM ABOUT FREE WILL

And this brings us finally to the last group of views one finds about free will. This is to deny the phenomenon altogether. We have already described a view called 'hard determinism.' Recall: this is a version of incompatibilism in which one believes that determinism is true and, as a result of reasoning like the Consequence Argument, one concludes free will does not exist. A stronger position, one that is compatible with hard determinism, is a position the philosopher Derk Pereboom has labeled **hard incompatibilism**. This is the view that yes, free will is incompatible with determinism, but it is also incompatible with indeterminism, because in an indeterministic world, everything that happens is arbitrary, or a matter of chance, and so beyond anyone's control. The hard incompatibilist doesn't need to have a view about whether the laws of nature are deterministic or indeterministic. He will say that, either way, free will couldn't exist.

Hard incompatibilism: the view that free will is incompatible with both determinism and indeterminism and so free will is impossible.

Some who have thought seriously about this issue are not very bothered by this. For example, the psychologist Daniel Wegner, in his book, *The Illusion of Conscious Will*, argues that we lack free will, but that this is something we can live with because all that matters to our lives is that we as humans maintain the illusion that we are free agents. The illusion is sufficient to keep us engaged and see our lives are meaningful.

However, one might worry that a lot is lost if we are forced to give up seeing ourselves and others as free agents. The biggest issue turns on the fact that it is almost unanimously agreed by philosophers that there is a necessary connection between free will and moral responsibility. One can only view oneself or someone else as morally responsible for his or her actions if those actions are up to him or her. If someone's actions aren't their own, then it is not reasonable to blame that person (if one judges these actions to be morally wrong) or praise the person either (if one judges these actions to be good).

It is not an esoteric philosophical point that free will is tied up with moral responsibility. We are familiar from everyday interactions with small children, the sick, or the developmentally disabled that sometimes someone does something one doesn't like, but it isn't right to blame that person since the act wasn't really in an important sense up to them. They couldn't have helped what they did. Similarly we all know that sometimes we do things not because we want to or because these are actions that are really the result of our free choices, and that when this happens, these are actions we don't really deserve to be held morally responsible for. We don't deserve to be praised for them. If you make the effort to phone up your grandfather every week, but not because you really want to, but because your parents threaten to remove your monthly allowance if you don't do so, then you hardly deserve praise for being the faithful grandchild.

In his book, *Living Without Free Will*, Pereboom does an earnest job of conceding the many radical consequences the loss of moral responsibility would seem to have for the way we live our lives and interact with others. If it were true that none of our actions were up to us and so we uniformly lacked moral responsibility, this would mean that we couldn't reasonably praise or blame anyone for anything they ever do. You wouldn't have reason to take pride in the successes in your life. You couldn't reasonably blame the thief, murderer, or rapist. You couldn't see the important relationships in your life, your friendships and loves, as stemming from another person's free decision to spend time with you and make sacrifices on your behalf.

This might cause some to rethink the denial of free will in the first place. This, after all, is a lot to give up. But, Pereboom argues, as surprising and challenging as it is to see ourselves this way, free will is something that must be given up since it is neither compatible with determinism nor indeterminism and these are the only two metaphysical options there are. (Indeterminism is after all just the denial of determinism!) In his book, Pereboom addresses the challenge of explaining how we might continue to see our lives and relationships as valuable even without the existence of free will; and how we might justify locking people up in jail and imposing other penalties, even if people are not actually morally responsible for any of their actions.

EXERCISE 9.4

Compatibilism, Libertarianism, Hard Determinism, or Hard Incompatibilism?

We have now see four major views on the topic of free will. Which position do you find most convincing and why? Which do you consider to be its most challenging rival? Why is your position preferable to that view?

SUGGESTIONS FOR FURTHER READING

Free will has for a long time been one of the most lively areas of research in contemporary metaphysics. There has been a lot written and there are lots of connections between this topic and related ones in the philosophy of mind and action, the philosophy of causation, and of course related topics in ethics concerning moral responsibility. There are several nice books containing introductions to the topic, especially *Free Will: A Very Short Introduction* by Thomas Pink and *A Contemporary Introduction to Free Will* by Robert Kane. The book *Four Views on Free Will* by John Martin Fischer, Robert Kane, Derk Pereboom, and Manuel Vargas presents a defense of

http://philosophy
commons.typepad.
com/flickers_of_
freedom/

four positions on the topic: compatibilism, libertarianism, skepticism about free will, and revisionism (Manuel Vargas's view that our commonsense conception of free will needs to be substantially revised, but not abandoned) side by side. Van Inwagen presented his Consequence Argument in *An Essay on Free Will*. There is also a blog entirely devoted to the topic of free will. It may be found at: http://philosophycommons.typepad.com/flickers_ of_freedom/.

NOTES

1   One can find this distinction in the first chapter of Kane's *A Contemporary Introduction to Free Will*.

2   This view has no relationship with the political libertarian position (the view in favor of a limited government) except for sharing a common name.

3   For an interesting discussion (and defense!) of this possibility, see Nancy Cartwright's excellent book: *The Dappled World*.

4   For a clear and comprehensive discussion of this debate, see David Z Albert's *Quantum Mechanics and Experience*.

5   Macroscopic objects are those large enough to be seen with the naked eye.

6   In Chapter 7, we discussed a couple of salient philosophical senses of the word 'possible': logically possible, nomologically possible. Lewis seems to be pressing the point that your having breakfast this morning was logically possible.

7   Frankfurt actually offered the case as a counterexample to what he called the Principle of Alternative Possibilities. This is the principle that one is only *morally responsible* for an act if one has the ability to do otherwise. So, this is strictly speaking not a principle about freedom but a principle about moral responsibility. As we discuss in more depth in the final section, however, there is a tight connection between the two phenomena.

8   See his "Freedom and Necessity."

9   See his *The Metaphysics of Free Will*.

10   See his essay "Human Freedom and the Self."

11   This isn't to say that this means the view is unproblematic or easy to understand. Indeed, even in Descartes's time (the seventeenth century) philosophers expressed puzzlement about how a nonphysical mental substance could affect anything in the physical world. See for example the correspondence between Descartes and Princess Elisabeth of Bohemia.

12   In his "Existentialism is a Humanism."

13   The butterfly effect is a common example used to illustrate chaotic behavior.

CHAPTER 10

The Metaphysics of Race

(with Allan Hazlett)

Learning Points

- Introduces the distinction between natural entities and those that are socially constructed
- Considers the ontological status of racial categories as a case study in social ontology
- Evaluates three views about the metaphysics of race.

RACE: A TOPIC IN SOCIAL ONTOLOGY

Suppose we are satisfied that merely fictional entities – like Pegasus – do not exist and that the entities described by natural science – like horses – do. Now consider marriages. To which category do they belong? On the one hand, it seems like a mistake to say that marriages don't exist, in the manner of Pegasus. Marriage is a real phenomenon, not a mere fiction like Pegasus. But, on the other hand, it seems like a mistake to say that marriages exist, in the manner of horses. Marriages do not exist independently of our social practices, institutions, and conventions – as John Searle puts it, marriages seem to exist only because we believe them to exist.[1] So what sort of entities are marriages then?

Academics from various disciplines speak of "social construction" when they encounter entities or phenomena that, on the one hand, cannot be dismissed as merely fictional, but that, on the other, are not part of the objective, mind-independent world. Along with marriage, things that are said to be socially constructed include gender, knowledge, science, nature, and race. Such entities or phenomena are part of a social reality that exists, in some to-be-articulated sense, in virtue of our social practices, institutions, and conventions. This talk of social construction and social reality raises many fascinating metaphysical questions. Are there any socially constructed entities? If so, which entities are socially constructed? Is everything socially constructed? What is the relationship between socially constructed entities and other entities? What is the relationship between "social reality" and reality?

In this chapter we'll introduce these issues by looking at a specific example of something that is often claimed to be a social construction: race. One reason for this focus is the fact that a large and heterogeneous set of things have been claimed to be socially constructed. It may not be possible to say anything sensible about social construction in general, without first considering a specific (putative) case. So in what follows we turn to the idea that race is a social construction, and to the metaphysical alternatives to this idea.

EXERCISE 10.1

Natural and Socially Constructed Entities

List five examples each of entities (or types of entities) that are socially constructed and those that are not socially constructed.

NATURAL AND SOCIAL KINDS

In his essay on "The Analytical Language of John Wilkins," Jorge Luis Borges asks us to imagine a certain encyclopedia, in which

> animals are divided into (a) those that belong to the emperor; (b) embalmed ones; (c) those that are trained; (d) suckling pigs; (e) mermaids; (f) fabulous ones; (g) stray dogs; (h) those that are included in this classification; (i) those that tremble as if they were mad; (j) innumerable ones; (k) those drawn with a very fine camel-hair brush; (l) etcetera; (m) those that have just broken the flower vase; (n) those that at a distance resemble flies.

This passage has fascinated philosophers interested in the idea of social construction. We can start to see why by comparing the classification of animals in Borges's encyclopedia with the classification of animals in contemporary biology, where animals are classified by phylum, by class, by order, by family, and by species. Someone using the categories of Borges's encyclopedia and someone deploying the categories of contemporary biology would come up with a different division of the same individual animals. The person using the categories of contemporary biology would come up with Figure 10.1.

While the person using the categories of Borges's encyclopedia would come up with Figure 10.2.

The reason all this is interesting is that there seems, at least at first glance, to be a metaphysical difference between our two systems of

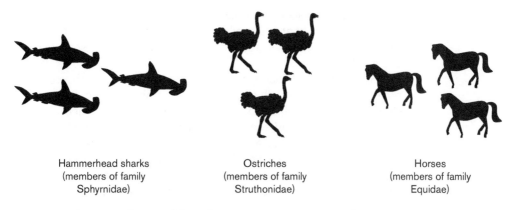

Hammerhead sharks (members of family Sphyrnidae)

Ostriches (members of family Struthonidae)

Horses (members of family Equidae)

Figure 10.1 Biological System of Classification

Animals that belong to the emperor

Animals that have just broken the flower vase

Animals that are trained

Figure 10.2 Borgesian System of Classification

classification. This difference isn't easy to articulate precisely. One way of putting it traces back to Plato's *Phaedrus*: the biological classification system seems to "carve nature at the joints," while the Borgesian system doesn't. That is to say, one classification carves entities up according to objective distinctions in the world, while the other does not. (Or, at least, the distinctions tracked by the former system seem more objective than the distinctions tracked by the latter system.) Contrast the periodic table of the elements – a system of chemical classification positing a hundred chemical categories (hydrogen, carbon, gold, barium, etc.) – with some random, arbitrary grouping of objects: all the things in your bedroom count as one chemical element, all the things in your kitchen count as another, and so on. Chemists at least think that what they are doing with the periodic table is carving things up according to objective distinctions that exist in the world prior to our taking an interest in them, whereas the alternative system of chemical classification just described would be doing no such thing.[2]

Another way of putting the present point is that the biological system groups animals into **natural kinds**, while the Borgesian system doesn't. As Quine argues in his essay "Natural Kinds," this notion is very closely related

Natural kind: a group of objects in which each member of the group shares some objective, mind-independent similarity.

to the notion of similarity. The biological classification system has grouped together animals that are similar to one another, while the Borgesian classification system has grouped together animals that are not similar to one another.

But not so fast! Although the animals that belong to the emperor aren't similar to one another with respect to their morphology – i.e., their form or structure – they are similar to one another with respect to their owner. And while the hammerhead sharks are similar to one another with respect to their morphology, they aren't similar to one another when it comes to ownership – or, indeed, when it comes to any number of properties they might have: their location, or their favorite kind of fish to eat, and so on. What makes classifying animals by morphology more "natural" than classifying them by ownership?

We might appeal here to the distinction between intrinsic and extrinsic properties. Recall, this is the distinction between properties that a thing has in itself, just because of how it is, as opposed to properties that a thing has in virtue of its relationships with other things. The property of being square is intrinsic because whether something has this property depends only on how that thing is in itself, whereas the property being ten miles from Lagos is extrinsic, because whether something has this property depends on its relationship to Lagos. It seems that the morphological properties of animals – properties like the color and size of their bodies – are intrinsic, while properties like being owned by the emperor are extrinsic. So perhaps we can articulate the metaphysical difference between our two systems of classification, one "natural" and the other not "natural," by saying that the biological system has grouped together animals that are intrinsically similar to one another, while the Borgesian classification system has grouped together animals that are not intrinsically similar to one another, even if they are extrinsically similar.

However, this move is complicated by the fact that in contemporary biology, organisms – animals at least – aren't classified by morphology. The reason the hammerhead sharks go together isn't their common form and internal structure. Rather, individual animals are members of a biological species in virtue of their relationship to other members of that species. The reason the hammerhead sharks go together is that they have the same ancestors and can breed with one another. So if our contemporary biological system is "natural," as opposed to the Borgesian system, it's not because the former but not the latter groups together animals that are intrinsically similar.

One response you might have to all of this is to reject the idea that there is a metaphysical difference between the biological system and the Borgesian system. But for many people, the intuition remains that the former tracks objective distinctions while the latter doesn't, or at least distinctions that are more objective than those tracked by the latter. So let's attempt to articulate what is distinctive about biological and other natural classifications, as opposed to the classification system implied by Borges's encyclopedia.

One way to get a grip on what is distinctive about natural kinds is to contrast them with what we'll call **social kinds**. The criteria for membership

Social kind: a group of objects in which each member of the group shares some similarity based in existing social practices, institutions, or conventions.

in a social kind make reference to social practices, institutions, and conventions, like culture and language. To say that some group constitutes a social, rather than a natural, kind is to say that their similarity depends on social practices, institutions, and conventions. The members of said group are similar only given the contingent fact that social practices, institutions, and conventions are the way that they happen to be. The members of natural kinds, by contrast, you might think, are not like that: the hammerhead sharks would be similar, regardless of the existence of social practices, institutions, and conventions.

It seems like biological species and the chemical elements of the periodic table are natural kinds, whereas groups like the bourgeoisie and professors seem to be social kinds. People who are wives, or people who are husbands, people who are single, seem to constitute social kinds (perhaps providing the sense in which marriage is a social construction). Finally, to borrow an example from Sally Haslanger, people who are cool seem to constitute a social kind:

> [T]he distinction . . . between people who are cool and people who are uncool . . . is not capturing intrinsic differences between people; rather it is a distinction marking certain social relations − i.e. it distinguishes status or in-group . . . The distinction does not capture a difference in the individuals so-called except insofar as they are related to me (based on my likes and dislikes), and its use in this context is determined not by the intrinsic or objective coolness of the individuals but by the social task of establishing a cohort.
>
> (Haslanger 1995, pp. 99–100)

Since the classification system that divides people into the cool and the uncool depends on our social practices, the categories of cool people and uncool people are social kinds. We might then take a category or property to be a **social construction** when its members constitute a social kind.

One reason why it is important to determine whether a particular group constitutes a natural or a social kind has to do with necessity and contingency.[3] Social kinds depend for their existence on social practices, institutions, and conventions. But, crucially, any given set of social practices, institutions, and conventions could have been different. Social kinds, unlike natural kinds, are neither inevitable nor unchangeable. This has profound consequences for our understanding of these groups. From a historical perspective, the existence of a particular social kind (or set of social kinds) is not the only possible course history could have taken, and from a political perspective, the existence of a particular social kind (or set of social kinds) is negotiable, something that could in principle be changed. In both these senses, when it comes to socially constructed groups, things could have been otherwise.

Social construction: a classification whose members constitute a social kind.

THREE VIEWS ABOUT RACES

With this conception of social construction in hand, let us consider the claim that race is a social construction. We shall understand this claim as saying that racial classification is a social construction, that racial categories are socially constructed, and that particular races or racial groups – white, black, American Indian, Samoan, and so on[4] – are social kinds. We can bracket the question of whether individual "racialized" people – that is to say, people who are classified as members of a race (more on which below) – are socially constructed, in some sense, as well as the question of whether the very idea of race is socially constructed. And we will remain neutral on the question of universals discussed in Chapter 2. When we ask whether racial categories are socially constructed, we may be asking if there are universals corresponding to our categories that depend on social relationships. Or, if we prefer nominalism, we may ask whether there is a more or less natural class that corresponds to these categories.

The claim that races are social kinds is endorsed by many contemporary academics. But it has been sparsely defended in the history of philosophy, and goes against many people's common sense.[5] The historical and contemporary non-academic consensus has held the view that races are natural kinds. The most influential version of this consensus is that races are biological categories.

What makes something a biological category? Biological species evolve when there is geographic isolation that leads to exclusive mating, eventually resulting in a group of individuals who cannot produce viable offspring with any individuals outside that group. But this process of exclusive mating can create genetic variation that falls short of the inability to produce viable offspring with others. Think, for example, of the different breeds of dogs. Although all members of all breeds are members of the same species, *Canis lupus*, and thus are able to produce viable offspring with one another, the members of each breed are morphologically, genetically, and historically similar to one another, as opposed to members of other breeds. The species *Canis lupus* includes wolves, but also the subspecies for domestic dogs, *Canis lupus familiaris*. This includes greyhounds, golden retrievers, dachshunds, and the rest. Although the members of different breeds of dogs can interbreed, we recognize them nonetheless as members of distinct biological categories because of their morphological, genetic, and historical similarities. So species are one kind of biological category, but we also recognize more fine-grained biological categories. (One might wonder how fine-grained biological categories can be.)

We'll articulate the view that race is a biological category as follows:

> *Biological realism about race*: Races are natural kinds; in particular, racial categories are biological categories, akin to (but perhaps not quite the same as) subspecies or breeds.

For the biological realist, races are akin to species, subspecies, or breeds. In this sense, races amount to real, objective categories in nature.

To what are races akin, for the social constructivist, that is, the theorist who says that race is a social construction? The example of cool and uncool people is instructive here. The social constructivist can argue that racial classification is essentially hierarchical, that is, essentially racist. Just as it is part of what it means to call someone "uncool" that you disapprove of that person, social constructivists argue that racist connotations are built into the meaning of terms for non-white races. The system of racial classification is designed to enforce a social hierarchy, with white people at the top. It has been argued that the idea of race and thus the division into the categories of, for example, white and non-white, emerged in the seventeenth and eighteenth century European academic world alongside the development of African slavery in Europe's New World colonies. Just as attributions of coolness are used to mark an in-group cohort, as against an out-group, racial attributions are used, so the argument goes, to identify white people as the norm and non-white people as the "other."

Haslanger articulates a social constructivism about race, according to which "races are those groups demarcated by the geographical associations accompanying perceived body type, when those associations take on evaluative significance concerning how members of the group should be viewed and treated" (2000, p. 44). It is the second clause that is most important to distinguish social constructivism: for Haslanger, to be a member of a race is to be *racialized*, which is to be systematically subordinated or privileged, in virtue of being perceived as "appropriately occupying certain kinds of social position" (p. 44). This doesn't exclude the input of biological features into the classification. These social distinctions are at least partly attributed in virtue of one's having certain morphological features. However, racial classification, according to this view, is not merely a matter of biological classification. Social factors play an essential role.

The system of racial classification, for the social constructivist, can usefully be compared to the caste system in India. A person's caste, like her race, is inherited from her parents and cannot be changed. Traditionally, castes were organized in a hierarchy, so that some occupied a higher social status than others meaning only they could practice certain trades or interact in certain circles. For example, Brahmins were priests; Dalits were a lower caste. To the outsider, caste distinctions may not mark objective (e.g., biological) differences between people, and this is because caste is merely a social construction. For someone immersed in a society structured by a caste system, caste might appear to be something other than a mere "social reality." But, this appearance is misleading. The social constructivist argues that the case of race is analogous. Racial distinctions seem to mark biological differences between people, but in fact racial differences are merely part of our social reality. So we should contrast biological realism about race with:

> *Social constructivism about race*: Races are social kinds, more akin to castes or to the cool people.

According to the social constructivist, race isn't biologically real, and so it doesn't correspond to an objective categorization in nature. It only exists as part of social reality.

Before turning to the arguments for and against these views, we need to consider a third option. In some sense, biological realists and social constructivists agree about the reality of race. Both parties agree that (for example) some people are white and that some people are black; what they disagree about is the nature of racial categories: do they pick out natural kinds or social kinds? You might want to reject this common assumption about the reality of races.

As the social constructivist can agree, we sometimes get things wrong when it comes to the categories we use: we can mistake a category that picks out a social kind for a category that picks out a natural kind. But we also sometimes employ empty categories, categories that pick out no real kind at all. Consider the category of witches. During the early modern period, around 50,000 people were executed in Europe and North America on the grounds that they were witches. As with attributions of uncoolness or caste status, accusations of witchcraft may have been used in some cases to enforce social hierarchies or to mark an out-group. However, although we may not be inclined to say that there are no uncool people or that there are no Dalits, we are inclined to say that there are not, and never have been, witches. The eliminativist makes the same claim about racial categories that we are inclined to make about the category of witches. There are not, and never have been, witches, although there have been people who were called 'witches.' The eliminativist says that there are not, and never have been, black people and white people, although there have been, and still are, people who are called 'black' and 'white.' So we can add a third view to our list of options:

> *Eliminativism about race*: There are no races. Racial attributions are false. The case of race is analogous to that of witch-hood. There are no witches and witch accusations are false. Race is neither biologically real nor socially real.

Social constructivists and eliminativists agree that races are not natural kinds. They disagree about the reality of races, more on which in the final section.

EXERCISE 10.2

Social Constructivism vs. Eliminativism

Why does it sound correct to many to say that there are no witches and yet wrong to say that there are no cool people? If neither category is natural, then in what sense could one category be "real" and yet the other is not? What could this attribution of reality come to?

THE ARGUMENT FROM GENETICS

It can seem like biological realism about race is obviously true. Can't we just *see* that people are racially different? Voltaire wrote that only a blind person could doubt that there are different races. This section and the following two sections consider three arguments against biological realism about race, which will at least undermine the idea that biological realism is obviously true. We will not take a stand on which of the three positions outlined above is correct; our aim is merely to give a sense of what speaks for and against those positions.

We first need to be clearer about what the biological realist is committed to when she maintains that racial categories are biological categories. If races are natural kinds, racial categories are not random and arbitrary groupings of people. Biological realism seems to be committed to what Kwame Anthony Appiah calls **racialism**, which is:

> the view ... that there are heritable characteristics, possessed by members of our species, which allow us to divide them into a small set of races, in such a way that all the members of these races share certain traits and tendencies with each other that they do not share with members of any other race.
>
> (Appiah 1992, p. 13)

Racialism: the view that there are heritable characteristics possessed by members of our species which permit a division into a small set of races.

Importantly, racialism is not merely the view that people can be classified according to their morphological differences. Everyone – even social constructivists and eliminativists – agrees that people can be classified according to their morphological differences. (Although all will add the caveat that the existence of people of mixed race, people who "pass" as a race seemingly not their own, and people who identify and are identified as members of a particular race but who don't have the morphological features taken to be definitive of that race make racial classification based on morphology problematic.[6]) But racial oppression could hardly exist if there were not some way for racists to identify their targets!

One can accept morphological differences between people while rejecting biological realism about race. Recall the classification of people as cool and uncool. This is a paradigm example of a social classification. Yet there are morphological features that also distinguish the cool from the uncool: the cool people wear their hair a certain way, wear the right kind of clothes, and so on – they can be picked out by their appearance, and the distinction between the cool and the uncool is in many cases obvious. But cool people do not make up a natural kind, because membership in this category is determined by something more than these morphological features. The critic of biological realism says the same about races, but she does not deny that people are morphologically different in various ways that might be roughly mapped by our racial categories.

Consider some arbitrary morphological category, for example, one that picks out people who are redheaded and freckled. As Appiah argues, this isn't a biological category, and the reason is that the morphological criteria for membership in this category aren't correlated with any biologically important features of a person. Racialism sees racial differences as tracking something more than mere morphological differences: the morphological criteria for race membership are indicative of an underlying suite of biological features – a set of "traits and tendencies" which includes more than just morphological features. These involve genetic features that cannot be uncovered by simple observation, for example the presence or absence of certain genes.

In fact, Appiah argues, given what biologists know about genetics, racial categories do not have one key property of natural kind categories:

> Apart from the visible morphological characteristics of skin, hair, and bone, by which we are inclined to assign people to . . . racial categories . . . there are few genetic characteristics to be found in the population of England that are not found in similar populations in Zaire or China . . . [G]iven only a person's race, it is hard to say what his or her biological characteristics (apart from those that all human beings share) will be, except in respect of the "grosser" features of color, hair, and bone . . .
> (Appiah 1992, pp. 35–36)

Racial categories do track certain morphological differences. "But that," Appiah argues, "is not a biological fact but a logical one," since these criteria are merely morphological (p. 36). Being a member of the redheaded-and-freckled group is correlated with the morphological criteria for membership in that group, but that is not a natural kind, one that corresponds to a significant biological difference. But if "real" races are just like the group of people are who redheaded and freckled in all relevant respects, then these aren't natural kinds either. In other words:

The Argument from Genetics

1. If racial categories were biological categories, there would be genetic differences between races, beyond those related to morphology.
2. There aren't genetic differences between races, except for those related to morphology.

Therefore,

3. Racial categories aren't biological categories.

How might the biological realist resist this argument? One possibility would be to challenge the second premise. Consider the success of race-based medicine. To take a very simple case, black people are more likely to get sickle-cell disease. The reason is that carrying the gene that can lead to sickle-cell disease also makes one less likely to catch malaria, such that people whose ancestors evolved in areas where malaria is relatively common are more likely to carry the gene that can lead to sickle-cell disease.

Black people are more likely to have ancestors who evolved in such areas, because malaria is most common in sub-Saharan Africa. Here is a relevant genetic difference, not one relating merely to morphology. This seems a good reason to reject the second premise from the argument from genetics.

Alternatively, the biological realist might challenge the first premise of the argument from genetics. Robin Andreasen, for example, argues that races are "ancestor-descendent sequences of breeding populations, or groups of such sequences, that share a common origin."[7] On her view, races are subspecies of *Homo sapiens*, given a "cladistic approach to subspecies." (1998, p. 200). **Cladistics** is the dominant approach to classification in contemporary biology, which carves up categories based on the shared evolutionary histories and (resultant) common genetic profiles of individuals. A cladistic system of classification classifies organisms in terms of their evolutionary history and genetic profile. Rather than a system of racial classification based on morphology and genetics (which is what Appiah targets), Andreasen proposes a system that groups individuals based on their shared history (and genetic profile). We will return to her proposal below.

Cladistics: an approach to classification in contemporary biology, which carves up categories based on the shared evolutionary histories and (resultant) common genetic profiles of individuals.

EXERCISE 10.3

The Argument from Genetics

Evaluate the argument from genetics. Is this argument sound or unsound?

THE ARGUMENT FROM RELATIVITY

If there are any natural kinds, they are absolute. If chemical elements are natural kinds, then there is one absolutely correct periodic table, not a plurality of equally correct periodic tables, one that is correct for me, another that is correct for you, and so on, or one that is correct for my culture, or that is correct for your culture, and so on. Only one periodic table can be correct. However, systems of racial classification do not seem to be like this: it seems that there are a plurality of equally correct systems.

We can see the problem by trying to list the races. For the seventeenth century writer François Bernier, one of the first people to write about race, there were four: a race comprising Europeans, North Africans, Indians, and Americans; an African race; an Asian race; and "the Lapps." In 1765 Voltaire proposed seven races: "the whites, the negroes, the Albinoes, the Hottentots, and Laplanders, the Chinese, [and] the Americans," while Kant's 1777 list had four races (but not Bernier's four): white (including Arabs, Turks, and Persians), "Negro," "Hun," and "Hindu." W.E.B. DuBois (in 1897) had eight: "the Slavs of eastern Europe, the Teutons of middle Europe, the English of Great Britain and North America, the Romance nations of Southern and Western Europe, the Negroes of Africa and America, the Semitic people of Western Asia and Northern Africa, the Hindoos of Central Asia and the Mongolians of Eastern Asia."[8] Different people are apt to give different answers to this question. Consider the system implied by the 2010 United States census, as shown in Figure 10.3.

When the census is conducted in other countries, the list of races is different. For example, in 2011, South Africa offered four options: Black African, Colored (i.e., "mixed race"), Indian or Asian, and White. In 2000, Brazil offered five: White (branca), Black (preta), Yellow (amarela), Brown (parda), and Aboriginal (indigena). Some censuses speak of ethnicity rather than race. Thus in 2001, Bulgaria's census offered three "ethnic groups" as choices: Bulgarian, Turkish, and Gypsy, while England's offered the options: White, Mixed, Asian or Asian British, Black or Black British, Chinese, or "any other ethnic group." The 2010 U.S. census had a separate question as to whether a person is "of Hispanic, Latino, or Spanish origin," which is standardly understood as a question about ethnicity rather than race. (The distinction between ethnicity and race is a murky one.)

Could any of these different systems of racial classification be the correct one, in the way that the periodic table of the elements is the correct system of chemical classification? You might think that the answer to this question is "No." If that is right, racial classifications are not absolute – there is no one correct way to divide people up in terms of race. In addition, even if we were to agree on a common list of categories, there are differences

9. What is Person 1's race? *Mark* ☒ *one or more boxes.*

☐ White
☐ Black, African Am., or Negro
☐ American Indian or Alaska Native – *Print name of enrolled or principal tribe.* ⤵

☐ Asian Indian   ☐ Japanese   ☐ Native Hawaiian
☐ Chinese   ☐ Korean   ☐ Guamanian or Chamorro
☐ Filipino   ☐ Vietnamese   ☐ Samoan
☐ Other Asian – *Print race, for*   ☐ Other Pacific Islander – *Print*
  example, Hmong, Laotian, Thai,   *race, for example, Fijian, Tongan,*
  Pakistani, Cambodian, and so on. ⤵   *and so on.* ⤵

☐ Some other race – *Print race.* ⤵

Figure 10.3 2010 U.S. Census

EXERCISE 10.4

Races

Which way of drawing up a list of racial categories seems correct to you?

when it comes to the membership of the different races. Bernier included Indians and Americans (i.e., American Indians) in the white race because he thought their darker skin was merely the result of the harsher sun in their native environments. In Britain, 'Asian' refers to Indians and Pakistanis, but in America it refers only to East Asians.

The upshot of all of this is that different people employ different systems of racial classification, and that there are differences between contemporary systems and historical systems as well as differences between contemporary systems used synchronically in different places. However – and this is the important bit – none of these systems seems any more correct than any of the others. On what grounds could we maintain that one of these systems has gotten it right, when it comes to describing "the races"? They all seem to be equally good (or bad) ways of classifying people. Unlike the periodic table, there's not one system that correctly carves up reality. But if races were natural kinds, then there would be such a system. In other words:

The Argument from Relativity

1. If races were natural kinds, there would be one correct system of racial classification.
2. There exist multiple, equally correct systems of racial classification.

Therefore,

3. Races aren't natural kinds.

Again, both premises of the argument may be challenged. In particular, a realist like Andreasen might challenge the second premise. Based on the work of geneticists studying human evolution, Andreasen proposes the cladistic system of racial classification as shown in Figure 10.4.

Figure 10.4 represents our best theory as to the historical evolution of human beings. Unlike the systems of classification described above, this one is based on our best science, so it has a claim to be correct among a plurality of competitors. Andreasen's insight is to treat these cladistic groups as races. There are two important features to note about Andreasen's system. First, it does not match up with the system of racial classification

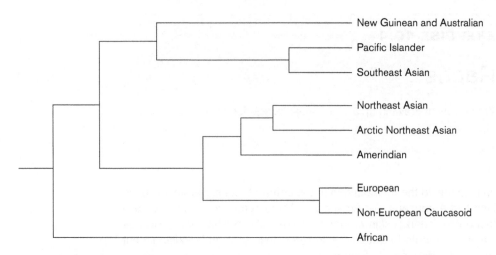

Figure 10.4 Cladistic System of Racial Classification

employed by most people. As Andreasen admits, "the folk category 'Asian' is not a cladistic race" (1998, p. 212). Second, if races are subspecies – or, indeed, if they are anything like the other categories of contemporary biology – they will be dynamic, that is, subject to change over time. Human beings have an ongoing history of mating in groups – i.e., most people are such that they are most likely to mate with some subset of the total human population – which has had various causes, including geography and culture. Races exist in virtue of this ongoing history. Were our practice of isolated group mating to end – as seems likely so long as global travel continues to be common – races would cease to exist. All individuals would end up with a shared common set of ancestors. Less dramatically, for the biological realist, what races there are might change: the races of today might not be the races of tomorrow. This conflicts with commonsense conceptions of race.

This is no problem, Andreasen argues, because "the existence of biological races does not depend on our folk taxonomy being right" (1998, p. 213). The critic of biological realism might challenge this assumption. Science often corrects common sense, rejecting commonsense classifications. The category "fish" was used for centuries, even millennia, to include cephalopods (whales), certain aquatic molluscs (octopus, squid), as well as (sometimes) mermaids. None of these are fish, according to contemporary biology. Science corrects common sense. But you might think that when scientific categories are *too* different from folk categories, what we have is not a correction of commonsense categories, but rather a rejection of commonsense categories.

We can see an example of this principle at work if we consider two systems of classification intended to explain and predict human behavior: the signs of the zodiac, posited by astrologers, and the five-factor model of personality, posited by psychologists. The former divides people into 12 groups (Pisces, Leo, Gemini, and so on), based on their date of birth, and offers explanations and predictions of their behavior on the basis of their astrological sign. The latter classifies people according to five personality traits (openness, conscientiousness, extraversion, agreeableness, neuroticism), and offers explanations and predictions of their behavior on the basis of said classifications. The five-factor model has been extremely useful in predicting and explaining human behavior. Five-factor personality differences have been found to be correlated with a variety of mental health and genetic differences, among others. By contrast, the signs of the zodiac are utterly useless for predicting and explaining human behavior. Now here's the point: no one would say that the signs of the zodiac are real, but that astrologers had them wrong: they've got nothing to do with your date of birth, and instead of 12, there are five, and instead of each person having one sign, each person has some degree of each of the five, and so on. The five-factor model of psychology didn't *amend* astrology, showing us what the signs of the zodiac really are, in the way that contemporary biology amended our commonsense theory of fish, showing us what fish really are; the five-factor model supplants astrology.

But now we have to decide: does the division of human beings offered by contemporary genetics and evolutionary biology amend our folk theory of race, showing us which races there really are? Or does it supplant our folk theories of race, showing us that the concept of race is bunk? Critics of biological realism argue for the latter view.[9] Contemporary biology doesn't reveal that race is radically different than we took it to be; it reveals that, so far as biology goes, there is no such thing.

EXERCISE 10.5

The Folk Theory vs. Biological Theories of Race

Could contemporary genetics amend our folk theory of race showing us which races there really are? Or does it rather supplant our folk theories? How could one decide the answer to these questions? What does this say about the Argument from Relativity?

THE ARGUMENT FROM ANTI-RACISM

The historical and contemporary non-academic consensus has been that races are natural kinds. But this view has been held in conjunction with various other false and morally problematic views about race. The appeal of biological realism is sometimes thought to be undermined by appeal to the fact that the concept of race has an (ongoing) racist history.

Consider a version of racialism[10] – cultural racialism – according to which it is of the essence of the various races to engage in different cultural practices. Think of the stereotype of Latino people as especially passionate or emotional. For the cultural racialist, members of a race who engage in the characteristic practices of that race are paradigms of their kind, while members of that race who don't engage in those practices are exceptions to the rule. Many of the people who maintain biological realism about race are cultural racialists. But cultural racialism is false. Here again is Appiah: "differences between people in language, moral affections, aesthetic attitudes, [and] political ideology . . . are not to any significant degree biologically determined" (1992, p. 35). In addition, many of the people who maintained (or maintain) biological realism were (or are) *racists* – they saw (or see) some races as being better than others.[11] Historically, biological realism was often defended by white supremacists. It is difficult to separate the history of the concept of race – understood as a biological division of human beings – from the history of racism. The upshot is that biological realism is often associated with, and motivated by, various false views and morally problematic ideologies.

But can't biological realism be separated from these associations and motivations? Consider the contemporary slogan "Race is only skin deep." Couldn't someone coherently believe in real racial differences – perhaps morphological, as suggested by the slogan, perhaps historical and genetic – while rejecting cultural racialism and racism?

What seems to make the difference here is whether racial categories can be freed from any cultural racialist or racist presuppositions. Sometimes a presupposition is built into the meaning of a word. If you call someone a 'witch' you're implying that she made a deal with the devil. Given the historical and contemporary association of biological realism and cultural racialism and racism, you might think that something similar is true of our words for the races. Just as the term 'witch' cannot be freed from its presupposition about the devil, one might think that 'Latino' cannot be freed from its cultural racialist and racist presuppositions. We know this is true of racial slurs, but given the racist history of the concept of race, you might think that it is true of all racial language. Call this the argument from anti-racism.

The critic of biological realism could expand on this argument. Historical and contemporary commonsensical conceptions of race are rife with confusions. We discussed two such confusions above: (a) historical and contemporary common sense assumes that races are static, whereas all contemporary biological categories are dynamic, and (b) cases of commonsense racial categorizations that do not correspond to genuine biological categories, for example Americans typically treat "Asian" as a race, but there is no such biological category.

What emerges is a picture of our folk conception of race as riddled with errors and racist assumptions. But just as we must reject the existence of witches if we deny the assumptions that go along with the use of that category, it seems like we must reject at least the biological reality of race, if we reject our erroneous and morally problematic folk conception of race. Even if those accused of witchcraft in the seventeenth century really did have something in common, and even if that has something to do with their being accused of witchcraft, we would not say that this had vindicated the reality of witches. The folk theory of witches is just too riddled with error and morally problematic assumptions for us to ever accept the reality of witches. The critic of biological realism says the same about our folk theory of race.

EXERCISE 10.6

The Argument from Anti-racism

How might one state the Argument from Anti-racism in numbered premise form? How might the biological realist respond to the argument from anti-racism?

One point that might be contested is the idea that the biological reality of race is threatened by the fact that our words for the races have racist implications. The biological realist might grant this idea, but argue that these terms nevertheless pick out natural kinds. Consider the slur 'retard,' paradigmatically used to denigrate the developmentally disabled. Suppose this group forms a natural kind. On this assumption, the fact that 'retard' is a slur – that it is used this way is the reason why there are now many campaigns to stop its use – does not challenge the claim that it picks out a natural kind. The fact that our racial language is rife with erroneous and morally problematic implications, you might argue, is orthogonal to the question of whether races are natural kinds.

A CAUSAL ARGUMENT AGAINST ELIMINATIVISM

If you are convinced by any of the arguments of the previous sections against biological realism, you are still faced with a choice: social constructivism or eliminativism? Social constructivism says that races are real, but not natural kinds; eliminativism denies the reality of racial categories altogether. When we reflect on the confusions and morally problematic ideologies that have evolved hand in hand with our concept of race, the eliminativist's picture begins to look appealing: we thought there were these natural kinds – races – but it turns out that there are no such things, just like there are no witches. The presuppositions of our concept of race, like the presuppositions of our concept of a witch, just turned out to be false.

This section considers an argument against eliminativism, and an eliminativist reply.

Alexander's dictum: the entities that exist are all and only those that possess causal powers.

Many metaphysicians have endorsed a principle known as **Alexander's dictum**, according to which the entities that exist are all and only those that possess causal powers.[12] For our purposes here, we need only consider the 'all' part of this principle. The claim that we should count something as existing if it has causal powers seems almost undeniable. If the correct causal explanation of some event or phenomenon cites x as a cause, then x must exist. Otherwise, how could it be a cause? This thought can be applied to races: if they have causal powers – if they enter into correct causal explanations – then we should admit their reality.

There are at least two ways in which one might think that races have causal powers. First, consider the ongoing history of racism and racial oppression, which is constituted by real events. For example, suppose Sarah, a bank manager, suffers from an unconscious racist bias against Samoans. Maria, her employee, descended from ancestors from Samoa, has applied for a promotion at the bank. Sarah rejects Maria's application. We might ask: Why was Maria's application rejected? In such a case, it seems perfectly possible that among the causes of the rejection was the fact that Maria is Samoan. This, together with Sarah's implicit bias against Samoan people resulted in Maria's application being rejected. But if the fact that Maria is Samoan *caused* her application to be rejected, then races have causal powers. And if races have causal powers, then we should count them as existing. And that means we should prefer social constructivism to eliminativism.

Second, an important and much-discussed feature of racial categories is that they often, perhaps even inevitably, become part of people's identities. When systems of racial classification are employed in a society, people in that society come to think of themselves as members of a particular race. In many cases, a person's race is a deep part of one's self-conception, of his or her understanding of who he or she is. Our races seem to make a difference to the way we view ourselves from our own first-person perspective. For some people, this difference is profound and meaningful. How can something so central to someone's identity be unreal? If the fact that you are Samoan is an essential component of your sense of self, could it really be true – as the eliminativist claims – that you are not actually Samoan? Just as race seems to enter into correct causal explanations of racial oppression (as in Maria's case), it seems to enter into correct causal explanations of people's identities. But eliminativists would have to reject such causal explanations.

The eliminativist about race could reply by embracing the conclusion that race cannot enter into correct causal explanations and offer alternative explanations of the relevant events and phenomena. When it comes to racial oppression, the eliminativist could argue that a correct causal explanation of the fact that Maria's application was rejected would cite the fact that Sarah *thought* Maria was Samoan – and that this is enough to explain what we were inclined to explain by appeal to Maria's actually being Samoan. Just as the behavior of those involved in witch-hunts can be explained by appeal to their false beliefs about witches, the behavior of those involved in racial oppression can be explained by appeal to their false beliefs about race. When it comes to racial identities, the eliminativist could make a similar argument: someone's identity can be founded on a false self-conception. According to some historical accounts, one of the people accused of witchcraft at Salem actually believed that she had made a deal with the devil – i.e., that she was in fact a witch. And we can imagine someone who not only believes such an accusation, but internalizes it, such that being a witch becomes part of her identity. The eliminativist could offer this as a plausible explanation of racial identity: the internalization of a false system of classification.

We can draw at least two important conclusions from this discussion of the metaphysics of race. First, the metaphysical question about the reality of race cannot be answered without careful consideration of our best contemporary science, including genetics and evolutionary biology, as well as anthropology and sociology. Second, answering these questions about race requires consideration of issues in the (applied) philosophy of language. Are racist implications part of the meaning of our racial vocabulary? Are race terms more like empty terms like 'witch' or more like meaningful terms like 'fish,' whose folk extension needs amending by science? We cannot inquire after questions about the metaphysics of race without inquiring after questions in the philosophy of language, linguistics, biology, and other disciplines. If the metaphysical debate about race is representative of debates about social construction in general, then this conclusion generalizes: questions about social construction require input from disciplines, including the natural sciences, the social sciences, the philosophy of language, and linguistics.

We have assumed that nothing is both a social and a natural kind, which grounds our conception of social construction. This conception yields a tripartite distinction between natural categories, socially constructed categories, and empty categories; this corresponds to our three articulated positions about race: biological realism, social constructivism, and eliminativism. The assumption that nothing is both a social and a natural kind could be challenged. You might point to the categories of the social sciences as both socially constructed and natural.

Alternatively, for some philosophers, all categories are socially constructed, including (if not especially) those posited by scientists. We should tread carefully before accepting that view, however – and before accepting whatever conception of "social construction" leads to it. We should not, for example, say that everything is socially constructed because our language, which we use to speak about everything, is socially constructed. It would be rash to jettison the conception of social construction we have employed here in favor of one that dissolves the seemingly interesting distinction between natural kinds and social kinds, so long as that distinction can coherently be made out (as we attempted to do above). Making out such distinctions is one of the important tasks of the metaphysician.

SUGGESTIONS FOR FURTHER READING

Two essential sources on the philosophy of race are Robert Bernasconi and Tommy L. Lott's collection, *The Idea of Race* and Bernard Boxill's *Race and Racism*. For overviews of the question of the reality of race, see Joshua Glasgow, *A Theory of Race*, chapter 1, and Charles Mills, "But What Are You *Really?* The Metaphysics of Race," in his *Blackness Visible: Essays on Philosophy and Race*. On natural kinds, see W.V.O. Quine, "Natural Kinds," pp. 114–138 and Nelson Goodman, *Fact, Fiction, and Forecast.*

On social construction in general, see Ian Hacking, *The Social Construction of What?*, Sally Haslanger, "Ontology and Social Construction," and Ron Mallon, "A Field Guide to Social Construction." For defenses of social constructivism about race, see Lucius T. Outlaw, *On Race and Philosophy*, Charles Mills, *Blackness Visible: Essays on Philosophy and Race*, Sally Haslanger, "Gender and Race: (What) Are They? (What) Do We Want Them To Be?"

For defenses of eliminativism about race, see Kwame Anthony Appiah, *In My Father's House: Africa in the Philosophy of Culture* and Naomi Zack, *Race and Mixed Race*. For a defense of biological realism about race, see Joshua Glasgow, *A Theory of Race*. On the medical and genetic science relevant to the metaphysical race debate, see M.J. Bamshad and S.E. Olson, "Does Race Exist?"

NOTES

1   In *The Social Construction of Reality.*
2   Recall the distinction between sparse and abundant theories of properties in Chapter 2.
3   See Hacking, *The Social Construction of What?* pp. 5–9, and Mallon, "A Field Guide to Social Construction," pp. 94–95.
4   These examples of races come from the question about race on the 2010 US Census. Contemporary American culture generally recognizes three, sometimes four, main races: white, black, Asian, and (sometimes) Latino. There are numerous different systems of racial classification. As we will see in the section on the argument from relativity, which distinct races one recognizes can make a difference to which metaphysical view is plausible. Biological realism is not plausible when applied to the categories Asian or Latino.
5   The closest anyone came to defending this claim, prior to the twentieth century, was David Hume, in his 1742 essay "Of National Characters," where he argued that "national characters" are the result of "moral" (i.e., cultural) as opposed to "physical" (i.e., geographic) causes. But although Hume seems to have thought that the differences between Europeans were merely cultural, he did not extend this prescient view to other races.
6   Race membership seems to depend on things that would not make a difference to membership in a biological category. For example, the fact that Barack Obama is "black" and Tiger Woods is "multiracial" seems to have something to do with the fact that Obama identifies as "black" and Woods identifies as

"multiracial," and not to have anything to do with their racial background. Biological categories aren't subjective in that way.

7   "A New Perspective on the Race Debate," p. 200.

8   See references in R. Bernasconi and T.L. Lott eds., *The Idea of Race*.

9   See Joshua Glasgow, *A Theory of Race,* chapter 5. The anthropologist Ashley Montagu famously compared race to "phlogiston" – a non-existent substance posited by seventeenth century scientists to explain the process of combustion.

10 Recall that racialism is the view that human beings can be divided into a small set of races, such that members of each race share traits and tendencies with each other that they do not share with members of any other race.

11 By saying that racists "see" some races as being better than others, we do not mean to imply that racism is entirely, or even necessarily, a cognitive matter. In the sense that a person can be a racist, racism is a set of cognitive, affective, and practical dispositions. "Racism" is also an illuminating name for the ideologies, practices, and institutions that sustain racial oppression.

12 The principle is named after the British philosopher Samuel Alexander (1859–1938).

Glossary

Abstract: a classification of entities, examples include properties or mathematical objects.

Abstraction: 1. a psychological process of considering an object while ignoring some of its features; for example ignoring all other features of a table (its color, material, texture) to just consider its size; 2. the metaphysical relation of one entity being an abstraction from another, an entity just like the latter except lacking some of its features.

Abundant ontology: an ontology that posits a relatively large number of types of entities.

Abundant theory of universals (or properties): a version of realism about universals (or properties) that posits a relatively large number of distinct universals (or properties); in the extreme case, a universal (or property) corresponding to any term that is applied to a multiplicity of entities.

Actualism: the view that everything that exists actually exists, nothing is merely possible.

A-features: tensed features of events such as their happening in the past, present, or future.

Agent causal libertarianism: see **agent causation**

Agent causation: the view that human agents are sometimes causes.

Alexander's dictum: the entities that exist are all and only those that possess causal powers.

Analytic: see **analytic/synthetic distinction**

Analytic account: an account of what we mean.

The **analytic/synthetic distinction**: the distinction between analytic (or logical) methods and synthetic (or empirical methods) for verifying a statement.

A posteriori method: an empirical way of knowing a fact or proposition, one that involves observation or sensory experience.

A priori method: a way of knowing a fact or proposition that does not involve observation or sensory experience.

Argument: a series of statements in which someone is presenting reasons in defense of some claim.

A-series: an ordering of events in terms of their being past (or more past), present, or future (or more future).

Atheism: the thesis that God does not exist.

A-theory of time: the view that the A-facts are not reducible to the B-facts.

B-features: tenseless yet temporal features of events, e.g. one event's happening five years before or after another.

Biological realism about race: racial categories are biological categories.

Block universe view: the combination of the B-theory of time and eternalism.

Bound variable: a variable that is within the **scope** of some quantifier phrase.

Brutal composition: the view that there is no true, interesting, and finite answer to the **Special Composition Question**.

B-series: an ordering of events in terms of their dates and times and permanent relations of being earlier than, later than, and simultaneous with each other.

B-theory of time: the view that the A-facts of time are reducible to the B-facts.

Categorical features: features that just concern what an object is like actually in itself at a certain time.

Cladistics: an approach to classification in contemporary biology, which carves up categories based on the shared evolutionary histories and (resultant) common genetic profiles of individuals.

Class nominalism: the view that properties are to be identified with the classes of objects that instantiate them.

Compatibilism: the view that free will is compatible with determinism.

Conceptualism: the view that universals exist, however they are entities that depend on our mind's grasp of them.

Conclusion: the part of an argument that is being argued for, for which reasons are being offered.

Concrete: a classification of entities that is not abstract, examples include material objects like tables, planets, and rocks.

Contingent: what is neither necessary nor impossible.

Contingent a priori: truths that are neither necessary nor impossible and yet discoverable merely by reflection on the meanings of the terms or concepts involved in them.

Contradiction: any sentence or statement of the form P and not-P.

Conventionalism: a position that seeks to reduce modal claims to facts about what follows or does not follow from the conventions of our language.

Counterexample: an example that shows an argument is invalid, by providing a way in which the premises of the argument could be true while a conclusion is false; or an example that shows a statement is false, by providing a way in which it could be false.

Counterfactual: a conditional asserting what would have been the case had things gone differently than how we suppose they actually go.

Counterfactual theory of causation: a theory that reduces facts about causation to facts about what would have happened in various counterfactual circumstances.

Counterpart: a counterpart of one entity x is an entity that bears some salient similarity and causal relations to x.

De dicto modality: concerns the modal status of propositions (or dictums), whether they are possible, necessary, or contingent.

Deductively invalid: an argument is deductively invalid when it is possible for the premises of the argument to all be true while its conclusion is false.

Deductively valid: an argument is deductively valid when there is no possible way for the premises of the argument to all be true while its conclusion is false. The premises of the argument logically imply its conclusion.

De re modality: concerns the modal status of features of individuals, such as whether a certain feature of an individual is essential or contingent.

Determinism: the position that the laws are such that given any state of the universe, one can use them to predict with certainty what the state of the universe will be at any other time.

Diachronic identity: identity over time.

Dilemma: a choice between two options, each of which yields unattractive consequences.

Dispositional features: features about how an object might behave in various situations.

Domain of quantification: the set of objects over which the quantifiers range in a given context, the set of possible values the variables can take.

Efficient cause: what brings an object or event into being.

Empiricism: the view that our knowledge and understanding of our world comes entirely from experience.

Endurantism: the view that what persistence amounts to is strict numerical identity over time.

Enthymeme: an argument that is incomplete as stated and invalid, although it is easy to supply the missing premises that the argument would need to be valid. In the case of an enthymeme, the author left out the missing premises for fear of boring the reader or insulting his or her intelligence.

Epiphenomenon: an event that is the result of another event but that has no effects of its own.

Epistemicism: the view that vagueness is ignorance; it is not a matter of fundamental indeterminacy in the world or indeterminacy in what our words or concepts apply to, but our ignorance about what our words or concepts apply to.

Epistemic possibility: something that is compatible with everything that one knows.

Epistemological: relating to what we can know or be justified in believing.

Epistemology: the theory of knowledge and justification.

Equivalence relation: a relation that is reflexive, symmetric, and transitive.

Ersatz modal realism: the view that there are possible worlds (worlds that can play a similar role to the concrete worlds of the modal realist), but that these are not additional universes in the same sense as our universe.

Essentialism: the view that objects themselves, independently of any ways we may categorize them, have certain properties necessarily.

Essential properties (essences): properties that hold of an individual by necessity that make them the kinds of things they are.

Eternalism: the view that past, present, and future objects and events are equally real.

Exdurantism (the stage view): identifies the familiar material objects we ordinarily think of as persisting with temporary stages.

Existentialism: the view that it is the kind of things we do that determines our essences, the kind of people we are. We do not possess innate essences that determine who we are and what we will do.

Existential quantifier: ∃, a symbol of first-order predicate logic. When combined with a **variable**, it can be used to represent a statement to the effect that something exists that is a certain way.

External question: see **internal/external distinction**

External statement: see **internal/external distinction**

External time: distinguished from personal time in David Lewis's account of time travel, it is time itself.

Fictionalism: what is required for the truth of sentences in a given domain is to be understood by analogy with truths of fiction.

Final cause: the purpose or goal for which an object exists or why it is the way it is at a given time.

Forms: the universals that constitute the fundamental entities of Plato's ontology.

Four dimensionalism: the doctrine of temporal parts, the view that in addition to spatial parts, objects have temporal parts.

Framework (Carnapian): a linguistic system including rules of grammar and meaning.

Frankfurt case: a case in which intuitively one acts freely and so is morally responsible for an action, and yet one did not have the ability to do otherwise.

Fundamental metaphysical theory: a theory that aims at completeness in the sense that every fact about the world is either a part of that theory or it can be given an explanation completely in terms of that theory.

Fusion: see **mereological sum**

Grounding: the relation that one set of facts bears to another set of facts when the one metaphysically explains the other.

Growing block theory: the view that past and present objects and events are real; future objects and events are not.

Hard determinism: the view that free will is incompatible with determinism and so human beings lack free will.

Hard incompatibilism: the view that free will is incompatible with both determinism and indeterminism and so free will is impossible.

Humeanism about laws: the view that the facts about the laws of nature are reducible to facts about regularities in what happens in our universe.

Hylomorphism: the Aristotelian view that substances are complex objects made of both matter (*hyle*) and form (*morphē*).

Idealization: a false assumption introduced into a theory in order to make it simpler to use.

Identity of Indiscernibles: a metaphysical principle stating that necessarily, if any objects are qualitative duplicates, then they are identical.

Immanent: an entity that is located in space and time, where it is instantiated.

Incompatibilism: the view that free will is incompatible with determinism.

Indeterminism: the denial of **determinism.**

Indiscernibility of Identicals: see **Leibniz's law**

Indispensability argument: an argument for realism (Platonism) about mathematical entities from the premises that (1) we should be committed to all and only the entities that are indispensable to our best scientific theories, and (2) the claim that mathematical entities are indispensable to our best scientific theories.

Instantiation: the relation between a property and an entity that has that property.

Internal question: see **internal/external distinction**

Internal statement: see **internal/external distinction**

The **internal/external distinction**: the distinction between questions or statements that are evaluated from within a linguistic framework and those that are evaluated from outside the framework, that may be about the framework itself.

Intrinsic properties: properties objects have just in virtue of how they are in themselves, not how they are in relation to other things.

Invalid: see **deductively invalid**

Leibniz's law: the metaphysical principle that necessarily, if a and b are identical, then they must share all of the same properties.

Libertarianism: the view that free will is incompatible with determinism and so determinism is false.

Linguistic ersatzism: a form of ersatz modal realism that interprets possible worlds to be sentences or other linguistic entities.

Linguistic (or **semantic**) **vagueness**: vagueness that is the result of semantic indecision; there not being facts to determine precisely in all cases what our terms apply to.

Logical connectives: symbols used to build complex propositions out of simpler ones.

Logical positivism: a movement in philosophy originating in Austria and Germany in the 1920s; a movement critical of metaphysics, arguing that all knowledge of the world must originate in sense experience and logic.

Logical possibility: what does not entail any contradiction.

Logicism: the view that mathematics is reducible to logic.

Major conclusion: the final conclusion of an argument.

Maximal property: a property F is maximal if large parts of an F are not themselves Fs.

Mereological atom: an object lacking any proper parts.

Mereological nihilism: the view that there are no mereologically complex objects, only simples.

Mereological relations: part/whole relations.

Mereological sum: the mereological sum of some objects $x_1, x_2, \ldots, x_n$ is the object that contains $x_1, x_2, \ldots, x_n$ as parts.

Mereological universalism: the view that composition occurs for any spatially disjoint objects whatsoever.

Meta-ontology: the study of what one is doing, or what one should be doing, when one is engaged in an ontological debate.

Metaphysical explanation: see **grounding**

Metaphysical vagueness: vagueness that results from how the world is objectively, not how we think or talk about it; fundamental indeterminacy in what exists or what features things have.

Mind–body dualism: the view that there are two kinds of substances, minds (mental substances) and bodies (material substances).

Minor conclusion: a statement that is argued for on the way to arguing for an argument's major conclusion.

Modal claims: those that express facts about what is possible, impossible, necessary, or contingent.

Modal logic: the branch of logic that represents modal claims.

Modal properties: properties having to do with what is possible, impossible, necessary, or contingent.

Modal realism: the view that in addition to the actual world, there exist other alternative universes, possible worlds, just as real as our own; and that it is in virtue of the nature of these universes that our modal claims are true or false.

Model: a theoretical structure involving a basic set of representational devices accounting for a set of data.

Modus ponens: the logical form:

> If A, then B
> A
> Therefore,
> B,

where A and B are any propositions.

Moving spotlight view: a view that combines eternalism with the A-theory of time.

Naturalism: the view that it is within science itself that reality is to be identified and described.

Natural kind: a group of objects in which each member of the group shares some objective, mind-independent similarity.

Necessary a posteriori: truths that are necessary and yet known on the basis of empirical observation.

Nominalism: 1. the view that there are no such things as abstract entities; 2. the view that there are no such things as universals; 3. the view that there are no such things as mathematical entities.

Nomological possibility or necessity: possibility or necessity according to the laws of nature.

Numbered premise form: a way of stating arguments so that each premise as well as the conclusion are given a number and presented each on their own line.

Numerical identity (or **identity in the strict sense**): oneness, the sense of 'a is identical to b' meaning that a and b are the same object, that they are one.

Objection from Coextension: an argument against class nominalism that there are more properties than those that may be recognized by the class nominalist, since two predicates may have the same extension and yet refer to two distinct properties.

Objective: not depending on any individual's perspective, absolute.

Ockham's Razor: the principle that one should not multiply one's ontological commitments beyond necessity.

One Over Many: an argument for realism about universals that starts from a premise about some similarities between a group of objects and concludes that there is a universal (a one) that runs through these individual objects (the many).

Ontological commitments: the types of entities one ought to believe in, given the sentences he or she accepts.

Ontological dependence: when one entity depends on another for its continued existence.

Ontology: 1. the study of what there is; 2. a particular theory about the types of entities there are.

Openness of the future: the view that there are not any determinate facts about the future.

Origins essentialism: the view that the origins of material objects and organisms are essential to them.

Ostrich nominalism: a version of nominalism that denies the existence of properties and refuses to answer the question of what it is in virtue of which objects are similar or appear to have certain features.

Particular: any entity that may not be multiply instantiated.

Perdurantism (the worm view): the view that material objects persist by having temporal parts at different times.

Personal time: distinguished from external time in David Lewis's account of time travel, elapsed time as measured by the normal behavior of physical objects: ticks of a watch, aging processes of human beings, etc.

Physicalism: the view that physics alone can provide a complete description of what there is in our world and what it is like.

Platonism: 1. the view that there are such things as the Platonic **Forms**; 2. the view that there are such things as abstract, mathematical entities.

Possibilism: the view that at least some entities are not actual, but merely possible.

Possible worlds analysis of modality: an analysis of claims about possibility and necessity in terms of what is true at various possible worlds (including the actual world).

Predicate nominalism: a view denying the existence of properties. Predicates may be satisfied or not satisfied by objects, but there need be no property that exists to explain this fact.

Premise: a statement offered as part of an argument as a reason for accepting a certain claim.

Presentism: the view that only presently existing objects and events are real.

Primitivist theory of causation: a theory according to which causal facts are not reducible to any noncausal facts, including facts about regularities, laws, counterfactuals, or probabilities.

Principle of charity: a convention of philosophical debate to, when reasonable, try to interpret one's opponent's claims as true and her arguments as valid.

Principle of naturalistic closure: the principle that any metaphysical claim to be taken seriously at a time should be motivated by the service it would perform in showing how two or more scientific hypotheses, at least one of which is drawn from fundamental physics, jointly explain more than what is explained by the hypotheses taken separately.

Problem of temporary intrinsics: a problem raised for endurantism by David Lewis, who argued that the endurantist cannot account for change in an object's intrinsic properties.

Problem of the Many: a philosophical problem about the existence and identity of material objects introduced by the philosopher Peter Unger in 1980. The problem stems from the fact that ordinary material objects (like persons, rocks, tables, and stars) seem not to have well-defined physical boundaries. There are several precisely defined objects with determinate boundaries that may be associated with any ordinary material object. This raises the question of which if any of these precisely defined objects it is identical to.

Proper part: x is a proper part of y just in case x is a part of y and x is not identical to y.

Protocol statement: a statement that may be directly verified by sense experience.

Qualitative identity: the sense of 'a is identical to b' meaning that a and b share all of the same qualities (the same color, same shape, same size, etc.).

Racialism: the view that there are heritable characteristics possessed by members of our species which permit a division into a small set of races.

Realism about universals: the view that universals exist and they are mind-independent entities.

Realization: one object or objects realize another when the former plays the role of implementing the latter, e.g. when some hardware components implement a particular program.

Reductio ad absurdum: the method of proving a claim by arguing that the negation of that claim would entail a contradiction (an absurdity).

Reference class problem: this is the problem that the probability we assign to an event seems to depend on our way of conceptualizing it (placing it against a reference class) on a given occasion. This may vary depending on the context making it difficult to say what is *the* probability of the event.

Regimentation: the procedure of representing statements in symbolic logic to make it as clear as possible what follows from those statements.

Regularity theory of causation: a theory of causation that explains causal relations in terms of the regular occurrence of patterns of events.

Scope (of a quantifier): the part of the sentence containing the variables the quantifier is binding. In symbolic logic, the scope of a quantifier is either the part of the sentence immediately after the quantifier phrase (in a simple sentence like '∃xFx'), or the part of the sentence contained in the parentheses that immediately follow the quantifier phrase. (For example, in '∃x(Fx ∧ Gx) ∧ Hx,' the xs in 'Fx' and 'Gx' are contained in the scope of the quantifier. The x in 'Hx' is not.)

Self-forming actions: important actions in the life of a person that decide the kind of person he or she will be.

Semantic ascent: when, in order to address a question, a philosopher "ascends to the semantic plane," addressing first a question about the meaning of certain key terms in the original question.

Semantic theory: an account of a proposition's or set of propositions' meanings and truth conditions.

Sentential operator: a bit of logical notation acting on sentences or propositions to form more complex sentences or propositions.

Set nominalism: see **class nominalism**

Shrinking block theory: the view that present and future objects and events are real; past objects and events are not.

Simple: see **mereological atom**

Social construction: a classification whose members constitute a social kind.

Social kind: a group of objects in which each member of the group shares some similarity based in existing social practices, institutions, or conventions.

Soft determinism: the view that determinism is true and it is compatible with the existence of free will.

Sortal essentialism: the view that it is essential to objects what kinds of things they are.

Sortal predicate: a predicate that classifies an object as a member of a certain sort (or kind).

Sound: an argument is sound just in case it has all true premises and is deductively valid.

Sparse ontology: an ontology that posits a relatively small number of types of entities.

Sparse theory of universals (or properties): a version of realism about universals (or properties) that posits a relatively small number of distinct universals (or properties); in the extreme case, there are only universals (or properties) corresponding to types recognized by our fundamental physical theories.

Special Composition Question: the question for any xs, when is it the case that there is a y such that the xs compose y.

Surface freedom: being able to act in such a way that one's desires are satisfied.

Supervenience: one set of facts about a class of entities (the As) supervenes on another set of facts about a class of entities (the Bs) when there can be no change in the A-facts without a corresponding change in the B-facts.

Synchronic identity: identity at a time.

Synthetic: see **analytic/synthetic distinction**

Teleological cause: see final cause

Theism: the thesis that God exists.

Theory of abstract particulars: see trope theory

Thought experiment: a fictional case used in order to draw out consequences of use to the building of a scientific or philosophical theory.

Three dimensionalism: the view that although objects may have spatial parts, they never have temporal parts.

Transcendent: a transcendent entity is one that is not located in space or time.

Trope: an abstract particular, e.g. the shape of the Empire State Building.

Trope theory: the theory that properties are tropes, or abstract particulars.

Truthmaker theory: the theory that truths have truthmakers, some entities or sets of entities that make them true.

Two Object View: the view that material objects are numerically distinct from the matter of which they are made.

Ultimate freedom of the will: having the ability to satisfy one's desires and being the ultimate source of those desires.

Universal: a type of entity that is repeatable, that may be instantiated at multiple locations at once by distinct entities.

Universal quantifier: ∀, a symbol of first-order predicate logic. When combined with a **variable**, it can be used to represent a statement to the effect that everything is a certain way.

Use/mention distinction: a distinction between two ways in which a word or phrase may appear in a sentence. A sentence may use the linguistic item so that it plays its typical semantic role (naming some object if it is a name, modifying some object if it is an adjective, and so on). Or, a sentence may mention the linguistic item, using it to refer to itself. In cases where a linguistic item is being mentioned rather than used, a philosophical convention is to place the relevant word or phrase in single quotes.

Valid: see **deductively valid**

Variables: symbols like x, y, z, etc. used to stand in for other things in a sentence, called the values of the variable.

Verificationist theory of meaning: the meaning of a statement is given by its conditions of verification.

Verificationist theory of truth: a sentence is only capable of truth or falsity if it is capable of being verified or falsified.

To be **wholly present** at a time: to have all of one's parts exist at that time.

World-line: the path of any object through space–time.

Bibliography

Albert, David Z. 1992. *Quantum Mechanics and Experience.* Cambridge, MA: Harvard University Press.

Alston, William P. 1958. Ontological Commitments. *Philosophical Studies.* 9(1–2): 8–17.

Andreasen, Robin. 1998. A New Perspective on the Race Debate. *British Journal for the Philosophy of Science.* 49(2): 199–225.

Annas, Julia. 1981. *An Introduction to Plato's Republic.* Oxford: Oxford University Press.

Appiah, Kwame Anthony. 1992. *In My Father's House: Africa in the Philosophy of Culture.* Oxford: Oxford University Press.

Aristotle. 1984. *The Complete Works of Aristotle.* J. Barnes, ed. Princeton, NJ: Princeton University Press.

Armstrong, D.M. 1978. *Universals and Scientific Realism* (Two Volumes). Cambridge: Cambridge University Press.

Armstrong, D.M. 1983. *What Is a Law of Nature?* Cambridge: Cambridge University Press.

Armstong, D.M. 1989a. *A Combinatorial Theory of Possibility.* Cambridge: Cambridge University Press.

Armstrong, D.M. 1989b. *Universals: An Opinionated Introduction.* Boulder, CO: Westview Press.

Armstrong, D.M. 1997. *A World of States of Affairs.* Cambridge: Cambridge University Press.

Ayer, A.J. 1936. *Language, Truth, and Logic.* London: Gollancz.

Ayer, A.J., ed. 1959. *Logical Positivism.* New York: The Free Press.

Ayer, A.J. 1969. Freedom and Necessity. In *Philosophical Essays.* London: Macmillan.

Baker, Alan. 2005. Are There Genuine Mathematical Explanations of Physical Phenomena? *Mind.* 114(454): 223–238.

Baker, Alan. 2013. Simplicity. *The Stanford Encyclopedia of Philosophy* (Fall 2013 Edition). E. Zalta, ed. URL = <http://plato.stanford.edu/archives/fall2013/entries/simplicity/>.

Barnes, Elizabeth. 2010. Ontic Vagueness: A Guide for the Perplexed. *Noûs.* 44(4): 601–627.

Barnes, Elizabeth. 2012. Emergence and Fundamentality. *Mind.* 121(484): 873–901.

Barnshad, M.J. and S.E. Olson. 2003. Does Race Exist? *Scientific American.* December.

Benacerraf, Paul. 1973. Mathematical Truth. *Journal of Philosophy.* 70(19): 661–679.

Benacerraf, Paul and Hilary Putnam, eds. 1983. *Philosophy of Mathematics: Selected Readings*. Cambridge: Cambridge University Press.

Bennett, Karen. 2011. Construction Area (No Hard Hat Required). *Philosophical Studies*. 154(1): 79–104.

Bennett, Karen. forthcoming. *Making Things Up*. Oxford: Oxford University Press.

Bergmann, Merrie, James Moor, and Jack Nelson. 2008. *The Logic Book* (Fifth Edition). New York: McGraw-Hill.

Bernasconi, Robert and Tommy L. Lott, eds. 2000. *The Idea of Race*. London: Hackett.

Black, Max. 1952. The Identity of Indiscernibles. *Mind*. 61(242): 153–164.

Boolos, George. 1984. To Be is to be a Value of a Variable (or to be Some Values of Some Variables). *Journal of Philosophy*. 81(8): 430–449.

Borges, Jorge Luis. 1964. The Analytical Language of John Wilkins. In *Other Inquisitions 1937–1952*. Austin: University of Texas Press.

Boxill, Bernard, ed. 2001. *Race and Racism*. Oxford: Oxford University Press.

Carnap, Rudolf. 1932. The Elimination of Metaphysics through the Logical Analysis of Language. *Erkenntnis*: 60–81.

Carnap, Rudolf. 1950. Empiricism, Semantics, and Ontology. *Revue Internationale de Philosophie*. 4: 20–40. Reprinted in *Meaning and Necessity*. Chicago, IL: University of Chicago Press, 1956.

Cartwright, Nancy. 1999. *The Dappled World: A Study of the Boundaries of Science*. Cambridge: Cambridge University Press.

Cartwright, Richard. 1968. Some Remarks on Essentialism. *Journal of Philosophy*. 65(20): 615–626.

Chalmers, David, David Manley, and Ryan Wasserman, eds. 2009. *Metametaphysics: New Essays on the Foundations of Ontology*. Oxford: Oxford University Press.

Chisholm, Roderick. 1964. Human Freedom and the Self. Lindley Lecture. University of Kansas.

Collins, John, Ned Hall, and L.A. Paul, eds. 2004. *Causation and Counterfactuals*. Cambridge, MA: MIT Press.

Colyvan. Mark. 2003. *The Indispensability of Mathematics*. Oxford: Oxford University Press.

Craig, William Lane. 2000a. *The Tensed Theory of Time: A Critical Examination*. Dordrecht: Kluwer.

Craig, William Lane. 2000b. *Time and the Metaphysics of Relativity*. London: Springer.

Davidson, Donald. 1967a. The Logical Form of Action Sentences. In *The Logic of Decision and Action*. N. Rescher, ed. Pittsburgh, PA: University of Pittsburgh Press.

Davidson, Donald. 1967b. Causal Relations. *Journal of Philosophy*. 64(21): 691–703.

Davidson, Donald. 1970. Events as Particulars. *Noûs*. 4(1): 25–32.

Descartes, René and Princess Elisabeth of Bohemia. 2007. *The Correspondence between Princess Elisabeth of Bohemia and René Descartes*. Chicago, IL: University of Chicago Press.

Dowe, Phil. 2000. *Physical Causation*. Cambridge: Cambridge University Press.

Einstein, Albert. 2013. *Relativity: The Special and General Theory*. New York: Empire Books.

Feldman, Richard. 1998. *Reason and Argument* (Second Edition). New York: Prentice Hall.

Field, Hartry. 1980. *Science Without Numbers.* Princeton, NJ: Princeton University Press.

Fine, Kit. 1994. Essence and Modality. *Philosophical Perspectives.* 8. 1–16.

Fine, Kit. 2001. The Question of Realism. *Philosophers' Imprint.* 1(2): 1–30.

Fine, Kit. 2009. The Question of Ontology. In *Metametaphysics: New Essays on the Foundations of Ontology.* D. Chalmers, D. Manley, and R. Wasserman, eds. Oxford: Oxford University Press.

Fischer, John Martin. 1994. *The Metaphysics of Free Will.* Oxford: Blackwell.

Fischer, John Martin, Robert Kane, Derk Pereboom, and Manuel Vargas. 2007. *Four Views on Free Will.* Oxford: Blackwell.

Forrest, Peter. 1986. Ways Worlds Could Be. *Australasian Journal of Philosophy.* 64(1): 15–24.

Frankfurt, Harry. 1969. Alternative Possibilities and Moral Responsibility. *Journal of Philosophy.* 66(3): 829–839.

French, Steven and Kerry McKenzie. 2012. Thinking Outside the Toolbox. *European Journal of Analytic Philosophy.* 8(1): 42–59.

Gendler, Tamar Szabó and John Hawthorne, eds. 2002. *Conceivability and Possibility.* Oxford: Oxford University Press.

Glasgow, Joshua. 2009. *A Theory of Race.* London: Routledge.

Goodman, Nelson. 1983. *Fact, Fiction, and Forecast.* Cambridge, MA: Harvard University Press.

Hacking, Ian. 1999. *The Social Construction of What?* Cambridge, MA: Harvard University Press.

Hall, Ned and L.A. Paul. 2013. *Causation: A User's Guide.* Oxford: Oxford University Press.

Hardegree, Gary. 1999. *Symbolic Logic: A First Course* (Third Edition). New York: McGraw-Hill.

Haslanger, Sally. 1995. Ontology and Social Construction. *Philosophical Topics.* 23(2): 95–124.

Haslanger, Sally. 2000. Gender and Race: (What) Are They? (What) Do We Want Them to Be? *Noûs.* 34(1): 31–55.

Haslanger, Sally. 2003. Persistence through Time. In *The Oxford Handbook of Metaphysics.* M. Loux and D. Zimmerman, eds. Oxford: Oxford University Press.

Haslanger, Sally and Roxanne Marie Kurtz. 2006. *Persistence: Contemporary Readings.* Cambridge, MA: MIT Press.

Hawley, Katherine. 2010. Temporal Parts. *The Stanford Encyclopedia of Philosophy* (Winter 2010 Edition). E. Zalta, ed. URL=<http://plato.stanford.edu/archives/win2010/entries/temporal-parts/>.

Hawthorne, John and Daniel Nolan. 2006. What Would Teleological Causation Be? In *Metaphysical Essays.* Oxford: Oxford University Press.

Heidegger, Martin. 1993. What is Metaphysics? In *Martin Heidegger: Basic Writings.* D.F. Krell, ed. London: Routledge.

Heil, John. 2012. *The Universe As We Find It.* Oxford: Oxford University Press.

Heller, Mark. 1990. *The Ontology of Physical Objects: Four-Dimensional Hunks of Matter.* Cambridge: Cambridge University Press.

Heller, Mark. 2005. Anti-Essentialism and Counterpart Theory. *The Monist.* 88(4): 600–618.

Hinchliff, Mark. 2000. A Defense of Presentism in a Relativistic Setting. *Philosophy of Science.* 67(3): 586.

Hirsch, Eli. 2010. *Quantifier Variance and Realism: Essays in Metaontology.* Oxford: Oxford University Press.

Horwich, Paul. 1975. On Some Alleged Paradoxes of Time Travel. *Journal of Philosophy.* 72(14): 432–444.

Hume, David. 2000. *An Enquiry Concerning Human Understanding.* Oxford: Oxford University Press.

Hume, David. 2006. Of Natural Characters. In *Essays: Moral, Political and Literary.* New York: Cosimo.

Hylton, Peter. 2007. *Quine.* London: Routledge.

Ismael, Jenann. 2003. Closed Causal Loops and the Bilking Argument. *Synthese.* 136(3): 305–320.

Jackson, Frank. 1977. Statements about Universals. *Mind.* 86(343): 427–429. Reprinted in *Properties.* D.H. Mellor and A. Oliver, eds. Oxford: Oxford University Press, 1997.

Kalderon, Mark Eli, ed. 2005. *Fictionalism in Metaphysics.* Oxford: Clarendon.

Kane, Robert. 2005. *A Contemporary Introduction to Free Will.* Oxford: Oxford University Press.

Keefe, Rosanna and Peter Smith, eds. 1997. *Vagueness: A Reader.* Cambridge, MA: MIT Press.

Keller, Simon. 2004. Presentism and Truthmaking. *Oxford Studies in Metaphysics, Volume 1.* Oxford: Oxford University Press, 83–104.

Keller, Simon and Michael Nelson. 2001. Presentists Should Believe in Time-Travel. *Australasian Journal of Philosophy.* 79(3): 333–345.

Kenny, Anthony. 1963. *Action, Emotion, and Will.* New York: Humanities Press.

Kim, Jaegwon. 1976. Events as Property Exemplifications. In *Action Theory.* M. Brand and D. Walton, eds. Dordrecht: Reidel.

Kim, Jaegwon. 1984. Concepts of Supervenience. *Philosophy and Phenomenological Research.* 45: 153–176.

Kim, Jaegwon. 2010. *Philosophy of Mind* (Third Edition). Boulder, CO: Westview Press.

Koslicki, Kathrin. 2010. *The Structure of Objects.* Oxford: Oxford University Press.

Kripke, Saul. 1980. *Naming and Necessity.* Cambridge, MA: Harvard University Press.

Kuhn, Thomas. 1977. Objectivity, Value Judgment, and Theory Choice. In *The Essential Tension.* Chicago, IL: University of Chicago Press.

Ladyman, James. 2007. Does Physics Answer Metaphysical Questions? *Royal Institute of Philosophy Supplements.* 82(61): 179–201.

Ladyman, James and Don Ross. 2007. *Every Thing Must Go: Metaphysics Naturalized.* Oxford: Oxford University Press.

Langton, Rae and David Lewis. 1998. Defining "Intrinsic." *Philosophy and Phenomenological Research.* 58(2): 333–345.

Laplace, Pierre-Simon. 1951. *A Philosophical Essay on Probabilities.* New York: Dover.

Leonard, Henry S. and Nelson Goodman. 1940. The Calculus of Individuals and its Uses. *Journal of Symbolic Logic.* 5(2): 45–55.

Le Poidevin, Robin and Murray MacBeath. 1993. *The Philosophy of Time*. Oxford: Oxford University Press.

Lewis, David. 1973a. Counterfactuals and Comparative Similarity. *Journal of Philosophical Logic*. 2(4): 418–446.

Lewis, David. 1973b. Causation. *Journal of Philosophy*. 70(17): 556–567. Reprinted with postscripts in *Philosophical Papers: Volume II*. Oxford: Oxford University Press, 1986, 159–213.

Lewis, David. 1976. The Paradoxes of Time Travel. *American Philosophical Quarterly*. 13(2): 145–152. Reprinted in *Philosophical Papers: Volume II*. Oxford: Oxford University Press, 1986, 67–80.

Lewis, David. 1978. Truth in Fiction. *American Philosophical Quarterly*. 15(1): 37–46.

Lewis, David. 1981. Are We Free to Break the Laws? *Theoria*. 47(3): 113–121.

Lewis, David. 1983. New Work for a Theory of Universals. *Australasian Journal of Philosophy*. 61: 343–377.

Lewis, David. 1986. *On the Plurality of Worlds*. Oxford: Blackwell.

Lewis, David. 1993. Many, but Almost One. In *Ontology, Causality, and Mind: Essays on the Philosophy of D.M. Armstrong*. K. Campbell, J. Bacon, and L. Reinhardt, eds. Cambridge: Cambridge University Press.

Lewis, David. 2000. Causation as Influence. *Journal of Philosophy*. 97(4): 182–197.

Loux, Michael J. ed. 1979. *The Possible and the Actual: Readings in the Metaphysics of Modality*. Ithaca, NY: Cornell University Press.

Loux, Michael and Dean Zimmerman, eds. 2003. *The Oxford Handbook of Metaphysics*. Oxford: Oxford University Press.

McDaniel, Kris. 2007. Extended Simples. *Philosophical Studies*. 133(1): 131–141.

McKay, Thomas. 1999. *Reasons, Explanations, and Decisions: Guidelines for Critical Thinking*. London: Wadsworth.

Mackie, J.L. 1980. *The Cement of the Universe*. Oxford: Clarendon.

Mackie, Penelope. 2006. *How Things Might Have Been: Individuals, Kinds, and Essential Properties*. Oxford: Oxford University Press.

McTaggart, J.M.E. 1908. The Unreality of Time. *Mind*. 17(68): 457–474.

Maddy, Penelope. 1992. Indispensability and Practice. *Journal of Philosophy*. 89(6): 275–289.

Mallon, Ron. 2007. A Field Guide to Social Construction. *Philosophy Compass*. 2(1): 93–108.

Marcus, Ruth Barcan. 1967. Essentialism in Modal Logic. *Noûs*. 1(1): 91–96.

Marcus, Ruth Barcan. 1990. A Backward Look at Quine's Animadversions on Modalities. In *Perspectives on Quine*. R. Barrett and R. Gibson, eds. Oxford: Blackwell, 230–243.

Markosian, Ned. 1998. Brutal Composition. *Philosophical Studies*. 92(3): 211–249.

Markosian, Ned. 2004. A Defense of Presentism. *Oxford Studies in Metaphysics, Volume 1*. Oxford: Oxford University Press, 47–82.

Meiland, Jack. 1974. A Two-Dimensional Passage Model of Time for Time Travel. *Philosophical Studies*. 26(3–4): 153–173.

Mellor, D.H. and Alex Oliver, eds. 1997. *Properties*. Oxford: Oxford University Press.

Mills, Charles. 1998. *Blackness Visible: Essays on Philosophy and Race*. Ithaca, NY: Cornell University Press.

Montero, Barbara. 1999. The Body Problem. *Noûs*. 33(2): 183–200.

Outlaw, Lucius T. 1996. *On Race and Philosophy*. London: Routledge.

Papineau, David. 2012. *Philosophical Devices: Proofs, Probabilities, Possibilities, and Sets*. Oxford: Oxford University Press.

Paul, L.A. 2006. In Defense of Essentialism. *Philosophical Perspectives*. 20(1): 333–372.

Paul, L.A. 2012. Metaphysics as Modeling: The Handmaiden's Tale. *Philosophical Studies*. 160(1): 1–29.

Pearl, Judea. 2000. *Causality: Models, Reasoning, and Inference*. Cambridge: Cambridge University Press.

Peirce, Charles S. 1877. The Fixation of Belief. *Popular Science Monthly*. 12: 1–15.

Pereboom, Derk. 2001. *Living Without Free Will*. Cambridge: Cambridge University Press.

Pink, Thomas. 2004. *Free Will: A Very Short Introduction*. Oxford: Oxford University Press.

Plantinga, Alvin. 1992. *The Nature of Necessity*. Oxford: Clarendon.

Plato. 2005. *The Collected Dialogues*. E. Hamilton and H. Cairns, eds. Princeton, NJ: Princeton University Press.

Pojman, Louis P. and Michael Rea. 2011. *Philosophy of Religion: An Anthology* (Sixth Edition). Stamford, CT: Cengage Learning.

Putnam, Hilary. 1967. Time and Physical Geometry. *Journal of Philosophy*. 64(8): 240–247.

Putnam, Hilary. 1972. *Philosophy of Logic*. London: Allen and Unwin.

Putnam, Hilary. 1975. The Meaning of "Meaning." *Minnesota Studies in the Philosophy of Science*. 7: 131–193.

Quine, W.V.O. 1948. On What There Is. *Review of Metaphysics*. 2(5): 21–36. Reprinted in *From a Logical Point of View*. Cambridge, MA: Harvard University Press, 1980.

Quine, W.V.O. 1950. Identity, Ostension, and Hypostasis. *Journal of Philosophy*. 47(22): 621–633. Reprinted in *From a Logical Point of View*. Cambridge, MA: Harvard University Press, 1980.

Quine, W.V.O. 1951a. Two Dogmas of Empiricism. *Philosophical Review*. 60(1): 20–43. Reprinted in *From a Logical Point of View*. Cambridge, MA: Harvard University Press, 1980.

Quine, W.V.O. 1951b. On Carnap's Views on Ontology. *Philosophical Studies*. 2(5): 65–72.

Quine, W.V.O. 1960. *Word and Object*. Cambridge, MA: MIT Press.

Quine, W.V.O. 1969. Natural Kinds. In *Ontological Relativity and Other Essays*. New York: Columbia University Press.

Quine, W.V.O. 1980. *From a Logical Point of View*. Cambridge, MA: Harvard University Press.

Quine, W.V.O. 1981. *Theories and Things*. Cambridge, MA: Harvard University Press.

Rea, Michael, ed. 1997. *Material Constitution*. Lanham, MD: Rowman and Littlefield.

Reichenbach, Hans. 1956. *The Direction of Time*. Berkeley: University of California Press.

Rosen, Gideon. 1990. Modal Fictionalism. *Mind*. 99(395): 327–354.

Routley, Richard. 1982. On What There Is Not. *Philosophy and Phenomenological Research*. 43(2): 151–177.

Russell, Bertrand. 1905. On Denoting. *Mind*. 14(56): 479–493.

Russell, Bertrand. 1912/2002. *The Problems of Philosophy*. Oxford: Oxford University Press.

Russell, Gillian. 2008. *Truth in Virtue of Meaning*. Oxford: Oxford University Press.

Salmon, Wesley. 1994. Causality without Counterfactuals. *Philosophy of Science*. 61(2): 297–312.

Sartorio, Carolina. 2005. Causes as Difference-Makers. *Philosophical Studies*. 123(1–2): 71–96.

Sartre, Jean-Paul. 2007. Existentialism is a Humanism. In *Existentialism is a Humanism*. New Haven, CT: Yale University Press.

Schaffer, Jonathan. 2003. Is There a Fundamental Level? *Noûs*. 37(3): 498–517.

Schaffer, Jonathan. 2004. Two Conceptions of Sparse Properties. *Pacific Philosophical Quarterly*. 85(1): 92–102.

Schaffer, Jonathan. 2009. On What Grounds What. In *Metametaphysics: New Essays on the Foundations of Ontology*. D. Chalmers, D. Manley, and R. Wasserman, eds. Oxford: Oxford University Press.

Schaffer, Jonathan. 2010. Monism: The Priority of the Whole. *Philosophical Review*. 119(1): 31–76.

Schneider, Susan, ed. 2009. *Science Fiction and Philosophy*. London: Wiley-Blackwell.

Searle, John. 1995. *The Social Construction of Reality*. London: Penguin.

Sider, Theodore. 1993. Van Inwagen and the Possibility of Gunk. *Analysis*. 53(4): 285–289.

Sider, Theodore. 1996. All the World's a Stage. *Australasian Journal of Philosophy*. 74(3): 433–453.

Sider, Theodore. 2001. *Four Dimensionalism*. Oxford: Oxford University Press.

Sider, Theodore. 2003. Maximality and Microphysical Supervenience. *Philosophy and Phenomenological Research*. 66(1): 139–149.

Sider, Theodore. 2011. *Writing the Book of the World*. Oxford: Oxford University Press.

Sider, Theodore. 2013. Against Parthood. *Oxford Studies in Metaphysics, Volume 8*. Oxford: Oxford University Press, 237–293.

Sider, Theodore, John Hawthorne, and Dean Zimmerman, eds. 2008. *Contemporary Debates in Metaphysics*. Oxford: Blackwell.

Siegel, Susanna. 2011. *The Contents of Visual Experience*. Oxford: Oxford University Press.

Sklar, Lawrence. 1974. *Space, Time, and Spacetime*. Berkeley: University of California Press.

Sklar, Lawrence. 1992. *The Philosophy of Physics*. Boulder, CO: Westview.

Skow, Bradford. Forthcoming. *Objective Becoming*. Oxford: Oxford University Press.

Smart, J.J.C. 1963. *Philosophy and Scientific Realism*. London: Humanities Press.

Sosa, Ernest and Michael Tooley, eds. 1993. *Causality*. Oxford: Oxford University Press.

Stalnaker, Robert. 1968. A Theory of Conditionals. In *Studies in Logical Theory*. N. Rescher, ed. Oxford: Blackwell.

Stalnaker, Robert. 1976. Possible Worlds. *Noûs*. 10(1): 65–75.

Strawson, Galen. 1989. *The Secret Connexion: Causation, Realism, and David Hume*. Oxford: Oxford University Press.

Strawson, P.F. 1959. *Individuals: An Essay in Descriptive Metaphysics*. London: Routledge.

Strevens, Michael. 2007. Mackie Remixed. In *Causation and Explanation*. J. Campbell, M. O'Rourke, and H. Silverstein, eds. Cambridge, MA: MIT Press.

Szabó, Zoltán. 2003. Nominalism. In *The Oxford Handbook of Metaphysics*. M. Loux and D. Zimmerman, eds. Oxford: Oxford University Press.

Thomasson, Amie. 2010. *Ordinary Objects*. Oxford: Oxford University Press.

Tooley, Michael. 1990. Causation: Reductionism vs. Realism. *Philosophy and Phenomenological Research*. 50: 215–236.

Trogdon, Kelly. 2013. An Introduction to Grounding. In *Varieties of Dependence: Ontological Dependence, Supervenience, and Response-Dependence*. B. Schnieder, A. Steinberg, and M. Hoeltje, eds. Munich: Philosophia Verlag, 97–122.

Unger, Peter. 1980. The Problem of the Many. *Midwest Studies in Philosophy*. 5(1): 411–468.

Van Fraassen, Bas. 1989. *Laws and Symmetry*. Oxford: Oxford University Press.

Van Inwagen, Peter. 1986. *An Essay on Free Will*. Oxford: Oxford University Press.

Van Inwagen, Peter. 1990. *Material Beings*. Ithaca, NY: Cornell University Press.

Van Inwagen, Peter. 1998. Meta-Ontology. *Erkenntnis*. 48(2/3): 233–250.

Van Inwagen, Peter. 2000. Temporal Parts and Identity across Time. *The Monist*. 83(3): 437–459.

Van Inwagen, Peter. 2009. Being, Existence, and Ontological Commitment. In *Metametaphysics: New Essays on the Foundations of Ontology*. D. Chalmers, D. Manley, and R. Wasserman, eds. Oxford: Oxford University Press.

Wegner, Daniel. 2003. *The Illusion of Conscious Will*. Cambridge, MA: MIT Press.

Wiggins, David. 1980. *Sameness and Substance*. Cambridge, MA: Harvard University Press.

Wiggins, David. 2001. *Sameness and Substance Renewed*. Cambridge: Cambridge University Press.

Williams, D.C. 1951. The Myth of Passage. *Journal of Philosophy*. 48(15): 457–472.

Williams. D.C. 1953. On the Elements of Being: I and II. *Review of Metaphysics*. 7(1–2): 3–18, 171–192.

Williamson, Timothy. 1994. *Vagueness*. London: Routledge.

Wilson, Jessica. 2006. On Characterizing the Physical. *Philosophical Studies*. 131(1): 61–99.

Wittgenstein, Ludwig. 1922. *Tractatus Logico: Philosophicus*. London: Harcourt, Brace and Company.

Wittgenstein, Ludwig. 1953. *Philosophical Investigations*. G.E.M. Anscombe and R. Rhees, eds. Oxford: Blackwell.

Woodward, James. 2003. *Making Things Happen*. Oxford: Oxford University Press.

Zack, Naomi. 1993. *Race and Mixed Race*. Philadelphia, PA: Temple University Press.

Zimmerman, Dean. 2008. The Privileged Present: Defending the "A-Theory" of Time. In *Contemporary Debates in Metaphysics*. T. Sider, J. Hawthorne, and D. Zimmerman, eds. Oxford: Blackwell, 211–225.

Index

Locators in *italic* refer to figures/tables
Locators in **bold** refer to glossary definitions